Paul and the Politics of Diaspora

Ronald Charles

Fortress Press
Minneapolis

PAUL AND THE POLITICS OF DIASPORA

Scripture quotations are from the New Revised Standard Version Bible, copyright © 1989 by the Division of Christian Education of the National Council of the Churches of Christ in the USA. Used by permission. All rights reserved.

Cover design: Laurie Ingram

Cover image © Vanni Archive/ Art Resource

Library of Congress Cataloging-in-Publication Data

Print ISBN: 978-1-4514-8802-9

eBook ISBN: 978-1-4514-8975-0

The paper used in this publication meets the minimum requirements of American National Standard for Information Sciences — Permanence of Paper for Printed Library Materials, ANSI Z329.48-1984.

Manufactured in the U.S.A.

This book was produced using PressBooks.com, and PDF rendering was done by PrinceXML.

Contents

Abbreviations

Primary Sources

Acts	Acts
Add Esth	Additions to Esther
Apoc. Bar.	*Apocalypse of Baruch*
Cicero	
Flac.	*Cicero "Pro Flacco"*
Cor	Corinthians
Dan	Daniel
Deut	Deuteronomy
2 Enoch	Slavonic Apocalypse of Enoch
Ep. Arist.	*Epistle of Aristeas*
Esth	Esther
Ezek	Ezekiel
Gal	Galatians
Gen	Genesis
Isa	Isaiah
Jas	James
Jdt	Judith
Jer	Jeremiah

Josephus

AJ/Ant.	*Antiquitates Judaicae/Antiquities*
War	*Bellum judaicum/Jewish War*
Jos. Asen	*Joseph and Aseneth*
Jos	Joshua
Jub	*Jubilees*
Judg	Judges
Kgs	Kings
LXX	Septuagint
Macc	Maccabees
Matt	Matthew
Ne	Nehemiah
1 Pet	1 Peter
Phil	Philippians
Phlm	Philemon

Philo

Leg. Gai.	*Legatio ad Gaium*
Mos.	*On the Life of Moses*
Spec. Leg.	*De Specialibus legibus*
Plut., Cic.	Plutarch, *Life of Cicero*
Ps	Psalms
Ps Sal	Psalms of Salomon
Rom	Romans
Sir	Sirach/Ecclesiasticus

Strabo

Geogr.	*Geographica/Geography*
Thess	Thessalonians
Tob	Tobit

Secondary Sources

AJS	*Association for Jewish Studies Review*
CP	*Classical Philology*
ETR	*Études théologiques et religieuses*
HTR	*Harvard Theological Review*
NTS	*New Testament Studies*
JBL	*Journal of Biblical Literature*
JAAR	*Journal of the American Academy of Religion*
JECS	*Journal of Early Christian Studies*
JJS	*Journal of Jewish Studies*
JSJ	*Journal for the Study of Judaism*
JSJSup	Journal for the Study of Judaism Supplements
JSNT	*Journal for the Study of the New Testament*
JSNTSup	Journal for the Study of the New Testament Supplement Series
JSP	*Journal for the Study of the Pseudepigrapha*
JSPSup	Journal for the Study of the Pseudepigrapha Supplement Series
JSS	*Journal of Semitic Studies*
JTS	*Journal of Theological Studies*
LCL	Loeb classical Library
MTSR	*Method and Theory in the Study of Religion*
Neot	*Neotestamentica*
NICNT	New International Commentary on the New Testament
NovT	*Novum Testamentum*
RB	*Revue Biblique*
SBL	Society of Biblical Literature
SBLTT	Society of Biblical Literature Texts and Translations
SCI	*Scripta Classica Israelica*
SNTSMS	Society for New Testament Studies Monograph Series
SR	*Studies in Religion/Sciences religieuses*
WUNT	Wissenchaftliche Untersuchungen zum Neuen Testament

Acknowledgments

This work is a revised version of my Ph.D. dissertation undertaken in the Department for the Study of Religion at the University of Toronto, Canada. John W. Marshall and Terence L. Donaldson, my co-supervisors, and Ato Quayson the third member of my committee, are to be thanked for their guidance and academic rigor. It has been truly a tremendous privilege to work with such excellent scholars. It was also an honor for me to have Professor Fernando F. Segovia as my external examiner.

My thanks go to Joseph Bryant, Kathleen Gibbons, Ronald Hock, Calvin Roetzel, Shawn Kelley, Jennifer W. Knust, Emerson Powery, Ryan Olerft, Amy Fisher, Magnus Zetterholm, Shealah Stratton, Gosnel L. Yorke, Célucien Joseph, Dexter Callender, Stephen Sapp, Kate Ramsey, April Dobbins, J. Albert Harrill, Linsey Bergholz, and Will Arnal. These different people were generous enough with their time to read a chapter or more at different stages of this project. I am indebted to Marissa Wold of Fortress Press for her final editing of this project and I thank Neil Elliott for his interest in the project and for including it in the Paul in Critical Contexts series. Any shortcomings are, of course, my own.

My brothers and my sister—all of them excellent professionals in their own right—seem to have known all along what took me a long time to realize—namely, that I am cut for this kind of stuff called academia. I thank them for believing in me, even when I did not. We all are very thankful to our sweet and loving mother.

I would also want to thank particularly my wife, Manette, and my boys, Olivier and Sébastien. I do not have words to thank them enough for their patience in understanding that I need to take time for my academic work. It is only love that can make such sacrifices possible. It is to them that I dedicate this work.

Introduction

Paul was of course a diaspora Jew, but we rarely take seriously his diaspora identity in our interpretation of his thinking.
—Sze-Kar Wan[1]

One must further remember that Paul had consistently been carrying out his work in or near Jewish Diaspora settlements.
—Dieter Georgi[2]

Scholars have long recognized Paul was socially located within and fundamentally influenced by different, interdependent social worlds: the Jewish milieu of his ethno-religious origin, and also the larger Hellenistic-Roman worlds that had established significant political and cultural hegemony over the Mediterranean region.[3] Though Paul has been seen as existing in these worlds, the specific character of his diaspora existence has not been addressed in any systematic manner. To be clear, one may find a few scattered chapters dealing

---

1. Sze-kar Wan, "Does Diaspora Identity Imply Some Sort of Universality? An Asian-American Reading of Galatians," in *Interpreting Beyond Borders*, ed. Fernando F. Segovia (Sheffield: Sheffield Academic, 2000), 122. Wan's challenge is what initially prompted me to undertake this research project.
2. Dieter Georgi, *Remembering the Poor: The History of Paul's Collection for Jerusalem* (Nashville: Abingdon, 1965), 58–59.
3. Richard Wallace, *The Three Worlds of Paul of Tarsus* (New York: Routledge, 1998); Nicholas T. Wright, *Paul in Fresh Perspectives* (Minneapolis: Fortress Press, 2005); Camille Focant, "L'expérience paulinienne d'une identité en tension," *Revue d'Éthique et de Théologie morale* 271 (2012): 143–64.

with Paul as a diaspora figure, but there is not one monograph dedicated solely to the subject. Thus, Paul's relationships as an itinerant diaspora figure with localized communities of Christ believers in the Roman Empire are open to fresh interpretation. With this study, I attempt to demonstrate both the necessity and the value of studying Paul's diaspora politics within the complexities of first-century Diaspora Judaism.[4] *Politics* is used here in the sense of participating in social formation and being an agent in the messiness of social and cultural relationships. My main argument for this book is that Paul's diasporic condition was central to his life, mission, and social relationships. Paul's tactical adaptability and his interpretation of Christ stem primarily from his social and cultural posture in his interrelations with the largely gentile communities of his diasporic social locations.

4. Some important comparative studies with respect to Diaspora Judaism are Shaye J. D. Cohen and E. S. Frerichs, eds., *Diasporas in Antiquity*, Brown Judaic Studies, vol. 288 (Atlanta: Scholars, 1993); Gerrie ter Haar, ed., *Strangers and Sojourners: Religious Communities in the Diaspora*, Study of Religion and Mythology (Leuven: Peeters University Press, 1998); André Levy and Alex Weingrod, eds., *Homelands and Diasporas: Holy Lands and Other Places* (Stanford: Stanford University Press, 2005); Steven Vertovec, "Religion and Diaspora," *New Approaches to the Study of Religion*, vol 2: *Textual, Comparative, Sociological, and Cognitive Approaches* (New York: Walter de Gruyter, 2004), 275–303. See also Paul R. Trebilco, *Jewish Communities in Asia Minor*, Society for New Testament Studies Monograph Series 69 (Cambridge: Cambridge University Press, 1991); Louis H. Feldman, "Palestinian and Diaspora Judaism in the First Century," in *Christianity and Rabbinic Judaism: A Parallel History of Their Origins and Early Development*, ed. Hershel Shanks (Washington, DC: Biblical Archaeology Society, 1992), 1–39, 327–36; Andrew J. Overman and Robert S. MacLennan, eds., *Diaspora Jews and Judaism: Essays in Honor of, and in Dialogue with, A. Thomas Kraabel*, South Florida Studies in the History of Judaism 41 (Atlanta: Scholars, 1992). See also, in the same volume, Thomas A. Kraabel, "The Roman Diaspora: Six Questionable Assumptions," 1–20; for more, see John M. G. Barclay, "Paul among Diaspora Jews: Anomaly or Apostate?" *JSNT* 60 (1995): 89–120; and Barclay, "Paul: An Anomalous Diaspora Jew," in *Jews in the Mediterranean Diaspora: From Alexander to Trajan, 323 bce–117 ce* (Berkeley: University of California Press, 1996). For the dynamics between these different important poles (homeland and diaspora), see Isaiah M. Gafni, *Land, Center and Diaspora: Jewish Constructs in Late Antiquity*, JSPSup 21 (Sheffield: Sheffield Academic, 1997); and Willem C. van Unnik, *Das Selbstverständnis der jüdischen Diaspora in der hellenistisch-römischen Zeit* (Leiden: Brill, 1993). More important studies worth mentioning at this point include Siân Jones and Sarah Pearce, eds., *Jewish Local Patriotism and Self-Identification in the Graeco-Roman Period*, JSPSup 31 (Sheffield: Sheffield Academic, 1998); Shayne J. D. Cohen, *The Beginnings of Jewishness: Boundaries, Varieties, Uncertainties* (Berkeley: University of California Press, 1999).

My analysis of Paul as a diaspora figure does not explore the old debate of his birth place (Tarsus or Jerusalem) because it does not add anything to my overall argument. My interest instead is in Paul's social-relationships as an itinerant diaspora figure with localized communities of Christ believers (i.e., the contrast between a diasporic founder figure[5] and groups composed of both dispersed and nondiaspora peoples) within the Roman Empire. Paul qualifies as a Diaspora Jew because of his social location in Diaspora Judaism for nearly thirty years as an apostle to the nations, and because of his relationships as an itinerant figure among localized communities of Christ-believers within the Roman Empire.[6]

To probe Paul's diasporic condition and, by extension, his diasporic identity and modus operandi, I will utilize some analytical tools taken from modern diasporic studies, where questions and concepts of migrancy, movements across boundaries, cultural diversity, home and diaspora, native and stranger, diaspora space and interethnic identities, and translocal identification via the modality of religion are explored.[7] I am very aware of the many pitfalls facing any scholar using modern approaches to study texts and figures of antiquity. This is why careful considerations with regard to the specificity of the ancient contexts and ancient categories are important to consider and must be worked with appropriately. I do

5. See the recent monograph on the subject by James C. Hanges, *Paul, Founder of Churches: A Study in Light of the Evidence for the Role of "Founder-Figures" in the Hellenistic-Roman Period* (Tübingen: Mohr Siebeck, 2012).

6. John M. G. Barclay takes a similar position in "Paul among Diaspora Jews: Anomaly or Apostate?" *JSNT* 60 (1995): 90. For Barclay, "Paul counts as a Diaspora Jew in as much as he spent nearly all the last thirty years of his life in the Diaspora and it is in this geographical and social context that his mission and his theological reflection took place."

7. For example, see James Clifford, *Routes: Travel and Translation in the Late Twentieth Century* (Cambridge, MA: Harvard University Press, 1997), 244–77; Robin Cohen, *Global Diasporas: An Introduction*, 2nd ed. (Seattle: University of Washington Press, [1997] 2008); Avtar Brah, "Diaspora, Border and Transnational Identities," in *Feminist Postcolonial Theory: A Reader*, ed. Reina Lewis and Sarah Mills (New York: Routledge, 1995, 2003), 613–34; Stéphane Dufoix, *Diasporas*, trans. William Rodarmor (Berkeley: University of California Press, 2008).

not intend to *impose* modern understandings of diaspora on the study of Paul, but the use of modern interpretive tools to approach an ancient historical figure like Paul will provide the opportunity to reframe and reinterpret his life and work.

The methodological question I ask is this: What can we see that we did not see before when we approach some issues in Pauline scholarship through the interpretive model of diaspora studies? In other words, what is the payoff to different contexts or sites in Pauline studies? The goal is to engage these different disciplines (biblical studies and diaspora studies) in conversation, so that Pauline scholars may see a bit more texture in some well-known texts.[8] To accomplish this goal, I have selected three issues to illustrate how the tools of diaspora studies can be used as interpretive model: (1) the conflict at Antioch in Galatians 2; (2) Paul's dealings with the Galatians; and (3) Paul's collection project.

In the next section, I will first give a sense of the concept of diaspora in antiquity, especially during the Second Temple period in Judaism, and then describe some of the ways various insights from the theories of modern diaspora might be useful to illuminate the social situation of Paul in the ancient Roman Empire.

---

8. In the discipline of Pauline studies, there is little precedent to what I am doing. For example, see John G. Gager, *Kingdom and Community: The Social World of Early Christianity* (Englewood Cliffs, NJ: Prentice-Hall, 1975); Bengt Holmberg, *Paul and Power* (Lund: CWK Gleerup, 1978), and his *Sociology and the New Testament: An Appraisal* (Minneapolis: Fortress Press, 1990). See also Margaret Y. MacDonald, *The Pauline Churches: A Socio-Historical Study of Institutionalization in the Pauline and Deutero-Pauline Writings*, SNTSMS 60 (Cambridge: Cambridge University Press, 1988); Bruce Malina, *The New Testament World: Insights from Cultural Anthropology*, 3rd ed. (Louisville: Westminster John Knox, 2001). These scholars and others have made use of the social sciences to help us read Paul from a different theoretical perspective. Many of these pioneers were heavily criticized by theologians, biblical scholars, and sociologists who accused them of reductionism.

Theorizing Diaspora

The word διασπορά (from the Greek διά, "through," "from one end to the other," and σπείρειν, "to scatter like seed, to spread, to disperse"), taken from the Septuagint,[9] originally referred to the dispersion of peoples of Israelite or Judean heritage over the course of centuries as a result of forced displacement. However, the term also refers to the result of voluntary migration and relocation.[10] The Jewish experience of loss and dispersion from the ancestral home, and the forced exile to Babylon of a large part of the elite population following the destruction of the First Temple and Jerusalem in the sixth century BCE, constitute a central site to situate the concept of diaspora. From this angle, the term encompasses the social, economic, political, and cultural effects of Babylonian hegemony, along with the subsequent Persian colonial rule, Hellenistic military, cultural, and linguistic conquest, and Roman imperialism.[11] The Septuagint uses the word διασπορά to connote Jewish existence away from the ancestral promised land as the dynamic equivalent to the Hebrew word גלות, or *galut*, which uniquely expresses a spiritual reality of banishment, deportation, and exile by force. However, the two lexical entries are not exactly synonymous, in spite of the fact that they have coexisted in texts and can still be used interchangeably. The logic of the specific coinage of "diaspora" in the Septuagint for "migration" instead of keeping and relying on the term *galut*, which signifies particularly banishment, might be, as indicated by Josèphe Mélèze Modrejewski, because of the variegated diasporic Greek contexts of the translators.[12] The legend of how the translation

---

9. Deut. 28:25; 30:4; Isa. 49:6; Jer. 13:14, 15:7, 41 (34):17; Dan. 12:2; Neh. 1:9; Pss 138 (139); 146 (147); Judg. 5:19; 2 Macc. 1:27; *Pss. Sol.* 8:28, 9:2.

10. Erich S. Gruen, *Diaspora: Jews Amidst Greeks and Romans* (Cambridge, MA: Harvard University Press, 2002), 2.

11. John M. G. Barclay, *Jews in the Mediterranean Diaspora*; Barclay, ed., *Negotiating Diaspora: Jewish Strategies in the Roman Empire* (New York: T & T Clark, 2004).

of the Septuagint took place, as narrated in the *Letter of Aristeas*, situates it in Alexandria. It is, however, possible that some of the translations may not have emanated from Alexandria at all, but were translated or completed by scholars working in other diasporic centers.[13] The vocabulary of the Greek colonists for exile and emigration were similar, and the choice of the word *diaspora* captures the voluntary aspect of migrations—aligning thus the Jewish past with the Greek's.

It is important to note that many Diaspora Judeans did not see the condition of being away from the ancestral homeland as divine punishment, as described in some passages in the Jewish Scriptures—Ps. 137:1-6 being a common and lingering refrain to describe such a condition. Rather, many saw the Diaspora in a far more positive way (e.g., Jer. 27:4–7; Tob. 13:3–13; Philo, *Mos.* 2.232).[14] By the fourth century BCE, there were many Jewish diasporic settlements in Egypt and Greece. In fact, more Jews were living outside the region of Jerusalem than in it.[15] In Macedonia and Achaia, the earliest epigraphic evidence of their presence dates to the first half of the third century BCE.[16] The social contacts between

12. See Josèphe Mélèze Modrejewski, "How to be a Jew in Hellenstic Egypt?" in *Diaspora in Antiquity*, ed. Shaye J.D. Cohen and Ernest S. Frerichs, Brown Judaic Studies 288 (Atlanta: Scholars, 1993), 68–70.

13. See Tessa Rajak, "Surviving by the Book: The Language of the Greek Bible and Jewish Identity," in *Cultural Identity in the Ancient Mediterranean*, ed. Erich S. Gruen (Los Angeles: Getty Research Institute, 2011), 273.

14. It is interesting to note that in Josephus, both views are in sight. As a well-established diaspora writer when he works on the *Antiquities*, Josephus expresses a more positive perspective with respect to being in the dispersion (e.g., *AJ.*, 4.115, 14.110). However, in his earlier work (*Jewish War*), his understanding of the destruction of the temple and Jerusalem is that of punishment from God, driving the inhabitants into exile because of their sins. See Daniel R. Schwartz, "From Punishment to Program, From Program to Punishment: Josephus and the Rabbis on Exile," in *For Uriel. Studies in the History of Israel in Antiquity Presented to Professor Uriel Rappaport*, ed. Menachem Mor and Jack Pastor (Jerusalem: Zalman Shazar Center for Jewish History, 2005), 205–26.

15. See, in particular, Joseph Mélèze Modrzejewski, *The Jews of Egypt. From Rameses II to Emperor Hadrian* (Princeton: Princeton University Press, 1997); Tessa Rajak, *The Jewish Dialogue with Greece and Rome: Studies in Cultural and Social Interaction* (Leiden: Brill, 2002).

the Judeans in the Diaspora and their societies of settlement were considerable and open, which indicates that many or most Judeans in antiquity did not think of themselves as away from home. They were entirely "at home" while living abroad in their diasporic cities.[17]

Erich Gruen argues that the Judeans in their different local Greco-Roman cities did not define themselves as part of a Diaspora radically different from those in the ancestral homeland, nor did they lament for or feel embarrassed by being outside Judaea.[18] Most scholars argue that one should be careful to consider the complexities and the particular contexts of the different interactions between various Jewish communities in their Greco-Roman world. The daily experience and relationship between Judeans and non-Judeans varied from place to place.[19] Diaspora life was varied in terms of how individuals deployed multiple strategies to navigate between different identities (cultural, social, religious, and ethnic). Most Judeans were accommodated to their environment and integrated into their varied diasporic societies without losing the minimum cultural markers that set them as being part of their particular ethnic group (male circumcision, Sabbath observance, going to some major pilgrim festivals such as Passover, Sukkot-Tabernacles, the Feast of Weeks, and observing at least some of the Levitical dietary laws). The

16. See Irina Levinskaya, *The Book of Acts in Its Diaspora Setting* (Grand Rapids: Eerdmans, 1996), chapter 10.

17. See Gruen, *Diaspora*; John J. Collins, *Between Athens and Jerusalem: Jewish Identity in the Hellenistic Diaspora*, 2nd ed. (Grand Rapids: Eerdmans, 2000); Leonard V. Rutgers, *The Hidden Heritage of Diaspora Judaism*, Contributions to Biblical Exegesis and Theology, vol. 20 (Leuven: Peeters, 1998), especially in chapter 1, where he asks some critical questions regarding the issue. His research, based on archaeological and epigraphic evidence, aims to push scholars studying the Jewish diaspora communities of the ancient Mediterranean not to overstress the differences in practice and beliefs between different Jewish communities there, but instead to consider the number of issues agreed upon by Jews in many diasporic communities of the ancient world.

18. See Erich S. Gruen, "Diaspora and Homeland," in *Diaspora and Exiles: Varieties of Jewish Identity*, ed. Howard Wettstein (Berkeley, CA: University of California Press, 2002), 18–46.

19. See Tessa Rajak, *Translation and Survival: The Greek Bible of the Ancient Jewish Diaspora* (Oxford: Oxford University Press, 2009), 115.

communal life and activities around the different synagogues in the Diaspora also testify to the degree to which the realities of Diaspora were navigated with the view to maintain a certain cultural and religious distinctiveness.

Some Judeans in antiquity saw Jewish Diaspora communities as satellites ready to spread Judaism wherever they were located, with Jerusalem functioning as the mother *polis*.[20] Even so, it is important not to ascribe an anachronistic, organized "missionary movement" to first-century Diaspora Judaism. However, that does not preclude the possibility that some individual Judeans could have carried out preaching activities to proselytize others to their ancestral ways of life.[21] In the collective memory and imagination of most Judeans in antiquity, Jerusalem was the religious and theological center where Yahweh had put his name, and where his presence was made manifest (see e.g., 1 Kgs. 8:48; 9:3; Pss. 76:1–2; 87:1–3; 137:1–7; Isa. 49:14–16; Ezek. 43:6–7; Sir. 36:18–19).[22] For example, for Philo, Jerusalem is "the mother city (μητρόπολις) not of one country Judaea but of most of the others in virtue of the colonies sent out at diverse times to the neighboring lands."[23] Thus, those outside the mother city constituted, in following Philo, residents of daughter cities or satellite colonies responsible to act in solidarity with the social, intellectual,

20. See Sarah J. K. Pearce, "Jerusalem as Mother City in the Writings of Philo of Alexandria," in Barclay, *Negotiating Diaspora*, 19–37. She argues that Philo's concept of *mother-city* derives from the concept of *galut* rather than the Greek concept of colonization.

21. See Martin Goodman, *Mission and Conversion: Proselytizing in the Religious History of the Roman Empire* (Oxford: Clarendon, 1994), 87; Shaye J. Cohen, "Was Judaism in Antiquity a Missionary Religion?" in *Jewish Assimilation, Acculturation, and Accommodation: Past Traditions, Currents Issues, and Future Prospects*, ed. Menachem Mor (Lanham, MD: University Press of America, 1992), 14–23, and Collins, *Between Athens and Jerusalem*, 262–64.

22. Daniel Schwartz offers an interesting argument in "Temple or City: What Did Hellenistic Jews See in Jerusalem?" in *The Centrality of Jerusalem: Historical Perspectives*, ed. Marcel Poorthuis and C. Safrai(Kampen: Kok Pharos, 1996), 114–27. He argues that Diaspora Jews (including Philo) did not want to emphasize the importance of Jerusalem and its temple, or live under their shadow.

23. Philo, *On the Embassy to Gaius*, trans. Francis H. Colson, Loeb (Cambridge, MA: Harvard University Press, 1962), 281.

and religious character of the metropolis. There is, admittedly, an apologetic purpose behind what Philo said. He wanted to draw the attention of the Alexandrian Jews who were no longer attracted to the Jewish customs. Therefore, he borrowed the Greek colonization terminology, which his readers were familiar with, to draw their attention to the importance of the Jewish cult and customs. It is Philo's view, but it does not mean that other Jews would necessarily have described the Jerusalem-Diaspora relationship in this way or agreed with what he said.[24]

There was not a movement of return to Jerusalem for the Diaspora Judeans in antiquity. One would need to wait until the destruction of 70 CE to find such a movement in sectors of the social Jewish classes living in the Diaspora.[25] However, the concern for Jerusalem as an important symbolic center in the consciousness of most Hellenistic Jews was a clear and real indication of Jewish identity in the Mediterranean world in antiquity.[26] This interest was made manifest through the annual contributions that members of the Diaspora communities sent for the maintenance of the Jewish ancestral homeland in the form of the two-drachma temple tax.[27] The attachment to Jerusalem meant that Judeans afar and "at home" in the Diaspora still had a sense of empathy and social responsibility vis-à-vis Jerusalem. At times, there seems to have existed some conflicts of identity in terms of where one's economic help should go (to home

---

24. See Maren Niehoff, *Philo on Jewish Identity and Culture*, Texts and Studies in Ancient Judaism 86 (Tübingen: Mohr Siebeck, 2001), 17–24.
25. Collins, *Between Athens and Jerusalem*, 274.
26. For more on the dynamics of Judean Diaspora in antiquity, see Arkady Kovelman, *Between Alexandria and Jerusalem: The Dynamic of Jewish and Hellenistic Culture* (Leiden: Brill, 2005); Philip A. Harland, *Associations, Synagogues and Congregations: Claiming a Place in Ancient Mediterranean Society* (Minneapolis: Fortress Press, 2003); Harland, "Acculturation and Identity in the Diaspora: A Jewish Family and 'Pagan' Guilds at Hierapolis," *JJS* 57, no. 2 (2006): 222–44.
27. Gruen notices rightly that in addition to the annual temple contribution, wealthy Diaspora Jews would give considerable gifts as expressions of their deep reverence (Jos. *B.J.*, 4.567, 5.5, 5.201–5; *Ant.* 18.82, 20. 51–53); see Gruen, *Diaspora*, 347.

"here," or to the ancestral home "there"?), but sending the annual temple tax funds to Jerusalem seems to have always taken precedence over local economic situations.[28] The preference for Jerusalem resulted in the development of strained relationships between these Diaspora groups and the inhabitants of their local towns, who were upset that economic resources urgently needed for local festivals and the repair of public buildings were sent away to the "homeland" of the Judeans.

In the first century CE, the different Christ-believing communities understood themselves to be dispersed diasporic communities scattered throughout the world with an eschatological home in heaven.[29] The word *diaspora* appears in the New Testament corpus in the following places: John 7:35; James 1:1; and 1 Pet. 1. The ambiguity posed by a mythical return to the homeland in the Jewish case, and the experiences of millions scattered from and in search of "home," have contributed to a reconsideration of the concept of diaspora in modern times.[30] Today, scholars disagree on how to define *diaspora* in a way that does not restrict the concept to static dimensions, but recognizes the ebb and flow of global diasporic communities constantly moving across the globe. For Stéphane Dufoix,[31] the concept of diaspora functions more like a reference

28. See Barclay's analysis of the socioreligious situations of the Jewish communities in the Asian provinces in *Jews in the Mediterranean Diaspora*, chapter 9.
29. For example, Paul states in Phil. 3:20 "for our state and constitutive government is in heaven." I use here Richard S. Ascough's excellent translation. See Richard S. Ascough, *Paul's Macedonian Associations: The Social Context of Philippians and 1 Thessalonians*, WUNT 2:161 (Tübingen: Mohr Siebeck, 2003), 148.
30. For a thorough treatment of the historical development of the concept of *diaspora* and how it is and has been used and misused in multiple contexts, see Lisa Anteby-Yemini, William Berthomière and Gabriel Sheffer, eds., *Les diasporas: 2000 ans d'histoire* (Rennes: Presses Universitaires de Rennes, 2005); Stéphane Dufoix, *La Dispersion: Une histoire des usages du mot diaspora* (Paris: Éditions Amsterdam, 2012), and John S. Kloppenborg, "Judaeans or Judaean Christians in James?" in *Identity & Interaction in the Ancient Mediterranean: Jews, Christians and Others; Essays in Honor of Stephen G. Wilson*, ed. Zeba Crook and Philip Harland (Sheffield: Sheffield-Phoenix, 2007), 116–19. See also Jana Evans Braziel and Anita Mannur, eds., *Theorizing Diaspora: A Reader* (Cambridge, MA: Blackwell, 2003).

point than a definition. For him, the use of the term *diaspora* covers several illusions—the illusion of essence, the illusion of community, and the illusion of continuity—that need to be challenged and transformed in order to move beyond the analysis that these rarely explicit illusions carry with them. However, one might argue against Dufoix that community and continuity, even essence in certain contexts, are not illusions.

Rima Berns-McGown, critiquing and questioning different classical definitions of *diaspora* alongside various other scholars, understands the concept as an imagined space, as well as a space of connections.[32] For her, diasporic individuals balance connections between the imagined "mythic" homeland and the adopted land, and between the individual's diasporic identity and that of the wider communities. These balancing acts lead to a creative space in which identities, practice, and the performance of those identities are redefined.

The migration scholar Robin Cohen lists some common features of diaspora that one may readily compare to Paul's diasporic posture in the first century.[33] One is that of the "dispersal from an original homeland, often traumatically, to two or more foreign regions."[34] In other words, one of the reasons for foreign residence can be forced displacement, which can be experienced both from an external or internal standpoint. Cohen's comprehensive description of common features of diaspora does not mean every diaspora shares every trait

---

31. Stéphane Dufoix, "Notion, Concept ou Slogan: Qu'y a-t-il sous le terme de "Diaspora"? " in *Les diasporas: 2000 ans d'histoire*, ed. Lisa Anteby-Yemini, William Berthomière and Gabriel Sheffer (Rennes: Presses Universitaires de Rennes, 2005), 53–63. See also Dufoix, *Diasporas*; Kim Knott and Seán McLoughlin, eds., *Diasporas: Concepts, Intersections, Identities* (London: Zed Books, 2010).
32. Rima Berns-McGown, "Redefining 'Diaspora': The Challenge of Connection and Inclusion," *International Journal* 63 (Winter 2007–08): 3–20.
33. Cohen, *Global Diasporas*, 17.
34. Ibid., 124.

articulated. He constructs his ideal types of diaspora based on these common features. For example, he considers the Jews, Africans, and the Armenians under the category of *victim diaspora*. He states, "Diasporas are often formed not only by one traumatic event (the marker of a victim diaspora), but by many and different causes, several only becoming salient over an extended historical period."[35] He also considers other types of diaspora, including the *labor diaspora* experienced by indentured Indians; the *imperial diaspora* of the British; *trade diaspora* (e.g., Lebanese, Chinese); and what he categorizes as *deterritorialized diaspora* to "encompass the lineaments of a number of unusual diasporic experiences."[36]

Paul is outside of his ancestral homeland, but the places he travels to are not presented as alien territories; there is no evidence of trauma in him, and he was not part of a victim diaspora.[37] Whether Paul experienced any sense of displacement as a diasporic subject is difficult, if not impossible, for us to know. What we do know is that most Judeans in antiquity did not think of themselves as away from home or as victims of displacement, but that they felt entirely at home

35. Cohen, *Global Diasporas*, 123
36. Ibid., 124 (italics added).
37. Indeed, there can be traumatic experiences in diasporic subjects and communities that may result from being scattered away from one's homeland, as was the case for the Jews after the war of 66–70 ce. Many theorists, such as Stuart Hall and Paul Gilroy, argue the diaspora can be celebrated, and may be a place that allows one to realize one's self. Gilroy argues the "dual consciousness" of the African diaspora is the result of a complex transnational and intercultural multiplicity, and one that enables these people to transform the different cultures they occupy. In this manner, it is no longer sufficient, or even possible, for modern diasporic subjects to claim a site as representing the locus of the diasporic reality—be it racial, spatial, or cultural. In the diaspora, according to Gilroy, one inhabits many locations that are never stable but that are constantly moving, continually evolving, and persistently changing. This fluidity allows the hybrid diasporic subjects to infiltrate and alter the dissimilar and complex cultural sites they inhabit. In this sense, diasporic realities are seen as less of a struggle, and not so much as a constant traumatic experience, but are understood as sites offering possibilities to create fluid and effective versions of solidarity between dispersed groups. Gilroy's notion of doubleness and its complexity destabilizes unitary narratives, but seeks and celebrates a positive model of cultural hybridity that challenges the ideal of the modern nation-state in its desire for ethnic hegemony. See Paul Gilroy, *Between Camps: Nations, Culture and the Allure of Race* (London: Allen Lane, 2000).

in their diasporic social locations.[38] Like other Jews who lived outside in the Diaspora rather than in the Judean homeland, Paul was at home in the Roman cities of the eastern Mediterranean; he never expresses loneliness about or longing for his Judean homeland. His relationship with the mother city Jerusalem, however, is both complicated and fraught.[39] Paul does not consider a return to the ancestral homeland, although the place preserves its mythic allure and is reconfigured to fulfill a certain "myth" of return.[40] In this sense, what is imagined is the descent of "Jerusalem from above" in order to embrace those on earth who are the children of this envisaged realm above.[41]

Even if those in antiquity who moved around and settled outside their place of origins did not consciously think of themselves as living as part of a diaspora or construct a theory or philosophy of diaspora, the quotidian practice of their lives lends itself to our contemporary theorizing of diaspora. They had fluid and mobile identities; they were navigating several worlds without feeling cut off or stigmatized from communities "at home." Cultural diversity with an emphasis to local particularities, as rightly observed by Kathy Ehrensperger, "should be regarded as the default setting in analyses of cultural encounter in antiquity."[42] Modern diaspora theories are useful to this study but there are differences, as well as similarities, between modern diasporas and that of ancient Jewish Diasporas. It is dangerous, for example, to equate the center-periphery/Jerusalem-

---

38. See Gruen, *Diaspora*.

39. F. F. Bruce understands Paul's relationship with Jerusalem to be "ambivalent." See "Paul and Jerusalem," *Tyndale Bulletin* 19 (1968): 3–25. The ancestral Judean homeland remained a significant place in his understanding and (re)imagination. See chapter 4 for more on this.

40. See chapter 5 of this study for more on the dynamics of home, space, and diasporic identity. In that chapter, I propose Paul's collection trip to Jerusalem could, indeed, be conceived of as a "homecoming" of some sort in an analysis of the financial transfer and patronal exchange between non-Judean and Judean assemblies.

41. See chapters 3 and 4 of this study for elaboration.

42. See Kathy Ehrensperger, "Speaking Greek under Rome: Paul, the Power of Language," *Neotestamentica* 46, no. 1 (2012): 15.

Diaspora relationship in the ancient world with modern Zionism. Concepts like *ancestral homeland* and *diaspora* are located in this study in specific frames of reference in order to reframe some issues in Pauline interpretation.

Furthermore, for Cohen, "alternatively or additionally, the expansion from a homeland in search of work, in pursuit of trade or to further colonial ambitions"[43] may push toward occupying the space of the diaspora.[44] Paul moved around the Roman provinces in search of work and with a message about the resurrected Christ. The map he followed stemmed more from life's necessities than from anything else, although his movements were in accordance with Roman provincial nomenclature (Illyricum, Macedonia, Achaia, Arabia, Asia, Galatia, and so forth).[45] Paul's movements to major cities were not because of forced displacement or because he wanted to be an active model missionary with clear missionary strategies. Paul moved around as an artisan in search of economic opportunities. He was a preacher proclaiming a different understanding of Judaism with his new conviction that the death and resurrection of Jesus constituted the fulfillment of the law and the promises God made to Abraham. He moved around with a strong sense of ethnic group consciousness, and a sense of empathy and responsibility for those dying of hunger in the ancestral home, especially those who shared his same faith in Jesus. Paul's position within the discourses of history

---

43. Robin Cohen, *Global Diasporas*, 17.

44. Indeed, people did and do move in search of economic opportunities, and this is typified by Cohen as labor diaspora.

45. Chantal Reynier is only partly right when she states, "Même si le milieu juif joue son rôle, Paul définit sa mission dans le cadre des provinces romaines (Syrie, Cilicie, Galatie, Achaie, Asie, Macedoine) et par rapport à des régions ou à des peuples." See *Saint Paul sur les routes du monde romain: Infrastrustures, Logistique, Itinéraire* (Paris: Éditions du Cerf, 2009), 229. She is correct with regards to the geographical spheres of Paul's activities, but wrong in still holding on to the essentialist notion that portrays Paul as being totally in control over clear missionary strategies (notice her "*Paul définit sa mission*"). Also, throughout her monograph, she relies too heavily and uncritically on the book of Acts as an unproblematic source for historical data and, in doing so, misses the opportunity to better calibrate Paul's "univers géographique."

and culture stands in relation to his boundary crossings—fostered in large measure by economic necessities—with his redefined, reframed Judaism stemming from his christological determination and orientation, a point to be further developed in chapter 5.

For Cohen, a point widely attested to in many diasporas is "a strong ethnic group consciousness sustained over a long time and based on a sense of distinctiveness, a common history, the transmission of a common cultural and religious heritage and the belief in a common fate."[46] Paul sustains and maintains a strong ethnic group consciousness,[47] and the transmission of a common cultural and religious heritage, albeit a modified one, is very much in sight. Paul seems to have had serious concerns for other Judeans, which corresponds to Cohen's theory that diasporas have a common sense of empathy and coresponsibility with coethnic members in other countries of settlement, even when home has become more vestigial. Thus, many discussions deemed theological may also have a dimension that goes beyond and embraces the social and the political aspects. Paul had a strong sense of empathy and responsibility toward his coethnic members. The Diaspora enabled him to create novel rhetorical strategies as he negotiated his way around his social and political environments.

Additionally, according to Cohen, there is usually "a troubled relationship with host societies, suggesting a lack of acceptance or the possibility that another calamity might befall the group."[48] Paul's success as a preacher in the Diaspora with the burgeoning of many different cells of Christ believers seems to indicate a high degree of acceptance from the nations (although his acceptance could be nuanced, considering his troubles with the Corinthians). Paul's

---

46. Cohen, *Global Diasporas*, 17.
47. For example, Romans 9–11 is intensely personal.
48. Cohen, *Global Diasporas*, 17.

diasporic identity is defined not by a return to some sort of essence or purity, but by creating new fictive kinships and imaginative ways of being and becoming "all things to all people" (1 Cor. 9: 22).[49]

Cohen has suggested that "one of the common features of all diasporas is the idealization of the real or putative ancestral home and a collective commitment to its maintenance, restoration, safety and prosperity, even to its creation."[50] This is illustrated by modern diasporas that contribute economically, politically, and socially to their host societies, and influence the policies of both the countries of settlement and the ancestral homeland. For example, the Haitian Diaspora has provided vital economic resources and social contributions to the homeland so much so that it is viewed by many Haitians as being the "Tenth Department," thus viscerally connecting the scattered Haitian Diaspora to the nine geographic departments of the country.[51] In Paul's diasporic posture, he was deeply concerned about the materially poor in Christ in the ancestral home—a home needing reappropriation and reimagination.[52]

49. I am inspired here by Liew's analysis of 1 Corinthians, especially on page 106. See Tat-siong Benny Liew, "Melancholia in Diaspora: Reading Paul's Psycho-Political Operatives in 1 Corinthians," in *What Is Asian American Biblical Hermeneutics? Reading the New Testament* (Honolulu: University of Hawaii Press, 2008).

50. Cohen, *Global Diasporas*, 106.

51. See Edwidge Danticat, "Introduction," in *The Butterfly's Way: Voices from the Haitian Dyaspora* [sic] *in the United States*, ed. Edwidge Danticat (New York: Soho Press, 2001), xiv. The former liberation theologian (Jean Bertrand Aristide) who became president of Haiti in 1991 and 2004 called the "Tenth Department" a "bank," as the money sent from those outside to the mostly poor of the country is vital for the survival of most. See Nina Glick Schiller and Georges Fouron, *Woke up Laughing: Long-Distance Nationalism and the Search for Home* (Durham, NC: Duke University Press, 2001), 119. See also Philippe Zacaïr, *Haiti and the Haitian Diaspora in the Wider Caribbean* (Gainesville, FL: University Press of Florida, 2010). For a very helpful survey of the variegated Haitian Diaspora, the different situations in its host countries, and the equally important roles of each vis-à-vis Haiti, see Jana E. Braziel, *Diaspora: An Introduction* (Oxford: Blackwell, 2008), especially 39–47, 151–56, 180–87. Braziel remarks rightly that "Diasporic communities have been (and continue to be) vital sites for political resistance to globalization" but "that does not mean that diasporas—or some diasporic communities—cannot also be extremely conservative, nationalistic voices . . . in their home and host countries" (158). This kind of support can be in the form of money, intelligence, weapons, or other means to endorse ethnic, exclusionary, nationalistic revolutionary militant groups.

The relationships and the discourses in the diasporas are the loci of struggles different groups face as they try to negotiate life in traditions and cultures that are foreign.[53] As Avtar Brah remarks, "All diasporas are differentiated, heterogeneous, contested spaces, even as they are implicated in the construction of a common 'we.'"[54] The creative dynamics in diasporas invite the diasporic subjects and communities to negotiate the power relations of who speaks and who does not; who is mandated to speak on behalf of whom, in what terms and in what language; and who is empowered and who is disempowered in a specific sociopolitical formation. The complexities and tensions inherent in the diasporic condition cause one to maneuver between selecting and adopting some of the cultural values of one's cultural host, and making and remaking creative and positive spaces of identity through solidarity and criticism. Thus, the realities of diasporic subjects and communities constantly entail negotiating sociopolitical and cultural identities that are in perpetual flux. Such multilayered cultural and political realities cannot be summed up simply as single binary oppositions of present and past, foreign and familiar, or alien and home. In fact, the boundaries of inclusion and exclusion, of "us" and "them," are contested and reconceived under the important concept of *diaspora space*, as noted by Brah. She contends the diaspora space "is the intersectionality of diaspora, border, and dis/location as a point of confluence of economic, political, cultural and psychic processes. It addresses the global condition of culture, economics and politics as a site of 'migrancy' and 'travel' which seriously questions the subject position of the 'native.'"[55] In this sense, the diaspora space is occupied by all:

52. That will be illustrated in chapter 5 by looking at the collection project.
53. See chapter 3 on how this relates to Paul and others in the conflict at Antioch.
54. Avtar Brah, *Cartographies of Diaspora: Contesting Identities* (New York: Routledge, 1996), 184.
55. Ibid., 181. The term *intersectionality*, which was first theorized by the legal expert Kimberlé Crenshaw, is an important critical concept that helps in analyzing various categories of identity

both by the one who has not been anywhere else besides this place, and by the one who has moved around quite a bit and settled in this place. In this sense, there is no fixity of places; no identities are kept unmarked. Thus, diaspora space is a space where the different interrelationships are not mediated through the dominant culture(s) but are shaped, differentiated, and connected by the different crossings. A diasporic space must always be problematized in terms of race, racism, religion, class, gender, sexuality, education, and so on.

Also significant is how the rhetoric in the diaspora space, especially in terms of who speaks and who says what, can be framed, concocted, and appropriated to serve certain identities and particular ideological and socioreligious discourses. Paul's diasporic space is a social, dynamic, and fluid space composed of both diasporic and nondiasporic peoples. For example, the negotiation between the delegation from Jerusalem and the Christ-following Diaspora Judeans in Antioch in Galatians 2 is not solely over gentiles and divergent theological agendas. Rather, as argued in chapter 4 of this study, Galatians 2 concerns questions of inclusion and equality, home and diaspora, center and periphery, whose voice is heard, who can represent properly what constitutes the right way of living out of the ancestral traditions in a diasporic space, and how far Diaspora Judeans could allow themselves to go in negotiating their lives in non-Jewish environments.

Brah's concept of diaspora space defines communities that meet in the messiness of space—complicated by issues of gender, sexuality, race, economic status, education, religion—conceived as dynamic,

(gender, ethnicity, economic status, etc.). It purports to highlight the fact that identities are interconnected and need to be studied together. See Crenshaw, "Demarginalizing the Intersection of Race and Sex: A Black Feminist Critique of Antidiscrimination Doctrine, Feminist Theory and Antiracist Politics," reprinted in *The Politics of Law: A Progressive Critique,* ed. David Kairys, 2nd ed (New York: Pantheon, 1990), 195–217; and "Mapping the Margins: Intersectionality, Identity Politics, and Violence against Women of Color," *Stanford Law Review* 43 (1991): 1241–99.

contested, appropriated, and (re)defined by those who have moved in, and also by those who have never been anywhere else besides this place. "Diaspora space" is a flexible space "of/for theoretical crossovers that foreground processes of power";[56] it is a place where multiple aspects related to diasporic realities are taken into consideration, and where the different identities are not untouched, but shaped by the various crossings; it is the confluence of the sedentary and the nomadic.[57]

The evolution of the concept of *diaspora* as dynamic, mobile, and fluid is theorized as *hybridity*. The notion of hybridity is claimed by many recent theorists, such as Homi K. Bhabha and Stuart Hall, as providing a site of resistance to hegemonic and homogenizing forces and practices that threaten to nullify cultural diversities. For Bhabha, the hybrid site opens up a "Third Space of enunciation."[58] This space "in between" provides a way to understand the different struggles that come into play when defining authority, subordination, assimilation, and resistance in a particular colonial and diasporic situation. In the words of Bhabha, "It is the 'inter'—the cutting edge of translation and negotiation, the *in-between*, the space of the *entre* . . . —that carries the burden of the meaning of culture."[59] In this sense, it is in exploring the interstices of negotiation and calculated responses on the part of colonial and imperial subjects, as well as diasporic communities, that one might start to understand the complexity of colonial history and diasporic life.

I show in chapter 2 how the dynamics of the hybrid condition can be expressed by looking at the *Letter of Aristeas*. In the *Letter*,

---

56. Avtar Brah, *Cartographies of Diaspora*, 210.
57. In chapter 3, through an analysis of the the incident at Antioch (Galatians 2), I will show how the diasporic space of Antioch was in flux, multidimensional, and contested.
58. Homi Bhabha, "Cultural Diversity and Cultural Differences," in *The Post-Colonial Studies Reader*, ed. Bill Ashcroft et al. (New York: Routledge, 1988), 206–9.
59. Ibid, 209.

the author expresses a profound desire for a particular community to enter into better communication with the Hellenistic world at large by incorporating the best of "Jewish" and "Greek" cultures and modes of thinking without jeopardizing what they hold dear as part of their socioreligious fabric. It presents a "third space" of breathing "in between." My analysis of the *Letter* is done in a way to situate Paul in his diasporic posture as one living "in between" social realities and religious ideals.

For Stuart Hall, diaspora (or his coined word *diasporization*), is similar to musical improvisation performed by black jazz musicians and rappers in which new, dynamic, "cut-and-mixed" recombinations make the whole diasporic process similar to a powerful cultural play.[60] According to Hall, the diasporic experience "is defined, not by essence or purity, but by the recognition of a necessary heterogeneity and diversity; by a conception of 'identity' which lives with and through, not despite, difference; by *hybridity*. Diaspora identities are those which are constantly producing and reproducing themselves anew, through transformation and difference."[61] Thus, for Hall, the subversive force of this hybridization lies in its capacity to deconstruct the discourses of the powerful, and to decenter, destabilize, challenge, carnivalize, break, and recreate elements from the master codes of the dominant culture by making them into something new.[62] Hall's theorizing of diaspora places the concept in a more fluid, mobile mode. Movements across boundaries of becoming and being are ever-expanding improvisations capable of creating new and complex tapestries of playful art conveying

60. Stuart Hall, "The Question of Cultural Identity," in *Modernity and Its Futures*, ed. Stuart Hall, David Held, and Anthony McGrew (Cambridge: Polity Press, 1992), 310–14.
61. Ibid. And one must note how differently diasporic populations can view their situations, especially when they focus on the cultivation of purity.
62. One could also point out, in nuancing Hall's theorizing, that diaspora also produces discourses of power of its own.

continuity and rupture, similarity and difference.[63] In other words, Hall imagines and argues for a diasporic identity that generates new kinds of subjects who are constantly crafting novel ways of being and evolving.

For all the aforementioned theorists, understanding the concept of diaspora through the lens of hybridity provides a site of resistance to homogenizing forces, destabilizes unitary narratives, and seeks to situate diaspora as a generator of new and complex identities in order to deconstruct any hegemonic discourses. Following Hall's theorizing, Paul's diasporic identities within the pluralistic and complex diaspora spaces he occupies are constantly reformed by interactions with the different communities with whom he was in contact. Even though his identities are, at times, construed as permanently fixed, Paul's movements across boundaries require him to engage in ever-expanding social experiments in creative ways.

The Scholarly Context of This Study and Its Contribution to the Field

When surveying Pauline studies, one does not find any scholarly work devoted solely or specifically to Paul's diaspora existence.[64]

---

63. I develop this more in chapter 2.
64. Again, what I am referring to here precisely is the absence of any substantial scholarly work, such as a monograph, devoted entirely to study Paul as a Diaspora Judean within the Judaism of the first-century Mediterranean world. The investigation of looking at Paul as a Diaspora Jew, and doing so in conversation with contemporary studies of identity, ethnicity and diaspora, is just in its initial stages. For example, see Calvin J. Roetzel, "Oikoumene and the Limits of Pluralism in Alexandria Judaism and Paul," in Overman and MacLennan, *Diaspora Jews and Judaism*, 163–170; Daniel Boyarin, *Paul: A Radical Jew: Paul and the Politics of Identity*,Contraversions: Critical Studies in Jewish Literature, Culture, and Society (Berkeley: University of California Press, 1994); Philip A. Harland, *Associations, Synagogues and Congregations: Claiming a Place in Ancient Mediterranean Society* (Minneapolis: Fortress Press, 2003). For some reflections and analysis on Paul's dynamics of identity and ethnic/self-constructions, see Robert Seesengood, "Hybridity and the Rhetoric of Endurance: Reading Paul's Athletic Metaphors in a Context of Postcolonial Self-Construction," *Bible and Critical Theory* 1, no. 3 (2005), slightly revised in *Competing Identities: The Athlete and the Gladiator in Early Christianity*, Library of New Testament Studies (New York: T & T Clark, 2006),

Wayne A. Meeks's landmark volume offered fresh insights into Paul and his churches in their social settings and spearheaded the social-scientific studies of early Christianity; however, it does not pay any attention to the dynamics of diaspora existence, or how they could have played some role in Paul's dealings with the different urban communities with which he interacted.[65] Meeks refers to Jews in general in the Diaspora, but the specificity of Diaspora existence as related to the shaping of Paul's socioreligious postures and how Paul's diasporic social location could have influenced his theology are not within the purview of his analysis.[66]

Even though there is an essential link among postcolonial studies and diaspora studies,[67] only a few biblical scholars have produced an analysis using the latter; meanwhile, especially in the last twenty years, much work has been done using postcolonial studies, particularly in Pauline studies.[68] Stephen D. Moore's very helpful overview of postcolonial studies in biblical studies mentions the current shift, and describes the way postcolonial studies as a whole tries to take account of globalization within the parameters of its analysis; but he does not pay attention to diaspora studies in its

---

20–34; Denise K. Buell, *Why This New Race: Ethnic Reasoning in Early Christianity* (New York: Columbia University Press, 2005); Denise K. Buell and Caroline J. Hodge, "The Politics of Interpretation: The Rhetoric of Race and Ethnicity in Paul," *JBL* 123, no. 2 (2004): 235–51; Tat-siong Benny Liew, *What Is Asian American Biblical Hermeneutics? Reading the New Testament* (Honolulu: University of Hawaii Press, 2008); Benny Liew, "Redressing Bodies at Corinth: Racial/Ethnic Politics and Religious Difference in the Context of Empire," in *The Colonized Apostle: Paul through Postcolonial Eyes*, ed. Christopher D. Stanley (Minneapolis: Fortress Press, 2011); Gordon M. Zerbe, "Constructions of Paul in Filipino Theology of Struggle," in Stanley, *The Colonized Apostle*, 255.

65. Wayne A. Meeks, *The First Urban Christians: The Social World of the Apostle Paul* (New Haven: Yale University Press, 1983).

66. Ibid., especially 34–39.

67. See the different articles in *Interventions: International Journal of Postcolonial Studies* 5, no. 1 (2003).

68. See Fernando F. Segovia and Rasiah S. Sugirtharajah, *A Postcolonial Commentary on the New Testament Writings* (London: T & T Clark, 2007), and Stanley, *The Colonized Apostle*.

relationship to both postcolonial studies and globalization and migration studies.[69]

Daniel Boyarin's study of Paul—a bold foray into Pauline studies by a Talmudic scholar who took Paul's diasporic existence seriously—aimed to analyze him as a first-century Jewish cultural critic in the ways the apostle managed to articulate a particular diasporic identity.[70] Boyarin posits Paul as a radical social critic who negotiates the pitfalls inherent in a coerced Christian universalism and a marked Jewish ethnic difference. In Boyarin's view, Paul is a radical social critic because of his "discourse of radical reform" directed at Jewish culture. In this sense, his view has some affinities to what is argued below, although his grand totalizing vision of idealized diaspora in a Hegelian type of synthesis is far from the present project.[71] Also, Boyarin's (post)modern response to Paul, which, inter alia, leads to a critique of contemporary Judaism, is not part of the scope of this study.

Another scholar who has pushed and challenged others to take Paul as a Diaspora Jew seriously by reflecting on Paul's Diaspora identity is Sze-kar Wan.[72] Wan's work is particularly helpful for the ways in which he articulates Paul's ethnicity and diasporic posture within the Greco-Roman political landscape with a critical eye to the specificity of the socioreligious groups that formed his entourage. For example, Wan's essay on the collection project is a key dialogue

69. See Moore, "Paul after Empire," in *The Colonized Apostle*, 9–23.
70. Boyarin, *Paul: A Radical Jew*.
71. Ibid., 52ff. Boyarin's postmodern cultural studies approach places Paul as a cultural critic of a particular kind of (nonnormative) Judaism.
72. Wan, "Does Diaspora Identity Imply Some Sort of Universality?"; Wan, "'To the Jew First and Also to the Greek': Reading Romans as Ethnic Construction," in *Prejudice and Christian Beginnings: Investigating Race, Gender, and Ethnicity in Early Christian Studies*, ed. Laura Nasrallah and Elisabeth S. Fiorenza (Minneapolis: Fortress Press, 2009); Wan, "Collection for the Saints as Anticolonial Act: Implications of Paul's Ethnic Reconstruction," in *Paul and Politics: Ekklesia, Israel, Imperium, Interpretation*, ed. Richard A. Horsley (Harrisburg, PA: Trinity Press International, 2000).

partner in chapter 5 of this study. Wan asserts the collection is better interpreted from the background of the temple tax, especially in light of the numerous tensions it fostered between the Jews and Roman authorities. In this sense, Paul, the Diaspora Jew coming from abroad and accompanied by gentile followers, would find himself implicated in the local ambient frictions over divergent conceptions with regard to where to draw the social and ethnic boundary lines.

Fernando F. Segovia is also one of the few biblical scholars who has endeavoured to examine Paul from the perspectives of diaspora studies.[73] He situates the theoretical and historical framework of diaspora studies in its relationship to postcolonial studies in order to show how contemporary biblical and Christian studies can benefit from these methodologies, especially in light of the shift in the social makeup of Christianity today.

Some Pauline scholars are still puzzled over the place of Paul in the Diaspora. Carl R. Holladay notes that Paul never "employs the term or its cognates (see James 1:1; 1 Pet 1:1)."[74] The simple response is that one does not need to see a term actually being used to know the reality and experience lurking behind such a specific term are present. Words are far from being the only valid indicator of the presence or absence of a particular social reality. The diasporic existence was certainly a reality for many Jews of the Second Temple period, even when the word *diaspora* may not have been utilized or present in the consciousness of those in the Diaspora. As I argue in this study, Paul

73. See Fernando F. Segovia, "Interpreting beyond Borders: Postcolonial Studies and Diasporic Studies in Biblical Criticism," in Segovia, *Interpreting Beyond Borders*, 11–34. There is one forthcoming monograph on Paul's cultural identity that I am aware of, which draws from sociolinguistics and multilingualism studies. See Kathy Ehrensperger, *Paul at the Crossroads of Cultures: Theologizing in the Space Between* (London: T & T Clark, 2013).

74. See Carl R. Holladay, "Paul and His Predecessors in the Diaspora: Some Reflections on Ethnic Identity in the Fragmentary Hellenistic Jewish Authors," in *Early Christianity and Classical Culture: Comparative Studies in Honor of Abraham J. Malherbe*, ed. John T. Fitzgerald et al., SNT (New York: Brill Academic Press, 2003), 458.

was a Diaspora Jew among the nations navigating and negotiating the politics associated with such spaces and social groups with which he engaged.

There is value in examining Paul from the perspective of diaspora studies in order to consider how some issues in Paul can become clearer or be read differently. Calvin J. Roetzel has rightly argued Paul's social location in Diaspora Judaism "may be crucial to understand the dynamic of Paul's theology."[75] For Roetzel, "given Paul's upbringing in the Diaspora, his Diaspora Bible (the LXX), his Greek language, and his education in the Diaspora, one must respond that a consideration of Paul that does not take account of the influence of the Diaspora on his theology is . . . absolute nonsense."[76]

Gordon M. Zerbe has recently proposed a creative reimagining of Paul in a contemporary diasporic context:

> Being born to a family of Filipino migrant workers living, say, in Hong Kong and being sent back to his homeland for a proper education. There he would encounter a new religious movement that had sprung up in the hills of a remote part of conflicted and impoverished Mindanao and found a foothold in the capital city despite the "salvaging" of its founding prophet. In this reimagining, Paul would first zealously resist the new movement but then embrace it with equal zeal, proclaiming its message of a soon-to-be transformed world to people in the centers of commercial and political power. It should not surprise us that the last time we should hear of such a person is in a place of detention.[77]

One certainly needs to be cautious not to impose a modern understanding of diaspora and migrant workers on an ancient diasporic artisan such as Paul, and one must be careful in approaching the claims of Acts that lurk behind Zerbe's method with regard to Paul's biography. However, such a reimaginative project can be

75. Calvin Roetzel, "Oikoumene and the Limits of Pluralism," 182.
76. Ibid., 179.
77. Gordon M. Zerbe, "Constructions of Paul," 255.

helpful in dislocating, disrupting, destabilizing, and reframing a figure often essentialized as a spiritual guru, a hero in company of fellow heroes with the vision "to turn Caesar upside down."[78] Paul lived at least half of his life in the Diaspora. In the Diaspora, he associated freely with conquered peoples who were different from his ethnic background, and he adapted his behaviour to his audiences in order to share with them his reimagined and recalibrated Jewish faith and hope centered around the figure of Jesus (1 Cor. 9:21). In his diasporic sociopolitical location, Paul associated with the nations and he considered it his goal to create alternative cultural and religious associations where "there is no Jew or Greek, no slave or free, no male and female" (Gal 3:28) in Jesus the Christ.[79] Paul's diasporic experience and identity propel him to generate new social dynamics and new politics of identity between nondiaspora peoples and those scattered. For Paul, the whole conception of being a Jew, with a set of "identity markers" rooted in the Torah (circumcision, dietary laws, the Sabbath), seems to have been designed to create effective versions of solidarity between different ethnic groups that share the diaspora space under the Roman Empire.[80] If one follows Hall's analysis of interpreting diaspora as constantly generating new and complex

---

78. Davina C. Lopez, "Visualizing Significant Otherness: Reimagining Paul(ine Studies) through Hybrid Lenses," in Stanley, *The Colonized Apostle*, 89. The movement in Pauline scholarship of the last few years, mainly through the impetus of Richard A. Horsley and various collaborators, that sees Paul as a political partisan against Caesar is a very interesting, instructive and thought–provoking development in the ways in which sociopolitical aspects related to Paul and empire are emphasized. See, for example, the following works edited by Richard A. Horsley: *Paul and Empire: Religion and Power in Roman Imperial Society* (Harrisburg, PA: Trinity Press International, 1997); *Paul and Politics*; *Paul and the Roman Imperial Order* (Harrisburg, PA: Trinity Press International, 2004). However, portraying Paul, as Horsley does, as an anti-imperial figure, a political genius, a national hero, and a rebel offering elaborate ways to challenge the imperial power of his time fails to consider the apostle within his diasporic, flexible, and hybridized position in the first century under the Roman Empire. See Richard A. Horsley's commentary on 1 Corinthians in Segovia and Sugirtharajah, *Postcolonial Commentary on the New Testament Writings*, 220–32.

79. My translation.

80. I am using James Dunn's category. See his *Jesus, Paul and the Law: Studies in Mark and Galatians* (Louisville: Westminster John Knox Press, 1990).

ways of being and evolving, then Paul's diasporic experience and identity as a laborer in search of work and an itinerant preacher proclaiming the message of Jesus to the nations propelled him to utilize and maximize different networks in order to generate new social dynamics.[81] In this sense, the "apostle to the conquered"[82] seems to foster versions of solidarity among different ethnic groups, dispersed and nondiaspora peoples, through transformation and difference in order to create diverse, fluid, and ever-expanding alternative communities within the Roman Empire around the figure of Jesus.

Paul's status as a diasporic subject under Roman rule requires one to move prudently in assessing this particular imperial power. One needs to be careful not to impose an uncritical judgement of Rome as being only a brutal force in antiquity; indeed, it was possible to live relatively at ease under the imperial regime as a colonial or diasporic subject because of the benefits conferred by the empire. For example, trade expansion, security, and local crafts and industries flourished. There were brutal elements of Roman domination, to be sure, but other more benign aspects existed as well. The *pax Romana* did bring certain material benefits, and Roman-Hellenistic culture was

---

81. The use of kinship terms in different ancient associations to signify that one "belongs" to the "in-group" is well attested. See Halvor Moxnes, ed., *Constructing Early Christian Families: Family as Social Reality and Metaphor* (London: Routledge, 1997); and Carolyn Osiek and David L. Balch, eds., *Early Christian Families in Context: An Interdisciplinary Dialogue* (Grand Rapids: Eerdmans, 2003); Reidar Aasgaard, *"My Beloved Brothers and Sisters!" Christian Siblingship in Paul*, JSNTSup 265 (London: T & T Clark, 2004). Also see Philip A. Harland, "Familial Dimensions of Group Identity: 'Brothers' (ΑΔΕΛΦΟΙ) in Associations of the Greek East," *Journal of Biblical Literature* 124 (2005): 491–513, and "Familial Dimensions of Group Identity (II): 'Mothers' and 'Fathers' in Associations and Synagogues of the Greek World," *Journal for the Study of Judaism in the Persian, Hellenistic, and Roman Period* 38 (2007): 57–79. For Caroline J. Hodge, "This new language of kinship creates a myth of collective identity for the Gentiles, an identity that relates to, but does not become one with, a Jewish identity." See Hodge, *If Sons, Then Heirs: A Study of Kinship and Ethnicity on the Letters of Paul* (Oxford: Oxford University Press, 2007), 152.

82. Here I am borrowing Lopez's title, *Apostle to the Conquered: Reimagining Paul's Mission* (Minneapolis: Fortress Press, 2008).

intrinsically meaningful and appealing to many conquered peoples. Real history has many shades, and is not simply black and white.[83] It is necessary to keep in mind that Rome was not a totalitarian regime as we moderns understand it, since that was logistically impossible in premodern social conditions.[84] The ideal of total control of the colonial subjects, cohesion, and absolute military efficiency in the case of Roman rule is a myth. The Roman Empire did provide security for its people, its diasporic subjects, and its client states, although not as an ideal modern and universal society. Also, as highlighted by several recent works, the simple oppositions of accommodation versus resistance and Roman domination versus local upheavals need to be nuanced by considering the dialectical character present in such complex relations.[85]

The Plan of the Study

Paul's condition was unremittingly diasporic and this influenced all his relationships and activities. Three specific contexts of his life and work were crucially formed by the diasporic condition, namely (1) his negotiation of difference organized along ethnic lines within

---

83. See, among countless others, David Braund, *Rome and the Friendly King: The Character of the Client Kingship* (New York: St. Martin's Press, 1984); James Bryce, *The Ancient Roman Empire and the British Empire in India* (London: Oxford University Press, 1914); Peter Garnsey and Charles R. Whittaker, *Imperialism in the Ancient World* (Cambridge: Cambridge University Press, 1978); Peter Garnsey and Richard Saller, *The Roman Empire: Economy, Society and Culture* (Berkeley: University of California Press, 1987); Harrison Thomas, "Ancient and Modern Imperialism," *Greece and Rome*, 55, no. 1(2008); Keith Hopkins, *A World Full of Gods: Pagans, Jews and Christians in the Roman Empire* (London: Weidenfeld & Nicolson, 1999); Christopher Kelly, *The Roman Empire: A Very Short Introduction* (London: Oxford University Press, 2006).

84. See Andrew W. Lintott, *Imperium Romanum: Politics and Administration* (London: Routledge, 1993), 120.

85. See David J. Mattingly, ed., *Dialogues in Roman Imperialism: Power, Discourse, and Discrepant Experience in the Roman Empire*, Journal of Roman Archaeology Supplementary Series 23 (Portsmouth, RI: Journal of Roman Archeology, 1997); and Clifford Ando, *Imperial Ideology and Provincial loyalty in the Roman Empire* (Berkeley: University of California Press, 2000); David J. Mattingly, *Imperialism, Power, and Identity: Experiencing the Roman Empire* (Princeton, NJ: Princeton University Press, 2011).

the nascent movement of devotees to Jesus, (2) his conception and treatment of his primary audience as the nations—those who were ethnically other to his Jewish self—and (3) his organization of financial transfer and patronal exchange between non-Judean and Judean assemblies.

This study has six chapters. This introduction lays out the specific issues that can be read differently from the perspective of diaspora studies and the theoretical model(s) that inform this work. Throughout, I take Paul's identity as a Diaspora Jew seriously and employ modern diaspora studies carefully in order to reframe and rethink some key questions in Pauline interpretation. The theoretical engagement I undertake here clearly shows how complex and fluid the concept of diaspora is, and how it is important to take care in using such analytical tools to capture an ancient diasporic subject like Paul.

The first chapter contains an analysis of two works outside of Paul in order to build on the complex notion of hybridity, as developed by Homi K. Bhabha. The phenomenon requires one to give an account of tension and contradiction. In this chapter, I look at hybridity in the *Letter of Aristeas* and in Josephus's rereading of *Aristeas* in book 12 of his *Antiquities* in order to show how strategies of negotiating the diaspora space might have been utilized. I illuminate how diaspora was negotiated in the ancient Hellenistic Judaism of the Roman period, and situate Paul's own ways of negotiating his social and religious ideas and ideals in the Diaspora. The social, religious, and political realities of diasporic hybrid subjects and communities living "in between spaces" are important grounds to cover in order to understand the complexities of inhabiting the space of diaspora, negotiating such a space, and imagining "home" in ancient Hellenistic Judaism of the Roman period. By highlighting interactions, relationships, negotiations, social realities and ideals, "home," and the memory of home in the diasporic milieu, this chapter situates Paul as a diaspora figure within the matrix and complexities of first-century Diaspora Judaism.

The second chapter presents a description of Paul as a diaspora figure. The works of Jonathan Z. Smith, particularly on the practice of comparison, are used to situate Paul comparatively to other Diaspora Judeans. I also build on the indices developed by John M. Barclay and Philip A. Harland to represent ways of measuring some similarities and differences between Paul and other Diaspora Judeans. In that chapter, diaspora studies highlight the positionality of diasporic subjects and explain how diasporic figures negotiate spaces. Like anyone's identity, Paul's is complex, plural—not essentialized to fit a somewhat rigid, permanently fixed, distinctive "Jewish" identity in the Diaspora—and continually in the process of being forged and formed by his movement across cultural boundaries. To borrow from Stuart Hall, Paul's cultural identity "is not a fixed essence at all, lying unchanged outside history and culture. . . . It is not once-and-for-all."[86] Paul's social position in the Diaspora can be seen as having at least some bearing on how he develops certain theses (cf. Gal. 3:28) that all, regardless of their ethnic origins, gender, and social positioning, can be one within boundary-crossing communities. The cross-cultural mingling of different identities allows him to imagine, think through, and wrestle with issues of spaces, identities (social, economic, gender), cultures, and traditions, even if he still holds on tight to certain prejudices in his mapping of the world. Following Hall's theorizing, Paul's diasporic identities are constantly in the process of crafting novel ways of being and of evolving; his movements across boundaries enable him to engage in ever-expanding improvisation, capable of creating new and complex tapestries of continuity and rupture, similarity, and difference. By

86. Hall, "The Question of Cultural Identity," 237.

placing Paul squarely within the pluralistic character of the nations, one may observe that his identities in his diasporic social location are, although at times construed as permanently fixed, surreptitiously constructed in tension between stability and change, constantly formed and reformed by interactions with other communities in the Roman imperial order.

The introduction and chapters 1 and 2 constitute the theoretical part of this project, whereas chapters 3 to 5 flesh out Paul's diasporic condition by analyzing three specific contexts of his life and work that were crucially formed by this diasporic identity. The three specific contexts include: (1) Paul's interactions with other Diaspora Jews, especially in the Galatians 2 incident; (2) Paul's relationship with the nations, specifically his dealings with the Galatians; and (3) Paul's collection project, through an analysis of the concepts of *home*, *homeland*, and *space*.

The first issue in Pauline interpretation for which diaspora studies might provide further insight is Paul's interactions with other Diaspora Jews, many of who were also his coworkers (for example, Priscilla and Aquila, Barnabas, Apollos, Cephas/Peter, Timothy). These interactions, especially in the Galatians 2 incident, involve not only those who are Diaspora Jews and coworkers, but also non-Jews in Antioch—a major and cultured Greco-Roman city with a variety of people travelling into and out of it. Since there is so much uncertainty about the location of the communities of the Galatians, the situation in Antioch is much more grounded, as it provides the context of clearly a mixed group of Diaspora Jews and non-Jews.

In Galatians 2, Paul relates a situation that developed in Antioch resulting in an open confrontation with Peter. The situation involves (at least) three sets of Jews representing different relationships with the ancestral homeland (Jerusalem): Paul, a Diaspora Jew from the outset; Cephas/Peter, now itinerant outside Judea and Galilee (perhaps Barnabas falls into the same group, at least with respect to his reaction to the situation); and "certain people from James," newly arrived from Jerusalem. Here, the tools and insights drawn from diaspora studies—especially the concept of diaspora space—will help us sharpen our understanding of Paul's diasporized positionality in Galatians. Far from being at the periphery, the question of diaspora and of diaspora space, with all its entanglements, is at the heart of the conflict at Antioch. The concept of diaspora space, as developed by A. Brah, is a space where multiple aspects related to diasporic realities are not mediated through the dominant culture(s), but are shaped, differentiated, and interrelated by the different journeys. This concept helps to highlight issues of representation, power, and authority. The way in which the diaspora space is shared, negotiated, and made use of by Paul to establish his authority, his ideological, and particular spatial, temporal, social and theological understandings, is illustrative of the complexity of inhabiting such a place. The rereading proposed in chapter 3 is situated in the messiness of lives shaped by the tensions of the diaspora space, as different groups and subgroups of the early Jesus movement were divided and struggled to assume control and authority over the contested spheres of home and diaspora, center and periphery, alongside divergent sociopolitical and theological agendas and interpretations. Thus what becomes clearer under the generative insight from diaspora studies is that the incident at Antioch was not simply about gentiles but about two Judean social groups claiming the identity of being Jewish in that specific diaspora space, and who was authoritative or representative in this matter. The human social practices are thus presented in a way to show the flesh-and-blood realities of the different social groups in conflict and negotiation within the diaspora space they occupied. The usual theological logic to interpret the conflict will have to be modified in order to take seriously into account the complexity of social relations in the diaspora space.

The second issue in Pauline interpretation for which diaspora studies might provide further insight is Paul's relationship with the Galatians. Paul is a male traveler whose interactions with the nations he encountered was altogether ambivalent. In this way, as I develop in chapter 4, the intersections of diaspora and gendered rhetoric allow one to understand how paradoxical Paul's rhetoric toward the Other was. Increasingly, especially in the last decade, scholars in the field of diaspora studies have come to recognize the importance of studying the relational space of diaspora and gender, especially considering that the phenomenon of diaspora is inextricably linked to issues of gender.[87] In Pauline scholarship, the studies of Paul's relationships with the nations have not paid adequate attention to Paul's diaspora posture and his very gendered Roman rhetoric. Chapter 4 recalibrates Paul's position toward the nations. One may argue that the Romans/nations hierarchy is expressed through contrasting gender constructs of male/female and conquered/penetrated. The different monumental

---

87. See Braziel, *Diaspora: An Introduction*, 67. The concept of *gendered diaspora* has been developed to relationally and intersectionally contextualize the movements of peoples. See Roxana B. Leal, "What Are the Different Ways in Which We Can Understand Gendered Diasporic Identities?" *Zona Próxima*, 1 (2009): 170–83. The global maid trade phenomenon and the different nanny politics, or the issues of Caribbean nurses who migrate to Western urban centers, for example, have been particularly important in considering how gender is contextualized by historical and social circumstances. Categories such as race, class, nationality, education, literacy, migration status, and religion are also important areas of exploration and theorization in diaspora studies, with the view to illuminate some of the complexities of such social realities. One of the critiques James Clifford leveled against Paul Gilroy's brilliant mapping of the Black Atlantic in his now-classic *The Black Atlantic: Modernity and the Double Consciousness* (Cambridge, MA: Harvard University Press, 1992) is that it leaves out the question of gender. In Gilroy's analysis, one does not find any presence of subjects who are not males, nor does one find any nuanced picture of power dynamics that play out within the different diasporas. In fact, Gilroy does not mention at all those blacks who ended up in South America and mixed with the peoples who inhabited these different regions. The picture that Gilroy presents is one constructed by a black European male interested in certain regions and histories and not in others; the historical map that he draws does not complicate, or nuance, the relationship of different diasporas. See James Clifford, *Routes*, 266–67.

inscriptions of the Roman Empire, as indicated by Lopez,[88] were constant visual reminders and spatial narratives of the nations, imagined and written off as collectively female: conquered, penetrated, raped, pacified, and defeated under the violent force of their collectively male conqueror, Roman imperial power. But if it is true that Paul associated freely with the conquered peoples of the nations, he did so employing his own ethnic prejudices and stereotypes of those who were ethnically Other.[89] Paul's rhetoric, particularly in Galatians, is fraught with the tension between control and freedom. Paul is a diaspora figure among the conquered peoples of Rome, but he is not so much outside the imperial discourse because he constructs his message about the Lord Christ with the linguistic tools of the imperial propaganda of Lord Caesar. His discursive conflict between mimicking the Greco-Roman gender equation of masculinity and femininity to signify his missionary position with the nations, specifically in his dealings with the Galatians, and that of siding with the victims of imperial violence demonstrates how issues of space, of center and periphery, alongside the dynamics of authority, can play out in the diasporic social location. This means that the field of Pauline studies will have to take into serious consideration the connections between diaspora existence and gender constructs in weighing Paul's rhetoric and identities in his dealings with the Galatians.

---

88. Lopez, *Apostle to the Conquered.*

89. *Other* is used here in the sense of self-definition in an oppositional mode of relationship to a group (social, ethnic), a person, etc. This is a concept well known in postcolonial theory. Edward W. Said's *Orientalism*, 25th anniversary ed. (New York: Vintage Books, [1979] 2003) is a good place to start exploring this. In biblical studies, one may refer to the different entries on *difference* in Laura Nasrallah, and Elisabeth S. Fiorenza, eds., *Prejudice and Christian Beginnings: Investigating Race, Gender, and Ethnicity in Early Christian Studies* (Minneapolis: Fortress Press, 2009). Paul, in fact, until the end of his life, continued to view the gentiles in stereotypical terms as prone to all sorts of depraved acts (Phil. 2:15; Rom. 1:18–32).

Finally, in chapter 5, diaspora studies will provide further insight on the question of Paul's collection project through an analysis of the concepts of *home*, *homeland*, and *space*. As I mentioned above, and as I elaborate in this chapter, one of the common features of all diasporas is a collective commitment to the maintenance, restoration, safety, and prosperity of the real or recognized ancestral home.[90] Diaspora studies enables one to understand Paul's collection project as being clearly situated within the broader narrative of a diaspora figure committed to working for the restoration of and service to those inhabiting the ancestral "home." The different readings proposed on this specific issue in Pauline scholarship have not paid enough attention to how Paul's acute sense of geographical space could have had bearings on what motivated him to risk his life to move around and do what he could to help these poor Christ believers dying of hunger in the recognized theological center (Jerusalem). Locating Paul as a traveler negotiating social realities and religious commitments allows one to observe how space is signified and how authority is asserted in the diaspora. Taking these different realities seriously means that the usual theological preoccupations and interpretations of this issue need to be modified in order to make room for more worldly social realities. Thus, by taking the nitty-gritty of social realities in a diasporic situation seriously, the dynamics of ideals and beliefs—manifested through the collection project—are met with the view to articulating Paul's identities, mission, and social relationships.

The last chapter is a brief narrative of the project as a whole, highlighting its different areas of focus, the contribution of this study to the larger conversations within Pauline studies, and other venues of scholarship that can and need to be pursued in further research.

90. See Cohen's typology in *Global Diasporas*; Braziel, *Diaspora: An Introduction*; Michel S. Laguerre, *Diaspora, Politics, and Globalization* (New York: Palgrave Macmillan, 2006).

This chapter also highlights what it might mean to read Paul today because, to borrow Lopez's very apt phrasing, "all studies of the ancient world are ultimately also about how we might relate to that world,"[91] and, I will add, to our own. Indeed, the study of Paul can help us to understand what it might have meant to be human in the first century—Paul as an itinerant diaspora figure with localized communities of believers trying to negotiate spaces, socioreligious ideals, and social reality—as well as what it can mean to situate ourselves today socially, ideologically, and politically in search of spaces we can call "home."

Space is a key word that brings together the different issues upon which this study centers, and it offers a unity of focus among them.[92] The concept of diaspora space is important, as it helps to revisit the conflict at Antioch; the concept of relational space allows one to understand the intersections of diaspora and gendered rhetoric in Paul's relationships with the Galatians; and key concepts such as *home* and *homeland* are important in studying Paul's space-making rhetoric in his collection project. For David Harvey and others making this point, places and spaces are not fixed and stable, but are the locus of and for multiple contestations, configurations, and meanings.[93] The space(s) that Paul imagines and occupies—vis-à-vis other Diaspora Jews and groups composed of both dispersed and nondiaspora peoples—reveal how his spheres of authority, "home" and diaspora,

---

91. Lopez, "Visual Perspectives," in *Studying Paul's Letters: Contemporary Perspectives and Methods* (ed. Joseph A. Marchal; Minneapolis: Fortress Press, 2012), 100.

92. See David Harvey, "Space as a Key Word," in *The David Harvey Reader*, ed. Noel Castree and Derek Gregory (Oxford: Blackwell, 2006), 272–74. For different analysis on *space* as conceptualized and experimented in the Hebrew Bible and the Christian Scripture, see Michel Gourgues and Michel Talbot, ed., *Partout où tu iras. . . . Conceptions et expériences bibliques de l'espace,* Sciences bibliques 12 (Montréal: Médiaspaul, 2003). It is unfortunate that Paul's space making alongside his management and negotiation of spaces in his epistles—and not in Acts, as one chapter endeavors to study—are not within the purview of this study.

93. See David Harvey, *Cosmopolitanism and the Geographies of Freedom,* Wellek Library Lectures in Critical Theory (New York: Columbia University Press, 2009).

center and periphery, and social-theological positioning are negotiated and signified. He moves "in between" diaspora spaces and relational spaces in order to reimagine other spaces. Thus, Paul's relationships as an itinerant preacher striving to utilize and maximize different networks to generate new social dynamics among various ethnic and dispersed groups with localized communities of believers within the Roman Empire is readily open to fresh understanding. Since Paul's life and work were crucially formed by the diasporic condition, the aim of this study is to reframe, reinterpret, clarify, and illuminate our understanding of Paul's circumstances and some of the issues he faced within a more historically variable socioreligious, political, and diasporic context in his social relationships.

The scholarly enterprise of considering Paul and his diaspora politics is, admittedly, a complex one. Because all theories, especially in the social sciences, are partial, an interdisciplinary approach involving such disciplines as history, biblical studies, postcolonial studies, and diaspora studies is necessary to understand Paul as an itinerant diasporic worker proclaiming the message of Jesus and trying to make sense of it all within the Roman Empire. Although the focus of the present research is on Paul himself as a diasporic figure—with "his" communities inhabiting the diaspora space as well—there is an important need for readers trying to read Paul anew to no longer privilege him or his point of views, while viewing "other positions in caricature;"[94] rather, such readers must explore the complex identities and situations of Paul and the other equally important voices in the texts, many times subdued or silenced by Paul. Granted, such a reading is a challenge because it complicates greatly the power dynamics in and of Paul's letters. Reading this way

---

94. See Elizabeth A. Castelli, "Interpretations of Power in 1 Corinthians," in *Michel Foucault and Theology: The Politics of Religious Experience*, ed. James Bernauer and Jeremy Carrette (London: Ashgate, 2004), 21.

is also necessary to nuance our understanding of Paul's identities in the diaspora.

The multilayered approach undertaken in the present study is an attempt to go beyond the challenge that one is, inevitably, stuck in a house of interpretive mirrors where the "Pauls" one sees are determined by one's own theoretical vision. Some "Pauls" are, evidently, more credible or defensible than others because of the ways in which their accounts and questions cover and connect more of the available evidence. This is why I concur that we cannot simply allow for an anarchic plurality, because if we do so, our collective enterprise as scholars is in serious jeopardy. I maintain, however, that this uneasy way of approaching Paul as a nonhero Jewish Diaspora male artisan, negotiating ideas, ideals, realities, social relationships, and the specific issues he faced through an interdisciplinary dialogue, is important. The significance of it lies in the possibility of having the interpretation of the constructed heroic and mythic Christian apostle interrupted in order to point to other possibilities that might exist in interpreting the Pauline texts under study. This conversation is a risk worth taking if one wants to reevaluate Paul as a diasporic socioreligious figure of antiquity, and read him afresh today.[95]

In the present study, I approach Paul as a biblical-, Pauline-, religious-studies researcher with the aim to study human phenomena, behavior, material practices, and social relations and questions, as one might go about analyzing any other ancient text or figure. This is important, especially as the study of the New Testament and "Christian" origins moves more and more into the

---

95. Andrea Lieber proposes something similar to what I do in this study: "I suggest that reading antiquity through the lens of contemporary diasporas can reveal a more nuanced appreciation for the complexity of ancient diasporic existence." See Andrea Lieber, "Between Motherland and Fatherland: Diaspora, Pilgrimage and the Spiritualization of Sacrifice in Philo of Alexandria," in *Heavenly Tablets: Interpretation, Identity and Tradition in Ancient Judaism*, ed. Lynn LiDonnici and Andrea Lieber (Leiden: Brill, 2007), 195.

university—the very context of this project—and is to be considered in a religious studies milieu where Christianity is regarded comparatively to other religious traditions. From this perspective, the relationship of data in need to be tested by rational inquiry—without any appeal to personal or transcendent insights and traditional normative theology—becomes more and more persistent. The methodological challenge is to explore possible ways one may benefit from using diverse theories and methods in understanding an ancient diaspora figure such as Paul and the communities he was part of, while trying to understand how the data at hand could have made sense from the emic/theological/religious position. But as biblical, Pauline, and religious studies scholars—quascholars—there is no other way for us to do our work than to use the tools of explanatory analysis so as to read, interpret, classify, and organize the data (theological and otherwise) we have with the view to satisfy our scholarly quests, since we do not have any privileged access to any "inner" or "higher" workings of who and what we study. As William Arnal points it,

> Our job as scholars . . . is to provide *reasons* for the claims we make, *reasons* for our rejections or approvals of the conclusions of our scholarly colleagues—and these reasons should, at least in theory, be comprehensible, assessable and "testable" by our scholarly peers. By "testable" I do not mean experimental testability as is expected in the natural sciences. . . . I simply mean that our arguments should be of a sort that any reasonable person should be able to assess them: they should not appeal to personal preferences, transcendent insights, or data that cannot be accessed by others.[96]

Thus, the historical and the mundane social factors embedded in negotiating diasporic relations are what this project uncovers. This way of approaching the specific issues I noted above is undertaken to

---

96. See Arnal, *The Symbolic Jesus: Historical Scholarship, Judaism and the Construction of Contemporary Identity* (London: Equinox, 2005), 73–74 (emphasis in original).

show the different possibilities that an interdisciplinary approach may offer to Pauline studies in general and to the particular questions of interest here. The possibility of overworked texts becoming fresher and much more intriguing through the confluence of multiple interpretive tools may, I must admit, annoy and interrupt one's habitual reading, but the adventure can be ultimately worthwhile. In rearticulating the discourse of Paul alongside other voices—many times captured or silenced by Paul (or by some Pauline scholars)—and studying him through a critical dialogue that involves different methodological approaches, Paul's rhetorical claims are problematized and relativized.[97] I propose, along with others, that the importance of this uneasy way to approach him is worth doing if one wants to reevaluate Paul as presented to us in the generally accepted "authentic" Pauline letters, and read him anew in a very dynamic way.[98]

97. See Joseph A. Marchal, ed., *Studying Paul's Letters: Contemporary Perspectives and Methods* (Minneapolis: Fortress Press, 2012).
98. The problem of studying ancient texts is that we have only partial access to their sociopolitical and socioreligious world. Thus, a study of particular texts of antiquity needs, as will be exemplified in this book, to be approached from a variety of perspectives by using numerous tools of analysis to gain a fuller knowledge of the past and the issues raised. The still-cherished historical-critical approach in biblical studies, for example, is only a first step in recovering—partially, of course—what the text might have meant to the author(s) and to the audience(s) addressed. The historical, unbiased, and absolute truth of a given text is, however, impossible to find because we can arrive at only partial interpretations of texts. One thing apparent from studying Paul's letters is that any interpretation of his texts cannot be regarded as the final and absolute reconstruction of what Paul really said—contra N. T. Wright, *What Saint Paul Really Said* (Grand Rapids: Eerdmans 1997). Therefore, *any* attempt to uncover Paul's meaning(s) must be considered only a tentative interpretation of the meaning of the text, how it is rhetorically constructed, and how the text should be viewed as open to further analysis and interpretations. See, among other texts that support such an approach, Jacques Derrida, "Structure, Sign and Play in the Discourse of the Human Sciences," in *Writing and Difference* (London: Routledge, 1980), 278–94. See also Umberto Eco, *The Role of the Reader: Explorations in the Semiotics of Texts* (Bloomington, IN: University of Indiana Press, 1979); Peter Bondanella, *Umberto Eco and the Open Text: Semiotics, Fiction, Popular Culture* (Cambridge: Cambridge University Press, 1997). In other words, there is no decisive element or fixed interpretation to any of Paul's texts. Furthermore, many of the questions and answers of historical-critical criticism, which developed within the sphere of theology, are coherent and make sense only if one is engaged in theological thinking. Outside of theology proper, many if not most of the issues in Pauline studies remain problematic. The many arguments surrounding the notion of

justification by faith in Paul and the endless debates on the πίστις Χριστοῦ, for example, are theological pursuits stemming from certain theological problems or anxieties. See Michael F. Bird and Preston M. Sprinkle, eds., *The Pistis Christou Debate: The Faith of Jesus Christ* (Peabody, MA: Hendrickson Publishers, 2009). The researcher whose aim is to study these questions as one might go about analyzing other ancient texts might find himself or herself to be entering "holy" sites that can be explosive on many fronts because many of these theological issues (the ones mentioned here, for example) do not seem comprehensible outside of theology proper. And I readily acknowledge that this is a thorny issue to go around because the whole discourse about the so-called New Testament texts is within a theological context; Christian Scripture is religious literature, and to bracket this aspect out completely in critical scholarly interpretation raises the question of whether one is fully engaging the material in its genre as a religious text. See Sandra M. Schneiders, *The Revelatory Text: Interpreting the New Testament as Sacred Scripture* (San Francisco: Harper, 1991), 90. Thus one needs to struggle with the socioreligious aspect of the text in one's interpretation of it.

1

Negotiating Diaspora in Ancient
Hellenistic Judaism

Clearly, the mix of east and west, the cosmopolitan atmosphere, and the friendly encounter with Hellenism continued into the Roman period and thus shaped Paul's thinking. Here Paul learned Greek as his first language, received his education, and was influenced by Hellenistic rhetoric and Stoic philosophy. Here he also learned a Jewish religion that was profoundly affected by this rich cultural environment. This great cultural heritage that joined Hellenistic and Jewish influences ideally equipped Paul to translate a gospel that was fundamentally Jewish for the Hellenistic world.
—Calvin Roetzel[1]

This chapter constitutes a very important background of how insights from diaspora studies in relation to postcolonial studies may help one analyze differently some works and diasporic figures in ancient Hellenistic Judaism of the Roman period. The aim of studying Paul not only in the Greco-Roman context but also within

1. Calvin Roetzel, *Paul: The Man and the Myth*, Studies on Personalities of the New Testament (Columbia: University of South Carolina, 1998), 14.

the framework of ancient Judaism is to understand some of the different ways several ancient figures in ancient Judaism navigated and negotiated their diasporic sociopolitical situations.

Paul was a Diaspora Jew and the Scripture of the Diaspora was the Septuagint. Gustav Adolf Deissmann was the first to have described Paul as "a Jew of the Septuagint,"[2] and to have suggested that the Jewish Scriptures in Greek could have provided the primary cultural, historical, and theological contexts and influence for an understanding of the apostle's socioreligious thoughts and life. The best way to start exploring Paul as a hybrid diasporic Judean, then, is to start with his Scripture—which is itself already located in this hybrid site—through an analysis of the tale that purports to give an account, although brief, of the translation of that Scripture into Greek, the *Letter of Aristeas*.

The first half of this chapter explores how the complex notion of *hybridity*, as developed by Homi K. Bhabha, can shed light on *the Letter*. The dynamics of the hybrid condition expressed in the *Letter*, it is argued here, are captured in the forms of calculated negotiations, prudent affiliations, and idealized memory. There one encounters a profound desire for a particular community to enter into better communication with the Hellenistic world at large by incorporating the best of the "Jewish" and the "Greek" cultures and modes of thinking, without jeopardizing what they hold dear as part of their

---

2. See Gustav A. Deissmann, *St. Paul: A Study in Social and Religious History*, trans. Lionel R.M. Strachan, first English ed., (New York: Hodder and Stoughton, 1912), 92. The dynamics of Paul's theology via a comprehensive understanding of his Diaspora Bible (the lxx) was undertaken by Dietrich-Alexander Kochsome years later. See Dietrich-Alex Koch, *Die Schrift als Zeuge des Evangeliums, Untersuchungen zur Verwendung und zum Verständnis der Schrift bei Paulus* (Tübingen: Mohr Siebeck, 1986). For more on how the Septuagint relates to the New Testament, see Robert T. McLay, *The Use of the Septuagint in New Testament Research* (Grand Rapids: Eerdmans, 2003). On the complexity of Paul's use of Greek, see Kathy Ehrensperger, "Speaking Greek under Rome: Paul, the Power of Language," *Neotestamentica* 46, no. 1 (2012): 10–31.

socioreligious fabric. The *Letter* begs to present, and to inspire, a "third space" of breathing "in-between."

The second half of this chapter analyzes how Josephus—a diasporic Judean both similar and different from Paul in various ways—reread and rewrote the *Letter*. The analysis of Josephus's rereading of the *Letter* is also done within this overarching understanding of inhabiting the Diaspora, which leads to a discussion of how he negotiated his diasporic existence in the *Antiquities*. Josephus's interaction with the *Letter*, done within a reception history framework, aims to shed new light on the parts of the *Letter* omitted by Josephus, especially in light of his diasporic and political space. I will make use of a very interesting caveat from André Pelletier to make my point.[3]

The analysis of how such a diasporic Judean figure as Josephus negotiated his social and political realities will, then, be a way to start situating Paul in the ways in which he navigated and negotiated his own fluid and dynamic diaspora spaces of the ancient Mediterranean world. What becomes clearer under the applications of insights gained from both diaspora studies and postcolonial studies is that more than forging complicated theologies, as a diasporic hybrid subject living "in-between" spaces, Paul was busier trying to manage living between his socioreligious ideals and his social realities. His "homing" desires are not hard to find.

The different points that are highlighted in this chapter, namely, the reality of a) inhabiting the space of diaspora, which leads to b) negotiating the space of diaspora, and c) conceptualizing "home," reflect the three focused issues stated at the beginning of this project. Inhabiting the space of diaspora involves relationships and interactions with both dispersed and nondiaspora peoples;

---

3. See André Pelletier, *Flavius Josèphe adapteur de la Lettre d'Aristée. Une réaction Atticisante contre la Koinè* (Paris: Librairie C. Klincksieck, 1962).

negotiating the space of diaspora means balancing sociopolitical realities and different ideals, as well as maneuvering the dynamics of "here" and "there," center and periphery, representation and authorized voice(s). "Home" or "homing" desires reflects the longing for a relation that transcends geographical and temporal space(s).

Hybridity and the *Letter of Aristeas*

In order to understand the dynamics of the hybrid condition of the *Letter* in its ambivalence, I argue here that the multiple agencies in place to foster a certain version of Jewish identity in this diasporic social location are best captured in the forms of *calculated negotiations, prudent affiliations*, and *idealized memory*.

The narrative known as *The Letter of Aristeas* has been read from different angles: as propaganda or apologetic literature, as a historical window to the early history of the translation of the Septuagint, as a purely fictional work of literature, and as a charter myth of Diaspora Judaism.[4] My reading is a postcolonial one. I will look at this Jewish work as a hybrid project, which ran the risk of being rejected by both the Jews and the Greeks, in spite of the author's lofty goal of incorporating the best of the two cultures and modes of thinking.

The *Letter* starts with a problematic claim. It purports to give a "trustworthy narrative" (1)[5] of how the event of the translation of the Septuagint took place. The author seems to be aware of how difficult it might be for some of his readers to embrace such a claim,

---

4. See Victor Tcherikover, "The Ideology of the Letter of Aristeas," *HTR* 51 (1958): 59–85; Mary Ann L. Beavis, "Anti-Egyptian Polemic in the Letter of Aristeas 130–165 (The High Priest's Discourse)," *JSJ* 18 (1987): 145–51. For more recent studies on the ideology present in the work, see Sylvie Honigman, *The Septuagint and Homeric scholarship in Alexandria: A Study in the Narrative of the Letter of Aristeas* (New York: Routledge, 2003), and Andrew Kovelman, *Between Alexandria and Jerusalem: The Dynamic of Jewish and Hellenistic Culture*,The Brill Reference Library of Judaism 21 (Leiden: Brill, 2005).

5. The text used is R. J. H. Shutt's translation in *The Old Testament Pseudepigrapha*, ed. James H Charlesworth, 2 vols. (Garden City, NY: Doubleday, 1983–1985), 2:12–34.

for he emphasizes the "truthfulness" of his account again at the end of the narrative: "To tell lies concerning matters which are being chronicled is inappropriate: if I were to make a single error, it would be impious in these matters. On the contrary we narrate things as they happened, eschewing any error" (297). As scholars have long recognized, the accounts of the *Letter* may certainly contain windows of historical realities, but the work as it stands is mainly a fictional composition. The author, who pretends to be a Greek admirer of the surpassing wisdom of the Jews is, according to most scholars, a Jew. The intricate knowledge of Jewish practices and Temple worship indicate that he is a Jew writing to other Jews and to possible Greek sympathizers and onlookers.[6] It is also being recognized by many scholars that there is more in the narrative than the translation, which, in fact, occupies a very small place in the tale. The section actually depicting the description of and the manner by which the translators went about doing their work is brief, as one can read in the following excerpts:

> Three days afterward, Demetrius took the men with him, traversed the mile-long jetty into the sea toward the island, crossed the bridge, and went in the direction of the north. There he assembled them in a house which had been duly furnished near the shore—a magnificent building in a very quiet situation—and invited the men to carry out the work of translation, all that they would require being handsomely provided. They set to completing their several tasks, reaching agreement among themselves on each by comparing versions. The result of their agreement thus was made into a fair copy by Demetrius. (301–3a)

> Following the custom of all Jews, they washed their hands in the sea in the course of their prayers to God, and then proceeded to the reading and explication of each text. (305)

---

6. See Tcherikover, "Ideology"; John M. G. Barclay, *Jews in the Mediterranean Diaspora: From Alexander to Trajan (323 bce–117 ce)* (Berkeley: University of California Press, 1996), 148; Terence L. Donaldson, *Judaism and the Gentiles: Jewish Patterns of Universalism (to 135 ce)* (Waco, TX: Baylor University Press, 2007), 109.

Most of the narrative features the king enquiring from the Palestinian Jewish translator-sages about virtue and prudent ways of governing in a series of seven banquets. It is also obvious that the author is not trustworthy in the way he presents the translation project as being completed in seventy-two days by a team of seventy-two translator-philosophers with a ratio of six taken from each of the twelve tribes of Israel. The fanciful account and dialogues one gets from reading the narrative raises the question of the intent of the author in allowing fiction to masquerade as a historical account.

The program of the *Letter* seems to have the best of both worlds—Judaism and Hellenism. What is at stake for the author is to remain a Jew and be, in some sense, like the gentiles. It is this hybridity that I want to explore in the narrative of the *Letter*. To do so, I will delve mainly into the work of the postcolonial and literary critic Homi K. Bhabha. However, before proceeding, it is necessary to address the issue of interpretive anachronism. There is certainly a risk of anachronism in using a theoretical construct drawn from a more modern state of affairs to understand the ancient world, if postcolonial theories are applied in a way that is lacking the necessary nuances for analyzing other times and places.

The term *postcolonial* derives from a specific sociohistorical juncture. It is a literary approach of late modernity and it basically features a European imperialistic stance versus the two-thirds world.[7] One needs to bear in mind, however, that the phenomenon of narratives shaped by, and in response to, imperial powers and human migration is quite an ancient one. In fact, as an example, most of the writing of the Hebrew Scriptures took place in imperial contexts.[8]

---

7. As a good introduction to the subject see, among others, Robert J. C. Young, *Postcolonialism: An Historical Introduction* (Oxford: Blackwell, 2001); Bill Ashcroft, Gareth Griffiths, and Helen Tiffin, eds., *The Post-Colonial Studies Reader* (New York: Routledge, 1995).

8. Needless to say, there is considerable scholarly debate over the dating of the various texts and particularly over the formation of the canon. The Hebrew Scriptures were written gradually

Here, one needs to be precise on the sociological content of *colonial*—the Babylonian captivity, for example, is not that similar to British rule in India, European imperialism in Africa, the new world colonies, and so on. Likewise, ancient imperialism and modern imperialism exhibit a few salient differences.[9] This is why one simply cannot find direct correspondences between the different colonial and diasporic contexts present in literature of ancient times and modern examples of imperialist rule and migration situations. For this reason, the aim in this chapter is not to impose a particular theory on a given period, but to extract from postcolonial studies a useful analytical concept such as *hybridity* that can be beneficial in understanding a particular literary product of the past. Doing so requires attending to the historical specificities in recognizing, for example, that the alleged community to which the *Letter* was addressed was not living in their ethnic homeland under foreign domination, but as a Diaspora community outside their homeland, and that if we place the work in the later second century (i.e., after the Maccabean revolt),[10] their homeland was no longer under the rule of a foreign power. Indeed, one needs to be careful about the variances, as well as any commonalities in the ways postcolonial analysis are applied. That should not, however, deter one from taking advantage of some of the analytical tools that this theoretical lens offers, and the

over centuries in which Egyptian, Assyrian, Babylonian, Persian, and Greek empires had varying degrees of influence in the lives of the Hebrews. See David Carr, *Writing on the Tablet of the Heart: Origins of Scripture and Literature* (New York: Oxford University Press, 2005), which offers a very interesting argument about the shaping of the Hebrew Bible in the Hellenistic period.

9. See James Bryce, *The Ancient Roman Empire and the British Empire in India* (London: Oxford University Press, 1914); Evelyn Baring Cromer (Earl of), *Ancient and Modern Imperialism* (London: Oxford University Press, 1910); Thomas Harrison, "Ancient and Modern Imperialism," *Greece and Rome* 55 (2008): 1–22.

10. Though there is no broad consensus regarding the date of the work, the time period suggested here is still favored by many commentators. See Donaldson, *Judaism and the Gentiles*, 108 for a brief summary of the debate and for pertinent bibliography.

"hybrid" site that will be explored here seems to reflect very well the dynamics of a diasporic community as addressed in the *Letter*.[11] It is now time to start exploring what the notion of hybridity has to offer.

Hybridity

Bhabha has developed the concept of hybridity in building on M. Bakhtin's description of the "hybrid construction," and on Jacques Derrida's deconstructive approach to language and discourse. Bhabha's contribution lies in the highlighting of a deconstructive approach to the discourses of colonialism and their social instantiation. His aim is to capture the hybrid condition of the creative dynamics of negotiating life and discourse in the contentious mixing of traditions and cultures that colonial situations create. In Bhabha's words,

> In my own work I have developed the concept of hybridity to describe the construction of cultural authority within conditions of political antagonism or inequity. Strategies of hybridization reveal an estranging movement in the "authoritative," even authoritarian inscription of the cultural sign. At the point at which the precept attempts to objectify itself as a generalized knowledge or a normalizing, hegemonic practice, the hybrid strategy or discourse opens up a space of negotiation where power is unequal but its articulation may be equivocal.[12]

---

11. Examples where biblical studies scholars and scholars of religious antiquity have used Bhabha's understanding of hybridity as an analytical tool are growing at a very fast pace. See, among others, Ann L. Jervis, "Reading Romans 7 in Conversation with Post-Colonial Theory: Paul's Struggle toward a Christian Identity of Hybridity," *Theoforum* 35 (2004): 173–94; C. Antonaccio, "Hybridity and the Cultures within Greek Culture," in *The Cultures within Greek Culture*,ed. L. Kurke and C. Dougherty (Cambridge: Cambridge University Press, 2003), 57–74; Daniel Boyarin and Virginia Burrus, "Hybridiy as Subversion of Orthodoxy? Jews and Christians in Late Antiquity," in *Beyond Syncretism: Rethinking Religious Hybridity*,ed. Otto Maduro and Meredith McGuire) = *Social Compass* 52 (2005): 431–41. John M. G. Barclay also explores *hybridity* as a valuable concept to analysing ancient times and figures in the paper he delivered at the University of York Josephus conference in 2001, published under the title "The Empire Writes Back: Josephus' Rhetoric," in *Flavius Josephus and Flavian Rome*, ed. J. Edmonson, et al. (Oxford: Oxford University Press, 2005).
12. Homi Bhabha, "Culture's in Between," in *Artforum International* 32 (1993): 170.

This "open space" is what Bhabha calls elsewhere a "Third Space of enunciation."[13] Bhabha's "Third Space" represents a space of communication and negotiation between cultural diversity and cultural difference. As Bhabha puts it,

> The intervention of the Third Space . . . challenges our sense of the historical identity of culture as a homogenizing, unifying force, authenticated by the originary Past, kept alive in the national tradition of the People. . . . It is that Third Space, though unrepresentable in itself, which constitutes the discursive conditions of enunciation that ensure that the meaning and symbols of culture have no primordial unity or fixity; that even the same signs can be appropriated, translated, rehistoricized and read anew.[14]

In this sense, it is in exploring the interstice of negotiation (not simple acquiescence, assimilation or collaborative agreement, but meaningful exchange), the calculated responses on the part of colonial subjects, and also of diasporic communities, that one might start to understand the complexity of colonial history and diasporic life. This space in-between, or this "interstitial" agency, provides a way to understand the different struggles that come to play in defining authority and subordination, assimilation and resistance in a particular colonial situation. In the words of Bhabha, "It is the 'inter'—the cutting edge of translation and negotiation, the *in-between*, the space of the *entre* . . . —that carries the burden of the meaning of culture."[15] In other words, the colonial condition is a site that renders discourses of both affiliation and resistance to colonial power possible. The reality or condition of particular colonial subjects is, in following Bhabha's lead, one that forces them to construct multiple agencies—satire, mockery, mimicry, affiliation,

13. Homi Bhabha, "Cultural Diversity and Cultural Differences," in Ashcroft et al., *The Post-Colonial Studies Reader*, 206–9.
14. Bhabha, *Location of Culture*, 37.
15. Ibid, 209.

borrowing, resistance, memory, vilification, and blessing—in order to foster versions of historic memory, which give meaning to the narrative they hold in the minority positions they occupy.

On the basis of Bhabha's analysis of the hybrid condition and project one can decipher several clues for comparison and interpretation in the *Letter*. The social situation is that of diasporic settlement. Some of the questions arising from such social and existential conditions are the following: How far should one go in accepting the new social reality? How far to go in accepting new cultural elements, and in rejecting old ones acquired or received as part of the matrix of what constitutes "back home"? Or for that matter, where or what is home? The background to the *Letter* is Alexandria. In the midst of a gentile nation, the questions of assimilation, repudiation, and compromise became urgent for the author of the *Letter* to address. How, then, should the Judaism of the Dispersion adapt if it wants to flourish without ostracizing very Hellenized Jews, and without outraging very conservative Jews of Palestinian Judaism? What is the best way to present Judaism to the philosophically minded and sophisticated gentiles? What, if anything, is possible in terms of mutual assimilation?

The creative dynamics the author of the *Letter* proposes allow him to negotiate life and discourse in a tradition and culture that is perceived as different and foreign. He saw the danger that menaced some Jews by adopting possible extreme positions that could be fatal to the Judaism of this particular community in the Diaspora. One of these plausible positions would be to deny the gentiles any say as far as a certain comprehension of God is concerned. The second extreme position would be to deny Judaism any special religious appeal and to assimilate it with the religious understandings of the locals. The author finds the solution to this dilemma in two ways, and he lays out his answers right from the beginning. One of the solutions proposed

is that both Jews and gentiles worship, in essence, the same creator
God, though with different names attached to this God:

> These people worship God the overseer and creator of all, whom all men
> worship including ourselves, O King, except that we have a different
> name. Their name for him is Zeus and Jove. The primitive men,
> consistently with this, demonstrated that the one by whom all live and
> are created is the master and Lord of all. (16)

The second move, which seems to be directly addressed to those
Jews doubting the special place and character of Judaism, regards
the special place of the Torah. He shows that the translation of the
Jewish law into the language of power and of the dominant culture
is an indication of the equality of the foundations of Judaism, if
not its superiority, to other high religious and philosophical ways
of life. In fact, he demonstrates effectively throughout the tale that
all the philosophers and dignitaries of the kingdom in Alexandria
are very much impressed by the profundity of the Torah and by
the wisdom of the people living by its guidance (38, 235, 312–313).
Thus, Aristeas opts for an "in-between" spatial location à la Bhabha to
articulate his translation and negotiation of both affiliation with and
resistance to the social and political situation he faces with his Jewish
community. The multiple agencies in place to foster a certain version
of Jewish identity in this diasporic context are not simple assimilation
and blessing, or strong vilification of the social reality. Something
more nuanced and settled is presented. The dynamics of the hybrid
condition are captured in the forms of calculated negotiations,
prudent affiliations, and idealized memory.

Dynamics of the Hybrid Condition: Calculated Negotiations

The first thing that strikes the reader is the amount of time set aside
for, and eulogies devoted to, the king. Though it is now established

that the work was mainly an in-house correspondence, it appears that the author is very concerned about the ways power is portrayed throughout his piece, and with the way some readers might report on his work to the political power in place. So he is very prudent in how he constructs the relationship with the kingly figure in his text. At first, everything is orchestrated in the narrative to show respect for the king's authority, learning, and wisdom. Ptolemy II is presented as a very cultivated monarch who brings seventy sages from Jerusalem to translate the Jewish Scriptures for his superb library in Alexandria. The king is assured on more than one occasion that he already possesses wisdom and conducts himself in a manner worthy of admiration. In 276 one reads, "The possession of an acute mind and the ability to discern everything, that is an excellent gift from God—which indeed you possess, O King." And again in 282, "The man endowed with glory and wealth and power, who deep at heart is the equal of everyone. Just as you by your conduct deserve admiration, God giving you the gift of caring for these things." Similar statements regarding how the king is one who already practices good virtues and good government are found in 283, 285, 287, 290, even while the king himself still deems it important to ask the sages for advice during the different banquets. But, in the midst of all the praise of the king's high regard for learning, art (81), culture (124), justice (19), and his political clairvoyance (167), he is placed in a position subservient to the God of the Jewish people. In 132 one reads,

> (Eleazar) began first of all by demonstrating that God is one, that his power is shown in everything, every place being filled with his sovereignty, and that none of the things on earth which men do secretly are hidden from him, but rather that all the deeds of any man are manifest to him, as well as that which is to come to pass.

And gradually in the narrative, the king moves from the position of the powerful monarch who is praised and prayed for (45, 185), to that of one who does obeisance to the translator-philosophers (177) for their surpassing knowledge and wisdom, and finally to one who is urged to follow God (254). This is what one reads in these two texts respectively:

> When the king saw the delegates, he proceeded to ask questions about the books, and when they had shown what had been covered and unrolled the parchments, he paused for a long time, did obeisance about seven times, and said, "I offer to you my thanks, gentlemen, and to him who sent you even more, and most of all to the God whose oracles these are" (177).

> "You must know that God governs the whole universe with kindliness and without any anger, and you, O king, he said, must follow him" (254).

Thus, for the author of the *Letter*, being in a minority position in a foreign country and under foreign rule did not mean that God was not in control of things. Rather, it meant that the Jewish God was sovereign, and that any power was viewed in a powerless perspective under the overarching rule of God.

The calculated negotiations at play in this fictional rendering of the relationship between this Hellenistic ruler and the Jews are ambivalent. There is admiration and resistance, acceptance and challenge. The calculated negotiations offered in the text illustrate how discourse from minority, diasporic, and colonial (though, again, one needs to remember that this is not the case for the situation under consideration) subjects is a perpetual state of choosing when and how to affiliate, when or how to resist, when and how to mimic. Mimicry is, according to Bhabha, "at once resemblance and menace."[16] In

---

16. Ibid., 86.

other words, there is in such discourse the mixture of the familiar and the unfamiliar, the double articulation of appropriation and challenge, approval and mockery.

The author of *Aristeas* participates in this double articulation in placing his work as both Other, and familiar, as a literary creation that is both upholding a certain status quo of the time—the position of women as those "with poor reasoning powers" (250), for example—and challenging certain positions, even those coming from his own cultural and religious background—for example, in presenting the broad understanding of God as being, in nexus, the God the gentiles worship under different names.

Also, interestingly enough, the author recalibrates the position of the Jews as well throughout the narrative. The tale that begins with a group of emissaries presenting the case of the Jewish slaves forcibly deported to Egypt by Ptolemy I (12–27) ends with the translators as friends to the king, with unlimited access to the royal palace (317–21). The imaginative picture given of Greek power is one that is not only subservient to the Jewish God, but also one that is shared, in some sense, if not by all Jews, then by its elite representatives. The *Letter* presents the best elite candidates as Jewish ambassadors to the king, and as advocates to the king's power. The elders from Palestine are introduced as ἄνδρας καὶ παιδείᾳ διαφέροντας, ἅτε δὴ γονέων τετευχότας ἐνδόξων, οἵτινες οὐ μόνον τὴν τῶν Ἰουδαϊκῶν γραμμάτων ἕξιν περιεποίησαν αὑτοῖς, ἀλλὰ καὶ τῆς τῶν Ἑλληνικῶν ἐφρόντισαν οὐ παρέργως κατασκευῆς, "elite men of excellent education due to the distinction of their parentage; they had not only mastered the Jewish literature, but they had also made a serious study of the Hellenic culture as well" (121).[17] These elite men support the king's thirst for territorial conquest by advising

17. The Greek text is from André Pelletier in *Lettre d'Aristée à Philocrate* (Paris: Éditions du Cerf, 1962), 164; translation mine.

him to take and to keep whatever God gives him (223–24), and their advice concerning women is highly gender biased (250). This envisioning of the elite males sharing in the privilege of power illustrates the conundrum of a "hybrid construction" caught up in a relation of tension, of negotiating, of mimicking and of translating and interpreting cultural identities in a sociopolitical culture that can be in perpetual flux.

But, reading the *Letter* from a postcolonial perspective makes one wary of the presentation of the Jewish elites in the text. Though the description of the giving of gifts to the delegation from Palestine is part of ancient literary topos,[18] one cannot help noticing the similarity between the goal of the Roman imperial order in a different time to win "the support and active cooperation of the local elite by offering them benefits,"[19] and what one finds in the text of the *Letter* here. Recall that the whole narrative is presented as a communication from a highly placed gentile elite (Aristeas in disguise) to another fellow elite (Aristeas's fabricated half-brother). This way of representing himself, his alter ego, and the Jewish elites might suggest that the author, albeit imaginatively, envisions a world where the elites of this diasporic community could play and negotiate different social roles as leaders among the Jews in Alexandria and that, through them, the power in place could maintain a certain level of control over, or could benefit from, informed knowledge, on its Jewish population. But this is certainly too much conjecturing, and there was probably no such idea in the mind of the author. Let us now move on to consider how the hybrid subject affiliates to the social location in the *Letter*.

18. George W. E. Nickelsburg, *Jewish Literature between the Bible and the Mishnah*, 2nd ed. (Minneapolis: Fortress Press, 2005), 196.
19. See Peter Garnsey and Charles R. Whittaker, *Imperialism in the Ancient World* (Cambridge: Cambridge University Press, 1978), 254.

Prudent Affiliations

The hybrid diasporic Jewish community caught in the middle of a predominantly gentile population in Alexandria could not but affiliate with the ambient cultural environment in some measure. The whole translation project seems to subscribe to this logic. It is true that the author does not indicate the rationale behind the undertaking of the translation except to note that Demetrius, manager of the king's library, proposed it in order for them to have all the books in the world at their disposal (9). However, the text seems to indicate that the translation was a project to place the Jewish text in dialogue, if not in competition, with other philosophical texts that had influenced the Greeks. But to arrive at that place of entering into and participating fully in Greek culture and ongoing philosophical debates meant that there was no choice other than taking the language of the dominant culture. What the author of the *Letter* does is to assimilate the linguistic arsenal in which he finds himself, and utilize it to deconstruct the discourses of the Greeks with his own ethnic, religious, and philosophical discourse. In other words, the translation project, and as a matter of fact the whole narrative of the *Letter* itself, seems to show both the sceptic Jews in Alexandria and the very conservative Palestinian Jews in the homeland that it is possible to express the faith of the Jewish ancestors in a language other than Hebrew, and that it is possible to be a genuine and faithful Jew in the midst of a pagan culture in the Diaspora.[20]

I am not interested here in the Septuagint per se, but in the linguistic mediating space of articulation of a certain project.[21]

20. This is in accord with the whole thesis advanced by George E. Howard in "The Letter of Aristeas and Diaspora Judaism," *JTS* 22 (1971): 337–48.
21. See Sarah Pearce, "Translating for Ptolemy: Patriotism and Politics in the Greek Pentateuch?" in *Jewish Perspectives on Hellenistic Rulers*, ed. Tessa Rajak et al. (London: University of California Press, 2007), 165–89. Her article is quite insightful in the way she evaluates the work of Elias J. Bickerman regarding the translators of the Septuagint. In a nutshell, Bickerman had argued

Bhabha presents hybridity as a means by which the subaltern speaks the approved language of authority in order to present a riposte. The "Third Space" construction elaborated in the language of the prevailing power is a narrative of emancipation and not reclusion, of integration and not separation, of both borrowing from and resistance to. In this sense, the translation becomes more than the mechanical transaction between two languages, but rather the complex negotiation or translation between two cultures. For Bhabha, "translation is the performative nature of cultural communication"[22] in the sense that it is the process and condition that characterizes movements, dislocation, and relocation of people in different geographical and cultural settings. It follows that the translation work of the sages from Palestine, becomes, then, the translation of Palestinian Judaism coming into full dialogue and discussion with Alexandrian Hellenism. Through the translated Torah, the *Letter* seems to argue, the Jews will be able to integrate themselves fully with the cultural and the social Hellenistic world. For the author of the narrative, it is no longer time to flee from the intellectual hubris of the world, but to remain and thrive in it.[23]

Bhabha has used Derrida's deconstruction of Walter Benjamin's classic essay on translation ("Translation passes through *continua* of transformation, not abstract ideas of identity and similarity")[24] to construct a fresh concept of translation as an afterlife or as a survival act in the context of hybridity. To quote Bhabha,

that the translators of the Septuagint translated *for* King Ptolemy in the sense that their work was designed to please and not to offend the king. For Pearce, the arguments for the "patriotic" translators would need to be stronger to be convincing.
22. Bhabha, *Location of Culture*, 228.
23. So far in this chapter, I have emphasized the author as really conscious of the cultural processes embodied by the writing. However, when one reflects on the level of intentionality at which the hybridization of the *Letter of Aristeas* takes place, one realizes that it is prudent to consider also the point at which the writing itself may witness consciousness about its own cultural creations.
24. Quoted in Bhabha, *The Location of Culture*, 212.

> If hybridity is heresy, then to blaspheme is to dream . . . it is the dream
> of translation as "survival" as Derrida translates the "time" of Benjamin's
> concept of the after-life of translation, as *sur-vivre*, the act of living on
> borderlines. Rushdie translates this into the migrant's dream of survival;
> an *initiatory* interstices; an empowering condition of hybridity.[25]

Following Bhabha's lead, one can see the translators in the *Letter* not
only as cultural translators, but also as cultural ambassadors in their
act of rendering their religious identity (which is inseparable from
culture and ethnicity) into a different language and doing this in a
way that would make sense to the gentiles among whom the Jews
lived in Alexandria. The *Letter* also highlights the fact that its author is
a very sophisticated cultural translator and ambassador. He is at pains
to make sense of what might appear foreign, confusing, or simply
bizarre to the gentile readers (food laws, unclean animals,[26] and table
fellowship, for example), and he is eager to move skeptical, narrow,
and intolerant Jews to a more ecumenical stance. The *Letter* becomes,
then, a strange migrant's cultural act of survival, "an initiatory
interstices, an empowering condition of hybridity." Stated
differently, the hybridity of the project is being expressed in the
textual affiliation and translation of one culture to the other, of one
reality into another; the turning of one foreign element, the law
books of the Jews (9) in Hebrew, into the borderline of a diasporic
reality, that of Greek Hellenism in Alexandria.[27] This affiliation is

---

25. Ibid., 226–27.
26. Beavis's analysis of the author of the *Letter* trying to explain and to defend Jewish abstinence
from "mice" and "weasel" to Alexandrian Greeks is interesting. She shows that without a due
explanation to the Greeks there, the Jews might find themselves being confused with the native
Egyptians who also did not eat such rodents, along with cats, dogs, and ibises, because they
regarded these animals as manifestations of the gods. See Beavis, "Anti-Egyptian Polemic," 150.
27. I am well aware that recent scholarship on Judaism and Hellenism argues against the
traditionally static dichotomy between these two cultural entities. See for example J. J. Collins's
excellent treatment in his *Jewish Cult and Hellenistic Culture: Essays on the Jewish Encounter with
Hellenism and Roman Rule*, Journal for the Study of Judaism Supplements 100 (Leiden: Brill,
2005). One then needs to be aware that the rhetorical strategy of the text of the *Letter* may well
not be completely identical to the social, cultural, and historical circumstances of its context

embraced in a prudent way in order for the diasporic community to deflect any charge Palestinian Judaism might have against them of selling out their cultural, ethnic, and religious identity. The author of the *Letter* still celebrates who they are as Jews, while entering fully into the realization of what is becoming no longer a foreign entity, but, strangely, home, even if away from Palestine. However, in spite of this forward-looking gaze, the author still finds solace in a fading, but idealized, memory.

Idealized Memory

The author of the *Letter* addresses the narrative of the Jewish people by touching on the different fundamental pillars of the Jewish collective consciousness. The memory of the place of origin[28] and of the covenantal relationship with God permeates the whole narrative. The land of Palestine, the city of Jerusalem, the temple, and the high priest's vestments figure as ideals and are expressed with a certain tone of reverence and nostalgia (83–120). The author seems to be spellbound by the memory of the religious festivals in the following excerpt:

> Many thousands of animals are brought there in the festival days. There is an uninterrupted supply not only of water, just as if there were a plentiful spring rising naturally from within, but also of indescribably wonderful underground reservoirs, which within a radius of five stades from the foundation of the Temple revealed innumerable channels for each of them, the streams joining together on each side. . . . The ministering of the priests was absolutely unsurpassable in its vigor and the arrangement of its well-ordered silence. . . . Everything is carried

of origin where a clear-cut boundary between the purportedly different cultural entities of Judaism and Hellenism was difficult to establish. One of the aims in using Bhabha's notion of hybridity here is to sharpen our understanding of the *Letter* as a literary project presented to ethnic and cultural groups perceived to be fully distinct.

28. The suddenness of the embassy's presence in Jerusalem indicates that the whole event, including the depiction of Jerusalem, is a product of memory and should not be taken as a factual event.

out with reverence and in a manner befitting supreme divinity. . . .
Every man who comes near the spectacle of what I have described will
experience astonishment and amazement beyond words, his very being
transformed by the hallowed arrangement on every single detail.(88–89)

On the other hand, a fundamental event in the collective memory
such as the Exodus is also being celebrated and re-envisioned to serve
the purpose of the present conditions. The recent works of David
Dawson, Philip R. Davies, Sylvie Honigman, and Arkady Kovelman
serve well to highlight this motif in the *Letter*.[29] In a nutshell, what
these different authors demonstrate, in various manners, is the
underlying narrative structure of the Exodus in the *Letter*. The letter
is presented as a new Exodus, a replica or reversal, an antitype and a
pesher. One of the obvious differences between the biblical rendering
of the Exodus and that of the *Letter* lies in the portrayal of the foreign
ruler.[30] *The Letter*'s Alexandrian king is magnanimous, and has deep
respect and admiration for the Jews, their religion, and their God.
Contrary to the biblical account of the Exodus, this Alexandrian king
let the slaves go freely, but these Jews in Alexandria under Ptolemy
II did not feel any compulsion to go out of the country. Instead of
leaving Egypt in order to worship their ancestral deity, in this replica
of the Exodus the Jews bring Torah and the worship of their God to
Egypt to signify the victory of God over the king of Egypt at last.
The land of Alexandria was home. But not quite. In the words of
Arkady Kovelman,

---

29. See David Dawson, *Allegorical Readers and Cultural Revision in Ancient Alexandria* (Berkeley:
University of California Press, 1992); Philip R. Davies, "Didactic Stories," in *The Complexities of
Second Temple Judaism*,vol.. 1 of *Justification and Variegated Nomism*, ed. Donald A. Carson et al.
(Tübingen: Mohr, Siebeck, 2001), 99–134; Honigman, *The Septuagint and Homeric Scholarship
in Alexandria*; Honigman, "The Narrative Function of the King and the Library in the *Letter
of Aristeas*," in Rajak et al., *Jewish Perspectives on Hellenistic Rulers*, 128–46; Kovelman, *Between
Alexandria and Jerusalem*.
30. See Honigman, "The Narrative Function."

All in all, the Letter is not just a story of the translation of Pentateuch. It includes all the major contents of Exodus, from Egyptian enslavement of the Jews to the gift of Torah on Mount Sinai, from the construction of the tabernacle to the banquets of the elders. What looks like digressions on the surface is the real essence inside. What seems to be the plot is nothing but the upper layer, which is designed both to veil and to expose the essence of the book."[31]

Furthermore, the special idealistic position of Israel as "distinct from all other men" (152) is also being remembered and commemorated. For the author of the *Letter*,

> in his wisdom the legislator, in a comprehensive survey of each particular part, and being endowed by God for the knowledge of universal truths, surrounded us with unbroken palisades and iron walls to prevent our mixing with any of the other peoples in any matter, being thus kept pure in body and soul, preserved from false beliefs, and worshipping the only God omnipotent over all creation. (139)

It might appear rather strange and disturbing to some readers that such general cultural prejudice is celebrated in a work that has done so much to portray and to promote a very healthy hybrid consciousness throughout. This is, in fact, the observation of Mary Ann L. Beavis: "The insistence on the isolation of the Jews from the nations is striking in a document as philhellenic as Aristeas."[32] This ethnic chauvinism expressed by the *Letter* seems to go in the opposite direction of the postcolonial analytical approach of hybridity developed by Bhabha, which fosters multiple constructions of agency, as opposed to any binary division between "them" and "us", to any notion of cultural or racial purity, and to the productions of hierarchy. The postcolonial analytical category of hybridity aims at freeing the different discourses on religion, ethnicity, and culture

---

31. Kovelman, *Between Alexandria and Jerusalem*, 131.
32. Beavis, "Anti-Egyptian Polemic," 146.

from their habitual tendencies of othering whoever or whatever is, or seems to be, different from oneself by embracing and celebrating differences.

If one wants, however, to be clement and sympathize with the author by looking at the situation from a different angle, these different myths of origin and of uniqueness among the nations may be understandable and interpreted as functioning as powerful sacred forces serving to help this diasporic community make sense of complex realities.[33] Memory, in this sense, allows the community not only to preserve its ideals of purity, but also to affirm its cultural continuity in a different social location and structure. The memory projected is an idealized one and, maybe, a personal one. And here the *Letter* is most interesting for what it suggests about the imagination of its own author in relation to his projected audience, rather than for what many of his contemporaries might find appealing or, perhaps, even acknowledge as their social reality. In other words, the rhetorical strategy of the text allows the author to imagine only what might be; it does not enact, but only imagines, a different sort of world. Judaism and Hellenism in real life could have been very different from this hybrid dream of rejection and assimilation, and both groups could very well reject the projection of the *Letter*.

In the *Letter*, memory and the significance of distance come to play hand in hand. The author brings what the land of Palestine has to offer as authoritative in the matter of religious discourse and of good governance. Thus, the author presents anything that a Jew in Alexandria would want to adopt from Greek culture as already

---

33. See Mircea Eliade, *Myth and Reality* (New York: Harper & Row, 1963). There are certainly other ways to explain the position of the *Letter* concerning the unique religious relationship of his ethnos to his God, and the interpretation I take here is just one of the wide range of possibilities that exist.

existing in Judaism, albeit in a more complex or superior form. But the irony is that the idealized Judaism he wants to portray in the delegation from "home" (i.e., Palestine) is an enterprise that is not free from the influences and the flavors of Hellenism. The answers of the Jewish philosophers to the king's questions during the different banquets illustrate the attempt of the author to position the project as a hybrid one, for they comport both Jewish and Greek elements. Günther Zuntz captures the hybrid construction of the seven banquets very well when he states, "Greek in substance yet with some Jewish additions and, throughout, a Jewish veneer; Jewish in conception, outline and purpose yet, here too, with some points of contact with Greek literary traditions and day-to-day custom, this chapter in the *Letter* stands out, a symptom of the Greek impact upon Hellenistic Jewry."[34]

The answers the king receives from the translators are being presented as originating from Jewish wisdom, but one wonders at this point if any Greek reader would be duped by this tactic. On the other hand, one may also quibble about the reception of such a farce from the Jewish community. It is probably these difficulties in representation and in reception of such a work that led Victor Tcherikover to reach the following conclusion decades ago:

> The Letter of Aristeas appears as a typical work of Alexandrian Jewry in the Ptolemaic period. There is no unity in the book, as there was no unity either in the heart of the author or in the social class to which he belonged. Like most of the people who strive to be "citizens of two worlds," Aristeas did not actually belong to either of them. It is

---

34. Günther Zuntz, "Aristeas Studies I: 'The Seven Banquets,'" *JSS* 4 (1959): 21–36. See also the article by Jonathan A. Goldstein with the very apropos title, "The Message of Aristeas to Philokrates in the Second Century bce: Obey the Torah, Venerate the Temple of Jerusalem, but Speak Greek, and Put Your Hopes in the Ptolemaic Dynasty," in *Eretz Israel, Israel, and the Jewish Diaspora: Mutual Relations; Proceedings of the First Annual Symposium of the Philip M. and Ethel Klutznick Chair in Jewish Civilization, Held on Sunday–Monday, October 9–10, 1988*, ed. Menachem Mor (Lanham, MD: University Press of America, 1991), 1–23.

difficult to class Aristeas among the nationalist Jews; his Judaism is pale and colorless, imbued with foreign influences, and it lacks the inner warmth of a genuine national feeling. Even less does Aristeas belong to the Hellenes. His aspirations to be like the Greeks only emphasize the great distance between him and the true Greek intelligentsia.[35]

Thus, by positioning himself and his project as hybrid, the author of the *Letter* seems to run the risk of being rejected by both the Jews and the Greeks, in spite of his ideals to combine the best of the two cultures and modes of thinking. This intriguing duality in Aristeas's cultural reaction in using outside sources and, at the same time, presenting Jewish wisdom as the ultimate standard of truth, illustrates well the ambivalence of the hybrid condition: both absorbing and resisting the socioreligious, political, and cultural milieu to present something "in-between." This "in-between" reality or positioning is an imaginative process, which goes beyond a simple duality of "us versus them," of "back home" versus "the adopted home," of simple assimilation and praise for the blessings or benefits enjoyed in the Diaspora, or even strong vilification of the present social and religious reality with its possible luring of bigotry and ostracism. It is a nuanced, risky position, where healthy criticism and constructive reflexion are possible in order to avoid intolerance and prejudice from all angles. It is this position that the author of the *Letter* tried to articulate, though at times one might wonder if he is totally freed from his own lies and chauvinism.

Conclusion

Read from a postcolonial angle, the *Letter* reveals itself as a hybrid project. The author has managed to argue for an "in-between" spatial location of the diasporic Jewish community in Alexandria. The

---

35. See Tcherikover, "Ideology," 84.

multiple agencies in place are captured in the forms of calculated negotiations, prudent affiliations, and idealized memory. The *Letter* offers a complex depiction of how a diasporic community could integrate and assimilate comfortably into the life of a host country, without losing any of what constitutes the essence of its cultural and religious identity. However, the project is a very difficult one to get across, as the conclusion reached by Tcherikover, for example, makes clear. For Tcherikover, clearly, the *Letter* has failed. But what would success look like? What exactly constitutes failure in the case of such a narrative? From whose perspective is success and failure to be judged? These questions are important, because for other readers the *Letter* might present itself as a healthy model of survival, of adaptation, and of success. But, again, who can determine what success is for an ancient literary creation such as *Aristeas*? It is necessary, then, to embrace the work as a hybrid project in its ambivalence, in its "Third Space of enunciation" à la Bhabha, in the ways it both rejects and embraces Alexandrian Greek Hellenism for different reasons.

In our present world where constant migration makes ways for cultures to be constantly created in transgressing old boundaries, the *Letter of Aristeas* has the potential of offering a way of being grounded in the adoption of new places and new languages without losing one's own culture and religion. In this sense, the *Letter* begs to present and to inspire a "third space" of breathing "in-between."

Now let us move on to consider how Josephus reread the *Letter* in his own diasporic social and political location.

Reading the *Letter of Aristeas* in Book 12 of Josephus's *Antiquities*

The *Antiquities* is a complex work covering Judean history and the Judean religion. It was addressed primarily to a Roman readership comprised of curious, interested sympathizers and converts (*Ant.* 1.8).

The historical and sociopolitical context of the author of the *Antiquities* is the Flavian Roman context of late first-century Rome.[36] The first edition of this magnum opus, which Josephus considered his noblest (κάλλιστα) enterprise (1.9), was completed and published in Rome in 93–94, in the thirteenth year of the reign of Caesar Domitian of the Common Era (*Ant.* 20.267). Josephus was writing after the destruction of the temple and he was reinterpreting the *Letter* in that context. There is a special relationship between the *Antiquities* and the *Letter,* since Josephus took as his model the high priest Eleazar, who likewise acceded to the request of a prominent gentile (Ptolemy II) eager "to have our Law and the political constitution (πολιτείας) based thereon translated into Greek" (*Ant.* 1.10). In his *Antiquities,* Josephus presents a summary of the constitution given by Moses (*Ant.* 4.196–301), and argues for the superiority of the Jewish *politeia* above all other political systems of government (e.g., *Ant.* 4.223–24).[37]

Here I explore how an ancient reader and writer such as Josephus read and then rewrote, summarized, and resignified another ancient text (*The Letter of Aristeas*) in his *Antiquities* from the angles of reception history[38] and of postcolonial historiography by arguing

36. See Tessa Rajak, *Josephus: the Historian and his Society,* 2nd ed. (London: Duckworth, 2002); Jonathan Edmonson, Steve Mason, and James Rives, eds., *Flavius Josephus and Flavian Rome* (Oxford: Oxford University Press, 2005).
37. See Daniel R. Schwartz, "Josephus on the Jewish Constitutions and Community," *SCI* 7 (1983–84): 30–52.
38. *Wirkungsgeschichte* (or reception history) can offer fresh insights into analyzing and understanding previous works. In this sense, individual readings are situated in a continuum of other readings and interpretations, which may put previously unnoticed aspects of a text into the light. Thus, there is an interest not only in texts, but also in the history of texts. For more on this hermeneutical approach, see Hans-Georg Gadamer, *Truth and Method,* ed. Trans. J. Weinsheimer and D. G. Marshall, 2nd ed. (New York: Crossroad, 1989). An earlier work, which has applied reception history as a methodology to the Josephan corpus, is the monograph by Heinz Schreckenberg, *Rezeptionsgeschichtliche und Textkritische Untersuchungen zu Flavius Josephus* (Leiden: Brill, 1977). In other words, the present reading is embedded in the continuum of readings and interpretations by considering the texts anew, and by positing that there is no particular reading or interpretation that should have an interpretive monopoly.

that, although Josephus maintained the specificity of his ethnoreligious tradition in his summary of the *Letter*, he does so in a less overt way. The main thesis I will pursue is that sociopolitical constraints in Josephus's diasporic socio-location guided his summary of the *Letter*. If Josephus imitated the magnanimity of Eleazar by sharing his ethnoreligious tradition with those who were eager to learn (φιλομαθεῖς) about the Judean constitution, law, and principal customs, he did not present his materials in the highly chauvinistic way of the high priest. Although Josephus maintained his bold claim that the Judeans had the noblest constitution in existence (1.15, 24), he managed, through the construction of different agencies—mimicry, affiliation, calculated negotiation—to move between assimilation and resistance in his summary of the *Letter*. The reading I propose here shows other possible ways of explaining Josephus's omissions and summary of the *Letter* by looking at the ways in which a Judean employed as a historian in the heart of the Roman political power negotiated his diasporic sociopolitical realities.[39]

The First Omission

Josephus presents a fairly elegant summary of the *Letter*.[40] He follows the sequence of the *Letter*, and one has no difficulty seeing that he had the text of Aristeas in front of him. For A. Pelletier,

> Ce qui le (Josèphe) pousse à y introduire tant de modifications, c'est *le désir de répondre aux goûts littéraires du public de Rome. C'est à partir*

---

39. See Tessa Rajak, "Josephus in the Diaspora," in *Flavius Josephus and Flavian Rome,* ed. Jonathan Edmondson, Steve Mason, and James Rives (Oxford: Oxford University Press, 2005), 79–97.

40. For an excellent comparative and philological work on Josephus's reading of Aristeas, see Pelletier, *Flavius Josèphe adapteur de la Lettre d'Aristée.* See also Shaye J. D. Cohen's *Josephus in Galilee and Rome: His Vita and Development as a Historian* (Leiden: E. J. Brill, 1979). In this classic work, Cohen similarly explores Josephus's retelling of not only his sources but his approach to historiography in general.

de cette préoccupation fondamentale que s'expliquent non seulement les transformations inévitables d'une *Lettre* en récit d'histoire, mais les corrections atticisantes, la tendance à uniformiser le style, à écarter ou moderniser le vocabulaire de certaines institutions anciennes, tandis qu'il maintient des termes de philosophie et de rhétorique qui ont cours dans le public cultivé. Si, par aventure, *quelque omission ou quelque changement peut s'expliquer par la prudence politique* du φιλορώμαιος, c'est, bien entendu, *parce que Josèphe doit la vie sauve et sa fortune aux Flaviens*, mais c'est d'abord pour s'accorder au conformisme du milieu cultivé auquel il destine ses Antiquités.[41]

For Pelletier, thus, on the one hand, the modifications are for the sake of the savant Roman audience (*le désir de répondre aux goûts littéraires du public de Rome*) and, on the other hand, some modifications in Josephus' text may be explained by political prudence (*prudence politique*). The line of argument I explore here builds on this important insight, but it has more to do with how Josephus negotiated his political and diasporic posture, from within which he read and summarized the *Letter* for his audience. The two texts are different. Although both texts were apologetic materials,[42] Josephus seems to be very careful in what he chose to include, to add, and most

---

41. Pelletier, *Flavius Josèphe adapteur de la Lettre d'Aristée,* 271; emphasis added.

42. In regards to the *Letter,* see Tcherikover, "Ideology," and Beavis, "Anti-Egyptian Polemic." For more recent studies on the ideology present in the work, see Sylvie Honigman, *The Septuagint and Homeric Scholarship in Alexandria,* and Kovelman, *Between Alexandria and Jerusalem.* For much of the twentieth century, Josephus's *Antiquities* has been considered to be an apologetic history. Recently, however, Steve Mason has challenged this view because he finds the description of Josephus as a Jewish historian and apologist to be too broad of a description. See Mason's "'Should Any Wish to Enquire Further' (*Ant.* 1. 25): The Aim and Audience of Josephus' *Judean Antiquities/Life,*" in *Understanding Josephus: Seven Perspectives* (Sheffield: Sheffield Academic Press, 1998). Mason's argument is solid. My understanding is, however, that there is a different kind of apologetic present. Although Josephus does not state it explicitly, it is clear that he works hard to portray the history of the Judeans in the best possible light. For this reason, I maintain that Josephus is doing apologetic work in his *Ant.,* and I am not arguing that he was not a *Jewish* historian, but the convincing arguments of Mireille Hadas-Lebel should push one to also consider the dimension of Josephus as a historian of Rome. See Mireille Hadas-Lebel, "Flavius Josephus, Historian of Rome," in *Josephus and the History of the Greco-Roman Period: Essays in Memory of Morton Smith,* ed. Fausto Parente and Joseph Sievers (Leiden: Brill, 1994), 99–106.

importantly, to exclude. The immediate concern is what Josephus chose to delete in his rendering of the *Letter*, especially the two major exclusions of 82–171 (including Eleazar's philosophical, apologetic, and even confrontational defense of the law), and 188–291 (the prolonged philosophical discussions between the king and the translators).

From 82–171, the *Letter* displays a distinct tone in its presentation of the concerns for cultic practices and cultural identity. The issues around food laws and animals deemed unclean are explained as "our express commands relating to religious observance/piety (εὐσεβείας) and justice" (131). The author returns to the issue of clean and unclean animals at different places in the section under study (144–51; 153–54; 161–65; 169–70). He is at pains to make sense of what might appear bizarre to his gentile readers. The focus on Jewish abstinence from certain animals such as "mice" and "weasels" (144), as mentioned earlier, could appear confusing, since the native Egyptians also did not eat such rodents, along with cats, dogs, and ibises, because they regarded these animals as manifestations of the gods.[43] The reasons given for the abstention of eating food deemed unclean are, first "to prevent our being perverted by contact with others or by mixing with bad influences" (142), and then because "we are distinct from all other men" (152). This belief or myth of ethnic purity and distinctiveness among other peoples, which is a characteristic of premodern articulation of indigenous religious identities (as well as most modern-day nationalisms), is matched with the memory of the "great and glorious" (155) deeds God did on behalf of the Judeans in the past (156–57).

Aristeas's other primary concern in the *Letter* is the worship of the true God, understood as the Jewish monotheist God.[44] 134 reads,

---

43. Beavis, "Anti Egyptian Polemic," 150.

"He (Eleazar) proceeded to show that all the rest of mankind ("except ourselves," as he said) believe that there are many gods" and "those who have invented these fabrications and myths are usually ranked to be the wisest of the Greeks" (138). There is, for the author of the *Letter*, seemingly no need to elaborate on the foolishness of the other nations (the Egyptians being especially targeted), since "their whole attitude (to life) is concentrated on these concerns" (140), in other words, false beliefs and the worship of the gods. Throughout this section, the author sketches a dichotomist image of "us" versus "them." "We" specifies what is special, glorious, historical, sensible and civilized, while "they" stand for what is ahistorical, nonsensical, and barbaric. The world consists of "them" and the "Others." They alone possess a monopoly status on the divine by means of a unique covenant with the true God. The whole discourse pictures a nation sufficient in itself and in no need of others, since it has God by its side. What is imagined is a series of binary divisions ("pure vs. impure," "Israel as the nation of God par excellence vs. the other nations," "true vs. false"), serves as a way to secure the constructed privilege and elite position of Israel among the nations. The gentiles cannot approach God unless they come to the Jewish understanding of this deity. There is no place in the author's understanding for dialogue with, or learning from the religious understanding of the Egyptians.[45] The author condemns them and projects the Egyptians

44. Strict monotheism (in the sense of a denial of all divine beings except YHWH, who is the only God) was foreign to Josephus. The point was that only one God should be venerated, not that other divine beings (angels, *daimons*, intermediary celestial beings, etc.) did not exist.

45. See Musa W. Dube, *Postcolonial Feminist Interpretation of the Bible* (St. Louis: Chalice, 2000). Dube is a postcolonial feminist African scholar. In this particular work, she proposes a set of questions one may use as an analytical grid for analyzing ancient texts in order to determine the degrees to which they can be categorized as imperializing texts. One of her questions is, "How does this text construct difference: Is there dialogue and mutual interdependence, or condemnation and replacement of all that is foreign?" Although there is dialogue in the *Letter*, the picture is complicated, as one party is represented as having the control of religious understanding.

as being in need of repentance and to come to the God of Israel. For the author of the *Letter*, God is on their side; the Other with unthinkable stories needs to come to them. This way of looking at the world is important to share with his fabricated correspondent brother: "Indeed, I consider that, on these matters, details of our way of life are worth narrating. Wherefore, in view of your love of learning, I have been induced, Philocrates, to expound to you the solemnity and characteristic outlook of the Law" (171).

Josephus and the First Omission

The first and most obvious reason for Josephus's first omission is that he has already gone through quite detailed matters of Judean law, and at considerable length, in *Ant.* 3–4. The work as it stands is quite lengthy (twenty volumes), and his audience has remained with him until volume 12! Josephus insisted that his audience was very interested in Judean law, which is why he, though exhausted by the project, completed it (*Ant.* 1.6–10). In the *Antiquities*, Josephus repeatedly refers to the laws and ways of living of the Jews, boasting that the law is the noblest constitution in existence (1.15, 24). For him, and for his audience, adherence to the ancestral laws is important. Josephus emphasizes how obedience to the religious laws and the ancestral rights leads to prosperity and blessings, whereas disobedience to the instructions and ancestral ways of living and being leads to disaster (*Ant.* 1.14). This logic would resonate well with an audience curious and respectful of an ethnic group with ancient customs, even if some of them were considered strange. Josephus, then, does not see a need to continue navigating the intricacies of the cultic system in his summary of the *Letter*, since he has done so at length in other accounts.

The second suggested reason in regard to Josephus's first omission is that of the divine privilege supposedly enjoyed by this specific group. In his particular sociopolitical location, the author of the *Antiquities* cannot posit, as the author of the *Letter*, that those of his audience who do not adhere to his Jewish way of living are defiled, or are in some sense inferior. Josephus has no choice but to mingle with a group different from his own ethnic background, and he cannot pretend that he is being perverted by being in contact with others or "by mixing with bad influences." Is it thus possible that Josephus's omission makes clear his attempt to mute the highly chauvinistic themes found in the *Letter?* While downplaying possibly offensive elements may have been part of Josephus's intentions for the omissions, the concept of ethnic purity and distinctiveness seen in the *Letter* also has a place in Josephus. Examples include his handling of the Pinchas episode (*Ant.* 4.139–59) and his consistent emphases in *Against Apion* (first half of book 1, latter half of book 2). He defends the idea of *amixia* (nonmixing with other nations) as mandated by Moses' law, along with distinctive diet and other customs. And Josephus defends this notion as being in keeping with ancient categories of citizenship, just as the Athenians and Spartans guarded their citizenship and purity. Hence, one cannot posit that the author of the *Antiquities* sees no room in his work for presenting himself as being in a special zone, while his audience would be viewed as ahistorical and nonsensical.[46] Josephus, a proud priest, who is addressing a readership that is interested in Judean's history and practices, places great emphasis on cultic activity (*Ant.* 3–4, especially). The description of Jerusalem and the Temple in 83–120

---

46. As a modern reader reading in my place, and as this study is informed by postcolonial sensitivities, I would well want to see that Josephus is not so much pushing his Judean agenda to a breaking point, that he would understand that the cultic details of one's religion are better expressed within one's inner religious circle. But that is not what the overall data present.

is left out in Josephus's summary, not because Josephus is opposed to positing Judean identity as superior and unique, but because this section of the letter repeats themes already present in Josephus's writing.

The Second Omission

The second section of the *Letter* that is omitted by Josephus (188–291) deals with prolonged philosophical discussions between the king and the translators. The segment in the *Letter* starts with the king asking for advice about good governance. After the response of each translator, the king shows satisfaction with regard to his inquiry and praises the virtues of the Jewish sages. The king is so impressed by the wisdom of the ambassadors that he "responded with prolonged hearty and genial applause" (220), and "with a loud voice the king complimented and encouraged them all" (235). And "the audience raised their voices in approval, and especially the philosophers, for these men far surpassed them in attitudes and eloquence, their starting point being God himself." The king's and the audience's good opinion of the sages is highlighted in other places as well (257; 261; 274; 277; 294). The praises of the king is reflected in the sages' admiration for the monarch.

This section is revealing in different ways. First, it displays an attitude toward the Other that is different from that of the first omission. Here, the Other, located in a powerful monarch in search of more wisdom, knows the importance of wisdom and where to look for it. Second, the Other distinguishes the superiority of the Jewish wisdom and holds it in high regard. Contrary to the essentialized Other of the first omission, here the Other is recognized as a powerful and wise ruler, who needs to be courted, someone whose conduct deserves admiration. Simply put, this powerful Other is "civilized," because he is, in many regards, "like us."[47] The *Letter* presents itself as a hybrid project, which one sees best in the forms of calculated negotiations, prudent affiliations, and idealized memory. Although the narrative is orchestrated to show respect for the king's authority, learning, and wisdom, nonetheless, it also challenges the king by placing him in a position subservient to the God of Israel (132). The *Letter* goes so far as to portray the king as one who does obeisance to the translator-philosophers for their surpassing knowledge and wisdom, and he is urged to follow God (177; 255). Thus, in the *Letter*, there is admiration and resistance, acceptance and challenge, ambivalence and mimicry.[48]

Josephus and the Second Omission

When it comes to Josephus's omissions and the reasons for them, we need to consider at least the most obvious reasons. He summarizes the narrative of the *Letter*, but omits the elaborate philosophical discussions. Are there parallels elsewhere in his writings? There is a fairly obvious parallel in his handling of what is called the biblical paraphrase. It is not a paraphrase of the Bible, because he does not deal with Psalms, Proverbs, Ecclesiastes, Job, and so on—the more philosophical, discursive texts. Of the narrative texts, he harmonizes and reduces parallel stories to one single narrative.[49] The most likely or probable explanation for why Josephus needed to keep the summary short is that he gives what he thinks is enough for what he

47. Edward Said's work is relevant here, as he demonstrates how the "Othering" of the Orient was made to conform to a prejudiced outsider interpretation. See Edward Said, "Orientalism Reconsidered," *Cultural Critique* 1(1985): 89–107.

48. See Bhabha's analysis of the phenomenon of colonial mimicry, where the colonial subject manifests both resistance and complicity in the complex relationship that exists between colonizer and colonized. See *Location of Culture*, 85–92.

49. On Josephus's (re)reading and (re)writing of the Hebrew Bible, see Louis H. Feldman, *Studies in Josephus' Rewritten Bible* (Leiden: Brill, 1998); *Josephus's Interpretation of the Bible* (Berkeley: University of California Press, 1998).

needed to convey, in order to move on to matters of importance in
his narrative. The reason he wants to keep things brief is tied to what
he understands as the task of a historian. Josephus understands the
work of a historian to be the narration of past events, which should
exclude extensive philosophical discussion (as such, not philosophical
themes or excluding him from devoting his work to natural
philosophy, *Ant.* 1.1.4 §18), extensive moral-rhetorical assessment,
and even predictions of the future. In a famous passage (*Ant.* 10.210),
he omits the interpretation of Nebuchadnezzar's dream, and he
collapses several dreams and visions from Daniel into one, because "I
have only undertaken to describe things past or things present, but
not things that are future." Several times in *J. W.* and in *Ant.* he pauses
to excuse himself for briefly going into some moral question that
is "beyond the laws of history." An alternate theory in this type of
historiographical analysis that might also account for this omission is
that Josephus's own copy of *Aristeas* (or his memory of *Aristeas*) was
abbreviated at this point.[50]

Having established the historical point that the most obvious
reason Josephus omits the elaborate philosophical discussions of the
Letter is that he does not consider the material appropriate to the
work of a historian, I want to move on in a bit further, in order to
consider how his rereading of the *Letter* might have been measured
by sociopolitical constraints in his diasporic socio-location. Josephus's
paraphrase of this section is interesting. We read in *Antiquities* 12.99,

---

50. A number of scholars have argued that since Josephus elsewhere makes explicit admission of
his omissions, we might deduce one of two things: either, the material in 83–171 was not in
Josephus's text of Aristeas, or that he deliberately omitted it and supplied his own transitional
sentence by joining the material of 82 and 171 with the following statement: "These then were
the dedicatory offerings sent to Jerusalem by Ptolemy. Now Eleazar, the High Priest, after
dedicating them to God and honouring the bearers, gave them gifts to take to the king and sent
them back to the king." These reasons are both likely explanations for Josephus's omission.

> But the king, after waiting for what seemed a sufficiently long time, began to philosophize and asked each one of them about problems of nature, and when, after considering the questions, they gave precise explanations concerning every single problem suggested to them for discussion, he was delighted with them and made the banquet last for twelve days, so that anyone who wishes to find out the details of the questions discussed at the banquet can learn them by reading the book which Aristeas composed on this account.

The impression given in *Ant.* 12.99 is that after having let pass what seemed to be a sufficient amount of time for the feasting (διαλιπὼν δ' ὁ βασιλεὺς ἐφ' ὅσον ἔδοξεν ἀποχρῶντα καιρὸν εἶναι), the king began "to philosophize and asked each one of them about problems of nature" (φιλοσοφεῖν ἤρξατο καὶ ἕκαστον αὐτῶν λόγους ἐπηρώτα φυσικούς). Josephus does not give any indication that the king was asking for advice as to good governance, but that he asked questions about φυσικούς (problems of nature) or that he was enquiring about "problems of moral philosophy."[51] According to Josephus, the king needed to occupy himself somehow and he did so, not by enquiring about how to be a good king as in the *Letter*, but by asking questions about matters that pertained to moral philosophy. The scene depicted here is that of a pleasant afternoon spent in conversation between a king and his wise visitors. Josephus's account, at least as I read it, seems to eliminate any sentiment of rapture on the part of the dignitary and audience regarding the profundity of the wisdom of the Jewish sages. There seems also to be in Josephus's account an erasure of any side having an advantage in the degree of wisdom possessed. The king was simply delighted with them, and that is all. Based on the mentioned changes and omissions in Josephus's summary, can it be inferred that he has a different conception of the Other? This inference is not supported by Josephus's summary. It

---

51. See Josephus, *The Antiquities of the Jews*, Book XII, trans. Ralph Marcus, Loeb Classical Library (Cambridge, MA: Harvard University Press, 1943), 49.

shows, simply, that Josephus remembered that he was in a position similar to the translators, namely, in the position of one who had to entertain, to discuss philosophy only when the power in place deems it timely, and a historian under a political power that, ultimately, controlled him.[52]

Negotiating Diaspora in the *Antiquities*

Josephus is prudent in the ways in which he approaches power. He is a colonial subject of the Roman Empire, who needs to negotiate between his socioreligious beliefs about the "uniqueness" of the Jewish people, and the political realities of Rome as the conqueror of the Jews.[53] As a spokesperson for his people, arguing for an idealized version of the antiquity of his ethnic group, Josephus is well aware that his position is complicated. Although he is a priestly aristocrat, and has a presumptive right to represent his people, Josephus is nonetheless not mandated or authorized by any of his ethnic group to undertake this project. In fact, because of his past acts as a renegade general, who lied in order to save himself, he would have appeared in the eyes of many of his Jewish contemporaries, who were living as colonial subjects under the Roman Empire in the Diaspora, as disqualified from doing so.

As one living in the Diaspora, Josephus might well have had a consciousness of a "home" that was located somewhere else, which

---

52. Note the similarity between Josephus and Joseph. Both are in a foreign place (Egypt for Joseph and Rome for Josephus as an imperial protégé and historian) and both are in the proximity of political power. They are both hybrid colonial elite subjects caught in a relation of negotiating the power they are serving. See Ronald Charles, "A Postcolonial Reading of *Joseph and Aseneth*," *JSP* 18, no. 4 (2009): 265–83.

53. On the question of how Jews/Judeans negotiated their Diaspora identity, see among countless others, Barclay, *Jews in the Mediterranean Diaspora*, and Erich Gruen's *Diaspora: Jews Amidst Greeks and Romans* (Cambridge, MA: Harvard University Press, 2002). Scholarly debates on issues of assimilation and acculturation are addressed at length in Barclay's cited work, and Gruen's highly critical of idealization of the Jewish Diaspora experience is a very good starting point.

we cannot have access to, but his home, in the sense of where he had continued residence, was in the heart of the political power of the Roman Empire.[54] He was well aware of the loss of his ancestral home, since he had been a general in the Jewish wars before being captured by the Romans. He witnessed the destruction of the temple and of Jerusalem, but the complexities involved in defining where "home" was for him are difficult to attest. He is a diasporic and colonial subject living "in-between" places, identities, and allegiances. This space "in-between" provides him a way to maneuver between assimilation and resistance by constructing multiple agencies in the sociopolitical sites he occupies.[55] Josephus is in the difficult position of having to please both his Jewish kinsmen and his Roman audience. He does not mention Ptolemy's bowing down before the Law seven times (177), nor does he mention the king's courtiers waiting on table for the translators (186), as one reads in the *Letter*. The contrasts between the *Letter* and its paraphrase in the *Antiquities* demonstrate the sociopolitical tendencies of Josephus, who glosses over certain possible sources of conflict, while creating new scenarios that present the figure of the king as important and dignified. In sum, Josephus's "remixing" of the *Letter* serves the larger apologetic goals of his magnum opus: to present the antiquities of the Jews in an ideal and idealized way.

Josephus cleverly refers anyone who is interested in the details of the philosophical discussions at the banquet to go to read the *Letter* in its original. In this way, he does not reveal that the *Letter* contains any materials that are or might be problematic to diasporic

---

54. This does not negate the fact that he still had, as a landowner, some connections with the homeland (*Vita* 422, 425).

55. A significant reference that offers us a picture of how Josephus would like to be perceived by his audience is his *Life/Vita*, which was added as an appendix to *Ant*. This work, in spite of Denis Lamour's argument that it was a mistake for Josephus to have written this piece, is an extremely important document of evidence for how Josephus understands himself "between Rome and Jerusalem." Lamour's arguments are in his *Flavius Josèphe* (Paris: Les Belles Lettres, 2000).

and colonial subjects.[56] The reader will have to decide. And Josephus, through this method, maintains his distance from a text that might have compromised his position as a friend to Roman aristocrats and as a historian.[57] Similarly, the apologetic agenda in his paraphrase could also lend itself to a hybrid reading, insofar as it idealizes the memory of the period in which the *Letter* was supposed to have been written, specifically idealizing it in the new, Roman context. Is it possible, then, that Josephus, in pointing interested readers to the *Letter's* philosophical discussions, subversively invites the readers to discover how political power can be negotiated, resisted, and challenged? A reader of the *Letter* could easily realize that the conversations between the king and the sages, although certainly of good tone, present a challenge to the political power, that in the end, the Jewish translators surpass the monarch and, in a sense, conquer him. Thus, there seems to be in Josephus's discourse the double articulation of appropriation and subtle challenge, approval and mockery. To return to the question posed above: Could it be that Josephus points the interested readers to the details of the *Letter* in order to indicate to them how to question the power in place, how to challenge it, and, eventually, how to conquer it, if even imaginatively?[58] Such intent on the part of Josephus would show the level of political astuteness of Josephus in negotiating and challenging his diasporic sociopolitical context.

---

56. It is true that the author of the *Letter* was also writing in the Diaspora, but his work, because it was addressed primarily to other Jews, could be more open than Josephus's *Antiquities* in its challenge to the sociopolitical culture at large.

57. Josephus was a historian associated with the Flavian court, but he was not a court historian in the normal sense of that term, e.g., the way that Nicolaus of Damascus was a court historian of Herod. Josephus did not write Flavian history, but Judean history, except incidentally in *War*. In this way, one can observe Josephus's dual identity and his rereading of the *Letter* as a Roman and Jewish historian.

58. With regard to a critique of Roman power in Josephus's works, one can also refer to Steve Mason's work on irony, "Figured Speech and Irony in T. Flavius Josephus," in Edmondson et al., *Flavius Josephus and Flavian Rome*, 244–88.

By shying away from any criticism in regard to the king in his rendering of the *Letter*, I am suggesting, Josephus's writing is measured by political constraint. He had to maneuver his rhetorical, social and political strategy in a way that was in agreement with the interests of the Romans.[59] As an apologist, Josephus was caught in the dilemma of sharing the history and culture of his people in the terms of the dominant culture. In other words, for him to represent and advocate his own Judean tradition, he needed to examine the power relations that underlay his sociopolitical location by presenting his particular ethnoreligious traditions and constitution in ways that have, in places, strong resonances with the basic Roman values of austerity and philanthropy.[60] As a diasporic historian residing in Rome, the heart of the empire, Josephus took upon himself the task of retelling the history of a recently defeated people. And this can be linked to the importance of historiography for diasporic colonized communities to recount and conserve their history in the complex cultural and political realities in which they often find themselves. In the case of Josephus, he gave himself the power to recount the story of his people in the terms of the Romans. His task was to negotiate his discourse with the diasporic ambiguity within which he found himself, and he did so by both presenting the history of his diasporic community in a way supportive of the Roman sense of cultural superiority and by reinstating the honour of his ethnic group. In other words, Josephus carefully crafted his discourse to elevate his own Jewish nation by, strategically, avoiding the extremely prejudiced discourse of the *Letter*. The complexities and tensions

---

59. For more on Josephus's shrewd negotiations of the sociopolitical realities of imperial Rome through the lenses of hybridity, mimicry, and irony, see David A. Kaden, "Flavius Josephus and the *Gentes Devictae* in Roman Imperial Discourse: Hybridity, Mimicry, and Irony in the Agrippa II Speech (*Judean War* 2.345–402)," *JSJ* 42 (2011): 481–507. The bibliography therein is excellent.

60. See Mason, "The Aim and Audience of Josephus' Judean *Antiquities/Life*," , 85.

inherent in the diaspora condition allowed Josephus to adopt the cultural values of his Roman hosts, while creating positive space to give his gentile audience a comprehensive summary of the origins, history, laws, political constitution, and culture of the Judeans.

Josephus, like the author of the *Letter*, wanted to maintain difference and otherness as the hallmark of the Jews, but he realized he had to do so prudently and differently. In his diasporic sociopolitical context, and as one addressing the Other situated in a position of power, he could not insist too adamantly on a special status for his people. The best Josephus could do was to negotiate the political power in place. In taking upon himself the task of writing the histories of his subaltern pasts, he deemed it important to give an idealized picture of his history by ways of a redefinition of agency.[61] One recalls Avtar Brah's remarks that "all diasporas are differentiated, heterogeneous, contested spaces, even as they are implicated in the construction of a common 'we.'"[62] The diasporic colonial situation was experienced and negotiated differently by Josephus on the one way, and by those who did not have the power and privilege he enjoyed, on the other. He has the leisure to write, the expertise of a privileged intellectual that is heard by his aristocrat friends and sympathizers, the power to be the representative of his people in the Diaspora.[63]

---

61. And here agency is understood as synonymous with resistance to relationship of domination, which is close to Bhabha's rubric of hybridity as revealing the tension between the resistance of the colonial subject and their coinciding affiliation with their colonizers.

62. Avtar Brah, *Cartographies of Diaspora: Contesting Identities* (New York: Routledge, 1996), 184.

63. Josephus seems to fit the description of Noam Chomsky's intellectual image: "Quite typically, intellectuals have been ideological and social managers, serving power or seeking to assume power themselves by taking control of popular movements of which they declare themselves to be the leaders." See *Language and Problems of Knowledge: The Managua Lectures* (Cambridge, MA: MIT Press, 1988), 165.

Conclusion

The immediate concern of this section of the chapter was to investigate the plausible rationale behind Josephus's omission of two major parts of the *Letter of Aristeas* in his paraphrase of this work in book 12 of his *Antiquities*. I have suggested that Josephus omitted the first major part because there was for him no necessity to elaborate on the intricacies of the cultic system, since he had done so elsewhere. The second major omission, which is aptly summarized and referenced by Josephus, shows that the author of the *Antiquities* wanted to focus on historical events and that he was prudent by portraying the whole segment as discussions about problems of moral philosophy between the king and the translators. Thus, as I suggested, Josephus's account erases any tensions that one might perceive in the text. He proceeded this way in order to continue to enjoy with his audience a rendering of Jewish antiquities that highlights the overall theme pursued in his work, namely, that of respect for the religious laws, and the ancestral rights of the Jewish people, who prosper when they obey, but suffer when they go astray from these prerogatives (*Ant.* 1.14). The argument in terms of situating Josephus within the space of diaspora is that his rereading of the *Letter* was measured by sociopolitical constraints in his diasporic socio-location. He negotiated his diasporic space by developing rhetorical, social, and political strategies in a way that was in agreement with the interests of the Romans. In so doing, Josephus managed to move between assimilation and resistance in his summary of the *Letter*.

One, necessarily, needs to place Josephus's works as well as the *Letter* in a larger context of the adapting of rhetorical Greek conventions, which the author shared with other writers of the time, including those who valorized Greek identity and/or Roman identity. Josephus was hardly unique in his defense of the superiority of his own people.[64] If the point is that Jewish writers like Josephus and (possibly) the writer of the *Letter* seek to defend and define Judean identity vis-à-vis other groups in their diasporic social locations, precisely because that identity was under siege by their more powerful neighbors, then this context is readily acknowledged and the present reading is situated within a very complex web of rhetorical construction of identities in the ancient Mediterranean world. One also needs to remember that the writer of the *Letter*, as well as Josephus, are both highly privileged—they are quite literate and can command a broad audience, if nothing else—and that is one of the main points of diaspora studies: to notice the complex web of power relationships within which persons in a colonizing, diasporic sociopolitical locations are positioned.

Summary

Inhabiting the space of diaspora, negotiating the social, religious, and political realities of such a space, while imagining "home" and other spaces in ancient Hellenistic Judaism in the Roman period, were important grounds to cover in order to start situating Paul squarely within the matrix and complexities of first-century Diaspora Judaism. The *Letter of Aristeas* was a good place for setting the study of Paul in the Greco-Roman diaspora since the *Letter* is itself already located in this hybrid venue. The author of the *Letter* was writing in the diaspora, and his work was addressed primarily to other Jews—both in and out of the Diaspora. In the *Letter*, the dynamics of the diasporic condition are captured in the forms of calculated negotiations, prudent affiliations, and idealized memory. Then, it was

---

64. See Tessa Rajak, *The Jewish Dialogue with Greece and Rome: Studies in Cultural and Social Interaction* (Leiden: Brill, 2002).

necessary to consider how Josephus—another diasporic figure close to and different from Paul in many ways—managed and negotiated his diaspora existence at the heart of the Roman political power. Josephus' summary, rewriting, and resignifying of the *Letter* in *Antiquities* 12, it was argued, was characterized by his adept way to negotiate the sociopolitical dimension of his work as a historian in his diasporic space by moving between assimilation and resistance.

The articulation of the three specific theoretical aspects articulated earlier were important to contextualize by highlighting how ancient figures navigated their sociopolitical situations, relationships, social realities and ideals, "home" and the memory of home, in the diasporic milieu of Hellenistic Judaism in the Roman period. The payoff of this chapter with regard to Paul is that he is relevant both to the study of first-century Judaism as well as to the study of the early Jesus movement. To categorize him solely within one tradition—to what has become Christianity—is clearly to miss out on the vitality and variety of first-century Judaism. Therefore, scholars interested in Diaspora Judaism in the Greco-Roman period need to pay more attention to Paul as a first-century Jewish itinerant diaspora figure within the Roman Empire. As a diaspora figure, Paul had to negotiate his visions of the true kingdom of God and a new humanity manifested in Jesus alongside the incongruity of dire social realities.

Let us now turn to provide a clear description of Paul as a diasporic figure.

2

Paul, the Diaspora Jew

The second conceptual problem comes when we attempt to move from this redescription to explanation, for we are left with a Paul who is disconnected, unique, insensible, largely incomprehensible in any but self-referential terms, a Paul who speaks only in idiolect.
—William E. Arnal[1]

It is hardly surprising that this anomalous Jew should meet both puzzled and hostile reactions in Diaspora synagogues.
—John M. G. Barclay[2]

This chapter contributes to my argument by bringing my conceptual framing of Paul into sharper focus, providing a clear description of him as a diaspora figure. I argue here that Paul's social positioning in the Diaspora allows him to imagine, think through, and wrestle with issues of spaces, identities (social, economic, gender), cultures,

---

1. William E. Arnal, "Bringing Paul and the Corinthians Together? A Rejoinder and Some Proposals on Redescribing and Theory," in *Redescribing Paul and the Corinthians*, ed. Ron Cameron and Merrill P. Miller (Atlanta: Society of Biblical Literature, 2011), 81.
2. John M. G. Barclay, *Jews in the Mediterranean Diaspora: From Alexander to Trajan (323 BCE–117 CE)* (Berkeley: University of California Press, 1996), 393.

and traditions. Paul's diasporic identities are constantly in the process of crafting novel ways of being and evolving; his movements across boundaries requires him to engage in ever-expanding improvisations susceptible to creating new and complex tapestries of continuity and rupture, similarity and difference.[3]

Analytical Models

In order to provide a clear description of Paul as a diasporic figure, I have chosen four distinct analytical models: (1) Jonathan Z. Smith's model for doing a work of comparison; (2) Philip A. Harland's appropriated model for measuring degrees of acculturation, degrees of structural assimilation, and cultural maintenance;[4] (3) John M. G. Barclay's categories of assimilation, acculturation, and accommodation to study Paul among other Diaspora Jews;[5] and (4) insights drawn from diaspora studies to situate Paul in the ways he negotiated spaces in the diaspora. Smith provides an important venue

3. William E. Arnal captures what I want to express here in a way only he can with his beautiful prose: "Paul, now, is understood not as a purveyor of ideas whose content he has received from others and passes along, but as *bricoleur*, who uses mythic content, forms, and fragments as he encounters them, to construct novel notions that address his own problems, issues, and circumstances" (emphasis in original). See Arnal, "Bringing Paul and the Corinthians Together?" 80. The description of Paul as a "bricoleur" is also used by Pierre-Marie Beaude, although he, contrary to Arnal's arguments and my own, seems to regard Paul's thoughts as unique, as he clearly bows to Paul's "sainthood." Here is how he frames his understanding: "La pensée paulinienne, singulière à bien des égards, s'établit donc dans l'espace fréquenté par nombre de penseurs, philosophes, rhéteurs, théoriciens et praticiens en tous genres. Cette situation construit un pont entre lui et ses lecteurs, qui avaient, en le recevant, des points de repère, plus ou moins précis, pour le situer dans leurs schémas culturels. Mais c'est maintenant au « bricolage» des interdiscursivités dans les lettres singulières de l'apôtre qu'il faut nous intéresser. J'entends par « bricolage » la façon dont Paul, riche, par écho ou réception directe, de tous les discours concernant les appartenances et les identités, crée son propre discours." See Pierre-Marie Beaude, *Saint Paul: L'oeuvre de Métamorphose* (Paris: Éditions du Cerf, 2011), 274.
4. See Philip A. Harland, *Dynamics of Identity in the World of the Early Christians: Associations, Judeans, and Cultural Minorities* (New York: T & T Clark, 2009), 13 and 102–4.
5. John M. G. Barclay, "Paul among Diaspora Jews: Anomaly or Apostate?" *JSNT* 60 (1995): 89–120, and Barclay, *Jews in the Mediterranean Diaspora*, 381–95. Barclay's model could have been included in that of Harland's because of the closeness of their analytical types, but a different entry is allotted to his contribution for the sake of clarity.

to situate Paul within the milieu of first-century Diaspora Judaism, not as out of the ordinary or unique, but as both similar and different from other Diaspora Jews; Harland's model for studying minority groups allows us to understand Paul's social integration, adaptation, and participation within different networks by examining his social locations in the Diaspora; and Barclay's indexes place Paul squarely within the Jewish Diaspora of the Mediterranean world. While this chapter builds on some of the results pertaining to the approaches of Smith, Harland, and Barclay, insights from diaspora studies help us to move beyond their limitations. Insights from diaspora studies will allow us to understand further the positionality of diasporic subjects and how diasporic figures negotiate spaces and identities.

Jonathan Z. Smith's Model

One figure who has done very important work on the practice of comparison, specifically in the history of religion (though he certainly does not have the last word on the subject), is Jonathan Z. Smith.

Method

In his book *Drudgery Divine*, Smith endeavored to conduct a kind of comparative analysis that is not apologetic, but instead is based on sound "disciplined enquiry."[6] For Smith, the way the term *unique* is used, particularly in religious studies, has given the impression that the comparative task is "both an impossibility and an impiety."[7] Admittedly, the task of comparison is not an easy one, and for Smith, "there is nothing 'natural' about the enterprise of comparison. Similarity and difference are not 'given.'"[8] Comparisons, thus, are

6. See Jonathan Z. Smith, *Drudgery Divine: On the Comparison of Early Christianities and the Religions of Late Antiquity* (Chicago: University of Chicago Press, 1990), vii.
7. Ibid., 38.

mental exercises engaged in by the researcher to find out what the similarities and the differences are. Again according to Smith, "comparison, as seen from such a view, is an active, at times even a playful, enterprise of deconstruction and reconstitution which, kaleidoscope-like, gives the scholar a shifting set of characteristics with which to negotiate the relations between his or her theoretical interests and data stipulated as exemplary."[9] Making a comparison, in this sense, does not mean that one does not find differences—one does, and needs to take these seriously—but the differences in social formations, negotiating spaces, ideologies, practices, powers, religions, social and economic status, gender roles, and so on, are organized, classified, and studied by and for the interest of the scholar. They are not deemed to be out of the ordinary, but are considered ordinary social behaviours in their remarkable complexities.[10]

To be clear about what I am doing with Smith's work, I am not interested in his taxonomic approach. Smith favours a triadic comparison formulated the following way: "X resembles y more than z with respect to . . . ," or "X resembles y more than w resembles z with respect to. . . ."[11] Applied to Paul as the x factor, one could say: Paul resembles Josephus (y) more than Philo (z) with respect to . . ., or, in terms of expression, Paul's writings (x) resemble *The Wisdom of Solomon* (y) more than (a specific w) resembles (a particular z) with respect to, say, idolatry. This rigid method, although it can be helpful in some contexts of socioreligious study, does not capture the complexity and dynamics of the diasporic relationships I am interested in, where there is a continuum of social relationships

8. Ibid.
9. Ibid., 54.
10. For more on what I am trying to articulate here, see Russell T. McCutcheon, *Critics Not Caretakers: Redescribing the Public Study of Religion* (Albany: State University of New York Press, 2001), 14–15.
11. See Smith, *Drudgery Divine*, 51.

interacting together in the destabilizing diaspora space.[12] I follow Gregory D. Alles, who has identified some of Smith's pitfalls in his work on failed persuasion and religious mystification.[13] By critiquing Smith, Alles allows the research on the comparative enterprise, as proposed by Smith, to gain further strength. One of Alles's concerns is Smith's stipulation that "comparison is interesting only to the extent that it manipulates Differences."[14] For Alles, the stipulation "is convincing only when it conflates several kinds of difference."[15] He understands Smith's proposal as a reaction against the kind of comparison seen as "the discourse of similarity," which was practiced by such comparativists as Mircea Eliade. But in spite of Alles's concerns about some of the conclusions reached by Smith, he places his comparative work on *Iliad* and the *Rāmāyana* in Smith's terms. Alles's work is not a genealogical enterprise in the sense of "which artifact came first and who borrowed from whom," but rather an analogical one.[16] Alles goes beyond Smith here, even as he endorses him. Smith, while rejecting genealogy, embraces taxonomy, which has no place in Alles's comparative enterprise; it has no place in my analysis, either. Smith's theory is inadequate *on its own* for what I am interested in, with Alles providing a possible fix to the kind of problem I am referring to.[17]

---

12. See my analysis of those types of tensions in the entanglements of the diaspora space in chapter 3. The fact that I am not pursuing a taxonomic comparison may certainly be seen by some readers as lacking in methodological rigour for providing a systematic comparison. But this is not so.

13. Gregory D. Alles, *The Iliad, the R_M_YANA, and the Work of Religion: Failed Persuasion and Religious Mystification* (University Park, PA: Pennsylvania State University Press, 1994).

14. Ibid., 6.

15. Ibid.

16. Ibid., 5.

17. This is certainly not the place to even attempt to wrestle in a more thorough way with Smith's gigantic scholarly work. To expand the conversation with Smith's work, see *Introducing Religion: Essays in Honor of Jonathan Z. Smith*, ed. Willi Braun and Russell T. McCutcheon (London: Equinox, 2008).

I am particularly interested in building on Smith's practice of comparison that does not privilege any particular social and religious entity. In the case of Paul, this means moving away from any hagiographical presentation of this particular Diaspora Jew to place him as one Jewish male itinerant preacher and worker among others, as he was deploying different strategies to negotiate social relationships with localized communities of Christ believers within the Roman Empire. This means viewing Paul as one itinerant diasporic figure who was trying to make sense of his ideal vision of new associations in Christ within the fluid and dynamic diaspora spaces he occupied; this means understanding Paul as one human being trying to make sense of his socioreligious experiences and theology.

Results

The aim of this type of comparison is to look for analogy or similarity with regard to social and cultural matrices, for discursive practices, for parallels in teaching methods, for models of interacting with others, for *savoir faire* and *savoir être*, and so on and so forth. The results stemming from that type of comparison would then not surprise the researcher when he or she finds similarities and differences. One may compare, say, Paul as one among the ancient philosophers, what we moderns may characterize as a "religious" thinker, or as a Stoic among others in order to show similarities and differences between him and the other figures being compared. Or one may look for analogies in how different figures or groups of antiquity that shared common sociocultural mores, rhetorical practices, and understandings of the world and themselves, and so on, immersed in common dynamics of identity, and were doing things both similar and different than Paul.

This type of comparison is not about a simple, or rather simplistic, equation that "this" *explains* "that," as Larry W. Hurtado seems to understand comparison when he looks at Philo in comparison to other diasporic figures such as Paul.[18] This comparative approach shows that Paul did not operate de novo, but that he was a participant in the different conversations—using similar and well-known terms from his Greco-Roman world (e.g., virtue in Phil 4:8, need for self-control and discipline in 1 Cor 7:5 and 9:25-7)—and ways of thinking of his time.[19] This way of approaching Paul would not put the apostle to the nations in any special category with regard to other Diaspora Jews, but defines him clearly as another ordinary, yet complex, diasporic figure of antiquity forging a new language, and busy engaging in social experiments in creative ways. *Ordinary*, as used here, does not mean uncomplicated, unsophisticated, or easy to describe. This is, in fact, what characterizes ordinary human beings

18. In his exact terms, "With all sincere appreciation for the importance of Philo and for the labours of those who devote themselves to study of him, neither Philo nor other second-temple Jewish texts 'explains' key features of earliest Christianity witnessed in the New Testament, in the sense of accounting for their appearance." See his article, "Does Philo Help Explain Early Christianity?" in *Philo und das Neue Testament: Wechselseitige Wahrnehmungen*, Internationales Symposium zum Corpus Judaeo-Hellenisticum, 1.–4. Mai 2003, Eisenach/Jena, ed. R. Deines and K.-W. Niebuhr, WUNT 172 (Tübingen, Germany: Mohr Siebeck, 2004), 92.

19. See, for example, Will Deming, *Paul on Marriage and Celibacy: The Hellenistic Background of 1 Corinthians* 7 (Cambridge: Cambridge University Press, 1995); Francis G. Downing, *Cynics, Paul and the Pauline Churches* (New York: Routledge, 1998); Troels Engberg-Pedersen, *Paul and the Stoics* (Louisville: Westminster John Knox, 2000); Kenneth A. Fox, *Paul's Attitude Toward the Body in Romans 6–8: Compared with Philo of Alexandria* (PhD diss., University of St. Michael's College, 2001); Emma Wasserman, "Paul among the Philosophers: The Case of Sin in Romans 6–8," *JSNT* 30 (2008): 387–415, and "The Death of the Soul in Romans 7: Revisiting Paul's Anthropology in Light of Hellenistic Moral Psychology," *JBL* 126, no. 4 (2007): 793–816; Troels Engberg-Pedersen, *Cosmology and Self in the Apostle Paul* (New York: Oxford University Press, 2010). Barclay, in reviewing that book in "Stoic Physics and the Christ-event: A Review of Troels Engberg-Pedersen," *JSNT* 33, no. 4 (2011): 406–14, admits that there are linguistic and conceptual resonances of Stoicism present in Pauline discourse, but argues that Paul's theology is "fundamentally incompatible with Stoicism" (413) since it is based on different premises, logics, and underlying narratives from those of Philo. See also, in the same issue of *JSNT*, Engberg-Pedersen's response (433–43) to Barclay's review. Again, one needs to go back to the basics of what a work of comparison entails for much-needed clarity when one is comparing Paul to another figure.

and their existence: they are complicated! Paul does not escape this fascinating aspect of what makes us human. Stating that Paul was an ordinary Diaspora Jew does not imply that he is not a distinctive figure or that he does not occupy a distinct social position. In other words, as a Diaspora Jew, Paul was ordinary—as spelled out here—and distinct.[20] The point I am making is that one cannot say Paul is extraordinary with regard to all other contemporary Diaspora Jews, nor can one affirm, in an unsophisticated manner, that he was just like everybody else. He was similar, but not the same.

Without insisting that Paul is unique, one may certainly highlight his differences from both Josephus and Philo, for example, in his

20. The wariness I express here is with statements such as, "Paul was a radical Jew" (Boyarin), or that "Paul was the second founder of Christianity" (Wrede). See William Wrede, *Paul* (London: Philip Green, 1907), 179. Wrede's thesis was picked up and developed by Hyam Maccoby, who believed that Paul was a thoroughly Hellenized thinker who blended some Hellenistic elements with the original Jewish teachings of Jesus for the purpose of myth making, and by doing so managed to transform the pure Jewish religion of Jesus into a corrupt and virtually pagan system, which became the origin of subsequent antisemitism. See Hyam Maccoby, *The Mythmaker: Paul and the Invention of Christianity* (San Francisco: Harper and Row, 1986) and *Paul and Hellenism* (London: SCM, 1991). For a thorough engagement and refutation of the arguments advanced by Wrede, Maccoby, and others portraying Paul as the second founder of Christianity, see David Wenham, *Paul: Follower of Jesus or Founder of Christianity?* (Grand Rapids: Eerdmans, 1995). Pamela Eisenbaum notices, rightly, that Paul "is not some sort of 'marginal Jew.'" See her "Jewish Perspectives: A Jewish Apostle to the Gentiles," in *Studying Paul's Letters: Contemporary Perspectives and Methods,*ed. Joseph A. Marchal (Minneapolis: Fortress Press, 2012), 137n6. I am also wary of the sort of identity construction that understands Paul as a Jewish apostle, yet as one who is unlike any others of his ethnic group within the larger cosmopolitan and Hellenized Greco-Roman world where he operates. This seems to be the type of Jewish identity that Jörg Frey proposes. See Jörg Frey, "Paul's Jewish Identity," in *Jewish Identity in the Greco-Roman World = Jüdische Identität in der griechisch-römischen Welt*, ed. Jörg Frey, Daniel R. Schwartz, and Stephanie Gripentrog, Ancient Judaism and Early Christianity, 72 (Leiden: Brill), 285–322. This particular identity of Paul, rightly criticized by Todd Penner and Davina C. Lopez, "is an ethnic foreigner in a dominant colonial society who manages to adapt and to assimilate to that larger culture, unlike the other Jews in his midst, perhaps even some 'Jewish Christians', who refuse to 'get along' and are, at the end of the day, 'stubborn'. Leaving such stubbornness behind, Paul, and the 'Gentile Christians' who are naturally the object of his so-called mission, evolve as a community with seamless ties to their larger milieu. As the 'fittest' in this environment, they ultimately are the ones who survive." See Penner and Lopez, "Homelessness as a Way Home," in *Holy Land as Homeland? Models for Constructing the Historic Landscapes of Jesus*, ed. Keith W. Whitelam, The Social World of Biblical Antiquity, Second Series, 7 (Sheffield: Sheffield Phoenix, 2011), 168.

contributions, and creative (re)interpretations of key tenets of his cultural ancestral values and practices in his diasporic social locations under the umbrella of the Roman Empire. This should not be done in a way that privileges Paul's voice, however important it might be or appear to be. Paul, thus, needs to be placed within the social processes of this very fluid early Jesus movement in conversation with other voices in the movement, with other Diaspora Jews, and other figures in the larger Greco-Roman world. In sum, a description of Paul as a diaspora figure should not be made by leaning in the direction of attributing a certain uniqueness to the apostle to the nations, which is quite unwarranted in any serious comparative analysis.

Philip A. Harland's Appropriated Model

To conceptualize the dynamics of identity with regard to Paul and to develop a model of diaspora applicable to him, one can build carefully on the analytical categories developed by Philip Harland and John M. G. Barclay. I will first show the model articulated and then the results with regard to Paul. In this way, both its values and deficiencies are highlighted.

Method

The first category elaborated by Harland is that of cultural assimilation, or acculturation, which has to do with the cultural interchanges and processes of boundary negotiation. This category lends itself to the sort of hybridization explained in the introduction, but that is addressed more directly in the third category below.[21]

---

21. In Harland's terms: "It is important to emphasize that in my theoretical framework here acculturation can progress significantly without the disintegration of a group's boundaries in relation to a larger cultural entity. . . . Another related concept is 'biculturalism,' which is used by Berry and others to a dynamic process involving the individual's participation in both the minority culture and the majority culture. . . . In the study of modern diasporas (a subfield of migration studies), a similar term is 'hybridity,' which implies the combination of ethnic or

The second category in Harland's set is about structural assimilation, or the degree to which social integration and participation within informal networks are worked out. In this theoretical model, there is a difference between acculturation and structural assimilation, which refers to the degrees to which a diaspora figure has been able to be socially integrated in order to participate within the social structures of the host culture. Such structures may be informal social networks (e.g., neighborhoods, associations) or formal structures (e.g., political, legal, social, or economic institutions).

Many scholars have used theories of acculturation and structural assimilation to understand the degree to which the negotiation and reframing of boundaries between local diaspora communities and the host society at large are undertaken. The Canadian sociologist Raymond Breton, for example, has developed the concept of *institutional completeness* to study the varying degrees different ethnic immigrant groups acquire or maintain in personal relations.[22] Within this analytical framework, it is shown that the immigrants' interpersonal network in their own ethnic community allows them to fulfill their psychological, social, and religious needs. In other words, the social integration and acculturation of immigrants to new social environments becomes easier through organized interpersonal networking within their own ethnic group. For Breton, "the degree of institutional completeness and the magnitude of the ethnic interpersonal network are interdependent phenomena."[23] In this sense, it is easier for a community with a high degree of institutional completeness to attract new immigrants within their particular ethnic category. The social cohesion of a particular ethnic community

other identities in a particular individual or group." Harland, *Dynamics of Identity in the World of the Early Christians*, 102.

22. See, in particular, Raymond Breton, *Ethnic Relations in Canada: Institutional Dynamics*, ed. and intro. Jeffrey G. Reitz (Montreal: McGill-Queen's University Press, 2005).

23. Ibid., 181.

allows it better ability to exert its influence on the interpersonal integration of the immigrant. That does not prevent, however, particular immigrants from choosing to associate more with groups outside their ethnic communities. There is accommodation on the part of diaspora subjects and communities to local cultural practices, but there can also be resistance to particular national ideologies. The degrees to which minority groups are completely assimilated in their host societies remain, interestingly, limited. As Milton Yinger has concluded, "Traces of ethnic variation can persist even after several generations of social and physical mobility."[24]

The third conceptual category one may look at is that of dissimilation (differentiation) or cultural maintenance, as articulated by Harland. This category, which is most clearly associated with the idea of hybridity, refers to the degree to which the native culture is retained. Put differently, hybridity provides a clearer way of understanding the phenomenon addressed by this category. This category is further subdivided: (a) "strong identification with both groups, which entails integration or biculturalism"; (b) "an exclusive identification with the majority culture, which entails assimilation"; (c) "identification with only the minority group, which entails separation"; and (d) "identification with neither group, which entails marginality."

Results

Harland's analytical categories of acculturation, structural assimilation, and cultural maintenance in cultural minorities—drawn mostly from sociological and anthropological studies—are helpful to situate Paul as a cultural minority belonging to different networks in the ancient Mediterranean. Even though some analysts may use

24. Milton Yinger, *Ethnicity: Source of Strength? Source of Conflict?* (Albany: State University of New York Press, 1994), 39.

this method to construe Paul's identities as permanently fixed, in terms of cultural assimilation they are, in fact, not essentialized or pure, and neither are the categories we use to talk about him. They do not stand alone and rigid; they all conflate and collapse in on one another; identity categories are fluid and contested, not fixed and obvious—they merge and blend a lot like our own identities in our own lives. Identity, to quote Jeremy Punt, "is not a predefined essence, a packaged and contained entity with fixed boundaries and definite silhouette."[25] Paul's identities are dynamic and multifaceted.[26]

In terms of structural assimilation, one may consider the degree to which Paul is integrated into Greco-Roman life by how he is able to travel, which implies a certain level of assimilation, and how he is integrated—to a certain extent—into various economic structures by finding work wherever he goes. It would certainly make a difference for this particular analytical category to know whether Paul found work within the Jewish Diaspora or within non-Jewish workshops. For example, in Acts, he works with the Jewish couple Prisca and Aquila (Acts 18:3). There is no indication that he worked among people of his own ethnicity when he mentions his arduous work in 1 Thessalonians (1 Thess. 2:9). Also, the reference to working with his own hands in 1 Cor. 4:12 does not indicate whether he worked within the Jewish Diaspora or within non-Jewish workshops. Paul develops a sense of belonging by associating with those who share his faith in his social locations in the diaspora—non-Judeans and other Diaspora Judeans—and those with whom he shares his hopes are part

---

25. Jeremy Punt, "Identity, Memory, and Scriptural Warrant: Arguing Paul's Case," in *Paul and Scripture: Extending the Conversation*, ed. Christopher D. Stanley (Atlanta: Society of Biblical Literature, 2012), 27.

26. David J. Mattingly uses the term *discrepant identity*, which to him is similar to the term *hybridization* to refer to the discordant and inharmonious identities experienced by different individuals and groups to the Roman Empire. He prefers this term in lieu of the much used *Romanization*. See Mattingly, *Imperialism, Power and Identity* (Princeton, NJ: Princeton University Press, 2011), especially chapter 8.

of his social networks as an artisan worker and itinerant preacher. Paul's mobility in the diaspora, and his ability to adapt to different ethnic groups (1 Cor. 9:19-23) propel him to create ever-expanding alternative cultural and religious associations through transformation and difference around the figure of Jesus.

Where would we place Paul with respect to these options as articulated by Harland in the third conceptual category? Paul's identities are relationally and socially constituted; they are also expressed through his activities. He is a Jew, a circumcised Israelite (Phil. 3:5), whose views (e.g., his modified and enlarged monotheism) and actions are not shared by most Judeans of his time or later; he is the apostle of Christ to the nations, a handworker, letter writer, social entrepreneur, and founder and nurturer of different localized communities of Christ believers. The workshop and the different social networks that he developed with diverse ethnic groups allowed him to be integrated tightly within the mostly non-Jewish communities he worked and preached among. As a diaspora figure, Paul stands somewhat outside the culture of the communities to which he is a missionary, yet he develops close relationships with the non-Jews in his different communities. Paul's social strategy of negotiating spaces and identities enabled him to foster transcultural and transnational fluid communities with ties akin to family bonds. However, one cannot state that there is in Paul "an exclusive identification with the majority culture." His thinking and active acts of theologizing are rooted in the traditions and Scriptures of his ethnic group; his identities are multiple but are essentially framed around Christ, who is the portal by which one enters into a new identity with the God of Israel.

In terms of identification, Paul does not identify with only his Jewish minority group, which entails separation. As we have seen, and I will elaborate upon later in this study, Paul needed to be able to move between different cultural groups and local customs and practices in order to determine which practices were acceptable in light of the broader cultural world (e.g., the issue of food consecrated to local deities). Also, as far as identification was concerned, it was necessary for him to move between different perspectives and attitudes to adopt vis-à-vis the Roman Empire.[27] Paul was a Jew expressing his understanding of Judaism in light of his socioeconomic religious experience,[28] and he struggled to convince other Jews that he was still operating inside of the parameters of a Judaism redefined around Jesus. Paul's vulnerable social position in the diaspora communities, and his too-flexible acceptance of cultural diversity—at least as perceived by many in the Jewish community—to the point of even undermining Jewish fidelity to the law (circumcision and food being of particular concern) makes him, in the eyes of many other Diaspora Judeans, a poor candidate for representing the community "properly" since he was not maintaining the necessary ethnic "differences" from outsiders. This different sense of belonging and being alienated, feeling accepted and yet rejected by most, is an existential condition that seems to shape many of Paul's moves and theology. His home is not from any place on earth—Phil. 3:20; his behaviour is flexible and adaptable to wherever and whatever social and ethnic group he is in contact with—1 Cor. 9:19-23; he is still very much attached to and in pain for his people, though they do not share his socio-theological convictions—Romans 9–11; and his collection project is extremely important to him, allowing him to serve the materially poor in Jerusalem—Gal. 2:10. Paul is

---

27. See chapter 4 of this book.
28. It is very difficult to move away from our modern compartmentalization of life as we try to capture an ancient figure where religious, social, and economic differences did not exist. It is probably better to use *social experimentation* instead of *religious experience*, as suggested by Ron Cameron and Merrill P. Miller. See *Redescribing Christian Origins*, ed. Ron Cameron and Merrill P. Miller, SBLSymS 28 (Atlanta: Society of Biblical Literature, 2004), 503.

in and out (Gal. 4:12); he is an outsider as well as an insider,[29] living like a gentile but thinking like a Jew.[30] He is one who, with others, participates in the shaping of place and space, culture and imagination, memory and identity.[31] He is at home, and a stranger out of place;[32] he finds solidarity among the mostly non-Judean members of his communities, yet he strives, or seems to crave, to find acceptance from his kinsmen. Merrill P. Miller is right: "Paul crossed and erased boundaries continually and then established his own boundaries that he most certainly wanted to defend (consider Galatians), while also insisting that he did not want to invade anyone else's turf (2 Cor 10:12-18)."[33]

Social connections between different networks in the diaspora facilitated the social integration of diasporic subjects within their own communities, and these networks also helped to further the growth of particular associations. Paul had an extensive network—Judean immigrant networks (especially important if we take into account

29. In the context of Paul's hybrid position in Romans 13, John W. Marshall notes, "Paul is both 'in and of' that world, working in relation to its centre from its margins, gathering and deploying its resources in the interest of his own programme, whether that means swimming with or against the current of imperial power in any particular moment. Though ambivalence is often a terror to dogmatics, it is the condition of colonial existence and thus Paul's." See Marshall, "Hybridity and Reading of Romans 13," *JSNT* 31 (2008): 174. William S. Campbell notes, "Sometimes it seemed as if this Diaspora-born Jew understood neither his own people's nor the Gentiles' traditions." See Campbell, *Paul and the Creation of Christian Identity* (New York: T & T Clark, 2006), 55.

30. See Merrill P. Miller, "Re: Paul," in *Introducing Religion: Essays in Honor of Jonathan Z. Smith*, ed. Willi Braun and Russell T. McCutcheon (London: Equinox, 2008). For Miller, "Paul's 'conversion' was an 'inversion': living like a Jew and thinking like a Gentile, he was now 'called' to make known God's sovereign decision to 'call' Gentiles as Gentiles, requiring him to live like a Gentile (Gal 2:14–15; 4:12a)," 350.

31. See Jeremy Punt, "Identity, Memory, and Scriptural Warrant," 25–53. Etienne Trocmé is right when he states, "la foi, les institutions et le culte juifs ne sont pas attaqués de l'extérieur mais critiqué de l'intérieur." See "Le Christianisme primitif, un mythe historique?" *ETR* 49, no. 1 (1974): 17.

32. I am thinking here of Edward W. Said's celebrated memoir *Out of Place* (New York: Vintage Books, 1999), where the author, candidly and openly, shares with his readers how he has always felt himself to be one who was continually "out of place."

33. See Miller, "Antioch, Paul, and Jerusalem: Diaspora Myths of Origins in the Homeland," in Cameron and Miller, *Redescribing Christian Origins*, 226.

the fact that the early Jesus movement had other Jewish adherents in some cities of the Roman Empire), occupational networks,[34] family networks (1 Cor. 7:13-16; 1 Cor. 16:9; Rom. 16:3–5; Philippians 1)—nevertheless, as noted by Miller, "*he was also an outsider everywhere he went*" (emphasis added).[35] The qualifier should be that Paul was still operating within Judaism, although a reimagined and recalibrated one. Paul entertains social relationships as an itinerant diaspora figure with localized communities of Christ believers (and to non–Christ believers as well). He was also a Diaspora Jew in social relationships with other Diaspora Jews (both Christ-believing members and not).

Thus, Paul is an expatriate who lives "outside of Judaism for the sake of gentiles and, in a longer perspective, for the sake of Jews."[36] He wants to show other Judeans in the Diaspora (Christ followers or not) that the nations can offer those away from their ancestral homeland a sense of belonging in the way they can accept one who is different from them (Paul being a prime example because he was, for example, accepted like an angel of God by the Galatians, 4:14), yet these Others can be made to be the same—at least in Paul's mind—in the sense of losing their ethnic essence as they are made, rhetorically and imaginatively, part of a mythic collective identity through Christ (Gal. 3:14). Clearly, the last point under the category of dissimilation (differentiation) or cultural maintenance does not apply to Paul. He

34. See Richard S. Ascough, "The Thessalonian Christian Community as a Professional Voluntary Association," *JBL* 119. 2 (2000): 311–28. He shows, convincingly in my opinion, that Christ's followers in the midst of first-century Thessalonica may well be considered a professional guild of hand workers (cf. 1 Thess. 2:9; 4:9-12) who Paul persuaded to join the Jewish God and his son Jesus as a new divine patron. See also Ronald F. Hock, *The Social Context of Paul's Ministry: Tentmaking and Apostleship* (Philadelphia: Fortress Press, 1980) and his more recent article on when Paul learned his trade and its bearing on his social class, "The Problem of Paul's Social Class: Further Reflections," in *Paul's World*, ed. Stanley E. Porter, Pauline Studies 4 (Leiden: Brill, 2008), 7–18.

35. See Miller, "Antioch, Paul, and Jerusalem," 226.

36. John W. Marshall, *Parables of War: Reading John's Jewish Apocalypse*, ESCJ, Studies in Christianity and Judaism/Études sur le christianisme et le judaïsme (Waterloo, ON: Wilfrid Laurier University Press, 2001), 196.

evidently did not entertain the marginality of some ethnic subjects to isolate themselves from both their communities and that of the place of establishment. He was not a marginal Jew, nor was he an anomalous one with respect to other Diaspora Jews.

John M. G. Barclay's Model

One may also consider how John M. G. Barclay developed a set of categories to understand Paul in comparison to other Diaspora Jews of the Mediterranean world. Barclay insists we must account for three different sociocultural axes: assimilation, acculturation, and accommodation.

Method

Barclay does not refer to cultural assimilation but to assimilation *tout court* in his scale of comparison. If for Harland and others cultural assimilation is equivalent to acculturation, for Barclay one may understand acculturation in a limited sense. By assimilation, Barclay means "the degree to which Jews in the Diaspora were socially aloof from, or socially integrated into, their environment."[37] Thus assimilation needs to be understood, in Barclay's analysis, in terms of social integration, especially with regard to education and aspects of cultural exposure in relation to the Greco-Roman world. Paul is placed high on this specific scale because of his willingness to associate with and to live "like a gentile" in his diasporic social location. Paul, in Barclay's analysis, ranks low on the acculturation scale, "overall perhaps higher than *Joseph and Aseneth* but not as high as *4 Maccabees* and very much lower than Philo."[38]

37. John M. G. Barclay, "Paul among Diaspora Jews," 94.
38. Ibid., 107.

In the context of acculturation—his second conceptual category—Barclay portrays Paul as an "anomalous" Jew at work in the diaspora, whose "position there is distinctly anomalous."[39] *Anomalous* is, admittedly, not synonymous with *unique*, and Barclay may have carefully chosen this term to sidestep some of the issues that Jonathan Z. Smith raises with regard to the positions holding up Christianity as sui generis. But Barclay's position as it relates to Paul in the Diaspora is very close to a position of placing Paul in a unique place.[40] Barclay asserts, accurately, that "Paul never lost his sense of belonging to, and even representing, the Jewish people and it was presumably this sense of loyalty which drew him back again and again to the synagogue."[41] The character of Paul as an "anomalous" Diaspora Jew within this specific set of comparisons, according to Barclay, is apparent in his "comparative lack of openness to Hellenistic culture"[42] and the ways in which he operates using a sort of "negative universalism."[43] He

39. Barclay, *Jews in the Mediterranean Diaspora*, 381.
40. In his review of Barclay's work, Stanley Porter is disappointed with Barclay's characterization of Paul as an anomaly, yet, ironically, falls into the methodological gulf of seeing Paul as being "in many ways a unique figure," *JSNT* 72 (1998): 128. Martha Himmelfarb does mention, with consent, Barclay's presentation of Paul as an anomalous Jew in her review, *Association for Jewish Studies Review* 23, no. 2 (1998): 247–50. In her words, "While Barclay does not say so, the explanation for this unusual configuration of characteristics is surely Paul's intense expectation of the imminent end" (249). There is no mention of Barclay's view of Paul in the reviews of Daniel R. Schwartz, *Classical Philology* 95, no. 3 (2000): 349–57, nor in Gideon Bohak's review in *The Classical Journal* 99, no. 2 (2003/04): 195–202. Carl R. Holladay accepts wholeheartedly Barclay's thesis that Paul "is an "anomalous Diaspora Jew" in some fundamental ways." See his "Paul and His Predecessors in the Diaspora: Some Reflections on Ethnic Identity in the Fragmentary Hellenistic Jewish Authors," in *Early Christianity and Classical Culture: Comparative Studies in Honor of Abraham J. Malherbe*, ed. John T. Fitzgerald et al., SNT (New York: Brill Academic, 2003), 456. Brigitte Kahl also subscribes to Barclay's "anomalous" proposal by describing this "anomaly" "as an uncommon hybridity that refuses, in the name of Israel's exodus-God and Torah, to assimilate Torah and Roman *nomos* or the universal claim of Roman law to hold supreme authority over both Jews and non-Jews alike." See Kahl, *Galatians Re-Imagined: Reading with the Eyes of the Vanquished* (Minneapolis: Fortress Press, 2010), 352n39.
41. Barclay, *Jews in the Mediterranean Diaspora*, 395.
42. Ibid., 391. Barclay conducted his analysis especially with regard to how, in Romans in particular, Paul undermines the cultural and religious claims of both Jews and non-Jews.
43. Ibid., 392.

insists that "in the spectrum of voices we have heard from the Diaspora, it is those we have placed in the category of 'Cultural Antagonism' which most approximate to the character of Paul's theology."[44] Paul, in this way, was willing to go to the other nations, but was not affected by their cultures and was, in fact, antagonistic with regard to their modes of being and behavior. According to this logic Paul, then, remains pure in his interactions with the ethnically other while actively engaging with them and participating in many norm-breaking activities (from the perspective of his cultural tradition), such as sharing a meal with them and eating foods that are taboo.[45] Paul's character and status as a Diaspora Jew should be treated, Barclay advances, as anomalous since,

> in his conceptuality Paul is most at home among the particularistic and least accommodated segments of the Diaspora; yet in his utilization of these concepts, and in his social practice, he shatters the ethnic mould in which that ideology was formed. He shows little inclination to forge any form of synthesis with his cultural environment, yet he employs the language of a culturally antagonistic Judaism to establish a new social entity which transgresses the boundaries of the Diaspora synagogues. By an extraordinary transference of ideology, Paul deracinates the most culturally conservative forms of Judaism in the Diaspora and uses them in the service of his largely Gentile communities.[46]

In other words, according to Barclay, Paul in the diaspora among his largely gentile communities does not make use of the distinctive markers separating a Jew from a non-Jew (presumably circumcision, dietary laws, and the Sabbath). But what does that entail in terms of his relationship with other Jews who also were living in the Diaspora and kept a sense of belonging to both cultures loosely

44. Ibid.
45. Another of Jonathan Z. Smith's critiques in *Drudgery Divine* is the methodological *immunization* of Christianity (and Judaism), i.e., keeping it "pure" from Hellenism. It is different than the claim of Christianity being sui generis, but unacceptable all the same.
46. John M. G. Barclay, *Jews in the Mediterranean Diaspora*, 393.

defined? Barclay seems to still hold on to Paul's "'anomalous" character even in the new essays that are included in his compilation.[47] He admits that one cannot consider any figure as "'typical', although comparisons may draw out distinctive traits,"[48] yet, he still resorts to surrounding Paul with a wall of protection from research tools such as postcolonial analysis deemed "inappropriate to Paul"[49] because, allegedly, "Paul's relation to Rome is subsumed under his relation to what he provocatively calls 'the present evil age' (Gal 1:14), on an apocalyptic stage newly configured by the Christ-event."[50] One may well understand the reluctance to use, unimaginatively and forcefully, modern interpretive tools to approach ancient historical figures such as Paul or Josephus, but it is rather strange that the opportunity to reframe and to reinterpret Josephus's negotiations of the political realities of the Roman power via the tools of postcolonial analysis is readily made use of—and brilliantly—by Barclay, whereas Paul's sociopolitical context and the structures of power in his time are shunned as being unsuitable to analyze using the lenses of postcolonial analysis.[51] The postcolonial theoretical movement—especially the work of the Subaltern Studies Group—was the result of quite specific forms of government and domination in Africa and the Indian subcontinent during the nineteenth and twentieth centuries. I admittedly concur that a too-quick concern with postcolonial issues can lead one to ignore basic historical questions and methods, yielding doubtful results. Postcolonial studies can, however, suggest models, questions, and

47. See Barclay, *Pauline Churches and Diaspora Jews* (Tübingen: Mohr Siebeck, 2011).
48. Ibid., 29.
49. Ibid., 33.
50. Ibid.
51. See his excellent commentary on the *Against Apion* (Brill Josephus Series and online). He also published a number of relevant articles (e.g., "The Empire Writes Back: Josephan Rhetoric in Flavian Rome," in *Flavius Josephus and Flavian Rome*, ed. Jonathan Edmondson, Steve Mason, and James Rives (Oxford: Oxford University Press, 2005).

paradigms to sharpen or refine one's historical analysis. This reticence on the part of Barclay to use postcolonial studies to understand Paul's form of "theopolitics" because it, presumably, occupies a category that "does not conform to our normal understandings of politics,"[52] strikes me as neotheological maneuvers to conserve on a pedestal the figure of one who came to us as the mythic, heroic, and giant "Saint Paul." It also seems to be an unbelievable commitment to protect a figure deemed "anomalous," in spite of the clear statement and admission that no figure is "typical." Thus, there is a necessity not only to challenge Barclay's unfortunate use of the term *anomalous* with regard to Paul, but also to argue for the appropriate use of postcolonial and diaspora tools to study Paul because sheltering him from the tools of postcolonial analysis, as Barclay tries hard to do, may prevent one from seeing some of the intricate social and political strictures and structures at play.

The third and last analytical frame in Barclay's features is that of accommodation.In Barclay's investigation, Paul, compared to other Diaspora Jews, is at the lowest end of the spectrum in terms of accommodation because of his highly antagonistic stance vis-à-vis Hellenistic culture and the gentile way of life in general. Also, for Barclay, "accommodation is to do with how *Jews used the acculturation they had acquired*, to what degree they allowed this to shape their understanding of their Jewish heritage" (emphasis in original).[53] For Barclay, Paul's accommodation to his cultural milieu is more problematic to evaluate since his "perspective on the world still operates in line with the traditional Scriptural excoriation of Gentiles, only sharpened by his apocalyptic dualism. (…) Paul's exposure to Gentile society and the success he enjoys in winning converts there does not cause him to reformulate his conceptual map of the world."[54]

---

52. Barclay, *Pauline Churches*, 33.
53. Barclay, "Paul among Diaspora Jews," 97.

In other words, Paul goes into the world as a herald of Christ, and he experiences a great deal of success among the gentiles as they show openness to receiving his message, but he himself does not change in his perception of them. His values remain unchangeable; his thought "represents not some cultural fusion with Hellenistic values but a wholesale re-evaluation of both Hellenistic and Jewish traditions from a new vantage point, created by his Christology."[55] In terms of his accommodation, then, according to Barclay, "Paul stands near the bottom of our scale."[56] What Barclay finds to be a great anomaly "is the way Paul combines this culturally conservative form of Judaism with a social policy which seemed to his contemporaries dangerously assimilative."[57] Barclay comments that

> Paul's attempt to redefine a "Judaism" without ethnicity and without preserving the national way of life enshrined in the "ancestral customs" was hugely influential for later Christianity, but was clearly, and understandably, judged a contradiction in terms by his Jewish contemporaries. . . . There were limits to the diversity of Judaism and Paul encountered them in the form of the synagogue lash.[58]

For Barclay, "Although he creates and addresses communities across ethnic and cultural boundaries, Paul's theology employs traditional Jewish categories. His heritage shapes his perceptions of the world, *even while its categories are violently redefined by the social effects of his mission*" (emphasis added).[59] Barclay sharpens his proposal with the following comments: "Comparison of Paul with other Diaspora authors only shows how little his theology is influenced by Hellenism."[60] One may ask, then: How can the categories with which

54. Ibid., 107, 108.
55. Ibid., 109.
56. Ibid., 110.
57. Ibid.
58. Ibid., 118, 119.
59. Barclay, *Jews in the Mediterranean Diaspora*, 389.
60. Ibid., 390.

Paul understands his traditional Jewish way of life be *violently redefined by the social effects of his mission* while his theology, in comparison with other Diaspora Jews of his time, shows little influence of the surrounding *social effects* of Hellenism? Perhaps the crux lies in how Barclay separates and distinguishes "categories of traditional Jewish life" and "theology."

Results

Barclay's approach is helpful in the sense that it provides a way to situate Paul as a diaspora figure in comparison to other Jews in the Mediterranean Diaspora. However, his typology-producing approach represents a model of comparison that is reified, which does not take into consideration the flexibility of diasporic identities and diasporic meaning making. Barclay insists that "in the spectrum of voices we have heard from the Diaspora, it is those we have placed in the category of 'Cultural Antagonism' which most approximate to the character of Paul's theology."[61] Paul, in this way, was willing to go to the other nations, but was not affected by their cultures and was, in fact, antagonistic with regard to their modes of being and behaving.

One may agree with Barclay that Paul kept his distinctive "Jewish" identity in the Diaspora, and appreciate how Barclay uses the specificity of different axes of comparison in his typology, but one can also argue against any essentialism that would portray Paul as permanently fixed by or in his ethnic identity.[62] Identities are complex, fluid, and contested, formed and constantly reformed by interactions with other communities, and continually in the process

---

61. Ibid.,392.
62. One quick note: Jewish is put in brackets here to move away from any fixity on identity, especially when "seeing 'Jewish' identity as just one of many dislocated *ethnē* in the Roman Empire." See Arnal, "Bringing Paul and the Corinthians Together?" 98.

of being forged, even when they "might be construed or represented as fixed."[63] In placing Paul within his diasporic spaces, one may observe how the margins in the destabilizing diaspora spaces he occupies are complicated, and how his identities, although at times construed as permanently fixed, are constantly reformed and surreptitiously formed by interactions with other communities as they are set in the Roman imperial order. Paul's language, at least in 1 Cor. 9:19-23, does not seem to sanction an identity posture that is fixed, and unmarked, since he became τοῖς ἀνόμοις ὡς ἄνομος.[64] The problem with Barclay's mostly unchallenged thesis is that it seems to belie the complexities within which Paul and his associations negotiated, managed, or navigated their identities in the variegated social milieu within which they lived. Like everyone's identities, Paul's are complex and plural.

Overall Summary

The categories of acculturation, structural assimilation and cultural maintenance, as articulated by Harland to explore the dynamics of

63. Avtar Brah, "Diaspora, Border and Transnational Identities," in *Feminist Postcolonial Theory: A Reader*, ed. Reina Lewis and Sarah Mills (New York: Routledge, 2003), 195.

64. A quick glance at a short letter such as Philemon, for example, shows how Paul sees his identity—or at least how he characterizes himself—as a prisoner (vv. 1, 9), an old man (v. 9), a father (v. 10), a future visitor (v. 22), and one surrounded by fellow prisoners and fellow workers (v. 23). In addition, he makes use of friendship conventions with the householder Philemon (especially in v. 8), acts as an advocate of the slave Onesimus (vv. 13-19), organizes his thoughts in the rhetorical form of an *ethopoiia* (vv. 8-10a, 10b-15, and 16-22), and lives his life confident of the providence of God, much like a Stoic (vv. 4-5, 22). It is possible to see how his identity changes if one compare this letter with Philippians, for example. Such concrete comparison clearly demonstrates the multiplicity of overlapping identities embodied by Paul in the context of his social worlds. On Philemon again: Why does Paul identify himself as an old man and Onesimus as his son? He draws on conventions, widely attested, of the need for sons (or children) to care for their aged parents. For more on this, see Ronald F. Hock, "A Support for His Old Age: Paul's Plea on Behalf of Onesimus," in *The Social World of the First Christians: Essays in Honor of Wayne A. Meeks*, eds. L. Michael White and O. Larry Yarbrough (Minneapolis: Fortress Press, 1995), 67–81 and "Paul and Greco-Roman Education," in *Paul in the Greco-Roman World: A Handbook*, ed. J. Paul Sampley (Harrisburg, PA: Trinity Press International, 2003), 198–227.

identity of Judean immigrants and ethnic groups, or the three different sociocultural axes (assimilation, acculturation, and accommodation), as deployed by Barclay to measure similarities and differences in situating Paul with regard to other Diaspora Jews, are both important indexes to consider. Overall, in terms of evaluating the two models, the set of indexes proposed by Harland seem to be more refined than that of Barclay's. Harland's model can be applied to diaspora figures and groups since cultural minorities are often—not always—part of a larger diaspora. However, this model does not take diaspora realities explicitly into account. Stating that does not mean that these categories are not useful. They are. There is real value in what Smith, Harland, and Barclay do. Smith and Harland are especially positive methodological partners in this chapter. As we have seen, they give us much-needed precision in ways to view Paul. The point where I depart from Smith, as I mentioned previously, is his taxonomic approach. Where I move further than Harland is that the complexities of diaspora existence are not within the purview of his analysis. Barclay's set of comparisons has a static view with regard to diasporic identity. Since this study explores Paul's social relationships and identities as an itinerant diasporic figure, we need to keep in mind that this specific diasporic identity exists alongside many interconnected identities that would have been part of Paul's life and experience. This is why Paul's diasporic identities cannot be placed neatly under any schemas or axes of comparison, regardless of whether they are the categories developed either by Harland or Barclay. For analytical purposes, we isolate, classify, and study particular aspects of reality, but social experience and relationships and identities interact together and are, as we all know, much more complex and messier than any study can pretend to exhaust. In other words, to use Jonathan Z. Smith's very apt title, *Map Is Not Territory*.[65] Certainly, one cannot simply revert to generalities—or vagueness—to situate Paul's identities. This is why specific issues, such as those considered in this book, and specific concepts—such as the concept of diaspora space applied in chapter 3 to the conflict at Antioch—are important to study in order to provide a more nuanced way of describing the situation of Paul as a diaspora figure and the ways in which he was negotiating spaces in the diaspora.

Negotiating Spaces in the Diaspora

Diaspora studies offer another way of looking at identity that goes beyond any taxonomic and rigid model of diasporic identities. They make room to understand how diasporic subjects negotiate the intricacies of inhabiting the diaspora space. Consequently, it is important to pay attention to the complexities involved in Paul's negotiation of his identities. Diaspora describes nonessentialist and plural identities that are in process, even when these multiple sites of identities might be construed as untouched. The positionality of diasporic subjects and how diasporic figures negotiate spaces are two key insights from diaspora studies, which can build carefully on the analytical categories developed by Philip Harland and John M. G. Barclay. The question of how Diaspora Jews and Jewish communities, and especially literate and more elite Jews, constructed a modus vivendi with Roman society and realities is a vital one. Stating that, I do acknowledge that among Diaspora Jews, those whose writing is preserved in Greek are not a representative set. Only elite Jewish writers surviving from antiquity and preserved mostly by Christians are referred to here. Latin authors, epigraphic materials, and archaeological evidence are also needed to situate Paul in the larger world.[66] With respect to Judaism in the first few centuries,

---

65. See Jonathan Z. Smith, *Map Is Not Territory: Studies in the History of Religion* (Chicago: University of Chicago Press, 1993 [1978]).

we may more simply and directly mean Jews who are living in the broader Roman world and Roman cities, not in Palestine. Josephus, for example, fits this description well, as does Philo. Thus Paul needs to be studied squarely within the Jewish Diaspora of the Mediterranean world in order to determine the degrees of similarity and difference that exist between him and other Diaspora Judeans.

Paul as a diaspora figure living "in-between" social realities and religious ideals may be carried out in comparison with Josephus and Philo, with respect to how they negotiated their identities from their specific diasporic spaces. I use Josephus and Philo as comparators to illustrate the kind of comparative approach articulated by Smith (minus the taxonomic element). That which we have learned from the *Letter of Aristeas* in the previous chapter (that is, the dynamics of the hybrid conditions that may be expressed through calculated negotiations, prudent affiliations, and idealized memory) may help us also in situating Paul as a diaspora figure.[67] Paul, like Josephus, is a diaspora figure within the Roman Empire—Josephus at the heart of the Roman power as a Roman historian, Paul as an itinerant worker and preacher at the periphery of Rome's power gaze—who needs to move prudently "in-between" places, identities, and allegiances in the social and political sites he occupies. He, like Josephus, had to craft his discourse carefully in his rapport with the nations and with Rome. Paul is trapped between, on the one hand, his beliefs

---

66. Since the study of Diaspora Judaism is an interdisciplinary enterprise, and since it requires expertise in different areas, I only indicate areas where my work on Paul as a Diaspora Judean within the matrix of the Mediterranean world can be expanded and strengthened. My training has been mostly textually based, therefore I do not think it wise to venture into areas of knowledge that I do not have the expertise to evaluate in these pages. The works of A. Thomas Kraabel are paths to follow and, with adequate training, his analysis and that of others employing archaeological and inscriptional evidence can be used carefully as a model to continue the study of Paul in the Diaspora. See *Diaspora Jews and Judaism: Essays in Honor of and in Dialogue with, A. Thomas Kraabel,*ed. J. Andrew Overman and Robert S. MacLenan, South Florida Studies in the History of *Judaism*41 (Atlanta: Scholar's Press, 1992).

67. See the next chapter for points of comparison between some of the dynamics highlighted in the *Letter* and Paul in the conflict at Antioch.

and ideals and, on the other hand, the incongruity of the social realities as part of a minority group under the Roman Empire. On the basis of Homi Bhabha's analysis of the hybrid condition and project one can decipher several clues for comparison and interpretation between how both Josephus and Paul lay out adopted strategies for both negotiating with and mimicking the power in place. What emerges is a tension between repudiating and assimilating, resistance and complicity, independence and dependence, admiration and resistance, acceptance and challenge,[68] subverting and reinscribing the imperial system through very gendered Greco-Roman rhetoric.[69]

Josephus lived the first half of his life in Judea; Paul went to Judea as an adult, and later left. In terms of structural assimilation Josephus is well integrated into Greco-Roman life. Josephus, as we have seen in the previous chapter, was a historian associated with the Flavian court, although, as mentioned previously, one can observe his dual identity as a Roman and Jewish historian in his writing of Judean history. Paul was less culturally assimilated than Josephus. Paul, unlike Josephus, does not have political power supporting him. But like Josephus, he does not have the support of most other Diaspora Judeans in how he goes about representing Judaism in the Diaspora (Josephus was viewed by most Judeans as a traitor, the self-appointed representative of their interests, and Paul was deemed by many antagonistic Judeans in various communities as a dangerous apostate who deserved the synagogue's punishment of lashes—2 Cor. 11:24).

One may also compare Paul to Philo since they both operate in the Diaspora and, therefore, invite for fruitful comparison on many fronts. In fact, no other Jewish writer symbolizes the fusion

---

68. See, for example, the different commentaries on the letters of Paul in *A Postcolonial Commentary on the New Testament Writings*, ed. Fernando F. Segovia and Rasiah S. Sugirtharajah (London: T & T Clark, 2007); see also Christopher D. Stanley, ed., *The Colonized Apostle: Paul through Postcolonial Eyes*, (Minneapolis: Fortress Press, 2011).

69. See chapter 4 of this study.

of Hellenism and Judaism more than Philo. Given that most Jews of the time period and in the context of the Diaspora were more or less completely Hellenized, one can understand how Philo might have been so immersed in Hellenized Judaism. These two traditions blended so well in his mind that it is difficult, if not impossible, to play one tradition against the other in his work. Erwin R. Goodenough remarks that Philo "read Plato in terms of Moses, and Moses in terms of Plato, to the point that he was convinced that each said essentially the same things."[70] For Philo, the basis for Jewish particularism is that God blessed this group of people with a superior formulation of Greek metaphysics, and it seems that the degree of the superiority of Judaism lay more in the possession of Torah, and that Torah itself became simply a way of expressing Greek thought.[71] Philo never ceased to be a dedicated Jew (and one could say the same for Paul); his Jewish piety, as in Paul's case, influenced what he would take from the Hellenistic culture. There are, effectively, basic similarities between Philo and Paul since they both shared the same scriptural texts,[72] and lived during the same period of time in the Diaspora,

70. Erwin R. Goodenough, *An Introduction to Philo Judaeus*, 2nd ed. (New York: Oxford University Press, 1962), 10.
71. See Ellen Birnbaum, *The Place of Judaism in Philo's Thought: Israel, Jews, and Proselytes*, Brown Judaic Series 290, Studia Philonica Monographs 2 (Atlanta: Scholars, 1996); Andrea Lieber, "Between Motherland and Fatherland: Diaspora, Pilgrimage and the Spiritualization of Sacrifice in Philo of Alexandria," in *Heavenly Tablets: Interpretation, Identity and Tradition in Ancient Judaism*, ed. Lynn LiDonnici and Andrea Lieber (Leiden: Brill, 2007), 193–210.
72. See Barclay's treatment of what comparing Paul and another Diaspora Jew (Philo) entails in *Divine and Human Agency in Paul and His Cultural Environment*, ed. John M. G. Barclay and Simon J. Gathercole (London: T & T Clark, 2006), 140: "The Jewish philosopher Philo and the Jewish apostle Paul were contemporaries whose paths never crossed and whose minds moved within startlingly different frameworks. Both, however, were profoundly engaged in the interpretation of the Jewish Scriptures [and a] comparison which gives attention to the differences as well as the similarities between these two figures seems well justified." See also, in this line, the recent published PhD dissertation of one of Barclay's students, Jonathan D. Worthington, *Creation in Paul and Philo: The Beginning and Before*, WUNT II 317 (Tübingen: Mohr Siebeck, 2011). For more on Paul and Philo, see Halvor Moxnes, *Theology in Conflict: Studies in Paul's Understanding of God in Romans*, NovTSup (Leiden: E. J. Brill, 1980); Bruce W. Winter, *Philo and Paul Among the Sophists*, SNTSMS 96 (Cambridge: Cambridge University Press, 1997); John M. G. Barclay, "Paul and Philo on Circumcision: Romans 2.25–9 in Social

although in different social, economic, political, and geographical spaces. Philo lived a life of privilege—serving as an official ambassador of his people when needed—in Alexandria Egypt. Only once did he visit Judea, whereas Paul continually moved in different Roman provinces throughout the Mediterranean world as an itinerant artisan and preacher.

The diasporic existence was experienced, signified, and negotiated differently by Paul and Philo. Power, privilege, and being mandated to stand among the leaders of the people in the Diaspora (Philo), or to be convinced by a revelation to bring the obedience of the Jewish faith to the nations (Paul, Rom. 1:5); these are the different postures the two men adopted to negotiate the issue of representation in the Diaspora. Both Paul and Philo are part of the same larger culture, but differ on fundamental issues because of their different basic presuppositions, social locations, and premises. It is in his soteriology, especially as related to time, history, and theological understandings that Paul's distinctiveness—distinctive in his own ways, as all humans are—is attested and, in this sense, he is very

---

and Cultural Context," *NTS* 44 (1998): 536–56; Peder Borgen, "Observations on the Theme 'Paul and Philo': Paul's Preaching of Circumcision in Galatia (Gal 5:11) and Debates on Circumcision in Philo," in *Die Paulinische Literatur und Theologie*, ed. Sigfred Pedersen (Arhus: Forlaget Aros, 1980), 85–102; Borgen, *Philo, John and Paul: New Perspectives on Judaism and Early Christianity*, Brown Judaic Studies (Atlanta: Scholar's, 1987); Borgen, "Some Hebrew and Pagan Features in Philo's and Paul's Interpretation of Hagar and Ishmael," in *The New Testament and Hellenistic Judaism*, ed. Peder Borgen and Sören Giversen (Aarhus: Aarhus University Press, 1995), 151–64; Klaus Haacker, "Die Geschichtstheologie von Röm 9–11 im Lichte philonischer Schriftauslegung," *NTS* 43 (1997): 209–22; Karl-Gustav Sandelin, "Philo and Paul on Alien Religion: A Comparison," in *Lux Humana, Lux Aeterna: Essays on Biblical and Related Themes in Honour of Lars Aejmelaeus*, ed. Antti Mustakallio, Publications of the Finnish Exegetical Society 89 (Helsinki: Finnish Exegetical Society, Helsinki/Vandenhoeck & Ruprecht, Göttingen, 2005), 213–46; Folker Siegert, "Philo and the New Testament," in *The Cambridge Companion to Philo*, ed. Adam Kamesar (Cambridge: Cambridge University Press, 2009), 175–209; Calvin J. Roetzel, "Paul and Nomos in the Messianic Age," in *Reading Paul in Context: Explorations in Identity Formation; Essays in Honour of William S. Campbell*, ed. Kathy Ehrensperger and J. Brian Tucker (London: T & T Clark, 2010), 120–27; Stefan Nordgaard, "Paul's Appropriation of Philo's Theory of 'Two Men' in 1 Corinthians 15.45–49," *NTS* (2011): 348–65.

different from Philo. Nevertheless, Paul was similar to Philo as he turns "a culturally closed concept such as the covenant, based on ancestral land and ethnic homogeneity, into a subaltern identity based on promise, not genealogy or land."[73] Philo considers himself to be a Κοσμοπολίτης among the wise and virtuous philosophers (e.g., *Mos.* 1.157; *Spec.* 2.45; *Agr.* 65), whereas Paul's πολίτευμα is nowhere to be found on this earth but ἐν οὐρανοῖς ὑπάρχει (Phil. 3:20). Thus, in both thinkers, there is no fixity, fixture on, or attachment to the land.

In his article, "Paulus und Philo als Mystiker? Himmelsreisen im Vergleich (2 Kor 12, 2-4; SpecLeg III 1–6)," Bernhard Heininger makes a very close comparison between Paul and Philo on the basis of the language these authors use to signify their ascent to a plane of existence that is other and higher than the earthly one.[74] Heininger highlights the similarity in terms of linguistic pattern (*Kommunikationsmuster*) in Paul and Philo's description of their amazing mystical experience, as well as the difference—as lived and as interpreted by them—present in such visionary journeys. For him,

> Entscheidend ist vielmehr der Umstand, dass Paulus und Philo offenbar vergleichbare außerordentliche Erfahrungen (weil beide die Himmelsreise als visionäres kommunikationsmuster wählen!) doch sehr unterschiedlich versprachlichen. An dieser sprachlichen Grenze findet auch der Exeget seine Grenze. Oder um mit Philo zu sprechen: Wir wissen zwar um das *Dass* (die Existenz) seiner religiösen Erfahrung, das *Wie* (die Essenz) bleibt uns aufgrund der traditionellen Sprache weitgehend verborgen. Nichts anderes gilt für Paulus.[75]

---

73. Sze-kar Wan, "Does Diaspora Identity Imply Some Sort of Universality? An Asian-American Reading of Galatians," in *Interpreting Beyond Borders*, ed. Fernando F. Segovia (Sheffield: Sheffield Academic, 2000), 123.

74. See Bernhard Heininger, "Paulus und Philo als Mystiker?" in *Philo und das Neue Testament*, ed. Roland Deines and Karl-Wilhelm Niebuhr, WUNT 172 (Tübingen: Mohr Siebeck, 2004), 203–4.

75. Ibid.

Christian Noack, for his part, looks at how the fluid *sozialenSysteme* of Hellenistic Judaism plays a role in the antithetical characterization of foolishness and wisdom in Philo and Paul.[76] Here, the focus is on the *specificity* of the diasporic social milieu as having a certain bearing on the creative innovation of Philo and Paul in their interpretation of folly and wisdom:

> Philo und Paulus haben sich als zwei Zeugen für die beeindruckende Kreativität des hellenistischen Judentums erwiesen. Die antithetische Beschreibung von Torheit und Weisheit liegt bei Philo (im Allegorischen Kommentar) in einer innovation, auf das Erkennen selbst zugespitzen „psychologischen" Weise, bei Paulus in einer besonders auf das kommunikative Zusammenleben ausgerichteten „soziologischen" Weise vor.[77]

Indeed, Paul was different than Josephus and Philo on different scales with respect to how they negotiated their diasporic spaces—certainly occupying a distinct social position—but that is the very nature of comparative work; namely, that one does find differences, similarities, points of puzzlement, and even surprises that are carefully marked by the interested scholar as data in need of classification, categorization, and explanation. Again, to go back to the theoretical discussion articulated in the first half of this chapter, a description of Paul as a diasporic figure should not be made in leaning in the direction of attributing a certain uniqueness to the apostle to the nations, which is quite unwarranted in any serious comparative analysis. One uses comparison to look for similarities and differences among other figures and social practices in antiquity, and they are all important data for the interested scholar. One may certainly see complexities, differences, and novel ways in Paul's socio-rhetorics, as he was busy

---

76. See Christian Noack, "Haben oder Empfangen: Antithetische Charakterisierungen von Torheit und Weisheit bei Philo und bei Paulus," in Deines and Niebuhr, *Philo und das Nue Testament,* 283–307.

77. Ibid., 304.

engaging in social experiments in his diasporic socio-locations, but one may not for these reasons put him in any special category with regard to other Diaspora Jews. It is possible for one to find as many differences and similarities when comparing Paul with other Diaspora Jews or when comparing Pauline groups with Diaspora Jews with respect to how they deployed and negotiated their diasporic identities.

A comparison of Pauline groups and Diaspora Jews shows clearly both similarities and differences, as many similarities as differences, and there are no unproblematized, perfect fit correspondences between, say, the different *ekklēsiai* associated with Paul and the other social groupings such as the Diaspora synagogues, different associations, *thiasoi*, and *collegia* of the first-century Greco-Roman world, along with the mysteries, households, and the philosophical schools.[78] The point, as made very clear by John S. Kloppenborg, is that one needs to work on the specificity of the differences without holding on to one category or one specific figure as being *sui generis*. Kloppenborg, for example, shows how a close comparison can be made by using one clear phenomenon at work—conflict—in both

---

78. See John S. Kloppenborg, "Greco-Roman *Thiasoi, the Ekklēsia* at Corinth, and conflict management" in Cameron and Miller, *Redescribing Paul and the Corinthians,* 187–218; see also, in the same volume, Stanley K. Stowers, "Does Pauline Christianity Resemble a Hellenistic Philosophy?" In this article, Stowers analyses seven precise points where he argues one may find similar features between Pauline Christianity and Hellenistic philosophies. The points of similarities between Hellenistic schools and Pauline Christianity, according to Stowers, are that both groups "conceived of themselves as distinct and mutually exclusive *haireseis*, choices, or sects" (229); "contrary to conventional thinking" (230) with "dramatic reorientation of the self" (231), which results in "a new technology of the self" (232). Also, Stowers points to "the development of the notion of the wise man" (233) in both the Hellenistic philosophical schools and Pauline Christianity as well as intellectual practices that made reference to self-giving, in this venue, "rise to nontraditional and radical social formations" (235). One may not be convinced by all of Stowers's conclusions, but the case for similarities between Pauline groups and philosophical schools with regards to particular aspects, practices, and ways of self-understanding is made in a very helpful manner. The argument here is not that Pauline groups *were* philosophies, but rather that there are similarities between Pauline Christianity at Corinth and philosophies.

the Corinthian ἐκκλησία and ancient associations. What appears in that type of controlled comparison is the degree of similarities and differences in which the phenomenon of conflict is managed in these different social groups. For Kloppenborg,

> The phenomenon of conflict within the Christian group and Paul's strategies for conflict management fall within the spectrum of conflict management seen in other *collegia*. There are, of course, noteworthy features of the Corinthian *ekklēsia* too. A significant Judean component seems to be indicated by the choice of meeting time, and the use of the Tanak within the association; yet its conduct and geographical orientation do not appear typical of Diaspora synagogues. There are some similarities with domestic *collegia*, though the *ekklēsia* seems to have experimented with transfamilial assemblies too, a practice that offered the occasion for serious conflict. And though the group displayed some similarities with cultic *collegia* and may even have adopted some form of recognition of benefactors, Paul's efforts were directed to a certain levelling of status differences and concerted effort at the maintenance of *homonoia*.[79]

The point, thus, is to better understand the nature of conflict by positing the social dynamics of Pauline groups as being similar to other small groups in the ways in which they organized themselves and resolved their differences and divergences.[80] In this approach, one

79. Kloppenborg, "Greco-Roman *Thiasoi*,"216.
80. In his compiled essays on Pauline churches and Diaspora Jews (*Pauline Churches and Diaspora Jews*, 2011), Barclay makes a very comprehensive comparison between Paul's ἐκκλησίαι and the synagogues of Diaspora Jews in the Mediterranean basin. In this work, the focus is not on Paul per se but on social formations, social expression of identities, social practices, social strategies and negotiations between Diaspora Jews, early Christ followers, the Roman power and Roman religion. The questions Barclay poses and strives to answer in this latest work are the following: (1) How do the assemblies within the Pauline tradition compare as social groupings with the communities and Diaspora Judeans in the Mediterranean basin? How, across this comparison, was social identity created by significant practices in the respective communities and how were frontiers with "outsiders" defined and negotiated? (2) To what degree was the social identity formed and practiced in Pauline assemblies compatible with the social expression of Jewish identity in Diaspora communities? What structural components of social identification were shared between these sometimes overlapping groups, and where did points of tension arise? (3) How did Pauline churches invent and maintain a durable identity, despite deploying a smaller repertoire of differentiating practices compared to Diaspora Jews? What distinct "Christian"

moves away from any de novo phenomenon without making Paul's contributions banal and thus irrelevant; the differences between Pauline ἐκκλησίαι exist and are accounted for; the management of conflict from Paul is one of the shared strategies attested to in other similar ancient social groupings, yet the tweaking and efforts of Paul in his specific socioreligious context is different. In other words, one may consider Pauline groups and other social groupings, such as the diaspora synagogues and the different associations and philosophical schools of the first-century Greco-Roman world, in order to see the strategies utilized by these different social groups in conflict management. There are no simple correspondences or perfect fits. The researcher may be puzzled, intrigued, and surprised in his or her comparative analysis, but he or she should not see in Paul one who "speaks only in idiolect."[81]

Summary and Conclusion

Jonathan Z. Smith's comparative approach—without its taxonomic component—has helped us to situate Paul squarely as a Diaspora Jew within the matrix and complexities of first-century diaspora Judaism. One makes comparisons to look for similarities and differences, and they are all important data for the interested scholar. One may certainly see complexities, differences, and novel ways in Paul's socio-rhetorics as he was busy elaborating social experiments in his diasporic socio-locations, but one may not for these reasons put him in any special category with regard to other Diaspora Jews.

practices emerged, or how were practices apparently identical to those of nonbelievers invested with distinctly Christian meanings? (4) How did Diaspora Jews and early Christian assemblies negotiate their potentially awkward relationships with Roman power and Roman Religion? In particular, what stances and strategies can we discern in two contemporary but contrasting figures, Josephus and Paul?

81. William E. Arnal, "Bringing Paul and the Corinthians Together?", 81.

As we have seen in this chapter, Paul is not transcendent and incomparable to other Diaspora Jews; Paul, Josephus, and Philo are comparable, and they detach their identities from specific geographical locations. Paul is different from Josephus with respect to how he negotiates his diasporic spaces and because of how he is positioned in different social, economic, political and geographical spaces. Paul is similar to Philo, as both men never ceased to be dedicated Jews; they shared the same scriptural texts; they lived during the same period of time in the Diaspora, and were immersed in the same wider Hellenistic culture. The point is, without insisting that Paul be unique, marginal, or anomalous, one may highlight his distinctiveness, his differences from other Diaspora Jews, his contributions, and his creative (re)interpretations of key tenets of his cultural ancestral values and practices in his diasporic social locations. One can also underline the specificities of his social groupings without assuming that he and his groups were totally unprecedented phenomena.

The second important point was to provide a good description of the analytical models developed by Harland (in dialogue with Barclay) for discussing different degrees of acculturation, structural assimilation, and cultural maintenance in cultural minorities. Paul's social integration and participation within different networks (such as Judean, occupational networks, and family networks) allowed him to develop a sense of belonging in his diasporic social locations; his ability to adapt to different ethnic groups, his social strategy of negotiating spaces and identities with various groups composed of both dispersed and non Diaspora peoples made it possible for him to create ever-expanding alternative cultural and religious associations through transformation and difference around the figure of Jesus.

The third part of this chapter draws from insights of diaspora studies in studying Paul as a Diaspora Jew. The insights from diaspora studies that build on the categories adopted by Harland and the indexes of Barclay are that of the positionality of diasporic subjects and how diasporic figures negotiate spaces and identities. Paul's diasporic identities are a confluence of conflicting and contradictory identity factors from the diverse and different groups with which he is in contact, which makes it very difficult, if not all together impossible, to provide any simple and definitive answer to the vexing question of his diasporic identity and positionality. In Paul's different crossings, although there are clearly certain points where he is sternly fixed (e.g., sexual immorality and participation in what he deems to be idolatry), he had to be flexible enough to accommodate and modify his teachings according to the various social and theological contexts of his transcultural communities; he had to move "in between" diaspora and relational spaces in order to reimagine other spaces; he had to negotiate stability and change, identities in construction, and allegiances in the sociopolitical and religious relationships he had with the nations as an itinerant worker and preacher; he had to accept cultural diversity (1 Cor. 7:19; cf. 12:13) as a matter of fact in the fluid conditions he and his converts found themselves in. In other words, as he travels with a specific message, he adapts, shapes, redefines or, better, redraws the "insider" and "outsider" spaces and, in the process, he himself is shaped, albeit only in certain measures.

This chapter concludes the theoretical part of this project. The next section (chapters 3–5) will flesh out Paul's diasporic condition by analyzing three specific contexts of his life and work that were crucially formed by this diasporic identity, namely (1) Paul's interactions with other Diaspora Jews, especially in the Galatians 2 incident; (2) Paul's relationship with the nations, specifically his dealings with the Galatians; and (3) Paul's collection project, through an analysis of the concepts of *home*, *homeland*, and *space*.

3

Paul and Others in the Diaspora Space

My central argument is that diaspora space as a conceptual category is "inhabited" not only by those who have migrated and their descendants but equally by those who are constructed and represented as indigenous.

Diasporas are also potentially the sites of hope and new beginnings. They are contested cultural and political terrains where individual and collective memories collide, reassemble and reconfigure.
—Avtar Brah[1]

The issue at stake in this chapter is the Antioch conflict reported by Paul in Gal. 2:11-14. What becomes clearer under the generative insight from diaspora studies is that the incident in the very messy, multilayered, and contested diaspora space of Antioch was not simply about gentiles, but more about the mundane matter of two Judean social groups claiming the identity of being Jewish and struggling to control, and having authority over, the contested spheres of home and diaspora, center and periphery, alongside divergent sociopolitical

---

1. Avtar Brah, *Cartographies of Diaspora: Contesting Identities* (New York: Routledge, 1996), 181, 193.

and theological agendas and interpretations. I argue that, far from being at the periphery, the phenomenon of diaspora and of diaspora space, with all its entanglements, is at the heart of the conflict at Antioch.

The outcome of the Antioch incident was a defeat for Paul, given that Peter, Barnabas, and the other Judeans did not side with him, yet when he recounts the event in Galatians, he portrays himself as a man of courage who would not hesitate under any circumstance to defend the great principles of the truth of *the* gospel (or at least his understanding of it; 2:14). We have only Paul's version of the incident, and we are not informed of his actual reactions when he realised that he had not been able to keep Antioch of Syria, his cherished territory, under his own control. In other words, Paul attempts to configure himself in the conflict in Antioch in a manner that was directed toward specific ends, and one should not assume that Paul's description of the events at Antioch were without bias or self-interest. Did he feel trapped between his religious beliefs and ideals, and the social reality of being someone who needs to assert his authority before these "stupid" Galatians (3:1), who did not have full understanding of the situation anyway?

In a flash of brilliant insight, Larry W. Hurtado considers the following:

> Those Jewish Christians who insisted that Gentile converts had to undergo full proselyte conversion (including circumcision of males) may well have feared that to treat Torah–observance as anything less than mandatory for all could be seen as supporting the view that Torah-observance was not necessary for anyone. That is, Diaspora Jews (including Jewish Christians) who were concerned to maintain solidarity in Torah-observance over against other tendencies in Diaspora Jewish communities may have seen the Pauline position on the admission of Gentiles into Christian circles as implicitly supporting the sort of allegorizing Torah-observance that Philo criticised. In other words, Paul's Gentile converts may be thought of as having walked into

a family quarrel within Diaspora Jewish communities, unintentionally exacerbating it. If this line of inference is correct, what was at stake in the controversies over the admission of Gentiles to full Christian fellowship was not simply the terms of Gentile conversion, but was also the question of how far Diaspora Jews could allow themselves to go in negotiating their lives in non-Jewish environments.[2]

Hurtado sees that negotiation is integral to diasporic existence, and rightly gives voice to the possibility that diversity in Judaism partially prefigured a set of conflicts we see in the development of devotion to Jesus. Apart from the fact that the use of *Christians* in this quote is unfortunate, because it prevents one from understanding that this is an intra-Jewish dispute, several issues call for attention here: gentiles entering, or better, participating in, a diaspora space that is fraught with tensions of identity; identity formation; power contests between different Diaspora groups; and different manifestations of the dynamics of power; issues of representation; family quarrels within Diaspora communities; and the admission of gentiles being more about diaspora Judeans negotiating their lives in diasporic social locations than about gentile conversions per se. Let us pursue these questions separately in the following order: (1) issues of representation in the diaspora; (2) the diaspora as a space fraught with tensions; (3) the diaspora space as a place of solidarity and negotiations.

Issues of Representation in the Diaspora

In diaspora, issues of representation loom large: who can speak, who is mandated to speak, who does not speak, who represents (or who can embody) properly the people in their multiple attachments or

---

2. Larry W. Hurtado, "Does Philo Help Explain Early Christianity?," in *Philo und das Neue Testament: Wechselseitige Wahrnehmungen*, Internationales Symposium zum Corpus Judaeo-Hellenisticum, 1.–4. Mai 2003, Eisenach/Jena, ed. R. Deines, K.-W. Niebuhr, WUNT 172 (Tübingen: Mohr Siebeck, 2004), 85–86.

connections.[3] The diasporic situation is one where the discourse among the different diasporas can be concocted and appropriated with the view to serve certain social and ideological identities. I wish to note that the issue here is not about being flexible in diaspora, but about how far one can go without jeopardizing what constitutes, in the understandings of many coethnic friends and foes, the essence of one's culture, consciousness, and distinctiveness, and how one can claim being the legitimate representative of one's culture in such space. Paul occupies a fluid and complex social space in the diaspora that is replete with indigenous peoples, with many who were scattered away from families and homelands. He is in search of a "home" with other diaspora Judeans, many of whom are also his coworkers; he is busy trying to generate new social and dynamic networks among different ethnic and dispersed groups, using localized communities of believers within the Roman Empire. But in his efforts to develop social strategies that adapt to the culture at large, while maintaining a sense of belonging to his community and representing that community, the fine balance of interacting with the transcultural communities in their various social and variegated contexts is very difficult for him to maintain, or at least to convince others that he was maintaining. In the highly fluid conditions within which he works as a Diaspora Jew, Paul's conflict at Antioch reveals a layer that may be open to fresh analysis.

Paul is in the peculiar position of trying to represent his people in the Diaspora and wanting to have the blessings of the larger community. He struggles to convince the leaders of his socioreligious community in the Diaspora to legitimate him, although he claims he does not look for human approval (Gal. 1:10). Thus, on the one hand,

---

3. Rima Berns-McGown defines diaspora as a space of connections in two dimensions: a connection to an elsewhere (a "mythic" homeland) and a connection to here (the space one occupies). See "Redefining "Diaspora": The Challenge of Connection and inclusion," *International Journal* 63 (Winter 2007–08): 7–8.

he is convinced that he has a special mandate to go to the nations as a representative of Israel in order to share with them the blessings of Abraham. On the other hand, he wants to maintain solidarity with other Diaspora Judeans who, for the most part, treat him with great suspicion, particularly because of his too-flexible acceptance of cultural diversity (circumcision being of particular concern) and his very strange message of a modified and enlarged monotheism.[4] In this sense, Paul's vulnerable social position in the Diaspora communities makes him, in the eyes of many other Diaspora Judeans, a poor candidate for representing the community "properly" since he was not maintaining the necessary ethnic "differences" from outsiders. The configurations of power differentiate Paul's diasporic posture from other Jewish leaders of the Jesus movement in the Diaspora and from the Judeans coming from the circumcision party, as well as situating him in relation to other Judeans in the Diaspora who were not a part of this movement.

The Diaspora Space as a Space Fraught with Tensions

Diaspora space is defined by Avtar Brah as "the intersectionality of diaspora, border, and dis/location as a point of confluence of economic, political, cultural and psychic processes. It addresses the global condition of culture, economics and politics as a site of 'migrancy' and 'travel' which seriously problematizes the subject position of the 'native.'"[5] Diaspora space is thus a place that is

4. Admittedly, there was a plurality of views with regard to circumcision in antiquity, and various understandings regarding the degree to which gentiles should adopt Jewish customs and identity. For an examination of the interconnection between circumcision and genealogy in the Hebrew Bible, Second Temple Judaism, and the New Testament, see Matthew Thiessen, *Contesting Conversion: Genealogy, Circumcision, and Identity in Ancient Judaism and Christianity* (Oxford: Oxford University Press, 2011). Thiessen rightly remarks, "Paul's opposition to Gentile Christians' adopting Jewish customs and identity may be better understood as a variation on the genealogical exclusivism of contemporaneous forms of Judaism." Ibid, 147. See also Terence L. Donaldson, *Judaism and the Gentiles: Jewish Patterns of Universalism (to 135 ce)*. (Waco, TX: Baylor University Press, 2007).

129

perpetually in flux, constituted of multiple, fragmented identities, and articulating variegated roots,[6] routes, and rhizomes through every possible form of attachment.[7] Again, Brah: "Diasporas are also potentially the sites of hope and new beginnings. They are contested cultural and political terrains where individual and collective memories collide, reassemble and reconfigure."[8] In this venue, the important points to highlight are the different multilayered sociopolitical realities of those inhabiting the variegated geographical and cultural space. The concept of diaspora space, as proposed by Brah, defines communities that are met in the messiness of space—problematized by issues of gender, sexuality, race, economic status, education, religion—conceived as dynamic, contested, appropriated and (re)defined by those who have moved in, and also by those who have never been anywhere else besides this place. Thus, "diaspora space" is a flexible space "of/for theoretical crossovers that foreground process of power";[9] it is a place where multiple aspects related to diasporic realities are taken into consideration, and where the different interrelationalities and identities are not kept untouched, unmarked, but are shaped, differentiated, and interrelated by the different crossings.

The ways in which the diaspora space is shared, negotiated, and utilized by Paul to establish his authority and particular spatial, temporal, social, and theological understandings is illustrative of the

5. See *Cartographies of Diaspora*, 181.

6. In referring to roots here, I concur with Lisa Malkki that one should question "the romantic vision of the rooting of peoples," because the flip side of this is to consider some groups of people to be "rootless/restless," even pathological, for the alleged reason that their own soil does not nurture them. See "National Geographic: The Rooting of Peoples and the Territorialization of National Identity among Scholars and Refugees," *Cultural Anthropology* 7, no. 1 (1992): 30.

7. I use *rhizome* here in the sense of connection between multiple identities that are transformed through different and multiple social interactions. The sequence "roots, routes, and rhizomes" is used by Melanie Wright as the title for her article in *The Religious Roots of Contemporary European Identity*, ed. Lucia Faltin and Melanie J. Wright (London: Continuum, 2007), 29–39.

8. *Cartographies of Diaspora*, 193.

9. Brah, "Diaspora, Border and Transnational Identities," in *Cartographies of Diaspora*, 210.

complexity of inhabiting such a place. Paul, because of his understanding that time is short, does not see any problem in reappropriating and reimagining a Judaism that is very loose in terms of some major boundary markers (circumcision, Sabbath, and dietary laws). He goes to the nations, and in his diasporic social locations enters into collusion with other Diaspora Judeans who do not have his particular understanding of time. To be clear, especially if one wants to keep Paul's interaction with other Diaspora Judeans and other interpretations *within* ancient Judaism, other Diaspora Judean groups would agree with Paul's contention that non-Jews who affiliate with Jews and God must live according to the standards that apply to the Jews—non-Jews are not under Torah technically, but they may keep Torah righteousness as appropriate—except, for these other Diaspora groups, the end of ages has not arrived yet. Conversely, other Judeans who believed in the resurrection of Jesus and were moving around the empire did not share Paul's view on several fundamental issues. Some disagreed with Paul on how far one should go in opening the new understanding of Judaism in light of the Christ event. Consequently, if we consider the contestability of the diaspora space with the multidirectionality of understandings between Paul and other Diaspora Judeans (Christ believers and not), the intricacies of the diaspora space become clearer.

In the articulation of contested meanings and understandings one observes how negotiating one's multiple identities, consciousness, and attachments in a diaspora space that is perpetually in flux is fraught with tension and serious difficulties. Paul's identity is simultaneously an "other" from the Roman perspective, and a part of the "center" from the Jewish perspective, because he enjoys, with other Diaspora Judeans, the privileged heritage of Abraham's family, the gift of Torah, and the presence of the deity in Jerusalem.[10] Another identity may be deduced from the notion of Christ as new emperor and of Paul as becoming the imperial ambassador of a new empire and a privileged member—although not economically privileged—of a new theological center with nonbelievers now on the periphery, which would presumably include nonbelieving ethnic Judeans and Romans.[11] Thus Paul, as an imperial ambassador with a discourse that is framed, in large measure, with the rhetorical strategies of the Roman imperial machinery,[12] occupies the diaspora space with different ethnic groups (Judeans and non-Judeans who are dispersed and nondiaspora peoples) with the view to map new territories for his redefined Judaism.

The messiness of diaspora life often creates conflict over issues concerning authority to engage in (self-) definition. In the case of Paul, this manifests with respect to the apostle's permissive approach to Torah obedience among gentile converts, and through his authority and identity among Christ-following Judeans and non-Judeans in the diaspora space. I hope no impression is given here that I am making an assumption with regard to cultural identity that is maintained as a matter of *degree*, and that this was the concern

10. For variegated views on Paul's identities in various social, religious, and political contexts, see Kathy Ehrensperger and J. Brian Tucker, eds., *Reading Paul in Context: Explorations in Identity Formation; Essays in Honour of William S. Campbell* (New York: T & T Clark, 2010). See also Sze-kar Wan, "Asian American Perspectives: Ambivalence of the Model Minority and Perpetual Foreigner," in *Studying Paul's Letters: Contemporary Perspectives and Methods* (Minneapolis: Fortress Press, 2012), 175–90. Wan identifies Paul as a model minority and a perpetual foreigner, first in his diasporic socio-locations in the Roman Empire then as a member of the Jesus movement. For Wan, Paul's ambivalence vis-à-vis the empire is also manifest in his ambivalence toward the Jerusalem leaders who replicate the imperial structures, especially in the ways they treat Paul within the movement, namely as a perpetual foreigner. Although I admire Wan's fascinating reading of the Antioch incident from his own Asian American perspective, I find that his analysis could be nuanced a bit more. Paul, I argue here, also mimics the rhetoric of the empire against his opponents with the view to asserting his own authority and to controling the diaspora space of Antioch, which he takes to be under his jurisdiction.

11. Elisabeth Schussler-Fiorenza argues that conceptualizing Paul as a promulgator of a counterempire simply reinscribes the discourse of empire without undoing it: centers and peripheries may shift, and the main players' roles may be modified, but the discourse of center and periphery is untouched. See *The Power of the Word: Scripture and the Rhetoric of Empire* (Minneapolis: Fortress Press, 2007), 82–109.

12. See the following chapter on Paul among the nations.

among Paul's opponents in Antioch. One needs to be careful in not assuming that a clear and normative version of Judaism did exist for this period or that most Judeans in the homeland (say, farmers in Galilee or soldiers in Agrippa I's army) would have cared one way or the other about many of the issues that evidently troubled those from James and—to a certain extent—Peter as well. That is to say, the normative vision for Judaism that the cohort from Jerusalem seems to advocate was presumably not some platonic ideal of Judaism itself, but deviated from it to some extent. Such identity negotiations on the part of a variety of Judeans in the Diaspora clearly do occur within the homeland as well (one thinks, for example, of Judeans' adoption of various conquerors' cultures, ranging from Persian conceptions of the afterlife to the use of Charon's obol in the Roman era). Thus the question of which foreign practices are adopted and which traditional ones are dropped or reinterpreted is a matter of how they are prioritized in respective contexts. While Diaspora Judeans would find these priorities considerably different from those of their homeland (and acculturate accordingly), it does not entail that similar compromises were not made by Judeans in the homeland. The question, then, is why did *this* group from James take issue with *these* particular commandments and not, for example, Paul's peculiar conception of the Godhead (which at least nearly violates certain interpretations of the First Commandment), the mixed fibers in the gentile converts' clothing, and so on? Even Judeans calling for "purity" (with respect to what?) necessarily took in "foreign elements," even if they would deny they were doing so. If we adopt language of *degree* when discussing matters like *extent* of assimilation, *boundaries* of identity, and so forth, then our description of the "religion" practiced by Paul, James, Peter, and their assemblies becomes subject to the same sort of authenticity politics that they employ. These assumptions would require us to overlook the question of *why* table fellowship was an issue for τινας ἀπὸ Ἰακώβου. It is difficult to imagine how Judeans in the Diaspora would share meals at all without something resembling table fellowship—the same applies to the question of equality of fellowship before God, since in the Diaspora, it would seem necessary to treat gentiles equally at mealtime. Conversely, it seems that Paul did advocate some form of Torah obedience among gentiles (cf. Paul's description of the essence of the "gospel" in 1 Thess. 1:9-10, which condemns idolatry and advocates worship of a single God). To be sure, Paul's condemnation of sexual "immorality" and other issues does not really contain appeals to the Torah, but he nonetheless demands his converts to engage in some sort of Jewish identity that has its origins in the Torah, albeit with emphases that differ from James's representatives and Peter. Again, to reiterate the point, one needs to move away from any form of normativity with regard to a Judaism that would be readily applied to any social agent or social groups.[13]

Situating the Diaspora Space of Antioch

First century Antioch was a very important Greco-Roman *polis* with a large Jewish colony (Josephus, *J.W.* 7.43.45), and it possibly had social institutions that functioned like a synagogue (Josephus, *J.W.* 7.44–45).[14] Antioch became an important center of government (it

---

13. William E. Arnal seems to be saying something similar: "Real people—even Jews!—have different views and behave in multiple ways. Serious and sensitive historical scholarship should recognize this, and thus also recognize that generalizations are, precisely, generalizations. Thus even if Freyne is right that generally Galilean Judeans were 'Torah-true,' and even if Sanders is right that there was a form of 'common Judaism' in our period, it does not necessarily follow that these generalizations apply to any particular person or group of persons." See Arnal, *The Symbolic Jesus: Historical Scholarship, Judaism and the Construction of Contemporary Identity* (London: Equinox, 2005), 31.

14. See Anders Runesson, Donald D. Binder and Birger Olsson, eds., *The Ancient Synagogue from Its Origins to 200 ce: A Source Book* (Boston: Brill, 2008), 244. One needs to heed the excellent caveat of Anders Runesson that "the Christ-believing ἐκκλησία in Antioch was, as other

was the capital of the imperial province of Syria under Augustus) and, in spite of the many sanitation problems associated with such an ancient and overpopulated megacity (it possibly had over three hundred thousand inhabitants in the first century), it retained its place—a solid third after Alexandria and Seleucia on the Tigris—as a vibrant cultural center for many intellectuals, while offering a mixture of opportunities for commerce and travels, especially as it commanded one of the trading routes between the Mediterranean and the Fertile Crescent.[15] The ethnically diverse population of the city was mainly composed not of born citizens, but of free newcomers or slaves with different social and religious traditions, all of whom were claiming a place in the social milieu and associating in diverse ways around various guilds (professional, social, and religious) with the view to find a sense of belonging, identity, and honor in a foreign diasporic social location.[16]

Antioch was founded by Seleucus I about 300 BCE, and shortly after its foundation many Jews settled there.[17] The Jewish Diaspora at

'synagogues' were, within the frames of the civic rights of the Jews in the Roman Empire. It is important not to impose an anachronistic view on Christ-believing Jews as not belonging to the Jewish people and not sharing their status in this early period." See also A. Runesson, *The Origins of the Synagogue: A Socio-Historical Study* (Stockholm: Almqvist & Wiksell International, 2001), 172n9.

15. In the late Roman Empire one meets a famous school of rhetoric there with leading representatives such as Themistius and Libanius. See Mason Hammond, *The City in The Ancient World*, assisted by Lester J. Barton (Cambridge, MA: Harvard University Press, 1972), 215.

16. For a thorough historical overview of Antioch see Glanville Downey, *A History of Antioch in Syria: From Seleucus to the Arab Conquest* (Princeton, NJ: Princeton University Press, 1961); Jean Lassus, *"La ville d'Antioche à l'époque romaine d'après l'archéologie,"* in *Politische Geschichte (Provinzen und Randvölker: Syrien, Palästina, Arabien)*, ed. H. Temporini and W. Haase, *Aufstieg und Niedergang der römischen Welt*, 2.8, *Principat*, (New York: Walter de Gruyter, 1978), 55–102. See also Barclay, *Jews in the Mediterranean Diaspora: From Alexander to Trajan (323 bce–117 ce)* (Berkeley: University of California Press, 1996),242–44; Paul R. Trebilco, *Jewish Communities in Asia Minor*, Society for New Testament Studies Monograph Series 69 (Cambridge: Cambridge University Press, 1991); Irina Levinskaya, *The Book of Acts in Its First Century Setting* (Grand Rapids: Eerdmans, 1996), 127–35; Magnus Zetterholm, *The Formation of Christianity in Antioch: A Social-Scientific Approach to the Separation between Judaism and Christianity*, Routledge Early Church Monographs (London: Routledge, 2003); Isabella Sandwell, *Religious Identity in Late Antiquity: Greeks, Jews and Christians in Antioch* (New York: Cambridge University Press, 2007).

Antioch was considerable in the first century, numbering somewhere around sixty-five thousand. In terms of the social character of the Jewish diasporic community at Antioch, they were treated relatively well, and there were no overall antagonistic feelings toward them on account of their ethnic origins. The Jewish community at Antioch enjoyed some financial prosperity and were given certain rights and privileges, such as being exempt from participating in emperor worship. Here is how Josephus describes the situation of the Jewish diaspora community in Antioch in the first century:

> The Jewish race, densely interspersed among the native populations of every portion of the world, is particularly numerous in Syria, where intermingling is due to the proximity of the two countries. But it was at Antioch that they especially congregated, partly owing to the greatness of that city, but mainly because the successors of King Antiochus had enabled them to live there in security. For although Antiochus surnamed Epiphanes sacked Jerusalem and plundered the temple, his successors on the throne restored to the Jews of Antioch all such votive offerings as were made of brass, to be laid up in their synagogue, and, moreover, granted them citizen rights on an equality with the Greeks. Continuing to receive similar treatment from later monarchs, the Jewish colony grew in numbers, and their richly resigned and costly offerings formed a splendid ornament to the temple. Moreover, they were constantly attracting to their religious ceremonies multitudes of Greeks, and these they had in some measure incorporated with themselves.[18]

By the end of the first century there developed some tensions as to the place and the acceptance of this particular community in Antioch. There were no programmatic state persecutions of the Judaeans in the first century, but the anti-Jewish sentiments were alive and well in some quarters of the Roman Empire (in Alexandria, for example,

---

17. See Menahem Stern, "The Jewish Diaspora," in *The Jewish people on the First Century*, ed. S. Safrai and M. Stern, 2 vols (Philadelphia: Fortress Press, 1974), 1:117–83.
18. *The Jewish War*, trans. H. J. Thackeray, LCL (Cambridge, MA: Harvard University Press, 1997), 7.43–45.

which might be behind the quite pronounced desire of returning to the homeland among many Alexandrian Judeans).[19] In the third year of Gaius's reign (40 CE), according to the Byzantine sixth century chronicler John Malalas, there was an episode that started in a circus in Antioch and resulted in a great riot where "the Hellenes of Antioch fought with the Jews there in a faction brawl," which led to many Judeans being killed and their synagogues burnt.[20] This event, which coincided with Caligula's decree to erect a statue of himself in the Jerusalem temple, with its evocation of the Maccabean crisis, according to Stephen A. Cummins, "would have been fresh in the memories of the Antiochene Judeans during the period in which the early church began to emerge within their city."[21] The strained, and often chaotic, relationships of the different social and ethnic groups did not, however, prevent these groups from having social rapports and collaboration, if not mutual fascination, with one another and, in their relationships with the Judeans, to even express curiosity and

19. See Peter Schäfer, *Judeophobia: Attitudes toward the Jews in the Ancient World* (Cambridge, MA: Harvard University Press, 1997).
20. See Elizabeth Jeffreys, Michel Jeffreys and Roger Scott, eds., *The Chronicle of John Malalas, A Translation* (Sydney: Australian Association for Byzantine Studies, 1986), 244.15–245.1, p. 136. Although it is true that Malalas's reports are often doubtful, this episode seems to be true. See the discussions and evaluations of the sources in E. Jeffreys, *Studies in Malalas*, Byzantina Australiensia, 6 (Sydney: Australian Association for Byzantine Studies, 1990), 167–216; for more on the Judean population in Antioch and the different interactions with the other ethnic groups, see Glanville Downey, *A History of Antioch in Syria: From Seleucus to the Arab Conquest* (Princeton, NJ: Princeton University Press), 192–95; Carl H. Kraeling, "The Jewish Community at Antioch," *JBL* 51 (1932): 130–60.
21. Stephen A. Cummins, *Paul and the Crucified Christ in Antioch: Maccabean Martyrdom and Galatians 1 and 2* (Cambridge: Cambridge University Press, 2001), 106. That frame of mind may have had some influence on some Judeans in Antioch in their ways of negotiating their lives in their own diasporic social location. And here Calvin J. Roetzel's suggestion on how the situation at Alexandria may have had a bearing on how Paul reads and understands the setting of the diaspora seems to be apropos: "While Paul did not borrow directly from the Alexandrian community, that community provides a useful model, nevertheless, for understanding how Diaspora Jews balanced loyalty to the Jewish Torah, the temple and the land with attraction to the Hellenistic culture." See "*Oikoumene* and the Limits of Pluralism in Alexandria Judaism and Paul," in *Diaspora Jews and Judaism: Essays in Honor of, and in Dialogue with, A. Thomas Kraabel*, ed. J. Andrew Overman and Robert S. MacLenan, South Florida Society for Humanistic Judaism 41 (Atlanta: Scholars Press, 1992), 163.

admiration for some aspects of the Judeans' ancestral ways of life in this fascinating diasporic space (*J.W.* 7.45).[22]

When some refugees scattered because of persecution—in connection with the murder of a certain Stephen—they brought the teachings concerning Jesus to Antioch, and Acts tells us (Acts 11:19-21) that Antiochenes accepted this message and became followers of Christ.[23] The association of Christ followers in Antioch became an important and dynamic center for the nascent movement, and teachers like the Cypriot Barnabas, who had some connections in Jerusalem, was sent to Antioch to oversee the work. Paul is taken alongside him for the organization and development of this group, and they both went to Jerusalem in order to clarify the divisions of territory and tasks, as well as some issues faced by the community of Christ believers in Antioch (Acts 15).

The Conflict at Antioch as a Family Quarrel within the Diaspora

It is not clear why Peter journeyed from Jerusalem to Antioch, but the δὲ that introduces Gal. 2:11-14—the focus of my analysis—is adversative and refers to the prior understanding of labor division and autonomy: Paul and his associates are recognized (ἰδόντες, Gal. 2:7, and γνόντες, 2:9) as having been entrusted with the gospel of uncircumcision (τὸ εὐαγγέλιον τῆς ἀκροβυστίας), just as Peter had with that of the circumcision (καθὼς Πέτρος τῆς περιτομῆς, 2:7).[24] In the words of James Dunn, "They had recognized the validity of

---

22. The Jewish community at Antioch was very open to non-Jews who were impressed by their monotheism and ethics, and who were interested in learning about the Jewish ancestral faith and traditions in the Jewish synagogues in the city.

23. Justin Taylor, building on Downey's suggestion (*A History of Antioch*, 192–95) that the disturbances in Antioch at that time would have been a result of missionaries from Jerusalem, proposes, in a rather intriguing way, that the label *Christians* attached to the Christ-followers recorded in Acts 11:26 would have been attached to the Christ followers by the Roman authorities at the end of Gaius's reign to signify a group engaged in seditious and criminal activities. See Justin Taylor, "Why Were the Disciples First Called "Christians" at Antioch? (Acts 11:26)," *RB* 101, no. 1 (1994): 75–94.

different forms of the gospel in different contexts (among Jews for Jews, and among gentiles for gentiles), and had agreed not to try to preach or enforce their understanding in the other's context."[25] The conflict started when Peter, who "prior to the arrival of some from James [used] to eat with members of non-Jewish nations, but when those from James came he began to draw back and separate himself fearing those of the circumcision" (Gal. 2:12; πρὸ τοῦ γὰρ ἐλθεῖν τινας ἀπὸ Ἰακώβου μετὰ τῶν ἐθνῶν συνήσθιεν, ὅτε δὲ ἦλθον, ὑπέστελλεν καὶ ἀφώριζεν ἑαυτόν, φοβούμενος τοὺς ἐκ περιτομῆς).[26] Because of that behavior, dubbed hypocritical by Paul, the one mandated as missionary to the nations opposed Peter to his face since, according to him, Peter was κατεγνωσμένος (had been condemned and found guilty) (Gal. 2:11).[27]

Observing the situation from the lenses of diaspora analysis, as it is presented to us thus far, several points appear clear. First, one observes territorial division of ancestral home (Jerusalem) and diaspora

24. This is what Terence L. Donaldson calls "Paul's sense of territory." For Donaldson, "Paul seems to have a sense of territory commensurate with this elevated view of his own role. Indeed, such a sense would almost necessarily be implicit in the apostolic agreement of Galatians 2:1-10." Paul's "territorial consciousness" makes him believe that "he has jurisdiction in the whole Gentile world; although, for the sake of his mission's overall success, Paul chose to restrict his activity to unevangelized areas." See the article by Donaldson, "The Field God Has Assigned: Geography and Mission in Paul," in *Religious Rivalries in the Early Roman Empire and the Rise of Christianity*, ed. Leif E. Vaage, Studies in Christianity and Judaism/Études sur le christianisme et le judaïsme(Waterloo, ON: Wilfrid Laurier University Press, 2006), 127, 129.

25. James D. G. Dunn, *The Theology of Paul's Letter to the Galatians* (Cambridge: Cambridge University Press, 1993), 38.

26. See E. P. Sanders, "Jewish Associations with Gentiles and Galatians 2:11-14," in *The Conversation Continues: Studies on Paul and John in Honor of J. Louis Martyn*, ed. Robert T. Fortna and Beverly R. Gaventa (Nashville, TN: Abingdon Press, 1990) 170-88.

27. The social location is an assembly, or perhaps even a symposium that, often, served as spaces of debates. One is reminded, for example, of Lucian's *Symposium*, in which the Cynic Alcidamas comes uninvited and is met with ridicule and rejection. In a way, Alcidamas is seen at the periphery of what it means to be an educated person or even a philosopher. See Lucian, *The Carousal* 46. Also, Athenaeus's debate of deipnosophists over what it means to be educated, i.e., who is (those who can recite a line of poetry for any occasion) and who is not (those who cannot or reject this definition, in this case the Cynic Cynulcus). See Athenaeus, *The Deipnosophists*, book 13.

(Antioch in Syria), of the management of center (Jerusalem as the symbolic center of Jewish religion, recognized by all, but in the process of being redefined by Paul in order to be appropriated differently) and periphery.[28] Second, there is the aspect of negotiating the social situation of diasporic settlement, in the sense of how the Judaism of the Dispersion (albeit a Judaism reframed around Jesus) should flourish without ostracizing very Hellenized Judeans, and without outraging Judeans such as τοὺς ἐκ περιτομῆς.[29] In this manner, as highlighted by Hurtado and others,[30] the dispute between the different parties arguing back and forth in Galatians was about the roles assigned to the non-Judeans as they were being given entrance

28. While Merril P. Miller's take on the symbolic function of *Jerusalem* in the Antiochene conflict differs from mine, it nonetheless grapples with similar questions. See "Antioch, Paul, and Jerusalem: Diaspora Myths of Origins in the Homeland," in *Redescribing Christian Origins*, ed. Ron Cameron and Merrill P. Miller (Atlanta: Society of Biblical Literature, 2004), 177–235. Miller's thesis in this important essay is that "*any historical reconstruction of the Jerusalem groups and its leaders to be won from the data of Paul's letters, in particular from Gal 1-2, must be wrested from competing mythic imaginations of 'Jerusalem' of diaspora Jews engaged in projects of teaching, recruitment, and community formation among Jews and Gentiles in Hellenistic cities outside Palestine,*" 181, emphasis original. Luther H. Martin, in the same volume ("History, Historiography, and Christian Origins: The Jerusalem Community," 271), asks some very pertinent questions with regard to Jerusalem: "What is the place given to 'Jerusalem' in the myth-making activities of the Pauline and the Lukan communities (keeping in mind the question of the dependency of the latter on the former) and in the subsequent environment of Christian mythic formations? How did 'Jerusalem' come to be the widely accepted 'root metaphor of the imagination of Christian origins'?" (here quoting Miller, "'Beginning from Jerusalem . . . ': Re-Examining Canon and Consensus," *Journal of Higher Criticism* 2, no. 1 [1995]: 3). It would have been very useful if Martin would have pursued some answers to these questions.
29. The work of Craig Hill reminds us that we should not view non-Pauline groups coming from Jerusalem as severe and legalistic, whereas Paul's groups are favored to being open and liberal. One should always attest to the complexities of the different groups and understand that the degree of conservatism or of liberalism in social religious groups is always relative and relational. See Craig C. Hill, *Hellenists and Hebrews: Reappraising Division within the Earliest Church* (Minneapolis: Fortress Press, 1992), 193–96. Also, as we are reminded by Shaye Cohen, "It is a mistake to imagine that the land of Judea preserved a 'pure' form of Judaism and that the diaspora was the home of adulterated or diluted forms of Judaism." See Cohen, *From the Maccabees to the Mishnah*, 2nd ed.; Louisville: Westminster John Knox, 2006), 29.
30. See, for example, Etienne Trocmé, "Le Christianisme primitif, un mythe historique ?" *ETR* 49, no. 1 (1974): 17; Sze-kar Wan's Galatians commentary in *Postcolonial Commentary on the New Testament Writings*, ed. Fernando F. Segovia and Rasiah S. Sugirtharajah (London: T & T Clark, 2007).

by two different self-conscious Jesus-believing Judeans. Thus Paul's redefinition and realignment is couched within a Jewish world view, and did not create a new people as such alongside Judaism, but inside it.

Peter's reaction could be interpreted as one trying to navigate his ways between variegated practices. He is in the complicated diaspora space at Antioch where Paul is strategically placed, and is one influential leader among those in charge of this community, yet in terms of division of tasks and of social responsibility Peter is accountable not primarily to Paul but to τοὺς ἐκ περιτομῆς. Prior to the arrival of those with whom he had certain social duties, authority, and enjoyed a certain reputation with, he had no qualms about eating with the nations. Certainly the Diaspora Judeans (followers of Christ and nonfollowers of Christ) would have been somewhat divided on their perception of Peter's associations with the ἔθνη. Some (and Paul would be one of them) would not see any problem with him having table fellowship with the nations, while others would be offended—although an extreme form of ethnic nationalism was very unlikely to be an issue at Antioch, since most Hellenistic Judeans were well integrated into the larger society.[31]

But since Peter—himself an authority figure and one whose presence would signify the authority that Jerusalem represents in the perception of many (Judeans and non-Judeans) in the Diaspora —was under Paul's authority in Paul's "zone of operations,"[32] going with what Paul would have deemed acceptable would not have been presented as an issue to him. The problem then began when

31. Markus N. A. Bockmuehl suggests that many first-century Greek speaking Jews at Antioch would be very lax in observing the halakic rules. See *Jewish Law in Gentile Churches: Halakhah and the Beginning of Christian Public Ethics* (Edinburgh: T & T Clark, 2000), 58–59. Magnus Zetterholm argues for the existence of both more conservative and more liberal Hellenistic Jews. See Magnus Zetterholm, *The Formation of Christianity in Antioch* (London: Routledge, 2003).

32. Philip F. Esler, *Galatians*, New Testament Readings (New York: Routledge, 1998), 139.

certain people from James came. Gradually,[33] one may conjecture in sympathy with Peter, after assessing prudently the situation and probably not willing to offend the strict sentiments of those belonging to the circumcision party, Peter, in a very pragmatic mode, withdrew from eating with some members of the nations when the representatives from James came to pay a visit in order to observe how things were being conducted in the Diaspora under the leadership of Paul. They are from the theological center; they are from the party that opts for some stability in this very flexible early Jesus movement, at least as far as they operate with and among those who are nonboundary crossing Judeans like themselves in Jerusalem.[34] Now if one posits the real possibility that the visit to Antioch might have had as its goal trying to place the communities in Antioch more in conversation—or in line, depending on how one wants to look at the conflict—with a larger socio-theological discourse within ancient Judaism, and avoiding any potential threats or persecutions from some factions in Jerusalem, then one may situate Peter's reaction in a more logical terrain than its caricatured presentation by Paul. Peter is one of them, but he finds himself doing, in the eyes of this delegation, what is clearly not proper. The fact

33. I follow Longenecker's understanding of the imperfect ἀφώριζεν as indicating a gradual separation of Peter from those with whom he was having fellowship. See Richard N. Longenecker, *Galatians*, WBC 41 (Dallas: Word Books, 1990), 75. Aliou Cissé Niang speculates that "the inceptive imperfect signaled that Peter's progressive withdrawal from table-fellowship could have been the result of much debate between James' emissaries and Paul." See Aliou C. Niang, *Faith and Freedom in Galatia and Senegal: The Apostle Paul, Colonists and Sending Gods* (Boston: Brill, 2009), 100. For a different understanding of the imperfect as indicating an ongoing practice, on the part of Peter, of withdrawing and of separating himself from the Antiochenes, see Martinus C. De Boer, *Galatians: A commentary* (Louisville: Westminster John Knox, 2011), 132.

34. This sentence is inspired by Merrill P. Miller's statement: "The Jerusalem group does not consist of Jews who are boundary crossers. They did not conceive of directing their own efforts to Gentiles, nor does a reading of Gal 1–2 convince me that they were likely to encourage or support those in their midst who might be inclined to do so. It is easier to imagine on their part a reticence toward the very efforts that were aimed at Gentile populations in the diaspora (cf. Matt 10:5–6). It is an important consideration that they did not reject the Antioch project." See Miller, "Antioch, Paul, and Jerusalem," 218.

that he is perceived by Paul to be afraid of the circumcision party could be explained not because of hypocrisy, as Paul in the thick of polemics implies it to be in Gal. 2:13,[35] but because of being at the wrong place (in the Diaspora, away from his own base and support group), and at the wrong time (when those from James—the pillar behind the delegation—showed up).[36] Peter tries to live in this

35. On the legacy of this text and on how charges of apostolic hypocrisy were developed in non-Christian and intra-Christian authors, see Margaret M. Mitchell, "Peter's 'Hypocrisy' and Paul's: Two 'Hypocrites' at the Foundation of Earliest Christianity?" *NTS* 58 (2012): 213–34. See also Nicholas Taylor, *Paul, Antioch and Jerusalem: A Study in Relationships and Authority in Earliest Christianity* (Sheffield: JSOT Press, 1992), 133: "Paul's ascription of hypocrisy to Peter likewise cannot be taken as reliable or objective in reconstructing the event, but reflects Paul's subjective, polemical, and anachronistic, perspective on the episode." Also, it is unwarranted to accept François Vouga's theologically motivated and unnuanced presentation of Peter as proven to be a transgressor (*übertreter*) who left "the truth of the gospel" (*die Wahrheit des Evangeliums*): "Der Bericht der Ereignisse in Antiochien begründet die Beurteilung des Verhaltens des Petrus: Indem er die Wahrheit des Evageliums verlassen und die Tischgemeinschaft abgebrochen hat, hat sich Petrus als Übertreter erwiesen." See Vouga, *An die Galater*, Handbuch zum Neuen Testament 10 (Tübingen: Mohr Siebeck, 1998), 53. It is, as a side note, interesting to notice that this incident was conceptualized and remembered by being turned into a chreia (χρεία) with a narrative beginning, whether by Paul at the time of writing or previously. The formal features of a chreia are there, essentially via the forms of "on seeing something" (εἶδον), and someone "said" (εἶπον) (Gal. 2:14) for the benefits of the speaker. See Ronald Hock and Edward N. O'Neil, *The Chreia in Ancient Rhetoric*, vol. 1: *The Progymnasmata*, SBLTT 27 (Atlanta: Scholars Press, 1986) and also from the same authors, *The Chreia and Ancient Rhetoric: Classroom Exercises* (Atlanta: Society of Biblical Literature, 2002).

36. I am following Peter Richardson's helpful analysis of the situation: "He [Peter] is in Paul's sphere of activity and is willing to adopt Paul's practice. However, when some from James arrive who hold a more rigorous view, the situation changes. It then becomes a matter affecting not just the Pauline mission to the Gentiles in a church surrounded largely by Gentiles, but includes also a consideration of the nature and basis of Peter's mission to the Jews. . . . The course of action he finally took was to give precedence to the pressures from the Jewish and Jerusalem side; he adapted his behaviour to the Jerusalem demands because that was the sphere in which his own role was primarily played." See Peter Richardson, "Pauline Inconsistency: 1 Cor. 9:19-23 and Gal. 2:11-14," *NTS* 26 (1979–80): 360–61. The provocative thesis of Dennis E. Smith goes against taking those "from James" as being a specific referent to James as the driving force behind this group. For him, "the terminology 'from James' would represent the fact that they are converts of James, related in the patron-client sense, rather than the idea that they were official emissaries. Their self-identity is related to their spiritual patron rather than to their local 'church.'" See Smith, 'What Do We Really Know about the Jerusalem Church?' in Cameron and Miller, *Redescribing Christian Origins*, , 248. One may wonder, then, if those "from James" only maintain a patron-client relationship with James, having no real mandate nor any sort of authority as representatives of the ancestral theological center under the leadership of James, why would Peter side with them? In other words, what would have been at stake for Peter to align himself with such a weak group?

vibrant cultural cosmopolitan city as τοῖς ἀνόμοις ὡς ἄνομος (recall Paul's statement in 1 Cor. 9:19-23); he had, like Paul, to be flexible enough to accommodate and to modify his behaviours according to the various social and theological contexts of the transcultural communities within which he was part of, as a visitor in Antioch; and he is not condemned by Paul for eating with members of the nations, but for withdrawing from eating with them when the delegation from the metropolis came.

The conflict seems to go beyond mere Torah observance (in this case eating nonkosher food with non-Judeans),[37] and to be more

37. There is no indication in the text to convince me to follow Esler's proposal that the "eating with" those in Antioch would only be in the context of the Eucharist. See Esler, *Galatians*,101–2. Esler is, in fact, following the views of many commentators such as Ernest DeWitt Burton, *A Critical and Exegetical Commentary on the Epistle to the Galatians* (New York: Schribner, 1920), 104; Hans Dieter Betz, *Galatians: A Commentary on Paul's Letter to the Churches in Galatia* (Philadelphia, Fortress Press, 1979), 107–8; James D. G. Dunn, *Jesus, Paul and the Law: Studies in Mark and Galatians* (Louisville: Westminster John Knox Press, 1990), 137–48. Although Ian J. Elmer does not follow the major commentators on the context of the meal as being eucharistic, since "neither in 2:11-14 nor in the rest of the letter does Paul make any allusion to the Eucharist" he, nonetheless, in a highly theological mode, thinks that "it [the Eucharist] could undoubtedly have served as a powerful lesson on unity among believers (cf. 1 Cor 10:17; 11:17-34)." See Elmer, *Paul, Jerusalem and the Judaisers* (Tübingen: Mohr Siebeck, 2009), 109. Paul is not explicit as to what kinds of dish were being served in front of Peter and those with whom he was having table fellowship. It could be that what the emissaries from James were having difficulties with was based upon their own ethnocentricism and prejudices that Judeans were not supposed to be eating with uncircumcised gentile sinners (cf. Dan. 1:8-16; Josephus, *Ant.* 4.137; 2 Macc. 6–7; 3 Macc. 3:4, 7; 4 Macc. 6:15, 17; *Jub.* 22:16; Tob. 1:10-13; Add. Esth. 14:17; Jth. 10:5; 12:1-20; *Jos. Asen.* 7:1; *Letter of Aristeas.* 142). In this sense, I am in agreement with Mark D. Nanos that the objection of the emissaries "was not to the inclusion of Gentiles at meals per se." For Nanos, what the people from James objected to was the acceptance of equality between Jews and gentiles as one before God. Mark D. Nanos, "What Was at Stake in Peter's 'Eating with Gentiles' at Antioch?" in *The Galatians Debate: Contemporary Issues in Rhetorical and Historical Interpretation*, ed. Mark D. Nanos (Peabody, MA: Hendrickson, 2002), 300, 316. My position is also shared by Merrill P. Miller, "Antioch, Paul, and Jerusalem," 213. For Miller, "What concerned Paul in the Galatian situation had nothing to do with dietary practices maintained by those 'in Christ' (to use Paul's language) who were Jews. Nor was he now particularly concerned about whether James and company recognized the meal practice at Antioch. The issue for Paul in writing to the Galatians was the undermining of the Jerusalem 'accord,' which acknowledged the integrity of the gospel he preached to Gentiles and its freedom from the imposition of Jewish covenantal law." Jae Won Lee, for his part, argues that in the sociohistorical context of the Antioch incident, Paul favors the non-Judean followers of Christ in face of dominant Christ-believing Judeans. See Jae Won Lee, "Justification of Difference in Galatians," in *Character Ethics and the New Testament*,ed.

concerned with territorial authority; that is, how a group from Jerusalem with its very strict understandings tries to control how gentile Antioch under a diasporic Jewish figure such as Paul needs to conduct its affairs. Paul's authoritarian military rhetoric demonstrates his awareness of the precariousness of his own authority in relation to the delegation and other authoritative teachers at Antioch, such as Barnabas (Acts 11:26, 13:1), who clearly did not side with him on this occasion.[38] When the group from Jerusalem comes, Peter goes to his field of authority, and the Diaspora Judeans sided with him. Now the authority of his party in this diaspora space becomes evident and Paul, to defend his turf and not be forced to surrender his assigned field, attributes this move to an intolerable compelling behaviour on the part of the Judeans to force the non-Judeans to become and to live like them. In a sense, Paul is presenting himself as the champion of the nations by telling the non-Judeans not to let their guard down and to defend themselves against a party that does not have their interest in sight. Positioning himself as standing in defense of Antiochenes' rights, the leader of the Diaspora division in the periphery, Paul attacks as well, because he feels that he has come under attack from the religious center via the circumcision party. Paul does not go after the delegation from Jerusalem, but stands head to head against the one whose influential behaviour has, in his mind, menaced to take over the members, the territory, and their God-given rights of freedom from the practice and directives of those of repute (οἱ δοκοῦντες), or those reputed to be pillars (οἱ δοκοῦντες στῦλοι εἶναι) (2:2, 6, 9).

Robert Brawley (Louisville: Westminster John Knox, 2007), 191–208. My argument, however, is that the power relationships—that is, in terms of theological positioning—of the Judeans on top of the non-Judeans remains, in spite of Paul's seemingly favoring the non-Judeans in the incident in Antioch. See the next chapter for more on Paul's positioning vis-à-vis the nations.
38. Nicholas Taylor does a very good analysis of the issue of authority in this whole saga, but he does not weigh in on how issues of border control, and how the complexities of diaspora negotiations might square in. See Nicholas Taylor, *Paul, Antioch and Jerusalem*.

The concept of diaspora, argues Brah, "centres on the configurations of power which differentiate diasporas internally as well as situate them in relation to one another."[39] And one can observe how the whole Pauline discourse in Galatians 2 is framed from the perspective of territorial power: who is in control; where does the border of authority of one lie (border maintenance); who speaks; who does not; which authority is asserted and contested in the fraught social realities of managing the diaspora space. Right from the beginning of the chapter, we observe a Paul who is engaged, discursively, in a military battle to protect his territory when he refers to those coming from Jerusalem: The false brothers (ψευδαδέλφους) came "to spy (κατασκοπῆσαι) on the freedom (ἐλευθερίαν) we possess in order that they might enslave/reduce us to slavery (καταδουλώσουσιν, 2:4). But we resisted (εἴξαμεν), and did not yield to subjection (ὑποταγῇ, 2:5). . . . So when those from James came, Peter gradually withdrew (ὑπέστελλεν) and separated himself because he was afraid (ἀφώριζεν ἑαυτόν φοβούμενος, 2:12). I opposed him to his face (κατὰ πρόσωπον αὐτῷ, 2:11)! The situation was so dire that even Barnabas was carried away in their hypocrisy (καὶ Βαρναβᾶς συναπήχθη αὐτῶν τῇ ὑποκρίσει, 2:13), but I shamed Peter publicly (ἔμπροσθεν πάντων, 2:14)."

In the battle for controlling the diaspora space, we heed here the battle cry of a general who admonishes his soldiers not to be deceived by militia that maneuvers, or tries, to take control of a territory that is duly the soldiers'! The political overtone of the situation is heightened if we build on R. Longenecker's proposal[40] (himself following R. Jewett)[41] that the Galatian "agitators" were Jews—although I would

---

39. Brah, "Diaspora, Border and Transnational Identities," in *Feminist Postcolonial Theory: A Reader*, ed. Reina Lewis and Sarah Mills (New York: Routledge, 2003), 617.

40. Longenecker, *Galatians*, 74.

41. Robert Jewett, "The Agitators and the Galatian Congregation," *NTS* 17 (1970–71): 198–212. See also, Stephen A. Cummins, *Paul and the Crucified Christ in Antioch*, 168. He offers a

not concur with him that these Judeans were not followers of Christ, since they were mandated by none other than James—motivated by fear of the zealot pressure in Palestine in the late forties and early fifties.[42] This delegation, in this sense, was composed of those who were largely motivated by a genuine concern to keep at bay all foreign elements in Judaism, and to oppose any Jewish sympathizer with gentiles, especially because they did not want to exacerbate any religiopolitical conflict between Christ followers and their fellow Judeans antagonistic to the Jesus movement in Jerusalem, and because of their understanding of the Jewish Diaspora communities as ready satellites to spread Judaism wherever they were located.[43] Thus, finding Peter having table fellowship with the gentiles in Antioch would clearly upset most, if not all, of those coming from Jerusalem.[44]

thorough analysis of Jewish nationalistic sentiments in first-century Judaism, particularly in chapter 2 of his monograph, "Maccabean Martyrdom in First-Century Judaism and Paul." He portrays Paul as a hero (contrary to my positioning of Paul), whose action stands in the line of Daniel and the Maccabean tradition (ibid., 162). See Mark D. Nanos's criticism of Jewett's thesis in *The Irony of Galatians: Paul's Letter in First-Century Context* (Minneapolis: Fortress Press, 2002), 208–11.

42. Craig Hill, analyzing Jewett's proposal, admits that "heightened fears of persecution might thus have played a role in the affairs" but he is not confident whether one can "know the degree to which, or even if, such a solution is true." See *Hellenists and Hebrews*, 130–31. It is attractive to think that pressure from the Zealots was a factor, and it may very well have been (although the Zealots' agenda would have been more about getting rid of the Romans than about pressuring a tiny group of Jesus followers). But, taking Hill's cautious approach, one cannot be dogmatic at all, especially when one considers that the nationalistic fervor against Rome was at its peak merely a decade later on the eve of the Jewish revolt in 66 ce. Sze-kar Wan, for his part, estimates that "James's impositions of rituals on the early Jesus followers was likely a necessary response to the political and ethnic unrest experienced in Jerusalem. The unrest would explode into full-scale revolt fifteen years later, but evidence suggests that unrest had been a constant feature of life in Jerusalem ever since Rome installed Herod the Great as a puppet king to rule Judea." See Wan, "Asian American Perspectives: Ambivalence of the Model Minority and Perpetual Foreigner," in *Studying Paul's Letters: Contemporary Perspectives and Methods* (Minneapolis: Fortress Press, 2012), 187.

43. Again, one needs to be careful to not ascribe an anachronistic "missionary project" to first-century Diaspora Judaism.

44. The phobias about table fellowship can be interpreted as anxiety over social relationships and as how, or where, to draw the lines between insiders and outsiders, exclusion and distancing, and between "othering" for the sake of identity and identity formation in the early Jesus movement. But, as clearly insisted and presented by Magnus Zetterholm, "*We cannot assume that these different groups of Jews held the same view of table-fellowship with Gentiles.*" See *The*

From their perspective, Peter and the other Judeans who were eating with the nations (we are not told if these were Christ's followers and members of Paul's groups at Antioch or not), acted as one of the gentiles (in the sense of flattening, or better, erasing any ethnic boundaries) and lived not as one who would be part of a group (that is, their group, the circumcision party [τοὺς ἐκπεριτομήν]) in advocating proper Jewish behaviors and customs amongst the nations. Peter, thus, in following this line of argument, acted the way he did because there were probable sociopolitical pressures and reasons behind this delegation that would endanger this fragile group of Judeans and Christ followers in search of stability and of recognition on the part of the wider society, especially on the part of the Zealots and temple authority in Jerusalem. In following this lead, Paul's language would have made a bit more sense as he felt he had to resist this delegation in the presence of the non-Judeans residing at Antioch, the very city that witnessed the beginning of the

Formation of Christianity in Antioch,150 (emphasis original). Also, as highlighted by several scholars (e.g., Tessa Rajak, *The Jewish Dialogue with Greece and Rome. Studies in Cultural and Social Interaction* (Leiden: Brill, 2001); Philip Harland, *Associations, Synagogues and Congregations: Claiming a Place in Ancient Mediterranean Society* (Minneapolis: Fortress Press, 2003), 219–28; Judith Lieu, *Christian Identity in the Jewish and Graeco-Roman World* (Oxford: Oxford University Press, 2004), there were considerable open social contacts and interactions between the Judeans in the Diaspora and their societies of settlement. The issue in the incident at Antioch, thus, goes beyond table fellowship, or the food that was being served. Hal Taussig proposes that it is quite plausible to understand the mixed eating of meals at Antioch as "social experimentation," especially considering that "by virtue of Paul's usage of the Jew/Gentile mix theme in 1 Corinthians, mixed ethnic eating became a conscious social experiment within Paul's circles at some point." See Hal Taussig, *In The Beginning Was The Meal: Social Experimentation & Early Christian Identity* (Minneapolis: Fortress Press, 2009), 167. One may also situate the incident within a larger framework of how various ethnicities jockeyed for space in the Roman empire. Strabo, for example, often comments in his tours of how the habits and customs of different areas set off one group from another and so gave them their particular identity. Often he cites some distinct practice—e.g., brushing teeth in a thin solution of urine (*Geography* 3.4.16; see also 4.4.3; 4.5.4; etc.). In this context, circumcision makes sense as it identifies Judeans in a world of many ethnicities. The philosophers who traveled with Alexander, on the other hand, came back and did not point out distinctive practices of the peoples they encountered but noted that all held the same values—justice, courage, self-control, and wisdom. Thus, in a rather quick comparative manner, one may consider the analogy of seeing those from Jerusalem as being aligned with Strabo's view, whereas Paul could well side with the itinerant philosophers.

attack against the Jewish people under the Syrian king Antiochus IV Epiphanes.

The fixation over Torah observance[45] by some in Jerusalem who may have been influenced by the Zealots' passion for freedom from the imperial order runs contrary to the flexible space and identities Paul is in need to constantly negotiate. The ones coming from Jerusalem may have certain misinformed views of those in the Diaspora as being, in general, lax and unorthodox. And even if they agreed to let Paul go to the nations with no other obligation than that he and his coworkers in the Diaspora would remember the poor (Gal. 2:10) without forcing the ancestral customs on the nations, they still fear that some in the Diaspora might adopt attitudes that leave their way of life so open that its distinctiveness becomes utterly meaningless.

Merrill P. Miller makes the interesting observation that "Paul's specialized knowledge of the traditions of the fathers gave him access to some elite Jewish circles, or their dependents, confirming him in his pursuits and making sense of divine sovereignty in terms of temple and covenant."[46] On a slight comparative note with the *Letter of Aristeas*, the whole narrative of which is presented as a communication from a highly placed gentile elite (Aristeas in disguise) to another fellow elite (Aristeas's fabricated half brother), the conflict at Antioch, observed from the angle of the Antiochene Christ believers, is presented as the socio-theological discussion between Judean elites—at least as far as special knowledge of the Judeans' ancestral traditions is concerned—over where the perceived elites of this diasporic community could play and negotiate different social

---

45. I am here appropriating and adapting Hengel's term *die verschärfung der Tora* to mean "Torah fixation." See Martin Hengel, *Die Zeloten: Untersuchungen zur Jüdischen Freiheitsbewegung in der Zeit von Herodes 1. Bis 70 n. Chr.* (Leiden: E. J. Brill, 1961), 231.

46. See "'Re: Paul'" in *Introducing Religion: Essays in Honor of Jonathan Z. Smith*, ed. Willi Braun and Russell T. McCutcheon (London: Equinox, 2008), 347.

roles as leaders among the Judeans and non-Judeans in this satellite colony and how, through them, the theological center (Jerusalem) could maintain a certain level of control over the development of its branches in Syrian Antioch.

The picture of the Antioch conflict recorded in Galatians 2 is that of diverse social and ethnic groups (natives of Antioch and immigrant newcomers, alongside those who have, for quite some time, established themselves in the important city of Antioch) observing the situation between these different Judean Christ preachers. The non-Judeans are, in a sense, already alienated from their previous lives and local social networks because of their belonging to the Judean Pauline groups, which would have vetted[47] their loyalties and their behaviors in order to belong to the god of Israel and to "become ethnically linked with Jews through baptism into Christ."[48] To put it slightly differently (and now with a mouthful), in a multiethnic city such as Antioch, where many gods constituted the essential fabric of the social and political function of the *politeia*, the participation of non-Judeans—readily welcome

---

47. One may notice that the verb δοκιμάζω (to test, to examine, to vet, and to approve) is the same that is used to refer to the examination of new members willing to enter into many ancient associations. For example, a new member entering the Iobackchoi club must be "approved (δοκιμασθῇ) by a vote of the Iobakchoi if he appears to be worthy and suitable for the Bakcheion" (δοκιμασθῇ ὑπὸ τῶν ἰοβάκχων ψήφῳ, εἰ ἄξιος φαίνοιτο καὶ ἐπιτήδειος τῷ Βακχείῳ). See John S. Kloppenborg and Richard S. Ascough, *Greco-Roman Associations: Texts, Translations, And Commentary*, vol. 1: *Attica, Central Greece, Macedonia, Thrace* (New York: Walter de Gruyter, 2011), 242, lines 35–37. For a very balanced presentation of the moral ethos of ancient associations, see also R. S. Ascough, *Paul's Macedonian Associations: The Social Context of Philippians and 1 Thessalonians*,WUNT 2:161 (Tübingen: Mohr Siebeck, 2003), 65–69, and "Voluntary Associations and the Formation of Pauline Christian Communities," in *Vereine, Synagogen und Gemeinde im Kaiserzeitlichen Kleinasien*, ed. Andreas Gutsfeld and Dietrich-Alex Koch, Studien und Texte zu antike und Christentum 25 (Tübingen: Mohr Siebeck, 2006), 177–81.

48. See Caroline J. Hodge, *If Sons, Then Heirs: A Study of Kinship and Ethnicity in the Letters of Paul* (Oxford: Oxford University Press, 2007), 148. One recalls Paul's ἑαυτοὺς δοκιμάζετε in 2 Cor. 13:5 and the appropriate behaviors the new converts were expected to adhere to—no worship of "idols"; evidence of self-mastery in conducting a life that is sexually restrained and continually examined, etc.

by Diaspora Judeans—in Pauline associations, which demanded exclusive worship to the god of Israel and "a radical modification of the self," would be quite taxing.[49] In the incident involving different Judean groups, they are tested with regard to the leaderships of Paul and that of the circumcision party. And, as the battle for the control of the diaspora space rages on, they are simply observers ready to see which side will win. Merrill P. Miller remarks that

> those in Antioch who shared an interest in renewing or continuing an effort to attract Jews would have taken the responsibility of the Jerusalem leaders not as an exclusion but as an invitation to link themselves to that responsibility. If Paul could come to imagine Jerusalem as the place of origin of the preaching of the gospel to the Gentiles, there is no reason why some in Antioch could not come to think of Jerusalem as the locus of authorization of the preaching of the gospel to diaspora Jews.[50]

The siding of most, if not all, diasporic Judeans Christ followers present at this particular situation with the emissaries from the Lord's brother confirm, as it were, to the non-Judeans observing the polarized polemical situation, that those from James are probably right, thus isolating Paul from them, as well as possibly pushing the apostle to take a significant turn in his missionary career.[51]

---

49. See Stanley K. Stowers, "Does Pauline Christianity Resemble a Hellenistic Philosophy?" in *Paul Beyond the Judaism/Hellenism Divide*, ed. T. Engberg-Pedersen (Louisville: Westminster John Knox, 2001), 100: "In Paul's thought, Gentiles in Christ must undergo a radical modification of the self because they have been fundamentally and consistently shaped by idolatry and *porneia*."

50. See "Antioch, Paul, and Jerusalem," 233.

51. See Ian J. Elmer on how the incident in Antioch most likely played a pivotal role in how Paul had to leave this particular diasporic space in order to find other spaces—certainly multilayered and contested in the complexities of the different groups he worked with—further afield from the growing influence of the circumcision party. See Elmer, *Paul, Jerusalem and the Judaisers*, 116 and 163. Although I do not share Wan's unnuanced siding with Paul, I appreciate how he expresses this turn in the relationship between Paul and the circumcision party: "The Opposition now decisively has the upper hand, and Paul is once again reduced to a wanderer, a perpetual foreigner in his own movement, consigned by the Jerusalem-Antioch metropolis to its periphery. Paul is excluded a second time, this time by members of his own group." See Wan, "Asian American Perspectives," 186.

The representative missionary amongst the nations steps up to defend his territory from any theology and/or sociopolitical behaviors that would undermine the hard-earned success of mission amongst the nations.[52] Paul wants to keep his gains, rally his troops, and project an image of himself to those inhabiting the diaspora space, who are watching him, as the one in charge: there is nothing to fear from those of Jerusalem; if there is any political, social, and theological threat stemming from these Judeans (perceived or real), it will be resisted and put under control; the flexible work, which began and prospered amongst the nations, is *the* gospel! (1:6-9). Now,

52. Under the heading of "Territoriality and the Conflict in Antioch (Gal 2:11-14)" James M. Scott explores, yet too briefly, how the incident at Antioch might have more to do with territorial control than with theological fine points. He, however, quickly dismisses this intriguing possibility with a turn of the hand and falls back on the much-too-usual theological explanation of the incident. James M. Scott, in what I feel like calling, after Donald Wiebe, a "failure of nerve," quips, "Of course, the issue that develops in Antioch after these men arrive runs much deeper than a merely territorial dispute" (159). Why "of course" after highlighting so well that "Paul evidently considers Peter and the men from James as intruders, infringing on his missionary territory by attempting to exercise control over an area that was outside their sphere of direct influence/jurisdiction"? The footnote to this sentence continues on the same path: "According to Acts 11:22, Barnabas had been sent to oversee affairs of the nascent church in Antioch before Paul became involved in the work. As a result of the Apostolic Council, however, the territorial jurisdiction of Paul was sharply divided from that of Peter, so that, from Paul's perspective, Peter should not have tried to exert his influence there." See James M. Scott, *Paul and the Nations: The Old Testament and Jewish Background of Paul's Mission to the Nations with Special Reference to the Destination of Galatians* (Tübingen: Mohr Siebeck, 1995), 158. The full reference to Wiebe's work mentioned above is "The Failure of Nerve in the Academic Study of Religion," *Studies in Religion* 13, no. 4 (1984): 401–22. A very recent book, which reproduces Wiebe's programmatic essay and compiles different essays in Wiebe's honor, aims to refine, elaborate, and to examine some of the failures of intellectual nerve in the academic study of religion. See William E. Arnal, Willi Braun, and Russell T. McCutcheon, eds., *Failure and Nerve in the Academic Study of Religion* (London: Equinox, 2012). The term *failure of nerve* goes back to Gilbert Murray, *The Five Stages of Greek Religion* (Oxford: Clarendon Press, 1925). Wiebe picks up the well-known term to articulate his criticism. I am grateful to Terence L. Donaldson for drawing my attention to that source. Atsuhiro Asano also envisages the possibility of how geographical boundaries could help in sharpening our understanding of the Antioch incident. It is not clear, however, what he means by saying that James's understanding of the land of Israel (Eretz Israel) might have prompted his action. See his *Community-Identity Construction in Galatians: Exegetical, Social-Anthropological and Socio-Historical Studies* (New York: T & T Clark International, 2005), 134n79: "Though the agreement was not specifically on geographical demarcation (Gal. 2.7-8), James' understanding of *Eretz Israel* may have influenced his action."

how Peter compels the non-Jews to Judaize (from Paul's perspective) in 2:14 (that is, to follow Jewish customs and Jewish ways of life, to live as Jews, which intimates that the non-Jews who are men would become circumcised)[53] by withdrawing from them when James's group comes, is not entirely clear from the immediate context of the text.[54]

Paul shows his great disappointment, especially with regard to an esteemed leader and former mentor such as Barnabas (Acts 11:19-25), who sided with the opponents and, in so doing, was undermining his very space of freedom (in Paul's understanding, Gal. 2:4), and of reputation.[55] Paul finds himself caught in the throes of conflicting identities, understandings, allegiances, and potentially dangerous political minefields when the group from James comes. The focus on political strategies utilized by Paul against those who come to "spy on his freedom" (2:4) shows how his discourse constructs and contests social identities in order to defend his territory that appears to be in peril. In other words, analyzing the tug-and-pull situation

---

53. Josephus, *J.W.* 2.454, 2.462–3 and Esther 8:17 lxx, as highlighted by Cummins, *Paul and the Crucified Christ in Antioch*, 185, where circumcision and following the whole law could be mutually reinforced. See also Plutarch, *Life of Cicero* 7.6; Josephus., *J. W.* 2.454, 463.

54. Several commentators suggest that Paul may have "the whole law" in mind, starting with circumcision, when he accuses Peter of Judaizing the nations. See, among others, Longenecker, *Galatians*, 78; Philip F. Esler, *Galatians*, 137 and Mark D. Nanos, "What Was at Stake in Peter's 'Eating with Gentiles' at Antioch?," 304. In this chapter (292–300), Nanos summarizes very well the prevailing views with regards to the precise character of the table fellowship in Antioch. But one may frankly ask: What is the correlation between the two? In other words, how does "this" (fellowshipping with the nations) signifies "that" (Peter's demand to the nations to become and live as a Jew)? For whatever reasons, since we do not have Peter's voice or reasons for withdrawing from them, and dispensing from looking at the situation only from Paul's perspective—now refracted by some time in which defeat has been turned into victory—it might be that Peter was not afraid of those from James. Maybe he was, or maybe he was not. We simply cannot assert one way or the other with any certainties. See also Paula Fredriksen, "Judaism, the Circumcision of Gentiles, and Apocalyptic Hope: Another Look at Galatians 1 and 2," *JTS* n.s. 42 (1991): 151–83; Fredriksen, "Judaizing the Nations," *NTS* 56 (2010): 232–52.

55. Barnabas, if we trust the reports in Acts, had some connections in Jerusalem (Acts 4:36-37; 9:27; 11:22), but his reputation as a trusted leader and teacher is among those at Antioch (Acts 15:2; Gal. 2:1). See Craig C. Hill, *Hellenists and Hebrews*, 105.

in Antioch from the perspective of contested cultural and political reconfigurations in the diaspora allows one to study how Paul's military rhetoric in engaging certain behaviors is not necessarily, or exclusively, over theological concerns, but may as well have to do specifically with the goal of maintaining control over his geographical jurisdiction.[56]

Paul still wants to hold on to his sense of being part of a grand mythic narrative and, even while shaming and blaming Peter publicly,[57] he manages to insert the point of assurance to the delegation from Jerusalem by playing a politics of difference. Confronting Peter, Paul charges the following: If you, being a Judean ('Ιουδαῖος) live as a gentile (ἐθνικῶς) and not as Jew ('Ιουδαϊκῶς), how can you compel (ἀναγκάζεις) the nations (τὰ ἔθνη) to Judaize ('Ιουδαΐζειν) (2:14)?[58] We are Jews by nature (φύσει) and not sinners from the nations (ἐξ ἐθνῶν ἁμαρτωλοί) (2:15). We observe at this juncture that his discourse is tainted by a very ethnocentric veneer, and that a family conflict within a certain branch of first-century Judaism in the Diaspora is taking place with the nations (i.e., those non-Judeans Christ believers socialized into Paul's communities) as silent spectators. And as Hurtado remarks, Paul's gentile converts may have, unintentionally, exacerbated the family quarrel within

---

56. Magnus Zetterholm, in spite of his robust sociological analysis of the conflict, and his clear agenda for analysing the situation from a different methodological approach, still manages to resort to theological conclusions. He considers the eschatological context of the conflict in order to suggest that what was at the heart of the conflict in Antioch was the tension of "*different concepts of covenantal theology.*" See *The Formation of Christianity in Antioch*, 156.

57. See Bruce J. Malina and Jerome H. Neyrey, *Portraits of Paul: An Archeology of Ancient Personality* (Louisville: Westminster John Knox, 1996), 48–52. For Malina and Neyrey, Paul is using typical and key ancient rhetorical tropes, such as encomium, in which one compares two different characters. Paul praises himself as being a virtuous and sincere person, while shaming Peter as one who acted out of fear and is a person pleaser, thus seeking to undermine and diminish Peter's reputation.

58. To Judaize refers to keeping and living in accordance to the ancestral customs of the Jews. See Josephus, *J.W* 2.18.2. It may also refer to non-Jews striving to follow some Jewish practices (Putarch, *Life of Cicero* 7.8). In the Antioch incident, Paul is scolding Peter for demanding that the non-Jews become and live like them, who are Jews by nature.

Diaspora Jewish communities, as each party scrambles to portray the best and legitimate side to offer to members of the nations what they estimate are the needed elements to enter into the family of Israel's god through the resurrected Christ.

As we have seen in a previous chapter, the author of *The Letter of Aristeas* portrays the delegation from "home," that is, Palestine, as having the authority in the matter of socio-religious discourse and of good governance (*Letter*, 121). This seems to be the same intent behind the delegation from the theological center in the Antioch case, namely, that they possess authority to oversee the works of the periphery in the Diaspora, and perhaps even add some "corrections," if need be. Paul, on the other hand, although he positions himself and his project in the Diaspora as hybrid in a similar vein to the *Letter*, does not esteem the delegation from the ancestral home as having the monopoly in terms of what should govern the social behaviors and theological discourse of those living in the Diaspora in Antioch. Ethnicity and geography seem to have been constantly in tension in Paul. He was a diasporic founder figure to many groups of the early Jesus movement—composed of both dispersed and non-Diaspora gentiles and few Judeans—whose identity was embedded in his multiple relationships. He was not inviting the gentiles to become Jews, yet he did not understand the gentiles as having anything meaningful to give up in terms of their own ethnic identity. He, in fact, opened up his own ethnic narrative by means of a collective ancestor (Abraham) to include the ones in the geographical spaces in which he was operating, without any regard to their own local and ethnic identities. Geography and ethnicity seem to be reordered in Paul's understanding of the world because of his conception of temporality. In his "in-between" diasporic posture and in his understanding of the shortness of time, Paul reimagined space and identities in the movements of being and of becoming, in negotiating and in navigating embedded social relations and narratives in anticipation of what he hoped was to come shortly.[59]

Paul's "space trouble" manifests itself in the flexibility of the space he inhabits and in the ways in which the category of *Jerusalem* is appropriated, redefined, and divided (one from above—Paul's mother and free; and one from below—Paul's opponents' mother and in slavery, Gal. 4:25-27).[60] Merrill P. Miller notices that "in displacing the Jerusalem community, Paul has substituted a utopian myth of origins for a locative myth. The true mother is nowhere on earth (cf. Phil 3:20), but one can catch a glimpse of her many offspring in Paul's labors (Gal 4:19), including those among the Galatians, that is, if they will heed Paul's warning (Gal 5:2)."[61] But one may also notice that even when Paul wants to detach himself from the delegation from Jerusalem, he does not seem able to not use their shared prejudices vis-à-vis the nations, nor can he forgo Jerusalem as a point of reference that, to him, signifies more than an abstraction or a symbolic homeland that can be made malleable and played with at will.[62] In this sense, the different spaces and places are unstable,

---

59. See chapter 5 of this study for more on this.

60. It is interesting, and somewhat intriguing, that the verticality expressed by Paul is the usual spatial image adopted in discourses related to the state, namely that the state occupies the "above" position while the grassroots of civil society works from the ground. See James Ferguson and Akhil Gupta, "Spatializing States: Toward an Ethnography of Neoliberal Governmentality," *American Ethnologist* 29, no. 4 (2002): 981–1002. It is not stated here that there is any clear correlation between Paul's spatial musings and that of the modern state's positioning, but, simply, that the language of verticality is considered to be interesting and intriguing, especially when one considers that the movement he was part of was at the grassroots level. But by the late Roman Empire such rhetoric of heaven coming down to earth (the city of God) will be readily utilized to serve the political hubris of the state (the Christian state) against "heretics" and all Others outside the walls of this "glorious" city with the view to maintain order and peace. See Averil Cameron, *Christianity and the Rhetoric of Empire: The Development of Christian Discourse* (Berkeley, CA: University of California Press, 1991).

61. Miller, "Antioch, Paul, and Jerusalem," 218.

62. This sentence may certainly convey an impression totally different from what I want to say. The false impression could be that Paul's task, a task at which he failed, was to overcome his particular attachment to prejudices against the nations (presumably because he was Jewish), though he should have (presumably because he was trying to be Christian—again, that is *not* my view); a formulation that contrasts the (selfish, particular) Jews with the (open, welcoming)

imagined, redefined, contested, appropriated, socially constructed, and articulate multiple meanings and complex configurations.[63] Jerusalem still retains its place as a "mother *polis*" and it still functions as a significant cultural site of identity, memory, and power—represented in the conflict in Antioch by those from James. Although Paul maps his territory as being the new socio-theological center by equating his opponents as belonging to the realm of slavery (Gal. 4:25), the importance of, and the significance of recognition from, Jerusalem is still obvious to him (Gal. 1:18-24; 2:6-7).[64]

Like the author of the *Letter of Aristeas*, Paul participates in this double articulation of Othering and of mutuality. He maintains his ethnic group in the center and as normative of human nature with a special relationship with the supreme God, yet he decenters the geographical place by positioning his territory as also being a center; a new center with its functions and directives stemming not from

Christians. I want to stress that these categories—often, but wrongly, deemed to be fixed, stable, and unproblematic identities—are far from my analysis. My arguments throughout this study are made in relation to the Diaspora Judaism of the first century and are not concerned with the construction in time and history of a heroic Paul who is stabilized in a fixed Christian book.

63. For more on this, see especially Akhil Gupta and James Ferguson, "Beyond "Culture": Space, Identity, and the Politics of Difference," *Cultural Anthropology* 7, no. 1(1992): 6–23. The focus of this article is to explore and to reevaluate the use of central concepts in anthropology such as *culture, cultural difference, space,* and *place,* which are often rarified by many anthropologists. The authors problematize the use and abuse of these concepts by showing how they are in fact very fluid and unstable notions. For example, the reality of border and the realities of those inhabiting such spatial location demonstrate how fictive and unsteady the concept of space can be.

64. Under the subheading "Paul and Jerusalem" in "'All Things to All Men': Diversity in Unity and Other Pauline Tensions' Frederick F. Bruce notices, rightly I think (although the usages of *Gentile mission* and *mother-church* are to my view problematic because, to put it simply, they accept into the ideological and mythical presentation of Acts), that "in the letter in which he [Paul] most categorically denies that his commission was in any way derived from the Jerusalem leaders, he tells how he visited them with Barnabas on one occasion and laid before them the gospel which he was preaching among the Gentiles 'lest somehow I should be running, or should prove to have run, in vain' (Gal 2:2). This implies that, if his Gentile mission be conducted without the fellowship of the mother-church, his efforts would be fruitless." See Bruce's article in *Unity and Diversity in New Testament Theology: Essays in Honor of George E. Ladd,*ed. Robert A. Guelich (Grand Rapids: Eerdmans, 1978), 96; see also Merrill P. Miller, "Antioch, Paul, and Jerusalem," 214.

humanity or from Jerusalem, but directly from God, who is about to invade the space Paul inhabits with a Jerusalem that is from above. It is interesting to note that as the author of the *Letter* held the status quo of his time by positioning women as those "with poor reasoning powers" (250), Paul also otherizes and effeminizes[65] the nations by calling the Galatians stupid (Gal. 3:1), which is the equivalent to being "with poor reasoning power," yet he wants to maintain, or at least to portray in a very idealistic mode, his community as being one in Christ Jesus formed on the basis of equality of all, regardless of one's gender, ethnicity, and social status (Gal. 3:28).

The Diaspora Space as a Place of Solidarity and Negotiations

One of Hurtado's insights is that the admission of non-Judeans in the Pauline groups may be more about Diaspora Judeans negotiating their lives in their diasporic social locations than about gentile conversions per se.[66] In agreement with Hurtado, one may query how the Pauline groups may effectively be more about Diaspora Judeans negotiating their lives in their diasporic social locations than about gentile admission and conversion in a fundamentally Jewish

---

65. See the next chapter for more on this.
66. The question of the gentile in Pauline studies is one that is at the heart of many scholarly discussions. The insider category of *gentile* is used tongue-in-cheek, as it is usually used in the literature, but since my argument turns around how multilayered the diasporic community is, the concept of *gentile* is a catchall for a lot of different people that risks obliterating exactly the distinctions this chapter is interested in making. Sometimes the category of *gentiles* is kept relationally, that is, as used by the insider's group. We know that many non-Judeans had a lot of sympathy for, and attraction to, the Jewish religion and way of life, because of its monotheism, ethics, and the inclusiveness of its community. See Terence L. Donaldson, *Judaism and the Gentiles.* One issue that needs more consideration is the degree to which the nations have played a role in the development and self-identity of Judaism in the Diaspora. The Boyarin brothers (Daniel and Jonathan) have proposed a theoretical and historical model of Jewish identity that would go beyond national self-determination in the sense that "Diaspora, and not monotheism, may be the most important contribution that Judaism has to make to the world, although we would not deny the positive role that monotheism has played in making Diaspora possible." See Jana Evans Braziel and Anita Mannur, eds., *Theorizing Diaspora: A Reader* (Malden, MA: Blackwell, 2003), 110.

movement. This is a way to move away from the usual picture of Paul and the nations—with Paul on top and defining the agendas and research questions to be investigated—in order to explore the question differently by considering the nations and Paul. What has he gained in going to the nations; what have the nations secured and provided for him; what are the mechanisms by which he finds a sense of purpose from the nations; in other words, what has the Diaspora, and existence in the Diaspora, done to Paul? In following Hurtado's lead, we can see that the Pauline position on the admission of gentiles without Torah observance runs contrary to other understandings amongst many Jewish Diaspora communities. The conflict in Antioch, which results in Peter, Barnabas, and the other Judeans consolidating the position of the visitors from Jerusalem (2:11-13), *may* have marked Paul's subsequent isolation[67] from a group he seems to have desired to have, at least, some recognition from.

One of the common features of diasporas listed by Robin Cohen is "a strong ethnic group consciousness sustained over a long time and based on a sense of distinctiveness, a common history, the transmission of a common cultural and religious heritage and the belief in a common fate."[68] In the case of Paul, he holds on to

---

67. Nicholas Taylor, *Paul, Antioch and Jerusalem,* 138; James D. G. Dunn, *The Theology of Paul's Letter to the Galatians* (Cambridge: Cambridge University Press, 1993), 72. Paul's account is only the account of one particular incident, and this is why I hesitate viewing this conflict as being emblematic of what was to follow (contra Hill, *Hellenists and Hebrews,* 147; Taylor, *Paul, Antioch and Jerusalem,*145–50., among others). One should, I think, take heed of William S. Campbell's cautionary conclusion with regard to the importance of the incident at Antioch: "Our contention is that this incident, whatever its significance, cannot possibly carry the weight attributed to it, and that even many newer approaches still retain remarkable similarities with the emphases of F. C. Baur and historic Paulinism (e.g., Dunn and Boyarin, although in many details reading the incident quite differently). Moreover, if it is allowed to continue to carry this significance, it perpetuates the making of Paul into the sectarian founder of a sectarian Christianity in strong discontinuity not only with Judaism, but even more seriously, with Christ." See Campbell, *Paul and the Creation of Christian Identity* (New York: T & T Clark, 2006), 51.

68. R. Cohen, *Global Diasporas: An Introduction,* 2nd ed. (Seattle: University of Washington Press, [1997] 2008), 17.

his ethnic group consciousness in his articulation of his different discourses. In other words, he maintains his loyalties to his ethnic consciousness and a sense of particularity in his different boundary crossings, while benefitting from the hospitality and from a sense of achievement of being a rather successful Jewish leader and preacher among the nations in his diasporic social locations. The common ancestral history that he shares with other Diaspora Judeans is maintained, albeit in a way not shared by most other Diaspora Judeans. Paul opens up his common ancestral history to a larger, almost cosmic dimension, by incorporating, in a very flexible move, all other histories. And in so doing, he at least rhetorically erases, perhaps unwillingly or without much thought, other histories for the sake of transmitting his own cultural heritage, albeit one that is redefined around the Christ. Thus, Paul's obsession with the heightened distinctive sense of his ethnic mythic past led him to play the politics of origins by disrespecting the history and condemning the culture of the non-Judeans who provide him a ready platform to experiment with his novel socio-rhetorics.

The image is that of several and different characters inhabiting the diaspora space and how they function in such a space. Judeans such as Paul or Barnabas, who are Christ followers and leaders in Antioch, are different from, say, a visitor like Peter and other Judeans (both visitors and settled who may be Christ followers or not). The diaspora space is the same; the understandings different; the belief of common heritage with other Diaspora Judeans is shared, but the diasporic consciousness is articulated differently. Paul still wants, however, to preserve, like other Diaspora Judeans, his national distinctiveness in their common history by working hard among the nations to convey the common cultural and religious heritage and beliefs in a common fate he shares in solidarity with other Diaspora Judeans.

The fine line of negotiation between the delegation from Jerusalem and the Christ-following Diaspora Judeans in Antioch is how, in the understanding of the culture carriers of "the traditions of the fathers," the predominantly gentile congregation should search for perfection in doing what is right, that is circumcision; the nations may certainly embrace the itinerant worker (in spite the social stigma attached to his portable trade)[69] and apostle, Paul, and an important visitor such as Peter; but this latter should refrain from having table fellowship with the ethnically Other in the Diaspora, especially considering his credentials, status, and his connections to, and representation of, Jerusalem. In sum, the conflict in Antioch was not solely, or particularly, over divergent theological agendas and interpretations, or simply about gentiles, but was, if not primarily, over questions of inclusion and equality, home and diaspora, center and periphery, native and stranger, diaspora and interethnic identities, solidarity and tensions between people of the same group occupying the same diaspora space, and over how far Diaspora Judeans could allow themselves to go in negotiating their lives in non-Jewish environments.

Conclusion

The aim of this chapter was to investigate Paul's interactions with other Diaspora Judeans through a nontheological reading of the dispute in Antioch recorded in a polemical mode in Gal. 2:1-14, or, at least, by not being overly preoccupied with theology. This chapter wanted to move away from any matter-of-fact statements that the incident in Antioch was more than about such "mundane" matters of controlling and having authority over space. The rather reticent, yet brilliant, insight of Hurtado, coupled with Brah's theoretical lenses

---

69. Ronald F. Hock, *The Social Context of Paul's Ministry: Tentmaking and Apostleship* (Philadelphia: Fortress Press, 1980), 25–26.

of diaspora space, has helped in observing the Antioch incident in sharper focus. The incident was explored from these different methodological angles in order to show how socially and materially entrenched human beings can engage in certain behaviors, and deploying certain rhetorics for specific material or social end.[70]

Finally, this chapter is not about repackaging in a nice and novel methodological fashion the conflict at Antioch. Its specific methodological challenge, rather, is to look for "mundane" explanatory accounts of the social behaviours, relationships, interactions, relationships, social realities and rhetorics of home and diaspora, center and periphery, alongside divergent sociopolitical and theological agendas and interpretations in the early Jesus movement. This way of approaching the different and important social actors in this movement in the context of first-century Diaspora Judaism allows one to examine how the dynamics of authority and subordination, resistance and complicity, independence and dependence, sociopolitical discussions, fears, beliefs, ideals and social realities were negotiated, contested, and appropriated in the multilayered diaspora space with the view to create new and different social spaces among the nations.

70. This sentence is inspired and adapted from Russell T. McCutcheon, *Critics not Caretakers: Redescribing the Public Study of Religion* (Albany: State University of New York Press, 2001), 88. In his words, "Despite the fact that the people we may study profess to be talking about other-worldly concerns, we as scholars have nothing to study but what we can observe in this world and what we can organize theoretically; therefore, what we observe and study are socially and materially entrenched human beings engaging in certain behaviors, maintaining specific social institutions, and deploying artful rhetorics for this or that material or social end."

4

Paul among the Nations

He [Augustus] lumped slaves and foreign subjects together as a class of humanity that existed to be exploited for the profit and comfort of the citizens of Rome.
—Clifford Ando[1]

You foolish Galatians! Who has bewitched you? Before your very eyes Jesus Christ was clearly portrayed as crucified.
—Paul, Gal. 3:1

In this chapter, I continue to employ the interpretive model I adopted for this study by contextualizing the diasporic identities and performance of Paul among non-Jews, specifically his dealings with the Galatians. In terms of the theoretical aspects articulated in the introduction, one can observe how the diasporic condition crucially formed Paul's relationships with the nations. As a diasporic figure, Paul's negotiation of his social, religious, and political realities was organized along ethnic lines; his many relationships as a missionary

---

1. Clifford Ando, *Imperial Ideology and Provincial Loyalty in the Roman Empire* (Berkeley: University of California Press, 2000), 300.

among the gentiles were embedded in his conception and treatment of those who were ethnically other. In this chapter, I show how Paul struggled between being a Diasporic gender-troubled Jewish male asserting his position of authority among the Galatians, and an emissary of Christ who accepted the reality of suffering while working actively in solidarity with these marginalized people to develop alternative, "new creation" communities based on mutual support, dignity, and love.[2] My aim is to work through an intersectional mode in order to uncover the tension within Paul's treatment of the nations in Galatians.[3] The purpose of an intersectional reading of Paul is to explore how his diasporic posture enhances different points of interest—his positionality vis-à-vis the Galatians, performance of gender, issues of power, and negotiations of identities—without making the diasporic reality a distinctive angle of perception. This means that the present chapter does not use diaspora analysis in any central way, although it is, in its own way, a small contribution to diaspora studies' often timid attention to gender as a category of analysis.[4]

In the first section, I look briefly at Paul's conceptualization of the gentiles by exploring the theological complexities that shape his relationship with those who are ethnically other. The second section analyzes Paul's theology and mission through the lens of gender in order to understand how his identities are expressed with respect to the Galatians, God, and the Roman imperial order. The third section shows that in Paul's struggles to assert his position of authority and defend his particular theological views, he uses the rhetorical

2. It is not at all my intention to portray one side of Paul (the "Jewish" side) in a negative light, and the other side (the one devoted to Christ) in a positive one. Throughout this study, I have endeavored to move as far away as possible from such simplistic and unhelpful notions.
3. On intersectionality as an important theoretical concept for analyzing various categories of identity simultaneously, see the introduction, note 53.
4. See the introduction.

devices of the Roman imperial machinery. As a result, he appears as a conquering male who does violence to the Galatians, and even to his own Scripture, in order to win theological arguments against his opponents. In the midst of his correspondence with the Galatians, however, he seems to have reflected on the nature of power and on how a delegate to the nations (εἰς τὰ ἔθνη) (Gal. 2:8) with a message of grace and peace from God should address his brethren in the faith of Christ they all share. The last section concerns the position of Paul's politics of identity in his interrelations with the Galatians.

Paul and the Gentiles

Paul does not conceive his work apart from his mission to the gentiles, and "one cannot understand Paul's particular theological vision without also gaining insight into Paul's self-understanding as Apostle to the Gentiles."[5] He defines Israel's relationship with God in connection to the ἔθνη, as if to signify that the alleged covenantal relationship they have with God could not, or does not, have any meaning if it is not calibrated within the parameters of their relationships with those who are ethnically other. In other words, it is through the restoration of Israel that the gentiles will be blessed. Paul and his ethnic group viewed the gentiles as being underneath them in terms of religious pedigree, because these Others are considered to be idolaters and sexually licentious.[6] Why, then, does Paul—himself on the periphery as far as the Romans are concerned—go to other peoples defeated and living under Roman rule? Is Paul's mission to the nations a way for him to create with them a movement of

---

5. Pamela Eisenbaum, *Paul Was Not a Christian: The Original Message of a Misunderstood Apostle* (New York: HarperCollins, 2009), 172.
6. Stating this, I am well aware of the polemical motifs that were part of self-definition for different ethnic groups in antiquity. See Jacob Neusner and Ernest S. Frerichs, eds., *"To See Ourselves as Others See Us": Christians, Jews, "Others" in Late Antiquity* (Chico, CA: Scholars Press, 1985).

international solidarity? Did Paul go to the ἔθνη so that he could experience in his very body what it means to be Other? In what sense, then, could Paul's message for the gentile nations be seen as a political threat to the Roman Empire when he proposes an alternative emperor—the Christ—instead of Caesar?

Davina Lopez has recently proposed to understand Paul's mission to the gentiles as a mission to the conquered nations. Lopez's study invites one to *reimagine* Paul as the mother of effeminized gentiles. She suggests that "Paul's birth pains are a symbol of the labor for a new creation of different relationships between Jews and other defeated nations at the bottom together, echoing his scriptural context and challenging his exilic situation under Roman rule."[7] Indeed, for Paul, to be in Christ is to participate in the new creation; it is to receive the promise of the Spirit and assume the quality of life that characterizes the new aeon of God's dealings with the human race, a veritable resurrection from the dead. In this theological sense, Paul's goal in preaching among the nations is to place men and women in what he perceives to be a new phase in world history by creating a new humanity. Paul's use of liberation language with respect to the "new creation" motif is revealing, and this language is not unique to him, although he develops the new creation idea in fresh ways and with new content.[8] This vision of new creation is, in its context, an alternative one that was bound to challenge other conceptions of world empire. But one might query whether Paul's new creation language was a message of liberation for the many non-Jewish individuals with which he had some relationship, or if it was not simply neocolonial rhetoric invented by a male Diasporic Jew imagining a different world. Lopez would answer that

7. Davina C. Lopez, *Apostle to the Conquered: Reimagining Paul's Mission* (Minneapolis: Fortress Press, 2008), 142.
8. See, for example, the work of Harry A. Hahne, *The Corruption and Redemption of Creation: Nature in Romans 8:19-22 and Jewish Apocalyptic Literature* (New York: T & T Clark, 2006).

Paul's discourse was aimed toward liberation. I have my doubts, even though I would not equate Paul's message to the non-Jews with any simple neocolonial rhetoric.[9]

Based on his eschatological understanding that time is short[10]—that is, he lives in the last generation before the impending return of Christ—Paul goes on to proclaim a Jewish message to the non-Jews, albeit a message deployed and centered around Christ.[11] He goes as a Jewish emissary to the nations to convince them to leave their local Greco-Roman cultic practices and join him and other Diaspora Judeans to follow the cult of another Jew who was not only conquered but also crucified. Paul sought to include the gentiles within the grand narrative of the Abrahamic covenant by means of faith in Jesus (Gal. 3:7). According to Paul, the story of Israel reaches its pinnacle in Jesus understood as the Christ, the end and purpose of the law (τέλος γὰρ νόμου Χριστὸς, Rom. 10:4). In light of this understanding and because of his genuine concern for his ethnic group, he installs himself as a missionary among those who are ethnically other with the aim to help his own people.[12] In other

---

9. See below for more on how I articulate Paul's position vis-à-vis the nations.

10. To understand Paul's eschatology as a whole, and to understand how his eschatology plays an important role in his theology, see particularly the works of Albert Schweitzer, Ernst Käsemann, and Johan Christiaan Beker. Beker, for example, has argued convincingly, in my opinion, that the main entrance to Paul's theology is to consider him as an apocalyptic prophet. See Johan C. Beker, *Paul's Apocalyptic Gospel: The Coming Triumph of God* (Minneapolis: Fortress Press, 1982); and *Paul the Apostle: The Triumph of God in Life and Thought* (Philadelphia: Fortress Press, 1980), especially chapter 8: "Paul's Apocalyptic Theology." Terence L. Donaldson observes that "Paul's logic is based not on space but on time: Israel's rejection has opened up a period of time during which the offer of salvation is extended to the Gentiles." See Donaldson, *Paul and the Gentiles: Remapping the Apostle's Convictional World* (Minneapolis: Fortress Press, 1997), 248.

11. Pamela Eisenbaum is correct when she states, "The primary difference between Paul and other diaspora Jews, Jews who either knew nothing of Jesus or attached no real significance to him, lies more with a different understanding of time and history than with theology." See Eisenbaum, *Paul Was Not a Christian*, 198.

12. This is, at least, how Paul understands the law and his mission in Romans. I concur that reading Romans *back* into Galatians is a bit anachronistic, especially if Romans was written when Paul was at a point in his life where he was reflecting on his mission, rather than in the midst of addressing local disputes (e.g., in 1 Corinthians and Galatians).

words, Paul understands his mission to the gentiles to fundamentally be a Jewish one. In this venue, Paul works hard among various non-Jewish groups for the sake of his people as he stirs up Israel's jealousy for God. By reaching out to the nations with his message about the death and resurrection of Jesus, his conception embraces the whole universe as being under an encompassing Jewish understanding of the world. For Paul, it is urgent to help God keep his promises to Israel,[13] and the mission to the nations is the way to achieve that. Stanley Stowers is correct to say that "Paul's Gentile assemblies seem to be vanguards and beachheads of Gentile renewal planted at strategic locations in various parts of the empire"[14] as "Paul does not think that the Gentile future can be divorced from the Jewish future."[15] Paul, thus, is portrayed and justified as one who *had* to go to the nations in order to secure peace and stability among them for their own good. This ideology is shaped by a desire to rescue the nations from their lack of self-control and their violent, sinful nature, and entice them to forge a commitment with the god of Israel via faith in the resurrected Christ.

Trying to situate early Christ-following communities in their wider context, Jonathan Z. Smith has helpfully suggested that one must pay attention not only to differences but also to the specificity of such differences.[16] In other words, Paul is different from the people of the nations to which he is a missionary, but the difference between them is nuanced by gender, race, ethnicity, and religion.[17] This

---

13. See Eisenbaum, *Paul Was Not a Christian*, 207.
14. Stanley K. Stowers, *A Rereading of Romans: Justice, Jews, and Gentiles* (New Haven: Yale University Press, 1994), 284.
15. Ibid, 287.
16. Jonathan Z. Smith, "What a Difference a Difference Makes," in *Relating Religion: Essays in the Study of Religion* (Chicago: University of Chicago Press, 2004), 251–302.
17. For a recent work exploring the link between ethnicity and religion, see Matthew Thiessen, *Contesting Conversion: Genealogy, Circumcision, and Identity in Ancient Judaism and Christianity* (Oxford: Oxford University Press, 2011).

difference that constructs Jew/gentile, male/female, Roman Empire/ conquered peoples, and Paul/his opponents as binaries, needs to be analyzed to consider how each is framed and "*how these signifiers slide into one another in the articulation of power*" (emphasis in original).[18] Paul is the representative of a tiny "sect" of Judaism, yet he imagines himself to be the true custodian of an authorized religious voice to the Greco-Roman world. Paul's status as a colonized and Diasporic Jew preaching about the life, death, and resurrection of another colonized Jew, not only to non-Jews, but also to colonizers of Jews and the nations in the larger Greco-Roman world, greatly complicates and nuances the power dynamics in and of his letters. I want to be precise here because this could be a point of contention, since the Judean war had not yet begun. There were rumblings and some incendiary policies (e.g., Gaius), but generally the Judeans were not subjugated in the way, say, Britannia had been under Claudius. Pompey did invade and sack Jerusalem in 63 BCE, but the preceding era under the Hasmoneans was a time when Judeans were "friends of Rome." After the Judean war, the Flavians deploy discourse that is sustained by the subjugation of Judea, as evidenced by "Judea Capta" coins. Paul positions himself as the sanctioned mediator able to redeploy Judaism by branding an odd—to most Judeans both of his time and later periods—"Christological monotheism,"[19] while the model that he presents to the nations under Rome's imperial order is one of pacific subjugation. In terms of the social character of his relationship with the non-Jews—particularly his dealings with the Galatians—Paul is one diasporic displaced body displacing other bodies.[20]

18. Avtar Brah, "Diaspora, Border and Transnational Identities," in *Feminist Postcolonial Theory: A Reader*,ed. Reina Lewis and Sarah Mills (New York: Routledge, 2003), 619.
19. See Nicholas T. Wright, *The Climax of the Covenant: Christ and the Law in Pauline Theology* (Minneapolis: Fortress Press, 1991), 114, 136.
20. This view of Paul will be elaborated upon below.

Paul's Gender Trouble

Another important aspect of Paul's diasporic posture worthy of consideration is how his identities are performed through his construction of gender. My interest is in how gender as a category interacts with other discourses, or how it is performed with and through other identity categories for particular effects. Gender is an important concept to consider since, especially in antiquity, it was intrinsically used to articulate and evaluate ethnicity. For example, Rome's myth of origins is clearly depicted in gendered terms.[21] Also, the different monumental inscriptions, sculptures, reliefs, and monuments of the Roman Empire in antiquity were constant visual reminders and spatial narratives of the nations, imagined and written off as collectively defeated (female) under the violent force of their collective (male) Roman conqueror. But if it is true, as Lopez argues, that Paul associated freely with the conquered peoples of the nations, his association with those who were ethnically other was based on his own ethnic prejudices and stereotypical views. In other words, those conquered by Rome were still being imagined by the Jewish Paul—the representative of yet another subjugated group—as beneath the apostle's own ethnic group in terms of access to the divine, and as being sexually unrestrained, possessing a base mind and deserving to die.[22]

---

21. See Yasmin Syed, *Vergil's* Aeneid *and the Roman Self: Subject and Nation in Literary Discourse* (Ann Arbor, MI: University of Michigan Press, 2005); see also Helen Callaway, *Gender, Culture, and Empire* (Urbana: University of Illinois Press, 1987).

22. See Jennifer W. Knust, "Paul and the Politics of Virtue and Vice," in *Paul and the Roman Imperial Order*, ed. Richard A. Horsley (Harrisburg, PA: Trinity Press International, 2004), 172. Stanley K. Stowers shows that Paul portrays the non-Jews as being unable to attain self-mastery. See Stowers, *A Rereading of Romans*, 42–82. For Stowers, this image of the gentile is "what moderns would call an ethnic cultural stereotype" (ibid., 109). For a very critical reading on the association between ethnic stereotyping and claims about sexual aberrations of the Others in the narratives of the Hebrew canon, see Randall C. Bailey, "They're Nothing but Incestuous Bastards: The Polemical Use of Sex and Sexuality in Hebrew Canon Narratives," in

Though male and embedded in a male chain of authority from God, Abraham, and Christ, Paul seems to signify the female body by birthing new worlds and new identities in his interaction and intersection with the nations. Paul is the mother to the Galatians, for whom he is in the pains of childbirth (4:19), as he is also a concerned and watchful brother (1:11; 3:15; 4:12; 4:28, 31; 5:11, 13; 6:1). This complicates the stance of Paul when trying to locate him between Rome and the communities he founded, as his identities are "performatively constituted."[23] In other words, Paul's gender is constructed, and its categories mixed, mangled, and made to function at once as a tool for maligning and disparaging, and also for nurturing and rearing his audience. Paul's gender is not about the transformation of one identity—the conquering male—into that of another—the so-called laboring mother among the defeated peoples.[24] Rather, Paul's gender is (to use Judith Butler's phrase) *troubled*.[25] In his relationship with the nations, he is both a broken, penetrated woman by the Romans and, at the same time, maintains a complicated, and at times, puzzling relationship with the imperial discourse as he tries hard to affirm his "masculinity" when he deems it

Reading from This Place, vol 1. of *Social Location and Biblical Interpretation in the United States*, ed. Fernando F. Segovia and Mary Ann Tolbert; (Minneapolis: Fortress, 1995), 121–38.

23. Judith Butler, *Gender Trouble* (New York: Routledge, [1990] 2006), 34.

24. This is the argument proposed by Lopez, see *Apostle to the Conquered*. Lopez's main argument is that manliness characterizes Rome with regards to the nations, which are imagined as women to be assimilated, dominated, raped, and pacified through military conquest. Reflecting on the gendered terms with which Romans and non-Romans are described in antiquity, Lopez proposes a "gender-critical re-imagination" of Paul's relationship with the gentiles through an examination of the ideology of conquest and universal domination in the Roman Empire (ibid., 6). Her thesis is that "the Pauline mission to the nations is a movement toward, and among, peoples destined to be defeated by Roman imperium, including the Jews" and that Paul's rhetoric "proposes overcoming a hierarchical dichotomy between Jews and Gentiles" (ibid., 172). Lopez uses the visual imagery of Roman imperial power in an extensive way in order to show how the imperial images both created and maintained the "natural" gender position of the Romans as penetrators and the nations as penetratees; her presentation of Paul as empire critical aims to reimage and reimagine him as confronting the Roman ideology of power with his message about Christ as he expresses his solidarity with the defeated peoples.

25. Butler, *Gender Trouble*, 172.

necessary in his dealings with the nations and his opponents.[26] In his relationships with the nations, Paul's gender posture is troubled when he becomes the (wo)man "evangelizing *Jew*, seeking to make ethnic Gentiles into 'citizens' of an 'imperial Israel.'"[27] Paul's "motherhood" among the nations is not necessarily to create an "impetus for alternative relationships among the defeated nations—Jewish and others,"[28] since his "feminine" performance, as Stephen Moore notes, "is simultaneously and paradoxically a demonstration of his masculinity."[29] And here one can note that Paul's masculine rhetoric is very present in Galatians in the ways he portrays both his opponents and his naïve, vulnerable, and dear Galatian children (4:17–20).

In keeping with queering his diasporic spatial posture, Paul seems to be playing it soft with the Romans in order to introduce a new master in the neighborhood of the nations. This new master, according to the apostle, can offer the femininized peoples of the Roman world greater peace and security by incorporating them into his own large-scale house, the fatherland and grand narrative of Israel. Thus, instead of seeing Paul simply in a position of solidarity with other nations, an interpretive imagining that is informed by a critical analysis of gender system allows one to consider Paul to be negotiating his way between different strong males—the Romans and

26. The following caveat from Penner and Vander Stichele is important to consider all along: "In our view, however, masculine identity in the ancient world must be seen as the starting point for understanding Paul's characterization of himself and the 'ideal' church that represents his embodied *ēthos*." Todd Penner and Caroline Vander Stichele, "Unveiling Paul: Gendering Ethos in 1 Corinthians 11:2–16," in *Rhetoric, Ethic, and Moral Persuasion in Biblical Discourse*, ed. Thomas H. Olbricht and Anders Eriksson (New York: T & T Clark), 236.

27. William E. Arnal, "The Collection and Synthesis of 'Tradition' and the Second-Century Invention of Christianity," *MTSR* 23 (2011): 210. Thus it is, in my view, important to scrutinize the intersections of power differentials, particularly how a "dual-axial" focus on gender and empire would inform one's reading of the Pauline corpus. I am influenced by my reading of Joseph Marchal at this point. See *The Politics of Heaven: Women, Gender, and Empire in the Study of Paul* (Minneapolis: Fortress Press, 2008).

28. Lopez, *Apostle to the Conquered*, 146.

29. Stephen D. Moore, *The Bible in Theory: Critical and Postcritical Essays* (Atlanta: Society of Biblical Literature, 2010), 291.

the resurrected Christ—with the view to gaining what is beneficial for himself, and to find out how the nations could have more pleasure under a new imperial and dominating Christ.[30]

The picture presented above can be nuanced by Daniel Boyarin's insights on the assumed position of the Jews as feminine, in order to present a "critique of male power through a mimesis of femaleness."[31] Boyarin claims that "the absence of *phallic* power is not a lack."[32] According to this author,

> Since making oneself less male on purpose through depilation was considered perverse, and the long foreskin was considered a sign of masculinity, circumcision, a deliberate "feminization"—in the very terms of their own cultural construction of the foreskin—would have seemed to these Romans just as perverse as depilation. Within Jewish culture, we suggest, the same representation, circumcision as feminizing, became positively marked.[33]

30. Consider the context of the statement in relation to the problematization of the view advanced by Davina Lopez.
31. Daniel Boyarin, "Unheroic Conduct: The Rise of Heterosexuality and Jewish Masculinity," in *Men and Masculinities in Christianity and Judaism: A Critical Reader*, ed. Björn Krondorfer (London: SCM Press, 2009), 100.
32. Ibid., 78.
33. Ibid., 88–89. Boyarin notes, "Hardly feminist, rabbinic Jewish culture thus refuses prevailing modes through which the surrounding cultures represent maleness as active spirit, femaleness as passive matter, a representation that has dominated much (if certainly not all) of European cultural imagination and practice. Maleness is every bit as corporeal as femaleness in this patriarchal culture. This refusal provides a partial explanation for how Jewish cultural imaginings could conceive a valued masculinity as being feminized in the terms of the dominant Roman culture. There is, however, a positive signification to 'feminization' as well. In a cultural system within which there are only two genders, the only way to symbolize 'refusing to be a man' (Stoltenberg 1989) may be an assertion that one is, in some sense, a woman. This represents, then, at least potentially, a positive oppositional identity to 'manliness' that is neither 'castrated' nor emasculate, because it does not read femininity as lack. . . . It is not the identification with women that bears here the 'feminist' potential but precisely the 'refusal to be a man.' The identification with women is an epiphenomenon of resisting manliness, but not one that implies 'castrated' status for either the unmanly man or the woman. Traditionally many Jewish men identified *themselves* as feminized, beginning with the Talmud and through an opposition to 'Roman' ideals of the male, and understood that feminization as a positive aspect of their cultural identity." See also ibid., 79–95.

In the case of Paul, however, his "feminization" seems to be of a different nature.[34] It is possible that the Galatians may have associated circumcision with self-mastery for men of physical courage, but Paul forbids them to do so by connecting circumcision to castration, making it thus a choice to become something undefined, a third gender, some gender-troubled effeminates, pseudo-men, or eunuchs, who are neither men nor women. As Fredrik Ivarsson remarks,

When Paul expresses his wish that his opponents should castrate themselves . . . [he] is implying that they are no real men, so they might just as well make themselves into the eunuchs that they actually are already. Paul characterizes the "circumcisers" as eunuchs, or maybe more specifically as *galli*. This characterization is consistent throughout the letter, as Paul accuses his opponents of cowardice and sexual licentiousness, which are stereotypical effeminate features of eunuchs and *galli*.[35]

Paul, according to Moore, "permitted his Jesus to enter him. 'I have been crucified with Christ,' he groans in Galatians, 'and it is no longer I who live, but it is Christ who lives in me [*en emoi*].'"[36] But the bottom line is that there *are* no females in the inner sanctum of

---

34. One may resist Boyarin's "feminization" in the act of circumcision since the penis of a Jew that is excised of the excessive flesh allows, according to Philo, "the semen to travel aright without being scattered or dropped into the folds of the foreskin (τό σπέρμα μήτε σκιδνάμενον μήτε περιρρέον εἰς τοὺς τῆς ποσθίας κόλπους), and therefore the circumcised nations appear to be the most prolific and populous" (Philo, *On the Special Laws, Books 1–3* trans. Francis H. Colson, Loeb Classical Library (Cambridge, MA: Harvard University Press, 1937), 1.7–10, p. 105. As Jennifer W. Knust states, "Romans may have asserted that circumcision was a form of genital mutilation, rendering the Jewish male body ugly, but the rabbis countered with the opposite point of view—circumcision made their bodies beautiful." See Knust, *Unprotected Sex: The Bible's Surprising Contradictions about Sex and Desire* (New York: HarperOne, 2011), 203. Circumcision, thus, allowed the Jewish man to be ready to enter into a pleasing covenantal relationship with God; and it allowed the penis to be more productive and direct in its work of procreation. So instead of a simple "feminization," the picture is more nuanced and complicated, as the Jewish man is both God's wife and one with a very productive and procreative penis that is not "clipped."
35. See Fredrik Ivarsson, "Christian Identity as True Masculinity," in *Exploring Early Christian Identity*, ed. Bengt Holmberg, WUNT 172 (Tübingen: Mohr Siebeck, 2008), 169.
36. *The Bible in Theory*, 296.

Paul's "gendered theology,"[37] and this type of theology so clouds his thoughts that he cannot develop his arguments without the gender construct. Paul revels in his understanding that the Son of God loves him and gave himself for him (Gal. 2:20). However, in this intricate love affair, "there are only males acting upon other males: God, Jesus, Paul."[38] And in his relationship with the nations, Paul proposes to the nations yet another imperial penetrator—the Christ—to demonstrate that the Christ finds in them no resistance to his domination. In this sense, Paul is a penetrated Diaspora Jew who is obsessed with his Lord, as he has already experienced the virility of the divine penetrator.[39]

In sum, Paul wants the nations to become like him: to be, first, subjected to the prowess of powerful males in order to become, secondly, like the masters, a man. Thus, Moore's observation seems to be appropriate at this point: "The redemption of femininity is accomplished through its transmutation into masculinity. . . . The story . . . is a saga of soteriological sex change. . . . It is a woman

37. I borrow this expression from Todd Penner and Caroline Vander Stichele, "Unveiling Paul," 236. The complete quote is the following: "Paul does not have a 'theology of gender,' but a 'gendered theology' that permeates all aspects of his discourse and thinking, resulting in, as Moore notes, a Pauline world that is devoid of significant female presence, especially in the 'inner sanctum of Pauline theology' (Moore, *God's Beauty Parlor*, 170)."

38. Moore, *The Bible in Theory*, 302. The only time Paul seems to show any interest in a female figure is to assert his own authority.

39. In a very bold move, Melanie Johnson-Debaufre and Laura S. Nasrallah in "Beyond the Heroic Paul" take issue with Lopez, who considers Paul as modeling a "*defeated*, and not heroic, male body" (Lopez, *Apostle to the Conquered*,138; emphasis in original). They challenge her thus: "Certainly in Galatians and elsewhere Paul presents his body as homologous to Christ's abused body. But is it possible, as some feminist scholars have argued, that Paul's assertion of his homology between his body and Christ's might be an *authorizing* move and thus another assertion of power, even if cast in a key different from that of the imperial masculinity depicted in statuary such as the *Prima Porta Augustus*? If we decenter Paul and assume that his subjectivity is embedded in his multiple relationships, should we not ask about the *variety of modes* of employing gender and one's own gender mutability for the purposes of persuasion? Paul's assertion of maternal status in relation to the Galatians would then need to be placed alongside his image of himself as a nurse in 1 Thessalonians and his self-depiction as a father with a punishing rod in 1 Corinthians." See *The Colonized Apostle: Paul through Postcolonial Eyes*, ed. Christopher D. Stanley (Minneapolis: Fortress Press, 2011), 328n41 (emphasis in original).

forever in the process of becoming a man."[40] It is clearly also a saga of a gender-troubled diaspora figure.

Paul's Violence against the Nations

The next aspect to study in contextualizing Paul's diasporic identities among the non-Jews is how he deploys his social relationships by means of different rhetorical moves to assert his authority and gain theological arguments. Lopez advances the argument that

> Paul's self-presentation of his former life shows what kind of man he was and is, and how he has changed. . . . The difference in Paul's activity after his revelation is not only that he believes in Christ, but that his image of self and behaviour towards others moves from sole dominator to among the dominated, and from impenetrable masculinity to penetrable femininity.[41]

Paul's complex, and even paradoxical rhetoric does not seem, however, to reflect any clear position about violence. In Galatians, for example, Paul's rhetoric is fraught with violence, as he is quick to utter divine curses on anyone who would preach to the Galatians a gospel contrary to what he preached to them (1:8, 9). Paul's commitment to the crucified Christ, and not to any other less violent

---

40. Moore, *Bible in Theory*, 295. Although the analysis is on Romans, Stephen Moore's insight is extremely important and needs to be wrestled with while we are engaged in queering Paul in Galatians: "Paul's discourse on *sin* in Romans is simultaneously a discourse on *masculinity*. Which in its turn means that Paul's Jesus, as the one who uniquely overcame sin, is implicitly held up as the supreme exemplar of masculinity for Jew and Gentile alike—a hypostatized Masculinity, if you will, to which all human beings can now aspire, whether or not they have been blessed with male genitalia. . . .*Righteousness in Romans is essentially a masculine trait*; it is, in fact, the very mark of masculinity. What then is *un*righteousness, sin, with its cunning accomplice, 'the flesh'? What else but loss of self-mastery, lack of masculinity—in a word, femininity. *Sinfulness, therefore, is essentially a feminine trait in Romans.* . . . Romans implicitly presents Jesus' submission to God as a model for the submission that should characterize the female's proper relationship to the male, as we have seen. Yet Jesus is not allowed to become mired in femininity, to sink into a softness, a flabbiness, from which he might lose his own hardness, his own manliness. For his spectacular act of submission is simultaneously a demonstration of self-mastery," 293–95, emphasis is in the original.
41. Lopez, *Apostle to the Conquered*, 133–34.

image of Christ available to him at the time—Jesus the prophet, Jesus the teacher, Jesus the healer, Jesus the glorious resurrected Son of God in heaven, and others—might be, as argued by Gager and Gibson, symptomatic of "Paul's own personality, his own predilection for images and symbols of violence."[42] According to Gager and Gibson, Paul's violent personality and his eccentric ideology regarding the gentiles as being violent and living in a world of violence attracted him to "those traditions within ancient Judaism that gave outlet and support to his prior inclinations."[43]

In Galatians, Paul indeed elaborates on how intensely (καθ' ὑπερβολὴν) he persecuted the assembly of God (τὴν ἐκκλησίαν τοῦ θεοῦ) and tried to destroy it (1:13) because of his zealous fervor (περισσοτέρως ζηλωτὴς)—or obsession—as he was a far more devoted student than his contemporaries to the traditions of his fathers (1:14). In other words, according to Paul's own testimony, his former way of living was marked by behavior that resulted in an intense persecution of Christ's followers. As we will see, the excess of zeal and the brutality that characterized the preconversion and calling of Paul is not absent in, at least, the rhetorical strategies used by this reenergized figure imbued with a renewed fanaticism directed to and for Christ in the epistle to the Galatians.

The language of 2:5 (οἷς οὐδὲ πρὸς ὥραν εἴξαμεν τῇ ὑποταγῇ) is, interestingly, reminiscent of the binary penetrator/penetrated, masculine/feminine I indicated previously. Paul's rhetoric of violence among the Galatians aims to silence the speech of those he perceives as false brothers (ψευδαδέλφους) in Gal. 2:4. Paul declares that "we" did not yield (εἴξαμεν), did not give in to subjection (ὑποταγῇ) (2:5), did not take a subordinate position under those who came "to

---

42. See their article "Violent Acts and Violent Language in the Apostle Paul," in *Violence in the New Testament*, ed. Shelly Matthews and E. Leigh Gibson (New York: T & T Clark, 2005), 19.
43. Ibid, 17.

spy (κατασκοπῆσαι) on the freedom we possess (τὴν ἐλευθερίαν ἡμῶν) in order that they might enslave/reduce us to slavery (καταδουλώσουσιν)" (2:4). Notice how the discourse is framed in Roman, military "manly" (*virtus*) violent tones, and how Paul affirms his own masculinity with regard to those who came, in his view, to sabotage his territorial conquest. Paul continues to show his bravado not only by dismissing the pedigree of whoever might seem to be important (2:6) but also by showing his active masculinity in the way he stood up to Peter (κατὰ πρόσωπον αὐτῷ) (2:11). Peter, according to Paul, acted like a poltroon because he was afraid (φοβούμενος)—unlike one who acts as a man—when those from the circumcision crowd (τοὺς ἐκ περιτομῆς) showed up (2:12). The description of the opponents to his gospel as cowardly can be seen as a way of feminizing them (claiming they are soft and passive). Paul's performance of masculinity is manifested in his firm resolution to resist his opponents by showing what a brave warrior he is, demonstrated in how he opposed Peter and scolded him publicly (2:11, 14).

Moreover, Paul's language in Gal 2:15, "We ourselves are Jews by nature and not sinners of the gentiles" (ἐξ ἐθνῶν ἁμαρτωλοί), is instructive of his stereotypical view of the nations and suggests "that for Paul the sinfulness of the Gentiles was a native conviction, part of his view of the world from the outset."[44] Paul wants to convince his gentile readers that he knows what is good for them, and he buttresses his apostleship by showing how he is connected to Christ. In Gal. 2:19, he claims that he has been "crucified with" (συνεσταύρωμαι) Christ. Stephen Moore's insights and questions with regard to Paul's crucified Christ are pertinent:

44. Donaldson, *Paul and the Gentiles*, 144.

What if the crucified Christ, as interpreted by Paul, were actually God's own (pri)son? The prison would contain a courtyard, however, and a scaffold would dominate the courtyard. For Paul's gospel of reform cannot simply be conflated analogically with the judicial reforms of eighteenth-century Europe. For the latter, the punitive liturgy of public torture had to be consigned once and for all to history. But for Paul, discipline remains indissolubly bound up with atrocity. Each believer must be subjected to public execution by torture: "Do you not know that all of us who have been baptized into Christ Jesus were baptized into his death?" (Rom 6:3). Paul refuses to separate torture from reform (cf. 1 Cor 1:18 ff.; Gal 2:19-21). Unless the believer is tortured to death in the (pri)son, he or she cannot be rehabilitated: "We know that our old self was crucified with him so that the sinful body might be destroyed" (Rom 6:6; cf. Gal 5:24).[45]

Paul's connection to, or better still, his courageous and manly participation in the violent act of Christ's crucifixion is his way of justifying himself to his audience as an authentic apostle of Christ in contradistinction to anyone else. Now Paul no longer lives, but Christ lives in him (2:20) (ζῶ δὲ οὐκέτι ἐγώ, ζῇ δὲ ἐν ἐμοὶ Χριστός). Paul assumes a new identity by allowing Christ to occupy his body. He is a zombie-like figure, a slave especially devoted to his patron deity, Christ (Gal. 1:10). In his magical world, he derails and shames the Galatians as ἀνόητοι Γαλάται: "Foolish, devoid of intelligence Galatians!" (3:1). In a diasporic situation where the ideals and beliefs of the Jesus movement are met with the nitty-gritty of the social realities, a frustrated Paul uses violence (in this case, verbal abuse) to engender fear and conformity. The pressure that came from various social and political realities exaggerates and amplifies tensions that might exist between Paul and his rival groups. Paul, the one possessed and penetrated by Christ, acts as an aggressor by verbally abusing the Galatians for the reason that they (outrageously) did not do as they were told, on the grounds that they questioned the credibility

45. See Moore, "The Divine Butcher," in *The Bible in Theory*, 162.

of Paul's gospel of freedom from the law. Paul remains in the supernatural register by asking the Galatians: "Who has bewitched (ἐβάσκανεν) you?" (Gal 3:1). In other words, he is asking who has used sorcery, a charm, or an amulet against them. Paul, the one possessed by Christ, is worried that the Galatians might be possessed by another mysterious force. He is determined to use different rhetorical means at his disposal to coerce them into accepting his authority over them. The discourse he adopts seeks to disrupt the resisting power of anyone in the community who would dare follow the theology of the rival emissaries. Paul does this by establishing his own power, and by finding pleasure in an authority structure that allows him to exercise control over them in a brutal although, at times, subtle mode.[46]

Paul's violence also manifests itself in how he relates to the Jewish grand narrative as being in covenant with God.[47] Paul fights to win his arguments against his opponents by calling, in Gal. 4:21;31, upon all his creative dexterity to offer a very startling interpretation of Genesis 16 and 21:8;21. Paul, without any second thought of the brutality with which Hagar, the young Egyptian female slave, was forced out of the home and into the desert, ingwatch her son dying of hunger and thirst,[48] equates her with his opponents. For him, his

---

46. See the analysis on the end of Galatians below.

47. Jeremy Punt would prefer to consider how Paul (re)reads the texts within his Jewish tradition as a form of memory. For him, "The apostle used texts from the Jewish tradition to foster, structure, maintain, and negotiate identity within his communities of Jesus-followers. . . . Reading texts as memory underlines that remembering the self is not about the restoration of some original self but rather about re-membering, of putting past and present selves together, moment by moment, in a process of provisional (re)construction." See Jeremy Punt, "Identity, Memory, and Scriptural Warrant: Arguing Paul's Case," in *Paul and Scripture: Extending the Conversation*, ed. Christopher D. Stanley (Atlanta: Society of Biblical Literature, 2012), 40, 41. Punt rightly observes (48) that in Paul's re-membering of texts he chooses what to re-member and what to ignore (e.g., Abraham's acts of unfaithfulness and machinations; his abusive—my term, not Punt's, who prefers to use "dismissive"—attitude toward Hagar and her son, and Sarah's determinative roles in different situations).

48. In the J tradition, she is the one who leaves Abraham's household on her own accord because she was mistreated by Sarai (Gen. 16:6).

challengers are currently making slaves of the Galatians, and he does not refrain in any way from asserting his own authority as the one who is the harbinger of freedom.

Paul considers those who will not follow his theological conclusions to be children born of slavery (sons of Hagar) and those who will not submit themselves to what he calls in Gal. 5:1 the yoke of slavery (ζυγῷ δουλείας) to be the children of freedom (represented by the free woman), whom he does not name but who are understood to be his children. Simply put, Paul compares those who do not share his theological sentiments to Hagar, who needs to be forced out, and those who accept his Christ to children of the free woman partaking in the blessings of Abraham (4:31). In other words, Paul, in siding with Sarah, participates in her terror of Hagar. Paul is angry at his rivals, and terrorizes whoever does not share his theological views by pushing them out of the household of faith. The tragedy for Paul's opponents, as for Hagar, is dreadful; her land is barren, a place where one starves and dies of thirst. Strangely, Paul goes out to the nations with his recalibrated Jewish message, and he is audacious enough to reverse the position of those of his nation who do not side with him to the camp of the gentiles.[49] Sarah used Hagar to satisfy her own agenda in the Genesis account, so Paul uses and abuses the story of Hagar and of the free woman to construct his own theological points against his opponents. Paul, acting in a way similar to Sarah, does not seem to care about the fate of Hagar or her children.[50]

49. Consider the whole Sarah-Hagar analogy as Paul's reversing of different roles. Paul states in 4:24: "Mount Sinai bears children who are to be slaves: this is Hagar." That, to him, represents the present city of Jerusalem (4:24). The Jerusalem from above bears children who are free. He considers himself not children of the slave woman, but of the free woman (4:31). He continues, "It is for freedom that Christ has set us free" (5:1).

50. My interpretation of Gal. 4:21-31(the Sarah-Hagar story) goes in the opposite direction of Lopez's (Lopez, *Apostle to the Conquered*, 154–62). Lopez also examines the so-called allegory of Sarah-Hagar in her article, "Visual Perspectives: Imag(in)ing the Big Pauline Picture," in *Studying Paul's Letters: Contemporary Perspectives and Methods*, ed. Joseph A. Marchal

Paul splits a territorial space like Jerusalem into two spheres: one from above and one from below. According to him, "Now Hagar stands for Mount Sinai in Arabia and corresponds to the present city of Jerusalem, because she is in slavery with her children" (Gal. 4:25). In other words, the Jerusalem from below is where Paul's opponents (Hagar) reside in slavery, whereas the Jerusalem from above "is free, and she is our mother" (4:26). In spite of the fact that Paul equates his opponents with belonging to mother Hagar, Mount Sinai, and the present Jerusalem—who generates slaves—the importance of Jerusalem is still obvious to him (Gal. 1:18-24). The Jerusalem that is above, which is free, chases the present Jerusalem that lingers in its mess, in its slavery under the law; the Jerusalem that is above—Paul's mother, mother Paul—pushes out the slave mother and her son, "for the slave woman's son will never share in the inheritance with the free woman's son" (Gal 4:30). He concludes this section with what seems very logical to him: "Therefore, brothers, we are not children of the slave woman, but of the free woman" (4:31). Paul's Jerusalem from above is invisible; it is the mythical transformation and reconfiguration of the ancestral place; it is heaven on earth, or better still, it is the desired fulfillment of the grand apocalyptic vision of a heavenly city of God (see, for example, Isa.

(Minneapolis: Fortress Press, 2012), 110–13. Her reading there is pretty much done from the same angle of her previous analysis, with one very important nuance worth quoting here at length: A "Jerusalem above" who "casts out the slave woman and her children" need not necessarily call up a picture of the safe haven for all people who wish to be liberated from empire. After all, another popular Roman image contributing to the construction of conquest as social reality is that of the winged Roman goddess Victory, who often appears as a woman "above" defeated personifications, declaring the Romans the winners of war and divine favor. Victory, as the "woman above" who appears at the conclusion of public visual narratives celebrating the "casting out" of the slaves, helps affirm the inevitability of empire, of an eternal hierarchy between those who conquer and those who are conquered. It would be outlandish to say that this image is, in effect, a depiction of Roman freedom. Victory might be rather inconvenient for those of us interested in the stability of an anti-imperial Paul, as she represents a visual option that he could appropriate, that "Jerusalem above" could very well express, and that an audience might "see" as they hear, read, or otherwise encounter Paul's rhetoric (Lopez, "Visual Perspectives," 112–13).

65:17-25; *2 Baruch* 4:2-7; *4 Ezra* 7:26; 8:52; 10:25-27; 13:36; *2 Enoch* 55:2), a new heaven and the new earth. Or is it a ghost-like city, a failed urban project with Paul as its zombie-like mayor and contractor?

In a very forceful manner, Paul tries to show that Israel's grand narrative was set in anticipation of Christ, who now establishes a new covenant. Hagar and Jerusalem from below represent the old covenant in the form of Paul's opponents, whereas Christ is Sarah, Paul, and Jerusalem from above, as well as those who adhere to Paul's message represent the new covenant (4:24).[51] For the purpose of winning the argument, Paul seems to cut off the very scriptural branches on which he sits while insulting the very nations—the idiotic Galatians (Gal. 3:1, 3)—to whom he preaches. He alleges that the only reason why his opponents are trying to compel the Galatians to circumcise is to avoid being persecuted for the crucifixion of Christ (6:12). They are, in this sense, weak and soft, as they try to avoid submitting to the deeds of violence that would then connect them to the grand drama of the violent act done to Christ on a

---

51. No wonder that "Gentile Christianity, in the name of Paul, did become arrogant, proud, and boastful against Israel." See John G. Gager, *Reinventing Paul: Israel and Gentiles in Paul's Gospel* (New York: Oxford University Press, 2000), 141. Paul, it is true, never came back in his later letters to the extreme positions he takes in Galatians. The "seed" vs. "seed*s*" argument is abandoned; the claim that those who lived under Torah are under a curse and in slavery (Gal. 3:13, 23) is off the radar; the assertion that those who belong to Hagar, his opponents, are excluded from the covenant is never referred to afterward. Instead, Paul shows real passion for his people and warns about gentile triumphalism in, for example, Rom. 11:17-24. Paul's extreme positions in Galatians, however, seem to have "provided the conceptual framework for the spiritualization of 'Israel' and the emergence of the displacement theology of the *adversus Judaeos* tradition." See Donaldson, *Paul and the Gentiles*, 306. The observation of the Boyarin brothers applies here as well: "In his authentic passion to find a place for the Gentiles in the Torah's scheme of things and the brilliance of the radically dualist and allegorical hermeneutic that he developed to accomplish this purpose, Paul had (almost against his will) sown the seeds for a Christian discourse that would completely deprive Jewish ethnic, cultural specificity of any positive value and indeed turn it into a 'curse' in the eyes of Gentile Christians." See Daniel Boyarin and Jonathan Boyarin, "Diaspora: Generation and the Ground of Jewish Identity," in *Theorizing Diaspora: A Reader*, ed. Jana Evans Braziel and Anita Mannur (Oxford: Blackwell Publishers, 2003), 87.

humiliating Roman cross. Paul is concerned with elaborating an alternative empire—one that comes with emperor Christ, who was crucified by the Romans but who is now resurrected and resides in the Jerusalem from above. The violence done by the Romans to Christ and Paul—recall that his scars are proof of him being crucified with Christ—is transferred by the apostle to his opponents, not only to his own scriptural narrative, but also to his children, the Galatians. Nowhere in Galatians do we find Paul presenting any clear resisting power against the hegemonic power of the Romans. Instead, as an itinerant diasporic figure with localized communities of Christ believers within the Roman Empire, he imitates the rhetorical strategies of the empire and imagines an otherworldly Jerusalem dislocating the earthly one. There is a tension in the text between acting like the Romans and siding with the victims of violence in order to denounce the ugly head of violence that, in fact, dehumanizes both the aggressor and the victim.

In this sense, Frantz Fanon's analysis of the black psyche in a white world might illuminate Paul's stance vis-à-vis the Roman Empire, at least with what we can infer from our reading of Galatians. Fanon distinguishes two types of colonial subjects, namely those who want to become like the colonizer, and those who want to find their "true identities" with reference to a certain mythical past. Fanon shows that the images construed by the colonized (either rising from a spirit of vengeance or supposedly informed by a certain cosmic myth) are largely "existential deviations" founded on the colonizer's construction of the colonial subject. For Fanon, "what is often called the black soul is a white's man artefact."[52] In other words, the colonized subject is trapped by the discourse of the empire. What can, on the surface, represent a liberating discourse is, in fact, enslavement

---

52. See Frantz Fanon, *Black Skin, White Masks* (New York: Grove Press, 1967), 16.

in the very game of the power. Fanon does not envisage any better position for the colonizer either. For him, the colonizer is also caught up in an enslaving reality. Fanon's project is to help both the black and the white to be freed from any alienation that prevents them from being fully human. For Fanon, the effects of colonialism can be devastating, socially and psychologically. In his words, "Face à l'arrangement colonial le colonisé se trouve dans un état de tension permanente. Le monde du colon est un monde hostile, qui rejette, mais dans le même temps c'est un monde qui fait envie. Le colonisé est toujours sur le qui-vive. . . . Il est dominé . . . infériorisé. Le colonisé est un persécuté qui rêve en permanence de devenir persécuteur."[53] Thus, according to the psychologist from Martinique, the colonial subject is always caught up in a relation of tension, of negotiating, of mimicking and translating his or her cultural identities in a sociopolitical culture that can be cruel, degrading, and in perpetual flux. Paul, in Galatians, tries to negotiate his grand theological vision of a cosmic Christ. He places Jerusalem from above as a new center of operation, the capital of an alternative empire, and an otherworldly reality that comes down with its grace and peace, while kicking away whoever opposes his gospel. Paul, in Galatians, deploys the linguistics and ideological arsenal of the empire as he envisions new creation communities and new humanity under Christ.[54] Nonetheless, he purports to do so by redefining an old one and by referring to a mythical past, albeit one that is modified, if not simply subverted and violated. Paul negotiates his grand theological vision of a cosmic Christ in order to displace any opposition he might face. Thus, "the human nomos becomes a divine cosmos, or at

53. Fanon, *Les Damnés de la Terre* (Paris: Librairie François Maspero, 1961, 1970), 18–19.
54. For situating Paul squarely *within* the wider Roman culture, see James A. Harrill, *Paul the Apostle: His Life and Legacy in Their Roman Context* (Cambridge: Cambridge University Press, 2012). Harrill rightly underlines, "Matters are much more complicated . . . than simply asking whether Paul was for or against Roman imperialism" (80).

any rate a reality that derives its meanings from beyond the human sphere."[55] The new emperor he proposes comes down from his place to get rid of anyone belonging to the realm of Jerusalem from below who still wants to keep Paul's converts in their grip. But the new emperor Paul introduces does not seem to be that much different from the emperor of Rome, at least in the way his grace and peace is announced.[56] The herald of Christ's gospel is a gender-troubled

---

55. Peter L. Berger, *The Sacred Canopy: Elements of a Sociological Theory of Religion* (New York: Anchor Books, [1967] 1990), 89.

56. The new emperor (Christ) is able to subject everything to himself since, according to Phil. 3:20 "our state and constitutive government is in heaven." I use here Richard S. Ascough's excellent translation. See Richard S. Ascough, *Paul's Macedonian Associations: The Social Context of Philippians and 1 Thessalonians,* WUNT 2:161 (Tübingen: Mohr Siebeck, 2003), 148. From this, we could infer that Paul may be imagining heaven's diasporic colony readying itself to occupy soon "this world," where Rome and other ancient associations establish their πολίτευμα. In this sense, Paul invites the Philippian Christ believers to become fictional diaspora figures by entering with him into a space where "home" is not a geographical entity imagined as fixed with clear boundaries, but an imagined and abstract space located in heaven. I am trying to build on Ascough's statement: "In Phil 3:20, Paul contrasts the Christian πολίτευμα, which is in heaven, with both the Roman πολίτευμα, which is in Rome, and, more immediately, the voluntary associations' πολίτευμα, which is in 'this world' (that is, it resides within the local group)." See ibid., 149. Joseph A. Marchal goes further in his analysis of Phil. 3:20 by indicating certain rhetoric of safety and destruction at play. In his words, "The contrast in fates through the safety/destruction dissociation is connected here with the political terminology of a group (*politeuma*), just as it was in the previous use of the related term (*politeuesthe*, 1:27–28)." See Joseph A. Marchal, *Hierarchy, Unity, and Imitation: A Feminist Rhetorical Analysis of Power Dynamics in Paul's Letter to the Philippians* (Atlanta: Society of Biblical Literature, 2006), 146n99. Thus Paul, along with the Phillipians, eagerly awaits a savior (ἐξ οὗ καὶ ἀπεκδεχόμεθα σωτῆρα, Phil. 3:20) from that mythic place located outside the sphere of here. The heavenly awaited hero, who is going to have everything subjected to his heroic power (ὑποτάξαι αὐτῷ τὰ πάντα), will transform their lowly bodies into glorious bodies similar to his (ὃς μετασχηματίσει τὸ σῶμα τῆς ταπεινώσεως ἡμῶν σύμμορφον τῷ σώματι τῆς δόξης αὐτοῦ κατὰ τὴν ἐνέργειαν τοῦ δύνασθαι αὐτόν, Phil. 3:21). The body-building imagery here is staggering, especially evident in the description of how the strong, "masculine" body of the heavenly hero interacts with the humble, "feminine" bodies of the Christ believers with the view to transform their lowly bodies into glorious, military ones that conform to the image of the new emperor. This imagery does not seem to be far away from Roman imperial social relations, where powerful Roman bodies are displayed as victorious over the weak, lowly, humble, female bodies of those conquered. Here the image seems to be suggesting that those Christ believers in Philippi, who are signified as conquered lowly bodies within the Roman categorization, will become the conquerors under a new and heavenly emperor ready to exercise "masculine" power to go and conquer with the company of the transformed and glorious bodies of heaven's diasporic subjects. In other words, the lived, messy, contested space, rife with imperial, racial, ethnic, religious, and economic conflicts of the Roman colony Philippi—including specifically Paul's imagined heaven's colony—is to be replaced by heaven

messenger, a diasporic messenger who clearly struggles to maintain his own cool.

Paul intimates that the Galatians have done him no wrong (Gal. 4:12). He reminded them of how they first met when he was forced to pass through Galatia on his way to another destination because of a weakness or disease of the flesh (ἀσθένειαν τῆς σαρκὸς) (Gal. 4:13). He reflects on the fact that they did not reject him because of the social stigma attached to his physical disability (4:14),[57] but that they would rather have done anything for him, even tearing out their own eyes to give to him if they could have done so (4:15). Joseph A. Marchal perceptively indicates that "these could be communities where weakness, receptivity, and/or fleshiness are recognized as 'feminine' but not necessarily inferior; or, alternately, where these matters matter less or materialize differently."[58] Paul invokes pathos by asking them if he has become their enemy by telling them the truth (4:16), and he shows that he does not want to lose them. According to Paul, what the others want "is to alienate you from us" (4:17). Paul seems to have realized that his earlier discourse was violent: "How I wish I could be with you now to *change my tone*

above with its own power projected to interrupt and invade the space below by rearranging bodies and by reimagining places and authority. The best, and very playful, work I know in connection to body building within the discipline of biblical studies is Stephen D. Moore, *God's Beauty Parlor: And Other Queer Spaces in and around the Bible*, Contraversions (Stanford: Stanford University Press, 2001). For more on the importance of space in interpreting Paul's letter to the Philippians, see Laura S. Nasrallah, "Spatial Perspectives: Space and Archaeology in Roman Philippi," in Marchal, *Studying Paul's Letters*, 53–74.

57. On Paul's disability, see Martin Albl, "'For Whenever I Am Weak, Then I Am Strong': Disability in Paul's Epistles," in *This Abled Body: Rethinking Disabilities in Biblical Studies*, ed. Hector Avalos, Sarah J. Melcher, and Jeremy Schipper (Atlanta: Society of Biblical Literature, 2007), 145–58. According to Albl, "In accepting Paul's gospel of the crucified Christ, the Galatians also accepted a positive interpretation of his disability. This disability was no longer an occasion to reject Paul, but rather an invitation to recognize the unity between the disabled Paul and the divine Christ—a unity effected by the very disability itself (sharing Christ's atoning death). The disability is thus interpreted not within the context of the demonic, but in the context of the divine" (ibid., 154).

58. See Joseph A. Marchal, "Queer Approaches: Improper Relations with Pauline Letters," in Marchal, *Studying Paul's Letters*, 223.

(ἀλλάξαι τὴν φωνήν μου), because I am perplexed about you!"
(4:20). So saying, he justifies his brutal tone on the basis that he
was perplexed that he might lose them to another group. Paul lost
his self-control and became angry; he showed his masculinity by
using harsh invective in order to (re)gain his feminine prize. But
in the middle of the letter, Paul switches his tone from that of the
forceful military penetrator who threatens to a concerned mother or
brother who seems to realize that he has gone too far. These are
his children in the faith, after all; his message is one of peace and
grace coming from God. Paul's tone, as he approaches the end of
the letter, becomes softer, even conciliatory. He relegates the issue of
circumcision to indifference, "for in Christ Jesus neither circumcision
nor uncircumcision has any value. The only thing that counts is
faith expressing itself, working through love" (5:6). Also, as he writes
in 6:15, "neither circumcision nor uncircumcision means anything;
what counts is a new creation." Gone is the discourse cursing anyone
who relies upon and observes the law (1:8, 9; 3:10); due penalty is
still reserved for his opponents (5:10); but no longer does Paul try to
humiliate his readers by publicly shaming them. Now, the emphasis
is on love and on supporting one another (6:2, 10).

Paul seems to realize that the best way to get his arguments across
is not to coerce but to persuade the Galatians by showing them what
they should do "for their own good." His softer tone might have
constituted a way to salvage the situation by rendering his arguments
more palatable in their ears. By cajoling them to do what he still
wants them to do, Paul's more sophisticated rhetoric throughout the
second half of the letter might be considered to be even deadlier. Paul,
however, might genuinely have realized in the middle of the letter
that he was wrong, that he was still using the rhetorical strategies and
tactics of masculinity, as dictated by his immediate environment. He
may have realized that he too was hurt, that he too was a victim of the

rhetoric of violence, and that it was not proper for him to bring God's grace and peace to the Galatians (1:3) through his language of war.[59] At the end of the letter, Paul admits to his frailty and vulnerability by inviting the Galatians to "see what large letters I use as I write to you with my own hand!" (6:11). Or, could it be that he wrote with large letters to assert, once again, his masculine apostolic authority (1:1) and through his motherly, yet controlling hands to declare, "Pay attention: this is your mother in the gospel speaking!"[60]

As 5:4, 12 and 6:17 show, Paul is "still very much entangled in the coils of violence."[61] He does not seem able to abandon completely the binary of male/female, penetrator/penetrated. He does not seem able to have a discourse that is free from manipulation, bitter sarcasm (5:12), and ugly pun (5:4), as he sees any opposition to him as being, ultimately, against Christ. Also, because his discourse is so imbued with bullying, even his most interesting insights with regard to power and his beautiful exhortation to "carry one another's burdens" (6:2) sound hypocritical. Paul's peace and mercy extends "to all who follow this rule" (6:16); as he explains, what matters is not the issue of circumcision versus no circumcision, but the new creation. Further, he does not want anyone to cause him any trouble or to bother him—his gender is troubled enough!—for "I bear on my body the marks (τὰ στίγματα) of Jesus" (6:17).[62] That is to say, "Despite the

59. I am here inspired by Calvin Roetzel's article "The Language of War (2 Cor. 10:1–6) and the Language of Weakness (2 Cor. 11:21b-13:10)," in *Violence, Scripture and Textual Practice in Early Judaism and Christianity*, ed. Ra'anan S. Boustan, Alex P. Jassen, and Calvin J. Roetzel (Boston: Brill, 2010), especially pgs. 95–96.

60. See Don Garlington, *An Exposition of Galatians: A Reading from the New Perspective*, 3rd ed. (Eugene, OR: Wipf and Stock, 2007). My analysis of the book as a whole is drastically different from his, but his interpretation of 6:11 is what inspires my thinking here.

61. Gager and Gibson, "Violent Acts and Violent Language," 16.

62. See Virginia Burrus, "Macrina's Tattoo," in *The Cultural Turn in Late Ancient Studies: Gender, Asceticism, and Historiography*, ed. Dale B. Martin and Patricia C. Miller (Durham, NC: Duke University Press, 2005). For Burrus, "the point is not only that such rhetoric symbolically inverts relations of power, but also that itself becomes, scarlike, a dense site—a deep surface—of complex and layered meaning, fusing (without quite confusing) rebellion and surrender,

reader's polite protests, Paul is stripping off his shirt once again as he says this, exposing the map of his missionary journeys that has been cut into his back."[63] He therefore justifies his violent discourse because of the violence done to him.

All in all, Paul's discourse stands embedded within the powerful dynamics of the empire: to conquer, to capture, to dominate, to silence, to shame, and to rape. But to understand Paul as solely a rapist of the nations would be clearly to misunderstand him. He was neither a "chauvinist nor a liberationist,"[64] neither a demon nor an angel,[65] but, simply something in between, a flexible hybrid (wo)man among the nations, a Diaspora Jew with "many conflicting convictions"[66] alongside his flashes of great insight with regard to the human condition, stemming from the complexity of power and social behaviours.[67]

Paul's Politics of Identity

Paul goes out to the defeated nations to offer them a rearticulated myth of Abraham's blessings when, from the point of view of the nations, Abraham could well be perceived as a conqueror by the

---

nobility and degradation, flesh and spirit, worldly and holy power. When '*their* mark' is read as '*God's* mark,' it may also be reclaimed as '*my* mark'—a self-willed inscription, even a defiant self-writing, that nonetheless necessarily retains an ambivalent connection to submission, transgression, and shame." Ibid., 105 (emphasis in original).

63. See Stephen D. Moore, "The Divine Butcher," 165.

64. Calvin Roetzel, *The Letters of Paul: Conversations in Context*, 5th ed. (Louisville: Westminster John Knox, 2009), 192.

65. I just cannot help thinking about Blaise Pascal's famous *Pensées* 358: "L'homme n'est ni ange ni bête, et le malheur veut que qui veut faire l'ange fait la bête."

66. See Heikki Räisänen, "A Controversial Jew and his Conflicting Convictions," in *Redefining First-Century Jewish and Christian Identities*,ed. Duo Herschel and Chancey Tatum (Notre Dame, IN: University of Notre Dame Press, 2008), 326.

67. To appreciate the complexity of Paul's gendered picture, see Penner and Vander Stichele, "Unveiling Paul." For Penner and Vander Stichele, "There is no area 'outside' of the realm of the Greco-Roman gendered cultural context in Paul; it is the cultural mode of discourse that Paul affirms, which is not to say that it is a 'patriarchal' or 'male' framework in toto, or that 'egalitarian' notions are in principle excluded. The picture is more complex than that" (235).

indigenous inhabitants of Canaan, who lost their land so that Yahweh's alleged promises to Abraham could be accomplished. The perception could also be directed toward Abraham's tribal deity. What is in Genesis is perhaps a reworking of the nomadic narratives of Abraham by later editors of the text, at a time when there were more urban settlements and the practices of colonization and imperialism more possible.[68] Here, one may refer to Musa Dube's trenchant observation: "If imperialism means 'to think about distant places, to colonize them, to depopulate them,' then at the core of ancient Israel's foundational story is an imperialist ideology, which operates under the claims of chosenness."[69] Paul now proposes the mythical grand narrative of the alleged conqueror, Abraham, to the defeated nations under Rome. Paul imaginatively constructs the fate of the nations by utilizing them to gain acceptance from his kinsmen. More explicitly, Paul uses his mission to the gentiles, and the success of his missionary endeavors, to gain acceptance from his people that the end time is indeed near because of the gathering of the nations into Israel's fold.[70]

What Paul seems to be doing among the defeated nations is enticing them to deny their past—although he would not want them to become Jews[71]—their culture and modes of being in the world, in order for them to be accepted by the Jewish god, now reoriented around the figure of Jesus, who becomes the new portal by which one enters this new identity in God. Paul proposes a "Christ myth" similar

---

68. See John V. Seters, *Abraham in History and Tradition* (New Haven: Yale University Press, 1975).
69. See Musa W. Dube, *Postcolonial Feminist Interpretation of the Bible* (St. Louis: Chalice, 2000), 17–18.
70. We have seen in the previous chapter how Paul still struggles to convince the leaders of his socioreligious community in the Diaspora to legitimate him, although he claims he does not look for human approval (Gal. 1:10).
71. Even though Paul is interested in his gentiles, he is against them trying to becoming Jews, while he places them within an Abrahamic genealogy; Paul strikes as one who says to the non-Jews: "Come . . . come closer. . . . No. Too close!"

to the national myths that Abraham and his descendants hold; neither tolerates alternative discourses. As Burton L. Mack has mentioned,

> Everything hinges on the Abraham-Christ connection. This is a marvelous example of myth-making strategy, seeking a pristine point of contact with a foundational moment of the past and making a connection that brackets all the intervening and recent histories of failure to achieve that ideal. In order to make his case, however, Paul had to press both the logic of the Christ myth and the plain sense of the Abraham stories much too far.[72]

The Other is constructed in such a way that she can be embraced and captured in order to serve as fitting illustration of particular theologies and discourses of identity. The genealogical construct that places Abraham as the father of all the nations aims to set the nations as belonging, not to the Roman Empire, but to Israel and to Israel's narrative. Paul reformats Israel's story to fit his grand theological vision of a new humanity, a new empire that is attached to, and is under, Christ. Thus, "Paul constructs a myth of collective identity for his gentiles: they can trace their beginnings not only to their baptism into Christ but also to their ancestor, Abraham."[73]

Paul refers to the Galatians as children of Abraham without any second thought about how he is thus erasing other ethnic, cultural, and religious identities. Paul's whole discourse is situated within a distinct Judeo-"Christian" framework that does not seem to care if the nations conquered by Rome may have any other understanding about how to approach God. Paul thus pacifies a bloody and very complicated relationship between Rome and its colonized subjects on the one hand and, and on the other, between the nations and

---

72. See Burton L. Mack, *Who Wrote the New Testament? The Making of the Christian Myth* (San Francisco: Harper, 1995), 118.

73. Denise K. Buell and Caroline J. Hodge, "The Politics of Interpretation: The Rhetoric of Race and Ethnicity in Paul," *JBL* 123, no. 2 (2004): 246. See also Caroline J. Hodge, *If Sons, Then Heirs: A Study of Kinship and Ethnicity on the Letters of Paul* (Oxford: Oxford University Press, 2007).

himself, the male diasporic Jew, migrant artisan, and preacher who is constantly navigating between his history, ancestral myths, social and religious ideals, and communities he has founded for the sake of theological gains. The apocalyptic myth that Paul inhabited, and on which he improvised, has major implications for the understanding of power in the unfinished world that this cosmic vision constructed. Paul makes a shift from the reality of displaced bodies—including his own—to controlling the bodies under his own authority with respect to satisfying the order of things under the Roman imperial order.

Paul is an itinerant diaspora figure whose identities in his interrelations with the Galatians are performatively constituted. He is indeed among the defeated nations by portraying himself as one who is also defeated; his body bears the marks of the empire and his audience is composed of defeated peoples. He, however, seems to have wanted to establish a new creation within a new realm and with a new lordship not that dissimilar to the one portrayed by Rome. Paul presents himself as one called by Israel's God to all the nations in order to present to them a new identity and a new politics of identity. For Paul, it is not about what the other nations are, but what he thinks they need; it is not about the fact that the nations are conquered by Rome, but that the nations are in need of new identities under a new lordship, that of Christ. Indeed, as Leif E. Vaage concludes, "This is finally what (Gentile) salvation means for Paul: adoption into the *familia* of the divine (Jewish) world monarch."[74] Paul proposes a more appealing myth to replace an old and established one. He does so by building on Israel's past mythical narratives to buttress his arguments and make the nations surrender to a new power, albeit a power that comes in the form of one crucified by the reigning power of

---

74. "Why Christianity Succeeded (in) the Roman Empire," in *Religious Rivalries in the Early Roman Empire and the Rise of Christianity*, ed. Leif E. Vaage, Studies in Christianity and Judaism/Études sur le christianisme et le judaïsme (Waterloo, ON: Wilfrid Laurier University Press, 2006), 270.

Rome. Paul seems to be imagining an alternative world, which is still defined by the old genealogical boundaries of insiders and outsiders, where "all non-Jews are thus flattened into a sameness, regardless of their self-constructed ethnicity, for no other reason than that they are different from insiders, the Jews."[75] Consequently, "in dividing humanity into Jews and non-Jews, he [Paul] subscribes to a *myth of otherness* to reinscribe the 'us'-versus-'them' mentality prevalent among some of his compatriots. In calling all Gentiles 'Greeks,' he is at the same time subscribing to a *myth of sameness*, in order to reinforce the Jewish-Gentile distinction."[76]

To Paul, as to the Romans, the nations exist to satisfy certain ideological and mythical spaces. For the Romans, the nations are there to be conquered; for Paul, they exist to be saved from their way of life in order to enter into a specific mode of being. Paul's idealistic but violent discourse manufactures, through a myth of innocence, a new hegemony among the nations by calling them to come under the lordship of a new emperor. His former expression of Judaism, in which he excessively persecuted the burgeoning Jewish sect of Christ's followers, is now replaced by becoming part of the movement he once tried to destroy and by advocating a radically altered version of his Jewishness to the scattered peoples of the nations. Paul imagines his recalibrated ethnic identity on top of any other identities; he metaphorically penetrates the nations while giving the impression of being in the trenches with them under Rome. He represents himself as an arch-soldier divinely ordained by the general, the master, the new emperor, Christ, to conquer the

75. See Sze-kar Wan, "'To the Jew First and Also to the Greek': Reading Romans as Ethnic Construction," in *Prejudice and Christian Beginnings: Investigating Race, Gender, and Ethnicity in Early Christian Studies*, ed. Laura Nasrallah and Elisabeth S. Fiorenza (Minneapolis: Fortress Press, 2009), 145.

76. See Sze-kar Wan, "Collection for the Saints as Anticolonial Act: Implications of Paul's Ethnic Reconstruction," in *Paul and Politics: Ekklesia, Israel, Imperium, Interpretation*, ed. Richard A. Horsley (Harrisburg, PA: Trinity Press International), 204 (emphasis in original).

nations. Even if one could argue that Paul was somewhat different, and to some extent, less of a violent man after his vision of a risen Christ than he previously was, one surely detects that there are vestiges of violence in Paul's language and attitudes toward those who are ethnically other.[77] In other words, Paul might have well rejected the model of violence he had formerly embraced, but he has not been able to move completely away from the rhetoric of violence. Paul, instead of presenting an alternative to the ideology and power structure of Rome, merely reproduces with Christ, as the mirror image of the Roman Empire with its imperial aims of domination, the relationship that was portrayed as natural by the Romans: being on top of the nations.[78]

As a result, by going to the nations Paul participates in a master narrative that portrays Israel as the nation that possesses, par excellence, the monopoly on the divine, monopolizing the true way of God in contradistinction to all other nations, which are envisioned to be in darkness. Paul participates in the hegemonic discourse of understanding himself to be a prophet like Jeremiah of old who goes out to proclaim "light" to the nations that reside in "darkness," and who gathers Israel back to Israel's God. What he dreamed of was the coming of the nations to the God of Israel, for the sake of the Jews, by ascribing a privileged status to his pedigree as a Jew because of his group's unique covenant with God. Though this view does not preclude the possibility that God does or may have a relationship with other peoples, it still maintains the uniqueness of one group over and above any other ethnic entities. In this sense, this kind of religious vision sees the nations coming under the banner of

---

77. See Calvin J. Roetzel's article, "The Language of War." Note also that in Rom. 15:19, Paul's conception of the world is quite Roman, a flattened oval, compressed on the north and south.
78. To explore how the image of Christ is patterned on the Roman emperor in Galatians, see Justin K. Hardin, *Galatians and the Imperial Cult: A Critical Analysis of the First-Century Social Context of Paul's Letter*, WUNT 2.237 (Tübingen: Mohr Siebeck, 2008).

Israel's deity as they embrace the faith and religion of Israel, which in Paul's case, is Israel's faith, hope, and narrative, modified and recalibrated around Christ.[79] In this framework, there is uniformity to and acknowledgment of what Israel, Paul, and Christ have to offer. The position of Israel, Paul, and Christ is that of one group with its exclusive mentality and a celebrated hero, enjoying the monopoly on matters of faith. The vision Paul proposes mirrors other myths of subjugation with its possibility—later confirmed— of becoming a tool of domination and eradicating other groups that could be perceived as "the enemy." Paul's vision is centered on Christ; it is a dream viewed as sufficient unto itself and in no need of understanding the identities of others, since Paul thought that he had the god of his fathers by his side in his reconfigured ethnic and religious identity in regard to the other nations.

According to Wan, "Given the social dynamics of the Galatians community, therefore, it seems best to see in the formulation 'in Christ there is no Jew or Greek' an attempt to erase the *power differential* in the new discourse."[80] In this sense, what Paul is calling and arguing for in the Galatians community "is for each cultural entity to give up its claims to power—as Boyarin suggests—in the creation of this new people, *without*, however, giving up its cultural specificities."[81] Lopez's argument goes in the same direction:

In the new mode of relationships among the defeated, the bodies on the bottom of a Romans/nations hierarchy should cease their perpetuation of divisions between one another and understand that there are larger dynamics of violence and persecution structuring their world. They

79. I appreciate Donaldson's caution that "Paul's statements about the Gentile mission stubbornly resist any attempt to force them into the Procrustean bed of eschatological pilgrimage patterns of thought." Donaldson, *Paul and the Gentiles*, 194.
80. Sze-Kar Wan, "Does Diaspora Identity Imply Some Sort of Universality? An Asian-American Reading of Galatians," in *Interpreting Beyond Borders*, ed. Fernando F. Segovia (Sheffield: Sheffield Academic, 2000), 126.
81. Ibid.

might realize that there are no divisions between them, as persecuted minority groups, that matter. . . . Paul brings the possibility of reconciliation *toward* the nations at the end of the earth, rather than imploring them to return to the geographic locality of a new Jerusalem *from* those same ends. He goes *out* to the frontiers to bring the news of an alternative central capital to the one they currently serve.[82]

Paul effectively seems to be working toward destabilizing and reworking identities in these communities. The apostle, who is himself not immune from the reality of violence (Gal. 6:17), would have every reason to align his theological visions with something other than the rhetoric and brutality of the Roman imperial order. The tension contained in Paul's treatment of the nations allows one to consider the possibility that by declaring in Galatians that "you are one in Christ Jesus" (Gal. 3:28), his purpose could well be to create alternative ways of being and relating to other cultural groups, as each one fully acknowledges the existence of the other "without each one forcing its own claims on the others."[83] Paul may well have had as his idealized goal to form new creation communities among the nations where he operates as a diasporic figure, in order to present an alternative vision in which justice would finally triumph; and that vision would be geared toward challenging other visions of world empire. In this framework, God would, through Paul's preaching among the nations, create alternative communities, even subversive ones, with countercultural values and concerns within a Roman context of marginalization and infighting among the various ethnic groups. But, as I pointed out previously, Paul does not seem able to detach himself completely from the seduction of violence. What he seems to be saying implicitly to the Galatians is "to serve one another in love" (Gal. 5:13), but to resist as strongly as possible

---

82. Lopez, *Apostle to the Conquered*, 150. Emphasis in original.
83. Sze-Kar Wan, "Does Diaspora Identity Imply Some Sort of Universality?" 126–27.

or to perform as virile males ought to, by erecting your phallic power against anyone besides me, Christ, God, or the powerful Roman authorities in order to shame publicly whoever does not accept and stand up for our gospel. Also, "love your neighbor as yourself," since the whole law is summed up in this single command (Gal. 5:14), but do not yoke yourselves as slaves to the law; stop being violent against one another, you violent and brainless Galatians (playfully adapting 5:15 and 3:1)! Otherwise, I will show you the full measure of my virility, my violence, in order to birth you, my dear brothers, as "docile bodies"[84] ready to be under my motherly control and to participate (in the sense of being crucified) as real men, in the violence done to Christ.

Conclusion

In this chapter, I have continued to employ the interpretive model adopted in this study by reading another issue in Pauline scholarship—Paul's relationship with the non-Jews, specifically his dealings with the Galatians—by paying close attention to Paul's diasporic posture. The important aspects of gender construction and performance of identity were contextualized in order to move within the complicated life of a diasporic subject such as Paul who tried to reconcile socioreligious ideals with social realities, and who was not always successful negotiating these different poles. The gendered Roman rhetoric that he used, and the ways in which he used the Scriptures of his tradition to negotiate his identities, enable us to understand the struggles he experienced to control his anger in his relationships with the Galatians and those he viewed as his opponents. He is a diasporic figure among the conquered peoples of Rome, but he is not so much outside the imperial discourse as he constructs

---

84. Michel Foucault, *Discipline and Punish: The Birth of the Prison*, trans. Alan Sheridan (New York: Vintage, 1977), 135–69.

his message of the Lord Christ with the rhetoric of the imperial propaganda of Lord Caesar. Such linguistic borrowing could be seen as standing against the power in place, or indicate that Paul is imagining and signifying a new world order. This new world order is the new humanity shaped in and around Christ for the purpose of hope and appeasement—I say appeasement here because without Paul's language of new creation or starting all over again, certain members of Paul's own communities could be tempted into desperate revolt against the imperial authority. But, curiously, this language of new world order from Paul would become, in time, the language of the power. Paul, in assimilating the language of the imperial power, would give a Christian rhetoric to support the policies of subsequent empires (Christian or otherwise) that would deprive alternative discourses of any positive value. His rhetoric of power has the imperial baggage—or should I say stamp—that renders it dangerous and devastating in the hands of powers, while being debilitating for the very poor and marginal communities he had hoped to help.[85] Paul may have been critical of the Roman imperial order, and his language may reflect a certain rhetoric of liberation, but by borrowing from the linguistic arsenal of the power in command, he remains dependent upon Rome's rhetorical strategies as he transfers the imperial ideology from one imperial power to another.[86] Paul, thus, in his diasporic social and political location

85. On this, see Averil Cameron, *Christianity and the Rhetoric of Empire: The Development of Christian Discourse* (Berkeley: University of California Press, 1991). Her brilliant analysis shows that the highly exclusivist message of the Christians was channeled through very sophisticated rhetoric imbued with the familiar themes and rhetorical techniques of Greco-Roman culture that eventually led to the totalitarian state of late antiquity.
86. A similar conclusion can be found in Sze-kar Wan, "'To the Jew First and Also to the Greek,'"146; Stephen Moore, *Empire and Apocalypse: Postcolonialism and the New Testament*, The Bible in the Modern World 12 (Sheffield: Sheffield Phoenix, 2006), 31. Leif E. Vaage states something similar with regards to the New Testament corpus: "Whatever transcendent truth the different writings of the New Testament might genuinely aim to project, the defining language of their vision remains rooted in the conventional rhetoric of Roman hegemony." See "Why Christianity Succeeded (in) the Roman Empire," 257. For a different understanding

mimics the master's strategies of intimidation to shame his opponents publicly with the view to promulgating his particular theological views. Paul envisages a cycle of imperial power and a counter emperor in his reappropriated Jewish myth making. Jesus is the new emperor against whom everybody else is measured; those in Christ—and following Paul's theological conclusions—are envisioned as participating in the new nation of God by which God's glorious future with the nations is achieved. Israel's religious claims of exclusivity toward the nations is embraced and celebrated by the diasporic figure Paul, around a constructed myth of being in Christ and through certain mythic narratives.

of the linguistic usage of Paul see, for example, Kathy Ehrensperger, "Speaking Greek under Rome: Paul, the Power of Language," *Neotestamentica* 46, no. 1 (2012): 10–31.

5

Paul's Travels as Transcultural Narratives: The Collection Project

Diaspora is different from travel (though it works through travel practices) in that it is not temporary. It involves dwelling, maintaining communities, having collective homes away from home (and in this it is different from exile, with its frequently individualist focus).
—James Clifford[1]

Μόνον τῶν πτωχῶν ἵνα μνημονεύωμεν, ὃ καὶ ἐσπούδασα αὐτὸ τοῦτο ποιῆσαι
—Gal. 2:10

The focus of this chapter is to revisit another difficult issue in Pauline scholarship, namely, the collection project. It is my contention that the various interpretations of Paul's collection have not paid sufficient attention to how the concepts of *home* and *homeland*, as well as Paul's

---

1. *Routes: Travel and Translation in the Late Twentieth Century* (Cambridge: Harvard University Press, 1997), 251. The caveat from James Clifford is important to note, as it clarifies different points related to the methodology adopted in this study.

acute sense of geographical space, might inform our understanding of his willingness to risk his life to move around to serve those inhabiting the ancestral "home." Since diaspora studies is keenly concerned with the dynamics of movements, it is well poised to shed new light on the connections between Paul's diasporic social locations and his attempt to restore and serve those inhabiting Jerusalem—especially those adherents sharing with him a bond in the resurrected Christ (Rom. 15:25; 26, 31; 1 Cor. 16:3).[2] Another generative insight from diaspora studies in this chapter is how the ancestral homeland is reappropriated and reimagined by the diasporic figure Paul in the issue of the collection. With the help of diaspora studies analysis I will demonstrate how Paul, as a member of one ethnic diaspora, is preoccupied to help Christ followers of his ethnic group located in his ancestral homeland, and how he goes about engaging other ethnicities to participate in his financial relief project. For Paul, Jerusalem still maintains a very important place in his reimagination, and it is reappropriated to serve his rhetoric of new creation (Gal. 4:25-26). Thus what is gained from using the tools and insight of diaspora studies in the context of Paul's collection project is the capacity to reread this issue from the perspective of social realities rather than solely from theological preoccupations, although theology cannot be neglected entirely. I will show at the end of the chapter how theology can still be engaged fruitfully, while not being too preoccupied by it.

I argue in this chapter that the collection project (mentioned in Gal. 2:10; 1 Cor. 16:1-4; 2 Cor. 8–9; Rom. 15:25-28) is at the heart of Paul's diaspora politics of a commitment to the restoration of and

2. Recall Robin Cohen's observation that one of the common traits present in diaspora subjects and diasporic communities is "the idealization of the real or putative ancestral home and a collective commitment to its maintenance, restoration, safety and prosperity, even to its creation." Cohen, *Global Diasporas: An Introduction*, 2nd ed. (Seattle: University of Washington Press, [1997] 2008), 106.

service to those inhabiting the ancestral "home," especially the poor invested in the resurrected Christ in a similar way as he is. I will begin by situating Paul as a diasporic figure through his travel practices; then the question of why Paul was so preoccupied with travelling for the collection project will be tackled in conversation with some major Pauline interpreters reflecting on the subject, before launching into the significance of why he was so eager to raise funds for the poor in Jerusalem through the lens of the concepts of *home*, of *time*, and *space*.[3]

Paul and Travel

The question of why Paul travelled and how his trips were funded has only recently been explored in ways that are not obscured by apologetic concerns.[4] The old romanticizing view of Paul as a formidable and ambitious traveler around the Mediterranean in the first century[5] is being challenged (replaced?) by a more mundane

---

3. Bruce W. Longenecker has recently argued that the best way to interpret Gal. 2:10 is in a generic way and not specifically with reference to the poor in Jerusalem. This interpretation is not shared here. See Bruce W. Longenecker, *Remember the Poor: Paul, Poverty, and the Greco-Roman World* (Grand Rapids: Eerdmans, 2010).

4. See especially Ryan Schellenberg, "'Danger in the Wilderness, Danger at Sea': Paul and Perils of Travel," in *Travel and Religion in Antiquity*, ed. Philip A. Harland, Studies in Christianity and Judaism, vol. 21 (Waterloo, ON: Wilfrid Laurier University Press, 2011), 141–61. Schellenberg's article develops Terence L. Donaldson's emphasis on contingencies of social "gritty realities" in determining the "geographical shape" of Paul's movements. See Donaldson, "The Field God Has Assigned: Geography and Mission in Paul," in *Religious Rivalries in the Early Roman Empire and the Rise of Christianity*, ed. Lief E. Vaage, Studies in Christianity and Judaism/Études sur le christianisme et le judaïsme(Waterloo, ON: Wilfrid Laurier University Press, 2006). See also the recent monograph by Timothy Luckritz Marquis, *Transient Apostle: Paul, Travel, and the Rhetoric of Empire*, Synkrisis (New Haven: Yale University Press, 2013). Marquis's study investigates how Paul signifies his apostolic role from that of a traveling figure with particular focus on 2 Corinthians 1–9.

5. See William Ramsay, *St. Paul the Traveller and Roman Citizen* (London: Hodder and Stoughton, 1896). Ramsay's work, as noticed by Robert Paul Seesengood has had a significant influence on many scholars with a more evangelical bent. Seesengood points out that "Ramsay's fingerprints remain indelibly stained onto the pages of F. F. Bruce's *Paul: Apostle of the Heart Set Free* (Grand Rapids: Eerdmans, 1977), and his influence on such evangelical Pauline scholars as Ben Witherington III is apparent. Indeed, Ramsay's *St Paul* was edited by Mark Wilson

view of Paul's movements: he traveled to major cities as an artisan in search of economic opportunities and not as an active missionary with clear missionary strategies.[6] Paul, the hero in Acts, undertakes his extended journeys (Acts 16:6-12; 20:13-16; 21:1-3; 27–28; 18:11-13) as an almost unscathed superhero in control of the times and circumstances (Acts 17:16-33; 27:27-44). Luke's hero manages, even as a prisoner, to have a composure that impresses Roman governors (Felix, Festus—"Paul, your great learning is driving you insane!" in 26:24—and Agrippa, Acts 24–25) and local authorities (13:7; 28:7-10). The hero of Acts is a Roman citizen (22:26)[7] who does not really have many difficulties with the Roman authorities, but has more problems with his fellow Judeans (13:50-51; 17:5-9;

and re-released as *Paul: The Traveler and Roman Citizen* by the evangelical press Kregel in 2001." See Seesengood, "Wrestling with the 'Macedonian Call': Paul, Pauline Scholarship, and Nineteenth-Century Colonial Missions," in *The Colonized Apostle: Paul through Postcolonial Eyes*, ed. Christopher D. Stanley (Minneapolis: Fortress Press, 2011), 335n23. See also Brigitte Kahl for a comprehensive critique of Ramsay's unabashedly Orientalizing discourse, "Galatians and the 'Orientalism' of Justification by Faith: Paul among Jews and Muslims," in Stanley, *The Colonized Apostle*, 209–17. For other early and influential studies based on the narrative tropes of Acts, see Basil Matthews, *Paul the Dauntless: The Course of a Great Adventure* (New York: Revell, 1916); Robert M. Pope, *On Roman Roads with St. Paul* (London: Epworth, 1939).

6. Traveling artisans are not necessarily diaspora figures, and a discussion of the nature of Paul's travel in relation to the collection project may not be apparent at first glance. However, the section below where I deal with Paul, the collection project, and home will help in clarifying the connection. Although Schellenberg is very cautious he basically says the same thing as above: "It may prove impossible to evaluate with any precision the extent to which economic opportunity motivated Paul's travels. At the very least, however, we can dispense with the idea that Paul restricted himself to cities because they somehow were representative of entire nations or because he strategically expected the gospel to filter out from the city to the countryside. Quite simply, cities would have given Paul his best hope of making a living." Schellenberg, "Danger in the Wilderness, Danger at Sea," 158.

7. I concur with Ekkehard W. Stegemann and Wolfgang Stegemann that "the Lukan picture of Paul represents a literary fiction, and for the estimation of the social position of the historical Paul, his own letters have priority. The historical Paul was a citizen of neither Rome nor Tarsus." See Ekkehard W. Stegemann and Wolfgang Stegemann, *The Jesus Movement: A Social History of Its First Century* (Minneapolis: Fortress Press, 1999), 302. For more extensive discussions concerning Paul's citizenship, see Jerome Murphy-O'Connor, *Paul: A Critical Life* (Oxford: Clarendon Press, 1996); Ben Witherington, *The Paul Quest: The Renewed Search for the Jew of Tarsus* (Downers Grove, IL: InterVarsity, 1998); John D. Crossan and Jonathan L. Reed, *In Search of Paul: How Jesus's Apostle Opposed Rome's Empire with God's Kingdom* (New York: HarperCollins, 2004), 5.

21:27-36; 23:13-22)—in spite of the fact that he obeys the law and conforms to the ritualistic demands made on him (21:26)—wherever he tries to bring the gospel of Christ.[8] The hero of Acts is under Roman care in a house arrest in Rome to fulfill the theological and ideological goal of Luke—the gospel is preached from Jerusalem to Rome—but in such an abode Paul is more like a resident philosopher sharing the wisdom of God revealed in his son with the different visitors he receives (entertains) in his place of seclusion (28:17-31). This image of Paul as the hero in control of his movements, and a traveler in different cities of the Roman Empire, serves Luke's foundational myth of a movement that is not offensive to the empire, but, rather, imitates it and is intelligible to its social, political, and cultural elite.[9]

Acts presents a hero-worship image of a Paul who, as a masculine and as a strong dominating figure, penetrates the shores and inlands of those lost in darkness.[10] One may, then, wonder how a

---

8. A few interpreters have recently situated Luke's position as engaging in subtle form of political subversiveness with regard to the empire. See Virginia Burrus, "The Gospel of Luke and the Acts of the Apostles," in *A Postcolonial Commentary on the New Testament Writings*, ed. Fernando F. Segovia and Rasiah S. Sugirtharajah (London: T & T Clark, 2007), 133–55; Kavin C. Rowe, *World Upside Down: Reading Acts in the Graeco-Roman Age* (Oxford: Oxford University Press, 2009).

9. To support this, see in particular Laura S. Nasrallah's chapter, "What Informs the Geographical Imagination? The Acts of the Apostles and Greek Cities under Rome," in *Christian Responses to Roman Art and Architecture: The Second Century Church amid the Spaces of Empire*, ed. L. S. Nasrallah (Cambridge: Cambridge University Press, 2010), 87–118.

10. The picture of Paul as a traveler discovering places is exactly the kind of hero figure the modern European biblical interpreter (mostly male) seems to have needed as a model in order to go explore and "civilize" the world in an ever-expanding colonial *mission civilisatrice*. One may recall the many representations of Africa as the "Dark Continent," and the many mission societies that sprung up mainly in the nineteenth century at the height of the European colonizing period with the view to "saving" the natives. See Christopher L. Miller, *Blank Darkness: Africanist Discourse in French* (Chicago: The University of Chicago Press, 1985); Valentin Y. Mudimbe, *The Idea of Africa* (Bloomington: Indiana University Press, 1994). A number of scholars have interpreted Luke's portrayal of the native islanders in Acts as credulous, superstitious, and prone to erroneous views. For example, see Robert C. Tannehill, *The Narrative Unity of Luke-Acts: A Literary Interpretation*, vol. 2: *The Acts of the Apostles* (Minneapolis: Fortress Press, 1989), 340–41; Ian H. Marshall, *The Acts of the Apostles* (Sheffield:

presentation of Paul as brutally treated, and utterly vulnerable to the whims of life's precariousness and unpredictability, might confront modern middle-class academics, who imagine the first-century wanderer as a good fellow they could easily invite for a lovely afternoon tea to discuss disembodied theological niceties. The picture presented in 1 Cor. 4:11, for example, is far from being glamorous: going hungry and thirsty, in rags and brutally treated, and in a state of homelessness (καὶ πεινῶμεν καὶ διψῶμεν καὶ γυμνιτεύομεν καὶ κολαφιζόμεθα καὶ ἀστατοῦμεν).[11] Again, many times Paul was subjected to the dangers and hardships of an ancient traveler: shipwreck, robbery, lack of sleep, hunger, and thirst (2 Cor. 11:23-27). He needed to find ways to sustain himself in the dire reality of a first-century itinerant worker.[12] He could not go to some places because of probable difficulties with local authorities (1

Sheffield Academic, 1992), 417; Joseph A. Fitzmyer, Acts of the Apostles (New Haven: Yale University Press, 1998), 782–83.

11. John T. Fitzgerald notes, "The verb ἀστατεῖν is a frequentative verb that expresses incessant movement. It depicts the life of the wanderer, constantly moving from place to place." See John T. Fitzgerald, Cracks in an Earthen Vessel: An Examination of the Catalogues of Hardships in the Corinthian Correspondence, SBLDS 99 (Atlanta: Scholars Press, 1988), 134.

12. Although Chantal Reynier is at times vague, does not problematize the theological and ideological agenda of Luke in Acts, and psychologizes with regard to her portraits of Paul, she, nonetheless, does have some good points: "Les voyages au 1er siècle doivent être pensés en fonction des espaces naturels et politiques et donc des échanges" (45); "Dans l'Antiquité, il n'existe pas de bateaux réservés uniquement aux voyageurs" (53); "Le voyageur antique ne peut circuler de façon isolée" (62); "Lors de ses nombreux voyages, Paul n'a sans doute pas toujours mangé a sa faim" (65); "Pour l'homme du 1er siècle, le voyage n'est pas de l'ordre de l'agrément" (66); "Le voyage, véritable épreuve aux dires des intellectuels qui l'ont pratiqué, a façonné la personnalité de l'Apôtre autant que la géniale expression de sa pensée" (69); "Même si l'on ne fait pas naufrage et si l'on ne rencontre pas de pirates, la mer demeure redoutable et difficile à supporter. Il faut y affronter les éléments: la mer démontée, le vent, le brouillard, le choc des vagues". . . . (84); "Il convient de souligner l'importance jouée par le port d'Ephese, véritable plate-forme pour Paul: il favorise les déplacements vers Corinthe et la Macédoine, il permet aussi les échanges épistolaires et le recueil de l'information" (152) ; "Ses voyages ont façonné sa personnalité et sa mission. . . . Les conditions de voyage offrent même à Paul la possibilité de murir sa pensée au cours des longues traversée ou lors des escales, ou encore à l'occasion de marches lentes et régulières" (218); "L' 'univers géographique' dans lequel Paul évolue fait de lui 'un homme de la mer.' Ce qui est paradoxal pour un homme issu du peuple juif qui, en tant que peuple, n'a jamais été poussé à naviguer" (220). See Chantal Reynier, Saint Paul sur les routes du monde romain: Infrastructures, Logistique, Itinéraire (Paris: Éditions du Cerf, 2009).

Thess. 2:1-2, 17-18),[13] or because he was not welcome by some local communities.[14] In other words, Paul's social realities as an ancient traveler and artisan were incongruous with the religious ideals that he might have had. Life for him as an itinerant worker and preacher in his diasporic social locations was grim and left him dependent on the support of others.

Approaching Paul as a diasporic figure through his travel practices also calls into question recent assertions that Paul was a champion of empire in the sense that he moved around by following and by mimicking the map of the Roman Empire.[15] Joseph A. Marchal, for example, following Musa Dube's theoretical framework for evaluating ancient texts based on their literary-rhetorical grounds,[16] inquires about "Paul's justification for his movement in the empire."[17] The question he adopts from Dube is the following: Does this text encourage travel to distant and inhabited lands, and how does it

---

13. Schellenberg analyzes several instances where Paul's itineraries were contingent, not to any particular "missionary motivation," but to life's "gritty realities." In the case mentioned in 1 Thessalonians, no modern reader is clear with regard to "the exact circumstances of Paul's separation from the Thessalonians," but "it seems likely that Paul's activities aroused the ire of local authorities, who may have been jittery about the potentially disruptive influence of these particular informal associations." See Schellenberg, "Danger in the Wilderness, Danger at Sea," 152. Also, Paul's inability to visit the Thessalonians, as shown by Schellenberg, was probably not because of any threat existing in the relationship between Paul and this association, but because of conflict with local authorities that prevented him from doing so, and "Paul set out from Philippi for Thessalonica unwillingly, was then forced to leave Thessalonica unwillingly, and was unable to return to Thessalonica when he wished" (ibid., 154).

14. Crossan and Reed, *In Search of Paul*, 161; Rainer Riesner, *Paul's Early Period: Chronology, Mission Strategy, Theology*, trans. Doug Stott (Grand Rapids: Eerdmans, 1998), 359.

15. That does not undermine the benefits the empire provided to Paul: would his moving around Roman *oikoumenē* (Illyricum, Macedonia, Achaia, Arabia, Asia, Galatia, etc.) have been successful without prior Roman conquest and pacification of the various areas in which he preached Christ? On Paul's very Roman (imperial) geography, see Wayne A. Meeks, "From Jerusalem to Illyricum, Rome to Spain: The World of Paul's Missionary Imagination," in *The Rise and Expansion of Christianity in the First Three Centuries*, ed. C. E. Rothschild and J. Schöter (Tübingen: Mohr Siebeck, 2013).

16. Musa W. Dube, *Postcolonial Feminist Interpretation of the Bible* (St Louis: Chalice Press, 2000), 57.

17. Marchal, *The Politics of Heaven: Women, Gender, and Empire in the Study of Paul* (Minneapolis: Fortress Press, 2008), 45.

justify itself? Analyzing Paul's rhetoric in the Philippians correspondence with regard to his movements around the Roman empire, Marchal concludes that the fact that "Paul twice justifies his travels in the name of progress echoes the historical rationale for colonization: empire is for the good of the subjects, a paternalistic, civilizing force of advancement. The imperial resonance of Paul's *parousia*, the term used for the arrival of a victorious emperor or the visit of an imperial administrator, then, may not be entirely coincidental."[18] Thus, according to Marchal, Paul, with his understanding of Jesus as a new emperor replacing the Roman emperor, covers the same territory as the Roman power. The image of Acts does not seem to be far away either in this configuration of Paul's movements, since he is portrayed as going from Jerusalem to occupy the political center, Rome.

However, Marchal does not consider other types of travelers, such as those moving around as exiles, immigrants, migrant workers, skilled artisans in search of economic opportunities, nor people traveling for business purposes, for reasons of health, journeying to gain experience and in pursuit of divine wisdom, and the homeless wandering from place to place, and so on.[19] Although his rhetoric is stamped with the Roman imperial rhetoric, Paul cannot, in my view, be compared to a Roman authority addressing a Roman *colonia* like Philippi. It is rather surprising that in spite of referring to "the conditions of travel,"[20] Marchal still does not pause to reflect on the specificity of these conditions and on how they might have had some

18. Ibid., 46.
19. There were of course other reasons for traveling in antiquity. See Lionel Casson, *Travel in the Ancient World* (London: Allen & Unwin, 1974); Jaś Elsner and Ian Rutherford, eds., *Pilgrimage in Graeco-Roman & Early Christian Antiquity: Seeing the Gods* (Oxford: Oxford University Press, 2005), and for an excellent bibliography, the recent work edited by Philip A. Harland, *Travel and Religion in Antiquity*.
20. Joseph Marchal, *The Politics of Heaven*, 91, 96.

bearing on Paul as a traveling artisan to the different communities with which he had some relations.

Building on Mary Louise Pratt's theoretical lenses of "contact zone"[21] and on Inderpal Grewal's adaptation of Pratt's conception,[22] Marchal argues, "These reformulations indicate the potential relevance for examining a colonia (like Philippi) in neither the periphery nor the center, as well as the ways in which gender factors into such imperial dynamics."[23] He continues with the same logic a couple of pages later: "Not only do the historical material conditions of this Roman *colonia* tend to reflect Pratt's and others' discussions of the contact zone, but Paul's letters, like Philippians, also seem to be expressions and negotiations of the colonized contact zone. Paul's role in these various communities depends upon his ability to travel and write about his missionary travels."[24] Again, one detects the influence of Acts in such an uncritical reading of travel. Marchal seems to collapse nineteenth-century travel literature with the narrative tropes of Acts to conclude, "In fact, knowing the travel literature of more recent empires, these kinds of arguments might summon various tropes of the colonial adventure hero, who endures trials and tribulations only to bolster his or her imperially racialized and gendered authority."[25] Overall, Marchal's critical study is thus

---

21. Mary L. Pratt, *Imperial Eyes: Travel Writing and Transculturation* (London: Routledge, 1992).

22. Inderpal Grewal, *Home and Harem: Nation, Gender, Empire, and the Cultures of Travel*, Post-Contemporary Interventions (Durham: Duke University Press, 1996).

23. Marchal, *The Politics of Heaven*, 93.

24. Ibid., 98. Melanie Johnson-Debaufre and Laura S. Nasrallah, criticizing Marchal's rather flat positioning of Paul as one similar to "a provincial governor or colonial administrator for the divine *imperator*" (*Politics of Heaven*, 50; this exact sentence—minus the italics—is repeated in Marchal's contribution to Stanley, *The Colonized Apostle*, 156), ask two pertinent questions, which reinforces my overarching thesis of locating Paul as an itinerant worker in the diaspora: "However, if we consider the social and economic status of both Paul and the communities to which he writes, might Paul's travels look more like the circumambulations of a migrant worker than the visits of a Roman imperial governor? Might they look that way to some contemporary communities, too?" See "Beyond the Heroic Paul," in Stanley, *The Colonized Apostle*, 329n47.

25. Marchal, *The Politics of Heaven*, 99.

trapped within a Lukan narrative and myths of Christian origins that muddy the very necessary corrective to the heroic presentation of Paul that is in view.[26]

In summary of the first point in this chapter, which has to do with the travel practices of a particular diasporic figure, it is clear the itinerant worker Paul traveled extensively—quite unusual for someone who was neither a merchant, a soldier, nor a Roman official[27]—between many worlds; he was tested by hardships and uncertainties and would have had to be supported by patrons and brothers in Christ in order for him to have moved around as he did. Even if he used language "rooted in the conventional rhetoric of Roman hegemony,"[28] he was not in any position to be compared with a Roman official sending letters to different coloniae. Paul's travels need to be studied in their specific historical sites and situated in the context of an itinerant diasporic preacher and worker, and self-described emissary of Christ to the gentiles (in Galatians and Romans) in need of funds to help him further his work, and to sustain himself in the precariousness of life. And it is precisely the precariousness of Paul's position that makes urgent the question of why Paul was so eager to travel for the collection project.

Paul's Transcultural Narratives

In this section of this chapter, the thesis to be developed is that Paul had a concern not for the ancestral home as such—which he

26. Luke's discourse effectively effaces the plurality of the different social networks and travelers in the context of a very diversified movement to focus on his hero. As noted by Johnson-Debaufre and Nasrallah, "Local networks of support and contested leadership are erased by the attention on Paul's dangerous, heroic, relentless move across much of the Roman *oikoumenē*." See "Beyond the Heroic Paul," 171.

27. Stating that, I acknowledge Justin Meggitt's point that "the experience of travel differed tremendously" and that one cannot view "travel *per se* . . . as a class indicator." See Meggitt, *Paul, Poverty and Survival* (Edinburgh: T & T Clark, 1998), 134.

28. Leif E. Vaage, "Why Christianity Succeeded (in) the Roman Empire," in Vaage, *Religious Rivalries in the Early Roman Empire and the Rise of Christianity*, 257.

reimagines, reappropriates and reconfigures to serve certain etiological goals—but a commitment, a zeal even (ἐσπούδασα), to remember and serve those poor (μόνον τῶν πτωχῶν ἵνα μνημονεύωμεν, ὃ καὶ ἐσπούδασα αὐτὸ τοῦτο ποιῆσαι, Gal. 2:10) in the "ancestral homeland" sharing the same engagement in the resurrected Christ as he did. The language of "service to the saints in Jerusalem" we find in Rom. 15:25, 26, 31 seems to indicate that only devotees of Christ are the object of his attention. Rom. 15:25: Νυνὶ δὲ πορεύομαι εἰς Ἰερουσαλὴμ διακονῶν τοῖς ἁγίοις. In 26 we have "to the poor of the saints": Κοινωνίαν τινὰ ποιήσασθαι εἰς τοὺς πτωχοὺςτῶν ἁγίων τῶν ἐν Ἰερουσαλήμ. In 31, Paul prays that his service in Jerusalem may be acceptable to the saints there (καὶ ἡ διακονία μου ἡ εἰς Ἰερουσαλὴμ εὐπρόσδεκτος τοῖς ἁγίοις γένηται). Thus, in this understanding, Paul did not go around collecting funds primarily for theological reasons, even if he made use of "spiritualized language of cultic piety"[29] to legitimize his fundraising efforts. Cultic rhetoric had become the convincing rhetorical device to engage material necessities.[30] This statement relates to Paul's organizing of financial transfer only. I am not in any way undermining the nature of Paul's theologizing, just as I am not divorcing Paul's theological motivations from sociological concerns. My point is this: Paul does

---

29. Dieter Georgi, *Remembering the Poor: The History of Paul's Collection for Jerusalem* (Nashville: Abingdon Press, 1965), 64.

30. Stating that, I acknowledge that of the nine explicit references to the "collection," only two explicitly invoke poverty as the issue at hand: "The poor among the saints at Jerusalem" (Rom. 15:25) and "That we remember the poor" (Gal. 2:10). In the latter case, the exact identity of the "poor" is left unspecified, but from the context one may presume that this is the materially poor *among the Jerusalem community* rather than the impoverished masses that is the concern. In another case, Paul references "the *needs* of the saints" (2 Cor. 9:12b). In the other six places, the reference is most often to the "saints" and to a "ministry" (διακονία) with no mention of poverty or need: the collection (τῆς λογείας) for the saints (1 Cor. 16:1); this ministry (διακονία) to the saints (2 Cor. 8:4); the ministry (διακονία) to the saints (2 Cor. 9:1); the ministry (διακονία) of this service (τῆς λειτουργίας) (2 Cor. 9:12a); traveling to Jerusalem, serving the saints (πορεύομαι εἰς Ἰερουσαλὴμ διακονῶν τοῖς ἁγίοις) (Rom. 15:25); that my ministry (διακονία) to Jerusalem may be acceptable to the saints (Rom. 15:31).

frame the process by which he undertakes his relief funds activities for his audience as a cultic act, but what the "collection" addresses are the economic problems those "back home" in Christ are experiencing. As a diaspora person who *shared fully in the bleak material existence that was the lot of the non-élite inhabitants of the Empire,*[31] he was busy organizing financial transfer in his diasporic social locations because the plights of those who were, in some sense, like him (economically and socioreligiously) "at home" in the ancestral home remained a deep concern to him.[32]

Paul is eager to remember the poor of the ancestral home—a home in need of reappropriation and reimagination since no place on earth can really fulfill adequately the place of home (Phil. 3:20)—because Jerusalem still retains an important and symbolic position in his imaginary and consciousness, in spite of issues he might have had with some from "back home." The point I am making is this: Paul is a poor apostle of Christ who, because of an acute sense of geographical space in which he understands a strong bond between Christ's adherents in his diasporic social locations and in Jerusalem, tries as hard as he could to get other poor to help those suffering at "home." In light of his diasporic constitution, one may conceive Paul's collection within a spatial dimension. In this venue, the collection becomes a crucial axis of covenant that represents a symbol or a spatial plane of entry by which he chooses, as a cultic official, to make his gentiles to be full participants into a specific Abrahamic narrative. Even if one does not want to succumb to Luke's theological

---

31. Meggitt, *Paul, Poverty and Survival*, 153 (emphasis original).
32. How poor Paul's communities were is a recent and lively debate that we may only make brief note of here. While a minority do hold vigorously to the "poor" status of Pauline communities (e.g., Meggitt), many hold to a modified view of Meeks's original thesis in *The First Urban Christians* (e.g., Bruce W. Longenecker, Gerd Theissen, Ekkehard Stegemann and Wolfgang Stegemann, Steven Friesen). Steven Friesen's article, "Poverty in Pauline Studies: Beyond the So-Called New Consensus," *JSNT* 26, no. 3 (2004): 323–61, provides one of the better overviews.

presentation that has the gospel of Christ progressing from one center (theological, Jerusalem) to the next (political, Rome), Paul seems to embrace a certain view of Jerusalem as being an important center that he cannot just shrug off. For instance, he characterizes his successful endeavors amongst the nations, leaving no more room for preaching in the regions, not from his diasporic posture, but from a specific geographic marker for his work: "From Jerusalem around all the way to Illyricum" (Rom. 15:19).

Richard Ascough has recently challenged the thesis that the early Jesus movement was a transcultural movement in contradistinction to the more strictly private character of ancient associations. He argues that the earliest Christ communities were essentially local groups similar to some ancient voluntary associations with very limited translocal connections.[33] With regard to Paul's collection project for the poor in Jerusalem, Ascough comments, "Paul's troubles with raising the money promised, and his rhetorical strategies in his letters to the Corinthians (1 Cor 8:1-15; 9:1-5), suggest that they, at least, remained unconvinced that they had a social and religious obligation to an otherwise unknown group."[34] Leif E. Vaage, in a different context—arguing against Richard A. Horsley's presentation of Paul in 1 Corinthians 8–10 as in the process of building an international alternative, egalitarian society—makes a similar statement:

> The difficulties, moreover, which Paul encountered in raising *his* collection for the poor in Jerusalem, suggest precisely not a sense of class solidarity or international consciousness on the part of the Pauline communities but, rather, the usual human reluctance to participate in projects of aid to total strangers. Paul's broad generalizations about

33. Richard S. Ascough, "Translocal Relationship among Voluntary Associations and Early Christianity," *JECS* 5(1997): 223–41. See also Ascough, "Voluntary Associations and the Formation of Pauline Christian Communities," in *Vereine, Synagogen und Gemeinde im Kaiserzeitlichen Kleinasien*, ed. Andreas Gutsfeld and Dietrich-Alex Koch, Studien und Texte zu antike und Christentum 25 (Tübingen: Mohr Siebeck, 2006), 176–77.
34. Ascough, "Translocal Relationship," 237.

support from Achaia and Macedonia are just that: rhetorical exaggerations.[35]

Ascough acknowledges that Paul certainly "would like to think that the congregations are connected, but this may not have been the case."[36] And, according to Ascough, Paul's use of the term *ekklēsia*, especially in his usage of the word in the plural as a designation for his churches, shows that, at least in Paul's mind, "there were connections among Christian groups within one or more provinces rather than simply within a town (i.e., Rom 16.16; I Cor 7.17; 11.16; 16.19; II Cor 8.1; 11.28; Gal 1.22; I Thess 2.14)."[37] But Paul, as noted also by Ascough, "never assumes his own communities are in contact with one another."[38] One notices quickly, in agreement with Vaage and others, that the collection project was *Paul's* collection. In Gal. 2:10, the report moves from "the only thing agreed on was that *we* should remember the poor" (μόνον τῶν πτωχῶν ἵνα μνημονεύωμεν) to "which also this very thing *I* was eager to do" (ὃ καὶ ἐσπούδασα αὐτὸ τοῦτο ποιῆσαι). Thus the translocal nature of this fund raising project was assumed not by any other but by Paul.

Furthermore, Paul does, at times, give the impression that he believes the movement he was part of had some translocal character (1 Cor. 1:2; Rom. 1:8), regardless of how localized the horizons were of the communities with which he had some rapport. Consequently, there is a difference between, on the one hand, the character of the Jesus movement—and here I would agree with Ascough with regard to the very limited translocal connections between the different local

---

35. Vaage, "Why Christianity Succeeded (in) the Roman Empire," 276–77. Emphasis in original. See Richard A. Horsley, *Paul and Empire* (Harrisburg, PA: Trinity Press International, 1997), 8: "In his mission Paul was building an international alternative society (the 'assembly') based in local egalitarian communities."
36. Ascough, "Translocal Relationship," 237.
37. Ibid., 238.
38. Ibid., 239n77.

groups that constituted this movement at its earliest stage—and, on the other hand, what Paul was doing and what he understood he was doing, which is not the same as what others may have thought he was doing. Merrill Miller suggests that what Paul says in Rom. 15:26-27, that Macedonia and Achaia were pleased to contribute, and that they owe it to those in Jerusalem to share their material blessings with them, since those in Jerusalem shared their spiritual blessings with them "is certainly what most diaspora Jews would have assumed to be the case about their relation to the temple in Jerusalem. One might, therefore, suppose that, in writing to the church in Rome, Paul has his own reasons at that point for thinking of the matter from the perspective of a diaspora Jew."[39] And this confirms perfectly what Robin Cohen proposes, namely that one vital element that generally characterizes diaspora is a deep concern and a collective commitment for the ancestral home with regard to its maintenance, restoration, safety, and prosperity.[40] In this case, the Diaspora Jew Paul takes upon himself, single-heartedly, to raise funds to help those from the ancestral home, and he uses theological arguments to convince the Christ believers of the nations to participate in this fundraising project. But his theological arguments do not always convince the members of the nations, or, more precisely, most of them where Paul travels to and is a part of, for they do not understand why they would have to be involved in such a project.

---

39. Miller, "Antioch, Paul, and Jerusalem: Diaspora Myths of Origins in the Homeland," in *Redescribing Christian Origins*, ed. Ron Cameron and Merrill P. Miller, SBLSymS 28 (Atlanta: Society of Biblical Literature, 2004), 187. I agree with this sentence as a whole, but the generalization of "most Judeans" leaves room for disagreement, since we really do not know what "most Judeans" thought or did in or out of the Diaspora.
40. Cohen, *Global Diasporas*, 1st ed., 106.

Dialogue with Some Major Proposals

This section will be a review of some major proposals with regard to Paul's collection project (Munck, Georgi, Nickle, Joubert, Wan, and Downs), while keeping the initial argument of this chapter in mind, namely that this specific financial project is situated at the heart of Paul's diaspora politics of an eager commitment to remember, to serve, and to restore the poor sharing the same faith in the resurrected Christ as him, who happen to inhabit Jerusalem, the ancestral "home." The different readings proposed by the major contributors, I will argue, have not paid enough attention to Paul's social realities in his diasporic situation as an important frame of interpretation; therefore, Pauline studies needs to take seriously Paul's diaspora politics to understand his collection project.

Johannes Munck's Thesis

For Munck, Paul, one called in a similar fashion as a prophet of the Old Testament, is "on his way from the Gentile world to show stubborn Israel the obedience of faith as it had become reality in the believing Gentiles. . . . The emissaries of the Gentile churches who went with him were to take their gifts to the poor of the holy city and thereby fulfil the prophets' promises of the last days."[41] According to Munck, the collection project had an eschatological purpose, namely that the coming of various gentile nations—the fullness of which is reached (Rom. 15:19), since Paul thinks in terms of nations and not in individual categories—with gifts to Jerusalem signified the fulfilment of what was announced by many prophets of old, namely, that the nations will flock to Zion by bringing their gifts.

The object of Paul's perilous journey with representatives from the nations is that Israel's jealousy might be stirred with the view

41. Johannes Munck, *Paul and the Salvation of Mankind* (Richmond, VA: John Knox, 1959), 308.

to its conversion. In Paul's plan of salvation, Jerusalem has always retained a special importance, and the collection to that place was not merely to alleviate certain material needs but also to encourage "the harassed Christian church in Jerusalem, situated in the midst of Judaism, whose mission to its fellow-countrymen, as Paul says, has led only to a realization of Israel's complete impenitence."[42] In Munck's program, we should consequently "imagine that after the salvation of the Jews there would be a short space of time in which the mission to the Gentiles, united with Israel, would experience the great things that are promised in the Old Testament."[43] In other words, in following Munck's arguments, the "full number of the Gentiles" (τὸ πλήρωμα τῶν ἐθνῶν, Rom. 11:25) in making with Paul the pilgrimage to Jerusalem has as its purpose to stir Israel to jealousy and, from that, to salvation. The collection project is in this sense situated between the understanding of the shortness of time in the last days, the importance of geographical space in salvation history, and the eschatological grand vision of the salvation of "all Israel" for the manifestation of Christ in glory, in order for God's historical drama of judgment and of salvation to be made manifest.

Munck's proposal is elegant, but suffers from several weaknesses. Its understanding of Judaism of the Second Temple period and its relationship vis-à-vis the gentiles is, as rightly observed and criticized by Donaldson, inadequate.[44] Donaldson raises some serious questions to which Munck's work does not provide any answers, or, if answered, are insufficiently addressed. For example, "How did Paul come to his convictions about the Gentile mission?"[45] and "How did Paul arrive at this inverted program of salvation?"[46] To these

---

42. Ibid., 302.
43. Ibid., 305.
44. Donaldson, *Paul and the Gentiles: Remapping the Apostle's Convictional World* (Minneapolis: Fortress Press, 1997), 20.
45. Ibid.

questions one may add, how would Paul's journey westward to Rome and Spain accommodate the pilgrimage scenario proposed? How would one explain the reticence of some communities to participate in Paul's collection project, considering the grand eschatological vision purportedly behind such an effort? Moreover, what would a decentering of both the so-called Pauline churches and "a Jerusalem Church" look like? By this I mean, how about envisioning various groups engaging in social contacts and projects via Paul's diasporic zeal to help those poor Jesus followers in his ancestral home? Paul, then, with his financial transfer coming from diverse and varied social groups with which he had some rapport, would not go to a particular center but to diverse and varied (especially in terms of socioreligious beliefs and practices) struggling communities of Judeans scattered in and around Jerusalem. Here I am musing with the thesis (thesis 7) proposed by Dennis E. Smith with regard to the so-called Jerusalem Council meeting:

> Jerusalem may simply be the location for the meeting as a central location for representatives from "the *ekklesiai* of Judea in Christ" to meet with the representatives from the Gentile mission. Whether one of the *ekklesiai* was actually in Jerusalem then becomes a moot point. Judeans in general, including those of Galilee, might claim Jerusalem as their ancestral "home," but there is not yet a clear indication that anyone is claiming eschatological primacy for Jerusalem.[47]

Following this intriguing insight, Jerusalem may still play the role of "ancestral home," but not the pilgrimage eschatological center that Munck envisages it to be. Furthermore, there is no specific Pauline text in relation to the collection project, which is the subject of interest here, that has any eschatological character with regard to the

---

46. Ibid., 21.
47. Smith, "What Do We Really Know about the Jerusalem Church?" in Cameron and Miller, *Redescribing Christian Origins*, 246.

pilgrimage of the nations to Jerusalem;[48] the list of the emissaries who accompany Paul is, problematically, taken from Acts and even there it is still problematic as presented. Although, as suggested by Merrill P. Miller, "some people from both groups may have viewed the activity in analogy with freewill offerings sent to the temple,"[49] there is no way to squeeze the collection project into the "Procrustean bed of eschatological pilgrimage patterns of thought."[50] Paul, in a single way, attributes the social project to his own undertaking and does not mention any delegate from the nations accompanying him to present the financial aid to the "poor among the saints" in Jerusalem (Gal. 2:10; Rom. 15:25, 31; 1 Cor. 16:1; 2 Cor. 8:4; 9:1).

One may now look further to see how the collection project is understood by another major contributor in the debate, Dieter Georgi.

Dieter Georgi's Thesis

The meaning behind the collection, according to Georgi, was "that the Jesus-believing community represented a new creation with its roots in the resurrection of Christ, and to stress that this community was neither the prolongation of nor an addition to the old world order."[51] The long and painstaking collection project, in this sense, is to convey a desire on the part of Paul and his associates among the nations to have a real partnership with those in Jerusalem.[52] Georgi envisages the collection as a great and public ecumenical act of economic solidarity—translated through the cultic language of Paul—between individual gentile congregations for the betterment of

---

48. See David J. Downs, *The Offering of the Gentiles*, WUNT 248 (Tübingen: Mohr Siebeck, 2008), 7.
49. "Antioch, Paul, and Jerusalem," 222. See also Downs, *The Offering*, 8–9.
50. See Donaldson, *Paul and the Gentiles*, 194.
51. Georgi, *Remembering the Poor*, 53.
52. Ibid., 54.

the sociological condition of a large group within the congregation in Jerusalem who are poor.[53] For Georgi,

> If Paul saw such a connection between the motif of the eschatological pilgrimage of Jews and Gentiles to Jerusalem and the collection (and its transference to that city), he must have considered the collection itself a signal of the last times. The history of the collection until then had certainly helped to create that impression; if Paul did ascribe such significance to the collection, he must have viewed its implementation and its transfer as a sign, not only to the world in general, but to the Jews in particular as well. But in this concept, the priorities in the order of the events pertaining to the last times had been reversed. The Jews were not preceding the Gentiles (as announced by Deutero-Isaiah), but rather the Gentiles were preceding the Jews.[54]

Thus Georgi, like Munck, ascribes to an eschatological pilgrimage scenario. The collection, in Georgi's interpretation, served as a manifestation that God has not forsaken the nations, that they are also his. It also suggests that the gentiles are in fact, contrary to other eschatological expectations, forerunners of God's salvation to Israel, and that their universal worship and service will provoke Israel to align its steps to the reversed eschatological salvation in process, for it is only through the salvation of the gentiles that Israel's salvation becomes itself a possibility. Indeed, the "promised pilgrimage of the peoples had begun to materialize, but without—indeed, in spite of—the majority of the Jews."[55] As mentioned in the above analysis of Munck's proposal, the eschatological scenario is problematic, to say the least, which then, inter alia, erases Georgi's subsequent argument about the eschatological reversal of the gentiles' salvation, which has as its aim to provoke Israel to enter into the surprising movement of God. Furthermore, there is no citation by Paul of the Deutero-Isaiah

53. Ibid., 75, 114.
54. Ibid., 100.
55. Ibid., 119.

texts that would substantiate Georgi's arguments. It is confusing that for Georgi, "the 'remembering' meant primarily an inner attitude—an attitude that was to be expressed through recognition, gratefulness, intercession by prayers, and, finally, financial aid as well."[56] Not only does he place the "remembering of the poor" at a very secondary level in his analysis, he does not pay the slightest attention to how ethnicity and the specificity of social location might have also played a role in these very material efforts on which Paul was embarking.

Keith F. Nickle's Thesis

Nickle's contribution is situated within Munck's and Georgi's eschatological setting in order to highlight the aspects of unity of all Christ's believers as signified in the collection project, for which Paul devoted an overwhelming amount of time and physical and mental energy. He highlights the fact that Paul considers the gentiles as debtors to Jerusalem (Rom. 15:24-27) and that the collection constituted a tangible proof of communion within the body of Christ. He also mentions the presence of a large delegation accompanying Paul—the first eschatological fruits of the nations streaming to Zion—for the delivery of such an important and presumably sizeable amount of money. But, upon reflecting on Paul's failure to actually mention such delegates, Nickle imagines that it was perhaps because he was afraid that "the delegation could be misunderstood from another perspective. The group accompanying him to Jerusalem could be judged a premature attempt to force the consummation of the End, instigated by Paul because he blamed the Jerusalem Christian for the ineffectiveness of their mission to the Jews."[57] Although he mentions briefly—and again in the context of delegates accompanying Paul—the dynamics of Jewish communities

---

56. Ibid., 42–43.
57. Keith F. Nickle, *The Collection: A Study in Paul's Strategy* (London: SCM Press, 1966), 140–41.

in the Diaspora, possibly appointing gentile men to bring the temple tax to Jerusalem, Nickle falls short from examining such dynamics and how tangible material concerns of those poor among Christ-believing communities in Jerusalem could have played a plausible role in how Paul would have carried out his work in or near Jewish Diaspora settlements. I am not inferring that that was what the social reality was. In fact, there is no evidence from Paul that such was the case—contra the thesis advanced by Karl Holl that Paul's collection was similar in aim to the temple tax levied from Diaspora Judeans and proselytes.[58]

The works of Munck, Georgi, and Nickle in relation to Paul's collection project have been very influential in the discussions on the topic, and many recent works have followed their lead in viewing the financial aid as stemming from Paul's zealous efforts to convince the different communities to help the poor in need in Jerusalem through a theological and eschatological framework of the nations flocking to Zion with their gifts.[59] One aspect that has not been dealt with by these different contributors is how the social and geographical spaces, ethnicities, and identities involved interacted with each other, and how they are constructed through the entanglements of Paul's collection project. Also, how did the social dynamics weave through

---

58. See Karl Holl, "Der Kirchenbegriff des Paulus in seinem Verhältnis zu dem der Urgemeinde," in *Gesammelte Aufsätze zur Kirchengeschichte* (Tübingen: Mohr Siebeck, 1928), 44–67. See Barclay, *Jews in the Mediterranean Diaspora: From Alexander to Trajan, 323 bce–117 ce*(Berkeley: University of California Press, 1996), 269. Cf. Cicero, *Flac.* 28.66–69; Josephus, *Ant.* 16.163–70; Philo, *Legat.* 156–57; 311–13.

59. See, among others, Roger D. Aus, "Paul's Travel Plans to Spain and the 'Full Number of the Gentiles' of Rom. XI 25," *NovT* 21 (1979): 232–62; Ed P. Sanders, *Paul, the Law, and the Jewish People* (Minneapolis: Fortress Press, 1983), 171; Thomas R. Schreiner, *Romans*, Baker Exegetical Commentary on the New Testament (Grand Rapids: Baker, 1998), 776–77; Don Garlington, *An Exposition of Galatians: A Reading from the New Perspective*, 3rd ed. (Eugene, OR: Wipf and Stock, 2007), 120; Sze-kar Wan, "Collection for the Saints as Anticolonial Act: Implications of Paul's Ethnic Reconstruction," in *Paul and Politics: Ekklesia, Israel, Imperium, Interpretation; Essays in Honor of Krister Stendahl,*ed. Richard A. Horsley(Harrisburg, Pa: Trinity, 2000), 191–215; Jae W. Lee, "Paul, Nation, and Nationalism: A Korean Postcolonial Perspective," in Stanley, *The Colonized Apostle*, 232.

Paul's rhetoric, and what effect did he purpose his highly theologized and cultic discourse to accomplish? The theological and apologetic agendas behind the above studies greatly obscure the exploration of the interweaving of these diverse and fascinating elements.

The next set of major interpreters to this conversation (Joubert, Wan, and Downs), with whom I will interact in the next three subsections, do offer ways to push the debate further in the direction of social history by paying closer attention to the social, cultural and associative contexts of Paul's collection project. But I still need to address the process of Paul's diasporic existence, his multiple struggles with the different communities he was asking for financial help from on behalf of the poor in Jerusalem through a multilocationality of space (geographical, cultural, temporal), and Paul's confluence of narratives that reimagine, redescribe, and reappropriate certain mythic discourses to justify his financial project.

Stephan Joubert's Thesis

Joubert aims to study the collection project from the interpretive framework of ancient Greco-Roman social-exchange relationships. Paul, according to Joubert, modified the model by inviting his communities to help the poor in Jerusalem not because that would buttress their honor or that they would be reciprocated in the future for their act of generosity, but out of a moral obligation vis-à-vis a group that was intrinsically linked to them through the same theological visions. Paul, for Joubert, situated his project within "a three-way reciprocal relationship between God, the Pauline communities and Jerusalem."[60] In this schema, the relationship is established from a sociological perspective (social exchange relationships), as well as stemming from a theological standpoint (the

---

60. Stephan Joubert, *Paul as Benefactor: Reciprocity, Strategy and Theological Reflection in Paul's Collection*, WUNT 124 (Tübingen: Mohr Siebeck, 2000), 216.

grace of God is bestowed on them through their act of service toward others in need) while the geographical aspect is also on the horizon (a gift and blessing is directed to a particular geographical site in order to enable them to be fully restored materially).

The social-exchange model proposed by Joubert is sophisticated and purports to move away from disconnecting social reality, socioreligious ideals, and the socioreligious functions of Paul's collection project. For Joubert, there was a complex rapport between Paul and the Jerusalem leaders, since "realising the potential which Paul missionary work showed in terms of alleviating the plight of the poor, and at the same time knowing that they were in the superior position within the relationship as benefactors to him and Antioch, [they] did not hesitate to indicate to him how to repay his debt of gratitude."[61] From this perspective, the pressure would then be on Paul to perform as a benefactor on behalf of the economically deprived members residing in Jerusalem. Although this is an intriguing presentation, it seems to presuppose a certain degree of influence of a central church holding a clear authority upon satellite communities and leaders in the Diaspora that would need to be substantiated. The "missionary model," which evokes a sense of having a "home base" and even being "sent out," along with notions of responsibilities that the one sent bears to those that sent him, does not seem far from Joubert's construction. But the proposal of Paul's collection project as an act of benefaction seems to at least present some interesting scope as it fits very nicely with what Robin Cohen observes about the role played by many diaspora subjects, even if the actual language of "benefaction" is not used by Cohen. Specific historical and economic conditions are attended to, as well as the moral and "religious" dimensions of Paul's collection project in Joubert's study; but the aspects of identity and imagination of

61. Ibid., 114.

home, as well as the dynamics of space realignments, could have been explored in order to show how social realities can be concocted, constructed, and made use of by theological socio-rhetorics to attain certain specific material results. Paul's diaspora politics of a commitment to the restoration of, and service to those inhabiting the ancestral "home," especially the poor sharing the same faith in the resurrected Christ, is clearly at work through his collection project.

Let us now move on to Sze-kar Wan's fascinating essay on Paul's efforts as engaging in anticolonial rhetoric to raise money on behalf of the "poor among the saints" in Jerusalem.

Sze-kar Wan's Thesis

Here is how Wan articulates his thesis:

My hypothesis is that Paul consciously pursued the collection as an ethnic Jew, a member of a minority group, a subaltern community under Roman rule. In Christ, the Jewish Messiah who had triumphed over all earthly and secular powers and potentates, he constructed a universalism along Jewish lines which in effect brought all Gentiles into the metararrative of Israel. This new narrative stood in opposition to and criticism of all Roman imperial, political, social, and cultural hegemonic forces, expressions, and institutions, including the patronage system.[62]

This proposal aims at advancing the conversation on the collection project further by paying close attention to issues of ethnicity as "a methodological starting point,"[63] alongside an interest in the Greco-Roman political landscape with a critical eye to the specificity of the socioreligious groups that formed Paul's entourage. The theological agenda and the dubious language of universalism mentioned may be worrisome, especially with regard to where the concept of universalism could lead to if left vacuous and undertheorized. The

---

62. See Wan, "Collection for the Saints," 196.
63. His term, ibid.

inclusion of the so-called gentiles into the metanarrative of Israel's story, however, is a solid point of investigation and of departure from the previous studies mentioned.

The sharp dichotomy between Paul's supposedly new narrative in contrast to, and criticism of, "all Roman imperial political, social, and cultural hegemonic forces, expressions, and institutions, including the patronage system" would have to be nuanced, since this "new narrative" was seemingly unable to develop away from the very gendered Greco-Roman rhetoric that othered and effeminized the non-Roman nations.[64] But we are only at the proposal. Let us move on further into Wan's main argumentation. It is unfortunate that Wan's analysis is done from Paul's perspective; that is, his study is conducted within the mantle of Paul's rhetoric and labels the preachers who oppose Paul as "detractors":

> The contested issue between Paul and the itinerant preachers in the Galatian church, for example, was precisely one of boundary. When Paul's detractors insisted that Gentile converts adopt the overt identity marker, namely circumcision, they were in effect drawing the boundary to coincide with the prevailing Jewish *ethnos*. Paul, for his part, taking the constructivist approach, modeled an entirely and radically new *ethnos* in which "there is no Jew or Greek, no free or slave, no male and female" (Gal. 3:28).[65]

Wan places ethnicity at the center stage in the discussion that took place in the so-called Jerusalem Council "between Jewish and Gentile Christians" (his terms, and put in quotation marks here because of the problematic and uncritical usage of such concepts).[66] He argues that, based on the alleged "victory for the missionaries to Gentiles"

---

64. See chapter 4 of this book.
65. Wan, "Collection for the Saints," 199.
66. See especially Anders Runesson, "Inventing Christian Identity: Paul, Ignatius, and Theodosius I," in *Exploring Early Christian Identity*, ed. Bengt Holmberg, WUNT 172 (Tübingen: Mohr Siebeck, 2008), 59–92.

the concession agreed on by the latter group was to contribute to the church in Jerusalem.[67] Wan justifies this proposal on the basis of μόνον in Gal. 2:10. The problem is that it was Paul's resolution to single-heartedly remember the poor that is in view here (ὃ καὶ ἐσπούδασα αὐτὸ τοῦτο ποιῆσαι). The form of this remembering for Paul eventually took shape through going to much trouble to gather the financial aid on their behalf, but this eagerness and zeal on Paul's part to remember the poor does not, ipso facto, translate into himself "conceding" to the Judean leaders in Jerusalem that he would have to undertake such a taxing collection project.[68] One obvious question then is the following: How would Paul remember the poor without campaigning for a collection project? For example, he could take upon himself the task to spur the sensitivity of those Judeans who, like him, occupy the diaspora space in their multiple social locations in order for them to intervene directly or indirectly on behalf of the poor in their ancestral metropolis. In fact, there existed financial commitments toward the homeland, in the form of the annual collection of money gathered at different local points in order to be taken to the temple in Jerusalem (*Ant.* 14.110–113; 18.311–312). The many local diasporic Jewish communities took this temple tax very seriously, since it created and reinforced the social and religious bounds, not only among themselves, but also between them and the Judean homeland. Paul could have tapped into that by asking individual Diaspora Jews to take upon themselves to provide for the welfare of the poor in Jerusalem. Or Paul could have shared the dire plight of the poor of Jerusalem with the social groups he was in contact with in his diasporic spaces, and he could equally

---

67. Wan, "Collection for the Saints," 199. *Concession* is his term.
68. I am well aware of the scholarly tradition that does see Gal. 2:1-10 as evidence that the collection project was something imposed on Paul by Jerusalem as part of a deal. See, for example, John C. Hurd, *The Origins of 1 Corinthians* (New York: Seabury, 1965). This is not the view I am arguing for.

use theological argumentations to show them the necessity of being part of a translocal movement. However, what translocal movement? some in his associations might well have asked, as they were much more interested in the local associations and the associative funds for local and immediate concerns.[69]

Furthermore, Wan estimates that the collection is better interpreted from the background of the temple tax, especially in light of the numerous tensions between the Jews and the Roman authorities that it fostered. Wan makes it clear that there is no evidence that Paul is conducting the collection project in a similar fashion as the temple tax imposed on the gentiles, although according to him, "it is possible that Paul might be borrowing terms from those associated with the temple tax to describe the collection."[70] The collection is presented in Romans 15, according to Wan, as a way to expand the boundaries "based on faith-centered reading of the Abrahamic covenant."[71] The high concentration of cultic language in Rom. 15:15-16, for example (a number of cultic metaphors in reference to the collection can also be found in 2 Cor. 8:1, 9-15) is interpreted by Wan to mean that Paul is presenting his collection in the form of "an offering of the Gentiles,"[72] following, without any hesitation, modification, or nuance, in the footsteps of the first major sets of interpreters encountered in this chapter that Paul's thinking was in line with the grand eschatological scenario announced by the

---

69. And that is the point of Richard Ascough when he states, "What confuses the Corinthians [about the collection] is not the fact that they have to donate, but that the monies are going to Jerusalem rather than the common fund of the local congregation." See Richard Ascough, *Paul's Macedonian Associations: The Social Context of Philippians and 1 Thessalonians,* WUNT 2:161 (Tübingen: Mohr Siebeck, 2003), 104. Paul could do all of that without embarking into a grand undertaking of a translocal economic project that he would have to supervise and deliver himself at great peril of his life and of his reputation.

70. Wan, "Collection for the Saints," 206.

71. Ibid., 203.

72. Ibid., 205.

prophets of old. To be fair to Wan, however, he does add a political dimension to this vision:

> Such a vision is, of course, political through and through, for it proclaims an all-encompassing sovereignty, to which all empires, including the Roman Empire, must pay obeisance. And Zion is the new capital to which all nations will have to make tributes. The Jewish universalism would serve as a form of resistance as well: the world-governing scope of the colonizers is thoroughly relativized and crippled by this eschatological fulfillment.[73]

Although the political dimension is advanced, the argument against such interpretations still holds, namely that in spite of possible echoes—especially in Rom. 11:12 and 15:12—of the eschatological tradition, there are no clear linkages between these texts and how Paul frames his different onerous travels as they are related to the collection project. Moreover, one needs to be prudent to not be swayed by Paul's own mythmaking through his social and theological rhetoric; his metaphors can portray himself and what he thinks he was doing in a certain positive light, which can be at odds with the reality of what was actually being done and from how what he was doing, or was attempted to do, was perceived by others.[74] In Wan's reading of the project, "Paul has constructed a new symbolic universe based on mutual obligation"[75] that is, in fact—and here it is a good point with which I am in agreement—based on "an essentially Jewish vision in which the Gentiles participate and that it is a Jewish institution (the temple?) into which Gentiles have

---

73. Ibid., 207.

74. In relation to Paul's perception of his own ethnic identity, Alan F. Segal states something similar: "Paul's own direct statements show that Paul thought he remained a Jew, although he did not continue to think of himself as a Pharisee. . . . What Paul thought he was doing is not the same as what others, in a less generous mood, may have ascribed to him." See Alan F. Segal, "The History Boy: The Importance of Perspective in the Study of Early Judaism and Christianity," in *Identity & Interaction in the Ancient Mediterranean: Jews, Christians and Others; Essays in Honour of Stephen G. Wilson* (Sheffield: Sheffield Phoenix Press, 2007), 235–36.

75. Wan, "Collection for the Saints," 209.

been incorporated."[76] Thus, and here I depart from Wan's analysis and expand a bit, it is a symbolic universe that is modeled on Paul's specific ethnicity; the status of the so-called gentiles as "the Other" remained intact, and they were subordinated to serve, through the collection project, a metanarrative of Paul's ancestral home, though that home needed to be reinvented, at least rhetorically—considering the heavy cultic language used with reference to the collection, especially in Romans 15–16, as highlighted by Wan and others.

In the last section of his essay, Wan focuses on 2 Corinthians 8–9 as an antipatronal appeal. His main point is that 2 Cor. 8:13-14 illustrates the notion of equity that Paul wants to impart on his communities. In this venue, their act of generosity on behalf of those lacking and in want (ὑστέρημα, 2 Cor. 8:14 and τὰ ὑστερήματα τῶν ἁγίων in 2 Cor. 9:12) would not be viewed as an obligation, but as an act of equity (ἰσότης) and of service in imitation of Christ who, through his poverty, makes them rich. Again, Wan's investigation is made without taking a distance from Paul's rhetoric, without weighing Paul's theological rationale in light of his ultimate motives—that of receiving benefactions from his gentile groups, and signifying a forum where his gentiles are depicted as participants in the covenant God made with Israel. We are not informed of the nature of Paul's relief project. However, one may query about the practicality, or the logistics, of undertaking any grand operation. For example, the size of the quantity of aid to be delivered and the amount of practical goods that could be assembled and transported seems to thwart any grand gesture. Thus, simply based on logistics, the collection does not seem to have been of major economic relevance. Also, my point is not to undermine the cultic and patronal elements present in Paul's language with regard to his relief effort, but to draw attention to the materiality of the collection, even when

76. Ibid.

its economic relevance may have been quite insignificant. The point is that one needs to gauge the almost obvious character of Paul's persuasive rhetoric that aimed to receive benefactions from these groups on behalf of the economically deprived Christ believers in Jerusalem. Wan proposes that the involvement of various congregations in the collection project was intentional on Paul's part to destabilize the patronal claim that any single community would have made if given the sole role of patron over the benefactees in Jerusalem in this important famine relief effort: "When there was a multiplicity of patrons, however, in competition with each other giving to the same client, the vertical structure became destabilized, resulting in a relativization of patronal power."[77] This is an argument from silence. How do we know that it was intentional of Paul to involve different churches in order to undermine the elite patron--poor client relationship that would have ensued from that? In fact, what we know is that Paul's financial practices seemed to have been quite controversial, and that it was a problem for him to actually persuade the different communities of Christ believers in his social diasporic locations to participate in this relief effort and for him to complete raising funds in a project these groups, for the most part, had no interest in.[78] Finally, with regard to Wan's perception of an anticolonial polemic in Paul's promotion of the collection in

---

77. Ibid., 214–15.
78. This last sentence is my own way of expressing what Ron Cameron and Merrill Miller state in a clearer way. Although what they say do resemble the argument advanced by Wan, I am not persuaded they are articulating the same thing: "Paul may not want to depend on the benefactions of patrons, when it comes to a matter so closely tied to the success of his mission, or, alternatively, there may not be enough wealth from such sources to carry through the collection. Depending mostly on his own labor surely has something to do with the desire to remain free of such dependencies. Moreover, 2 Cor 8–9; 11:7-11; 12:16 show that Paul's financial practices were controversial; evidently it required a great deal of persuasion to complete the collection, and we should not simply assume that all families or individuals participated. Finally, the collection is hardly free of ambiguities, including the intention to demonstrate through the collection the greater success, and thus the priority, of the Gentile mission in God's present plans, implying that in fact the collection is intended to be received as a benefaction requiring acknowledgment of Paul's mission and the honoring of it in Jerusalem."

Rom. 15:25-28, Calvin J. Roetzel rightly observes, "The problem is that the anti-colonial polemic of the text may be a bit too subtle. If that passage is seen as anti-colonial, then any affirmation that acknowledges the power and existence of the God of Israel could be read as anti-imperial as well."[79]

In spite of the criticisms one may have against Wan's thesis, in my view, his interpretation accounts for several important aspects that have not been touched on previously in the debates surrounding the collection project: ethnicity is at the forefront; the construction of a metanarrative based on certain ideology and perception of the so-called gentiles is presented; and the character of Paul's diasporic situatedness is taken into consideration. The next, and last, major contributor to be considered in this survey is David J. Downs's revised doctoral dissertation, *The Offering of the Gentiles*.[80]

David J. Downs's Thesis

Downs's study has the merit of offering a reading of Paul's collection efforts within a broad comparative manner à la Jonathan Z. Smith that does not pretend, or argue, that the collection has a unique character. In other words, Paul's collection project is firmly planted in its particular historical and associative contexts. Downs presents his thesis thusly:

See Cameron and Miller, "Redescribing Paul," in *Redescribing Paul and the Corinthians*, ed. Ron Cameron and Merrill P. Miller (Atlanta: Society of Biblical Literature, 2011), 291n151.

79. Calvin Roetzel, "Response: How Anti-Imperial Was the Collection and How Emancipatory was Paul's Project?" in *Paul and Politics* (Harrisburg, PA: Trinity Press International, 2000), 228.

80. There are, obviously, other major contributors, (e.g., David G. Horrell, "Paul's Collection: Resources for a Materialist Theology," *Epworth Review* 22 [1995]: 74–83; Horrell, "'The Lord Commanded . . . But I Have Not Used': Exegetical and Hermeneutical Reflections on 1 Cor 9:14-15," *NTS* 43 [1997]: 587–603; Justin Meggitt, *Paul, Poverty and Survival*.) The sample chosen in this chapter is, to my view, representative of the main routes the conversation on Paul's collection project has been taken. See the excellent and helpful survey of the history of scholarship on Paul's collection for the poor in Jerusalem in David J. Downs, *The Offering*, 3–26.

Using the theoretical perspective on "conceptual metaphors" developed by George Lakoff and Mark Johnson, I shall argue that Paul metaphorically frames his readers' responsive participation in the collection as an act of cultic worship, and in so doing he underscores the point that benefaction within the community of believers results in praise to God, the one from whom all benefactions ultimately come. This rhetorical strategy not only minimizes the competition for honor among the members of Paul's churches, it also suggests that even the very human action of raising money for those in material need originates in ἡ χάρις τοῦ θεοῦ and will eventuate in χάρις τῷ θεῷ (2 Cor 9:14-15).[81]

This thesis announces mainly three points: (1) the collection project will be studied through a specific metaphorical focus, and (2) the materiality of the project will be emphasized, but also (3) that the theological aspect of such undertaking will not be neglected. But from such an initial encounter with the work one may, not without any reasons, be concerned of theological agendas that might be lurking behind. How does one, or better, how *can* one, evaluate Downs's suggestion that "even the very human action of raising money for those in material need originates in ἡ χάρις τοῦ θεοῦ and will eventuate in χάρις τῷ θεῷ"? In other words, do we as scholars of religion—regardless of one's personal theological persuasion, traditions and religious/social commitments, and so forth,—have any access to certain χάρις τοῦ θεοῦ, which would eventuate in certain χάρις τῷ θεῷ? Do we not, after all—again, regardless of one's personal religious or theological convictions—only have what we can observe and read in order to categorize, to arrange theoretically, to construct and to deconstruct meanings to satisfy our own curiosities and that of those like us, who share our interests and questions as we try to make sense of the data we study, namely the "socially and materially entrenched human beings engaging in certain behaviors,

81. Downs, *The Offering*, 29.

maintaining specific social institutions, and deploying artful rhetorics for this or that material or social end"?[82] To be clear, this *etic* reading does not pretend to be the only one possible and it is not pretending to impose (well, how could it?) its understanding on the *emic* representations and motivations behind the phenomena under investigation.

Downs's study aims to occupy a middle ground between what he considers a concentrated theological reading of the collection project (e.g., the proponents for the eschatological reading and others such as Oscar Cullmann, Klaus Berger)[83] and that of a too-materialistic presentation (e.g., David G. Horrell, Justin J. Meggitt, in a lesser degree, Petros Vassiliadis).[84] He, rightly, rejects the collection as an eschatological event scenario, as well as rejecting the construal of the collection as an act of obligation on Paul's part. His sympathy lies more with the collection as serving the purpose of an ecumenical offering (close to Horrell's position), and the collection as material relief for some who were poor in the Jerusalem community. He examines the sociocultural context of the collection through a serious sociological comparative study of how ancient associations managed financial resources, benefactions, gift-giving and sharing practices in the Greco-Roman world.

Downs does criticize Wan's sweeping assertion that with the collection, Paul aimed to redefine ethnic boundaries by showing that "in spite of the unity of these groups accomplished through the gospel, Paul's distinction between these two ethnic categories

---

82. See Russell T. McCutcheon, *Critics Not Caretakers: Redescribing the Public Study of Religion* (Albany: State University of New York Press, 2001), 88.

83. Oscar Cullmann, "The Early Church and the Ecumenical Problem," *Anglican Theological Review* 40 (1958): 181–89, 294–301; Klaus Berger, "Almosen für Israel," *NTS* 23 (1977): 180–204.

84. Petros Vassiliadis, "The Collection Revisited," *Deltion Biblikon Meleton* 11 (1992): 42–48; "Equality and Justice in Classical Antiquity and in Paul: The Social Implications of the Pauline Collection," *St Vladimir's Theological Quarterly* 36 (1992): 42–48.

is nevertheless consistently maintained, for example, throughout the epistle to the Romans (cf. 1:16; 11:13; 15:7-9)."[85] More engagement, however, with some important issues raised by Wan (e.g., diasporic location) would have made his case stronger. Downs, in trying to illuminate Paul's metaphorical language, seems to be swayed by Paul's very metaphors and he, in a similar vein as Wan, although in not quite the same way, interprets Paul's collection as undermining the very stability of the Greco-Roman benefaction system:

> No mundane benefaction, the Jerusalem collection is represented as an offering consecrated to God. Additionally, in depicting the fund as an act of worship, a liturgy offered in the praise of God, Paul's cultic metaphors have the effect of downplaying certain aspects of the Greco-Roman benefaction system inimical to Paul's theological conception of the collection for the saints.[86]

But, to take a simple example, how would Downs evaluate Queen Helena's benefactions in light of this very general and especially theologically motivated statement? One recalls that Josephus mentions how Helena, King Izates's mother of Abiadene, provided significant benefactions to relieve the plight of those who were being oppressed by a severe famine (*Ant.* 20.51–53), which was caused by drought, in Jerusalem only few years prior (around 46/47 CE) to the request made to Paul as reported in Gal. 2:10.[87] Helena's acts of

---

85. Downs, *The Offering*, 16.
86. Ibid., 158. This sentence is similar but slightly different from what Barclay says: "Thus the collection, while designed to bind together Jewish and non-Jewish believers across huge geographical distances, also solidified the distinction between believers and 'the rest' among Jews in Judea itself." See John M. G. Barclay, "Money and Meetings: Group Formation among Diaspora Jews and Early Christians," in *Vereine, Synagogen und Gemeinde im Kaiserzeitlichen Kleinasien*, ed. Andreas Gutsfeld and Dietrich-Alex Koch, Studien und Texte zu antike und Christentum 25 (Tübingen: Mohr Siebeck, 2006), 121–22. This same line of argument is followed in the very recent article by Julien M. Ogereau, for whom "the sheer audacity and radical nature of Paul's project . . . was intended to transcend geo-political, socio-economic, and ethnic distinctions in a revolutionary way." See "The Jerusalem Collection as Κοινωνία: Paul's Global Politics of Socio-Economic Equality and Solidarity," *NTS* 58, no. 3 (July 2012): 360–78.

piety to the poor of Jerusalem seem to have been spurred by her
newly found faith in the Jewish religious ancestral way of life. It is
interesting to note that she did not need anyone to convince her with
any elaborate cultic language to undertake a charitable work —she
had corn and dried figs transported and distributed to the poor (*Ant.*
20.51; 101)—in a place that was in desperate need, with many dying
of hunger. And, at least to my knowledge, no one is claiming that
by this act of benefaction she meant to downplay "certain aspects
of the Greco-Roman benefaction system." Thus the differences in
social formations, in negotiating and reinventing spaces, religious
and social ideologies, powers, social and economic status, of mundane
concerns such as who would collect the money, for whom it was
being collected, and how proper financial accounting was to be
managed and guaranteed, are left unexplored.[88] The issues of interest,

87. The connection between Helena's grand gesture of generosity toward the poor in Jerusalem
because of her "desire to go to the city of Jerusalem and to worship at the Temple of God," (*Ant.*
20.49) and Paul's collection project has been made by Paul Barnett, as indicated by Joubert,
who also highlights the two situations as well. See Paul Barnett, *The Second Epistle to the
Corinthians*, NICNT (Grand Rapids: Eerdmans, 1997), 397n30; and Stephan Joubert, *Paul as
Benefactor*, 113. Regarding the Gal. 2:10 reference, for Downs, "the request of the leaders of the
Jerusalem church in Gal 2:10 *does not refer* to the collection that Paul later organized among the
Gentile churches of his mission (1 Cor 16:1-4; 2 Cor 8:1-9:15; Rom 15:14-32)." *The Offering
of the Gentiles*, 14 (emphasis original). Downs's argument is that the request of the Jerusalem
leaders referenced in Gal. 2:10—"remember the poor"—is not the same as the collection Paul
undertakes later. For him, Gal. 2:10 refers to the famine mentioned in Acts 11:27-30, which was
addressed when funds were sent from Antioch to Jerusalem in the hands of Barnabas and Saul.
He supports his position by stipulating that "it may be more accurate, then, to speak, as Martyn
does, of Paul's 'collections,' recognizing that Paul was in the delivery of a relief fund from
the church of Antioch . . . long before he organized a collection among the Gentile churches
of his own mission" (ibid., 34). Against Downs, I maintain that Gal. 2:20, 1 Cor. 16:1-4, 2
Cor. 8–9, and Rom. 15:25-35 refer to Paul's attempts to collect funds for the Jerusalem Christ
group. Separating out Gal. 2:10 seems to me to remove one of the strongest arguments that this
was about the poor at all. See Larry W. Hurtado's article on reading Gal. 2:10 as referring to
the collection project, "The Book of Galatians and the Jerusalem Collection," *JSNT* 5 (1979):
46–62.

88. The issue raised in 1 Corinthians 16, for example, as observed astutely by John S. Kloppenborg
and Richard S. Ascough, could well have "had to do with *who* would collect the money, *for
whom* it was being collected, and how proper financial accounting was to be managed and
guaranteed," instead of constantly turning to disembodied eschatological musings. See John
S. Kloppenborg and Richard S. Ascough, *Greco-Roman Associations: Texts, Translations, and*

which are needed to be studied and clarified for the interest of the scholar, are thus muddied, if not altogether left aside in Downs's comparative work, because of the seemingly too-encompassing theological interests that appears to guide his study:

> Paul's appeals to and discussion of the Jerusalem collection, which are addressed to those whose lives have already been transformed by the rectifying power of God, do not dwell on the logic of salvation. Yet in framing participation in the collection for the saints as an act of corporate worship and as a bountiful harvest produced by God, Paul implies that even this activity of human beneficence is one that depends on the χάρις.[89]

Paul, the Collection Project, and Home

Where was home? "Was a third trip to Jerusalem a homecoming for Paul?" are the questions Merrill P. Miller asks.[90] To this he answers, "No, it was just a way station."[91] But why such an eagerness on Miller's part to move away as quickly as possible from this fascinating query? Let us ponder a bit about the plausibility of Paul's collection visit to Jerusalem as more than "just a way station;" as Miller observes, "For Paul, beyond Jerusalem were Rome and Spain."[92] Probably realizing the force Jerusalem still plays in Paul's consciousness as being more than "just a way station," Miller seems to correct himself when he remarks, "Nonetheless, if Paul had persisted in a collection for the poor among the saints in Jerusalem and was bringing to the Holy city representatives of the Gentile churches, Jerusalem could not be thought of by Paul as merely a way station for the representatives of these churches. The collection had pedagogical aims, but also an

---

Commentary, vol. 1: *Attica, Central Greece, Macedonia, Thrace* (New York: Walter de Gruyter, 2011), introduction, 12 (emphasis original).

89. Downs, *The Offering*, 160.

90. Miller, "Antioch, Paul, and Jerusalem," 226.

91. Ibid.

92. Ibid.

epic dimension."[93] Analysing this question from diaspora studies, it becomes clearer that Paul's collection project and his collection trip to Jerusalem could, indeed, be conceived of as a "homecoming" of some sort for him; and with the full understanding that the diasporic experience, as Stuart Hall has observed, does not refer to identity that can only be secured in relation to some sacred homeland, and that "diaspora identities are those which are constantly producing and reproducing themselves anew, through transformation and difference."[94]

Home is a contestable and very fluid concept, which connotes more than a place of birth or physical locality; it is a special relation that one may entertain with any place that one might occupy; home "is a site from which and in which we construct self-identity and social relations";[95] it is a metaphorical "symbolic conceptualization of where one belongs."[96] "Home" "stands for a safe place, where there is no need to explain oneself to outsiders; it stands for community; more problematically, it can elicit a nostalgia that elides exclusion, power relations, and difference."[97] Home is plural; its complexities can be explored through the cut and mix of the different tunes and rhythms of life, to follow Stuart Hall's theorizing.[98] In sum, home "is not a fixed entity, space, or place with boundaries and/or borders, but is a fluid construction that is informed and mediated by an individual's life-stage, context and situation."[99] Paul goes "home"

---

93. Ibid., 226–27.
94. Stuart Hall, "Cultural Identity and Diaspora," in *Identity: Community Culture and Difference*, ed. Jonathan Rutherford (London: Lawrence and Wishart, 1990), 225.
95. Todd Penner and Davina Lopez, "Homelessness as a Way Home," in *Holy Land as Homeland? Models for Constructing the Historic Landscapes of Jesus*, ed. Keith W. Whitelam, The Social World of Biblical Antiquity, Second Series, 7 (Sheffield: Sheffield Phoenix Press, 2011), 154.
96. Ruba Salih, *Gender in Transnationalism: Home, Longing and Belonging among Moroccan Migrant Women* (New York: Routledge, 2003), 70.
97. Dorinne Kondo, "The Narrative Production of 'Home,' Community, and Political Identity in Asian American Theater," in *Displacement, Diaspora, And Geographies Of Identity*, ed. Smadar Lavie and Ted Swedenburg (Durham, NC.: Duke University Press, 1996), 97.
98. Hall, "Cultural Identity and Diaspora," 310–14.

with the collection but, as pointed by Brah, "home" "can simultaneously be a place of safety and terror."[100] The diasporic existence, made up of different crossings, rendered it difficult for Paul to locate and be established in terms of fixed territorial alignments. He brings "home" financial aid from the many places he has been to as a diasporic figure in order to signify that he belongs there somehow. "Home" is less about *place* and more about *relationship*, which is what makes the extended travels worth it for Paul. In his reappropriation of Israel's epic, he can no longer be bound to an earthly Jerusalem that is, in his view, bound in slavery (Gal. 4:25) of still holding on to the "old ways" whereas now is the new creation, a new time, a new era with Christ resurrected and coming back soon (Gal. 6:15; 2 Cor. 5:17; Rom. 8; 2 Cor. 1:8-11).[101] Paul is a man on a mission and the Jerusalem from below becomes itself diasporized in order to also play the role of a way station as he contemplates moving from Jerusalem to Rome and Spain. But, Jerusalem, in spite of all that is said, will always remain close to heart and cannot just be a way station as the preaching of the new creation is envisaged ἀπὸ Ἰερουσαλὴμ καὶ κύκλῳ μέχρι τοῦ Ἰλλυρικοῦ (Rom. 15:19).

The concept of diaspora is situated mainly in the context of different diasporic subjects and communities in their multiple

99. Carl E. James, "'I Feel Like a Trini': Narrative of a Generation-and-a-Half Canadian," in *Diaspora, Memory, and Identity: A Search for Home*, ed. Vijay Agnew (Toronto: Toronto Press Inc., 2005), 247–48.

100. Avtar Brah, "Diaspora," in *Theories of Memory: A Reader*, ed. Michael Rossington and Anne Whitehead (Baltimore: John Hopkins University Press, 2007), 289. The relationship of the diaspora to the homeland is, as suggested by Robin Cohen, both complicated and fraught (*Global Diasporas*, 2nd ed.,chap. five, "Diasporas and Their Homelands: Sikhs and Zionists"). The homeland can be invented or reinvented depending on the historical and socio-cultural contexts.

101. In his allegorical musing, Paul links Hagar as corresponding to the earthly Jerusalem and Sarah the heavenly Jerusalem (Gal. 4:22-26). Both women and the city are representations of the old and new covenants for Paul. See chapter 4, where I deal with Paul's symbolic interpretation a bit more.

experiences of movement—voluntary or involuntary—and in heterogeneous identities that cultivate a certain consciousness of a "home." Diaspora thus entails translocal, multilocal, cultural fluidity and transcultural consciousness. Although the places Paul travels to are not alien territories, they are not home. But neither is Jerusalem. "Home" is where he hopes to be, and strives for; "home" is out of this realm of existence. Paul longs to be released (ἀναλῦσαι) away from the body and be at home with Christ (τὴν ἐπιθυμίαν ἔχων εἰς τὸ ἀναλῦσαι καὶ σὺν Χριστῷ εἶναι, Phil. 1:23; καὶ εὐδοκοῦμεν μᾶλλον ἐκδημῆσαι ἐκ τοῦ σώματος καὶ ἐνδημῆσαι πρὸς τὸν κύριον, 2 Cor. 5:8). If most Judeans of his time were not thinking of themselves as away from home but felt entirely "at home" in their diverse diasporic social locations, Paul was a diasporic homeless man with, what Avtar Brah calls a "homing desire." For Brah, "the *concept* of diaspora places the discourse of 'home' and 'dispersion' in creative tension, *inscribing a homing desire while simultaneously critiquing discourses of fixed origins.*"[102] And the critique of discourses of fixed origins is done "while taking account of a homing desire, as distinct from a desire for a 'homeland.'"[103] The "homing of diaspora" needs not be understood exclusively in terms of searching for a home that is necessarily a geographical entity—or a mystic quest for origins—but as an imaginative process, as a memory, as a longing for something, as "a mythic place of desire in the diasporic imagination,"[104] and as, simply, a relation.

The tension between fixity and flexibility, "homing desire" and "homeland desire," is experienced by Paul as he moved across

---

102. See Avtar Brah, *Cartographies of Diaspora: Contesting Identities* (New York: Routledge, 1996), 193 (italics original). For Brah, "the problematic of 'home' and belonging may be integral to the diasporic condition, but how, when, and in what form questions surface, or how they are addressed, is specific to the history of a particular diaspora. Not all diasporas inscribe homing desire through a wish to return to a place of 'origin.'" Ibid.

103. Ibid., 16.

104. Ibid., 192.

geographical, historical, linguistic, cultural, and national boundaries around the cultural mixture of the Roman provinces in search of work, and as he encounters diverse social and ethnic groups (natives, artisans migrating in search of works, immigrants, slaves, freedmen, merchants, numerous associations from which he observes and learns, fellow workers, patrons, clients, etc.) with a message of the resurrected Christ. I hope I am not giving the impression of moving back to some older and unsophisticated scholarship, which viewed a sharp dichotomy between Diaspora/Hellenistic and homeland/Jewish mentality. Throughout this study, I have endeavored to present the flexible character behind these labels. What I want to express by my use of "homeland desire" is Paul's reimagined symbol as he uses what is there already in the form of the Judean ancestral "homeland" to express something other. The process of Paul's diasporic existence through "multi-locationality across geographical, cultural and psychic boundaries"[105] has helped him to become a complex hybrid element with multiple identities "where 'imagined communities' are forged within and out of a confluence of narratives from annals of collective memory and re-memory."[106] Jerusalem still maintains its mythic allure in his reimagination, but it is symbolically reconfigured with the view to serve his "space-making"[107] rhetoric of a free Jerusalem coming down from above and embracing those on earth—regardless of their ethnic identity—who are children of this

---

105. Ibid.
106. Ibid., 196. It is interesting to note, in passing, that whereas in the idealized memory of the author of the *Letter of Aristeas*, the ancestral land, the city of Jerusalem, and the temple are viewed in a state of plenty (88–89), the socioeconomic reality Paul confronts as he heads to Jerusalem with the collection is that of a barren ancestral land with many suffering from severe famine.
107. This concept, which is very useful to make my point, is borrowed from Ato Quayson who, however, uses it in a different context, that of colonial "space-making," defined by the author as being "first and foremost the projection of a series of socio-political dimensions upon a geographical space." See Ato Quayson, "Colonial Space-Making and Hybridizing History, or, 'Are the Indians of East Africa Africans or Indians?'" in *Diasporas: Concepts, Intersections, Identities*, ed. Kim Knott and Seán McLoughlin (New York: Zed Books, 2010), 245.

realm above through Christ (Rom. 15:25, 26, 31; 1 Cor. 16:3; Gal. 3:28; 4:26). In other words, the messenger to the nations is not committed to the restoration of the Judean "homeland" as such, but his determination is to remember (μνημονεύωμεν, Gal. 2:10) and to serve the poor from this space who share his epic vision of a re-creation of the local landscape (Gal. 4:25-26). The New Jerusalem, which is the recaptured and resignified product of a symbolic space, is imagined as invading the materiality of "home," thus interrupting a certain mythical discourse of centrality, in order to introduce a new mythic and cosmic center (a "safe place"?) that cannot be bound by time and space. In fact, according to Paul's very loaded theological and programmatic myth-making rhetoric, the whole cosmos, and not just one specific locale, will be redeemed—that is, for example, the main thrust of Romans 8—in order to share in the freedom of the glory of the children of God who will in turn have their inheritance in this entire new world.

Seán McLoughlin, reflecting on R. Cohen's suggestion that "Religions can provide additional cement to bind a diasporic consciousness" and that "their programmes are extraterritorial rather than territorial,"[108] opines,

> The suggestion here is that while in different time/space combinations religions indigenize and often reinforce territorial identifications, it is the ability to trump such processes with extraterritorial imaginings which is both especially salient and peculiarly well enabled in a globalizing world. Despite 'composite origins' (Stewart and Shaw 1994:18), the power of religions resides in their mythic, symbolic and ritual resources to narrate the idealized fictions and abstracted unities which seek to emphasize stability over flux and secure continuity through time and across space.[109]

---

108. Cohen, *Global Diasporas: An Introduction*, 1st ed. (Seattle: University of Washington Press), 189.
109. See Seán McLoughlin, "Muslim Travellers: Homing Desire, the *Umma* and British-Pakistanis" in Knott and McLoughlin, *Diasporas: Concepts, Intersections, Identities*, 224.

Manuel A Vásquez proposes that "Religion, then, is translocative, because it links the diaspora with the imagined homeland" in a sort of "Cosmization," which is "the irruption of the absolute time and space of the sacred into history and geography."[110] Notwithstanding the problematic usage of terms like *religion* and *sacred* as clear explanatory categories, the point is well made that there is in this fascinating cultural category that is problematically called *religion* a rupture of the absolute time and space that propels a reimag(in)ing of these spheres. In this vein, the diasporic subject Paul entertains a very complex relationship with space and time. Time is short, and the space can be redeemed and reimagined to narrate a different narrative.

Paul and Time

In Paul's theology—we cannot detheologize him completely, after all, since it is the language he thinks in—the events of the crucifixion and the resurrection are what structure the temporal scape as they continue to interrupt the past and forge an *in-between* messy present and continuous new creation. These important events (dubbed theologically the Christ event)[111] drive his different moves within his various cultural and social locations. In being sensitive to the apocalyptic substructure of Paul's active theologizing,[112] I suggest that

110. Manuel A Vásquez, "Diasporas and religion," in Knott and McLoughlin, *Diasporas: Concepts, Intersections, Identities*, 131.
111. This term is a very complex mythic marker for Christians that, for Burton L. Mack, "marks the center of the imagined world and its myth-ritual structure." See Mack, *Myth and the Christian Nation: A Social Theory of Religion* (London: Equinox 2008), 236.
112. It is within the apocalyptic context that Paul makes the claim that the eschaton has arrived with the advent, death, and resurrection of Christ, all of which have introduced, in Paul's understanding, the age of the Spirit (1 Cor. 15:23; 2 Cor. 1:22; 5:5; Rom. 8:23). In other words, the conceptual framework of Paul's theology is cosmic in proportion and apocalyptic: his main concern is with a new creation. The main arguments of Paul's preaching can be reduced to the following: (1) the advent of Christ in the fullness of the time; (2) his death and resurrection; (3) the Spirit; (4) the revelation of the mystery; and (5) the formation of a new people. To quote Beker: "Paul is not commissioned to proclaim an arbitrary apocalyptic blast to the world, but to prepare the world for the redemptive coming of God, the one who has already come to us in

Paul in his diasporic posture deems it particularly important to live "in-betweenness" and to anticipate the new creation[113] by collecting the money among the nations where he works and moves around for "the saints in Jerusalem." For Paul, in the "time that remains,"[114] in the possibility of even his own death before the much-anticipated Parousia of Christ (2 Cor. 1:8-11), he pushes on to go about carrying the collection project as "his religious duty"[115] toward his kinsmen, although it is distinctively directed toward "the saints" who are poor in Jerusalem, in anticipation of what is to come—for him as he finally would go "home," and for heaven's colony on earth to be ready and rejoice in the prospect of being fully restored in the New Jerusalem. Then the next stop for Paul is Rome and from there to "the end of the earth," as represented by Spain, in order for him to complete his "apostolic tasks."[116] This way, time and space meet and reinforce one another as new "space-making" is imagined, contextualized, and comes to effect through the continuum of a time that is itself interrupted by the Christ event, and thus shapes the contours of Paul's movements, thoughts, imagination, remapping, creative revisioning, and the collection project with the hope that *his* ministry to the saints

his Son, Jesus Christ." Johan Christiaan Beker, *Paul's Apocalyptic Gospel: The Coming Triumph of God* (Minneapolis: Fortress Press, 1982), 14.

113. I am alluding to the *already* and the *not yet* theological and eschatological tension: God, in Jesus, has inaugurated the new age with a renewed people living in "the presence of the future," awaiting the consummation of everything in the future, when God justifies the whole creation and put everything into rights. See George E. Ladd, *The Presence of the Future* (Grand Rapids: Eerdmans, 1974). See also the monograph by Ryan T. Jackson on Paul's conception of new creation, *New Creation in Paul*, WUNT 272 (Tübingen: Mohr Siebeck, 2010).

114. This is only to use Giorgio Agamben's fitting book title without entering into the intricacies of his reasoning, or without considering the performative aspect of his text in how the messianic/operational time ("the time that is left us," 68) does temporally. See Giogio Agamben, *The Time That Remains: A Commentary on the Letter to the Romans*, trans. Patricia Dailey (Stanford, CA: Stanford University Press, 2005).

115. Richard S. Ascough, "The Completion of a Religious Duty: The Background of 2 Cor 8:1-15," *NTS* 42 (1996): 584–99.

116. See Donaldson, "The Field God Has Assigned," 136, and "Introduction to the Pauline Corpus," in *The Pauline Epistles*, ed. John Muddiman and John Barton, The Oxford Bible Commentary (Oxford: Oxford University Press, 2010), 45.

in Jerusalem may be acceptable (ἡ διακονία μου ἡ εἰς Ἰερουσαλὴμ εὐπρόσδεκτος τοῖς ἁγίοις γένηται, Rom. 15:31).

Within this theological and temporal space spectrum, the collection project, which occupied and preoccupied him for many years, seems to have constituted a solid thread holding together many of his various and difficult travels, and may then be interpreted differently. It may signify not the coming of the gentiles to Zion, and not an act of mutualism in case Paul's communities might also need the financial help of Jerusalem.[117] Rather, the collection project may symbolically represent the restoration of part of the new temple of God (1 Cor. 3:16; 6:19; 2 Cor, 6:16) in dire need of help in Jerusalem—a significant corner of the re-created and resignified temple as it is situated in a symbolic place.[118]

Conclusion

The set goal in this chapter was to read anew Paul's preoccupations and various difficult travels for assisting economically the poor in Jerusalem through the lens of some basic concepts in diaspora studies: *home, homeland,* and *space.* My brief dialogue with some major interpreters in the history of scholarship on Paul's collection project was a way to test some of the different propositions in order to build on and try to advance the scholarly enterprise that is of interest to us. The different readings proposed on this specific issue have not paid enough attention to how Paul's acute sense of geographical space was an important motivating factor for him to risk his life in moving around and collecting funds to help these poor Christ

117. Justin Meggitt, *Paul, Poverty and Survival,* 164–78.
118. I am of course not referring to the physical temple in Jerusalem, which was then standing in good shape, but I am alluding to a different kind of temple Paul refers to in these different passages.

believers suffering from hunger in the recognized, yet reimagined, theological center (Jerusalem).

The first and major part of my reading of the collection project is not at all interested in the too-theological explanation that is usually expressed in explaining such relief effort. The conclusion of the chapter, however, shows what a theological reading, which is informed by the notions of space and time, may yield in assessing Paul's project. The dynamics of movements and of connections between inhabiting the diasporic social locations and that of the preoccupations for the welfare of those inhabiting the ancestral homeland are key factors to consider in order to understand the importance of the collection project for Paul. Taking these different realities seriously means that the usual theological preoccupations and interpretations of this issue need to be modified in order to make room for more this-worldly social realities. Thus by taking the nitty-gritty of the social realities in a diasporic situation seriously, the dynamics of ideals and beliefs—manifested through particular fund-raising activities—are met with the view to articulating and understanding better Paul's identities, mission, and social relationships. Inhabiting the diaspora space for Paul implies connections between "here" and "there." Negotiating the diaspora space means reimagining the homeland, while cultivating a "homing desire" and imagining other spaces.

6

———

Conclusions

Refusing to be disciplined by disciplinary tradition facilitates the spirit of crossing and mixing necessary to adapt eclectic, strategic, and pragmatic resources for analyses that resist a heritage that oppresses in history and in rhetoric, in image and in action, in the past and in the present, at "home" and "abroad."

—Joseph A. Marchal[1]

To go against the multiple and intersecting forms of hegemonic (ideo)logic that operate within our own discipline of biblical criticism, I would suggest that biblical scholars—minority or not—must also read across more worlds, whether in terms of discipline, gender, sexuality, race/ethnicity, and/or nation.

—Tat-siong Benny Liew[2]

Scholarship is about cultivating human flourishing, about giving an account of ourselves, who we want to be, what kinds of others we want

1. Joseph A. Marchal, *The Politics of Heaven: Women, Gender, and Empire in the Study of Paul* (Minneapolis: Fortress Press, 2008), 123.
2. Tat-siong Benny Liew, "Queering Closets and Perverting Desires: Cross-Examining John's Engendering and Trans-Gendering Word across Different Worlds," in *They Were All Together in One Place? Toward Minority Biblical Criticism*, ed. Randall C. Bailey et al. (Atlanta: Society of Biblical Literature, 2009), 281.

to construct, and what kinds of relations we choose to have with other humans and the world.

—Todd Penner and Davina Lopez[3]

In a field where so many important studies have been done on Paul, and where scholars really need to scratch their heads in order to find a small niche to work on a research project, it is surprising, at least to me, that the present study is the first full-fledged work that explores the specific character of Paul's diaspora existence, especially in ways enriched by insights from diaspora studies—in relation to postcolonial studies in terms of upsetting some received conclusions—and gender critical analysis. Paul's social relationships as an itinerant worker and preacher in the Diaspora with various communities of Christ believers and nonbelievers within the Roman Empire have been the focus of this project. Important aspects to investigate in this study were the Diaspora as a destabilizing space; the messiness of boundary crossings; the "cut-and-mix" hybrid positioning of diaspora subjects and communities in negotiating socioreligious ideals and social realities; the complexities of social positioning within different groups; and identities to construct and to transcend.

The main argument of this project is that Paul's diasporic condition was central to his life, mission, and social relationships. Paul was a diasporic male Judean of low social status negotiating different spaces; he was a devotee and interpreter of Christ among the nations; he was socially deviant, with little of an economic or political power base, and in the process of signifying a new empire under the authority of Christ in the first-century Mediterranean world. The notion of Paul as an itinerant preacher and worker in the Diaspora, needless to

---

3. Todd Penner and Davina Lopez, "Homelessness as a Way Home," in *Holy Land as Homeland? Models for Constructing the Historic Landscapes of Jesus*, ed. Keith W. Whitelam, The Social World of Biblical Antiquity, Second Series, 7 (Sheffield: Sheffield Phoenix, 2011), 172.

say, is an interpretive model that does not aim to answer all possible questions about Paul's identities and social relationships.

After laying down the theoretical and methodological framework in the introduction, the best way to start studying Paul as a hybrid diasporic Judean was to place him within the larger context of ancient diaspora Judaism in the Greco-Roman period. This emplacing was important for this project. Paul is relevant both to the study of first-century Judaism(s), as well as the study of the early Jesus movement. To categorize him solely within one tradition—that which has become Christianity—is to miss out on the vitality and variety of first-century Judaism; to relegate the study of Paul to solely, or principally, to students of the earliest Christianities is to imply certain essential differences between "Judaism" and "Christianity" that are historically problematic. Therefore, scholars interested in Diaspora Judaism in the Greco-Roman period need to pay more attention to Paul as a first-century Jewish itinerant Diaspora figure within the Roman Empire.

The *Letter of Aristeas* was a good place for setting the study of Paul in the Greco-Roman Diaspora, since the *Letter* itself already is located in this hybrid setting. The dynamics of the hybrid condition expressed in the *Letter*, I argued in chapter 1, are captured in the forms of calculated negotiations, prudent affiliations, and idealized memory. There one encounters a profound desire for a particular community to enter into better communication with the Hellenistic world at large by incorporating the best of the "Jewish" and the "Greek" cultures and modes of thinking, without jeopardizing what they hold dear as part of their distinct socioreligious fabric. The *Letter* begs to present, and to inspire, a "third space" of breathing "in-between."

Then, it was necessary to consider how another diasporic figure, Josephus, one close to but different from Paul in many ways, managed and negotiated his diaspora existence at the heart of the

Roman political power. Josephus, I argued, in his rereading and summary of the *Letter*, seemed to have omitted parts of the text because of sociopolitical constraints. In other words, Josephus's summary of the *Letter* in *Antiquities* 12 was characterized by his adept way of adapting to and navigating the sociopolitical dimension of his work as a historian in his diasporic space. By the way he constructs agencies, Josephus managed to negotiate his diasporic sociopolitical location by moving between assimilation and resistance in his rewriting of the *Letter*.

In chapter 2, I developed a description of Paul as a diaspora figure. The thesis of that chapter is that one is to consider Paul as both a complex and ordinary figure in the Diaspora. Attention to both similarities and differences does not have as its aim the underplaying of variations and distinctiveness, but to show that differences are as important as similarities. I utilized the works of Jonathan Z. Smith, particularly on the practice of comparison, in order to move away from any suggestions that a figure, be it that of the constructed Christian and mythic hero "Saint" Paul or not, can be seen as out of the ordinary. Paul, rather, needs to be studied as both similar and different to other Diaspora Judeans. I appropriated Philip A. Harland's model for studying degrees of acculturation, of structural assimilation, and of cultural maintenance in minority groups to help situate Paul's social integration, adaptation, and participation within different networks in his social locations in the Diaspora. John M. Barclay's categories of assimilation, acculturation and accommodation have also helped to place Paul within the Jewish Diaspora of the Mediterranean world. The insights drawn from diaspora studies, which were built on some of the results of Smith, Harland, and Barclay, have allowed me to situate Paul in more flexible ways, and to focus on his multiple identities and how he was negotiating spaces in the Diaspora.

With the ground of the theoretical layers of this study cleared, it was then possible, in chapter 3, to look at an overworked issue among Pauline scholars—the dispute at Antioch—through a different conceptual lens (diaspora space) that could offer, not a solution to the problems highlighted in the scholarly discussions, but instead different ways or angles of observation. The main argument, a simple one, but one that is not preoccupied with the usual theological conclusions on the subject, is that the real debate in Antioch was not so much about gentiles, but first, about two social Judean groups claiming the identity of "Jewish," and second, who was authoritative or representative to assume control over the contested spheres of home and diaspora, center and periphery, alongside divergent sociopolitical and theological agendas and interpretations. In other words, at the heart of the conflict at Antioch was the question of diaspora and of the complexities of lives lived in tension in the entanglements of the diaspora space they all occupied. The usual theological logic used to interpret the conflict at Antioch, in light of the analysis done in that chapter, ought to be modified, in order to take into account the messiness of social relations in the diaspora space.

What follows (chapter 4) in the narrative of this study is a recalibration of Paul's position toward the nations through an intersectional reading that uncovers the questions of gender and diaspora, gender and ethnicity, and gender and empire. One of the aims of that chapter was to resist any unambiguous, or unnuanced, picture of Paul as a diaspora figure among the nations. I contextualized Paul's gender construction and performance of identities by scrutinizing the tension between mimicking the discourse of the empire and of siding with the victims of imperial violence, which surfaces in his rhetorical moves with the Galatians. In light of the analysis undertaken in that chapter, the field of Pauline studies needs to take into serious consideration how the diaspora existence heightens Paul's rhetoric and identities in his dealings with the Galatians.

Chapter 5 immersed itself in another hot and difficult issue in Pauline scholarship, that of the collection project. To be fair and to understand the issue as clearly as possible, I briefly revisited a number of major contributors on the topic, demonstrating that the different solutions proposed were lacking or biased in one way or the other. The reading proposed in that chapter was informed by diaspora studies and, to a lesser degree, by theology, in order to understand Paul's plausible motivations in his different and difficult travels. Pauline studies will have to pay more attention to Paul's social realities in a diasporic situation in order to understand his collection project. The usual theological preoccupations and interpretations of this issue need to make room for more this-worldly social realities. Issues of "home," of time and space seem to have had bearings on Paul's motivations to risk his life to move around in order to do what he could to help the poor Christ believers dying of hunger in the ancestral home, before his own time of death came. Then, after the collection trip to Jerusalem, he would go to Rome and then to "the end of the earth," as represented by Spain, in order to proclaim the death and resurrection of Christ. But there is no clear historical evidence as to how the collection was received, since the last comments we have concerning this project are in Rom. 15:14-32. It seems rather tragic that his relief effort was probably rejected by the leaders of the Christ groups in Jerusalem (according to Acts 21:27-36); his plan, or hope, of going to Spain did not seem to have materialized either. Paul, the itinerant preacher and contested leader of Christ believers in the Diaspora, one with unusual zeal and socioreligious ideals, was never able to see materialized some of his cherished desires; for example, that of seeing numerous

Jews embrace, like many gentiles, his understanding of a redeployed Judaism with Jesus as the Christ, the τέλος (end and purpose) of the law; or that of proclaiming the death and resurrection of Christ to the ends of the earth. What we see, instead, is that his message, with the germ of imperialism that it itself had, became a weapon of mass destruction in the hands of mostly Christian male European leaders, with the view to manufacturing certain social spaces for controlling women, slaves, and to make others "Other."[4] The past nineteen to twenty centuries of history in interpreting Paul's letters has illustrated the hermeneutical choices usually made. Slaves, women, the poor, the "Other" were simply excluded or marginalized in the enterprise. The European colonialist project and the conditions of American colonialism illustrate this point well. The interpreters coming from these imperialistic centers have, in general, projected a colonialist reading of Paul in order to advance the interests of whites, males, slave owners, and those in positions of influence. Paul's captivity—or at least the early ecclesiastical attempt to control or neutralize him—within an artificial and confusing Christian canon may also have the effect of making even his most daring dreams, propositions, and insights lose much of their sparkle.[5]

---

4. See Fernando F. Segovia, *Decolonizing Biblical Studies: A View from the Margins* (Maryknoll, NY: Orbis, 2004). The growing body of works stemming from feminists, from postcolonial biblical scholars and from others with new, intriguing, and exciting ways of reading texts has increasingly drawn our attention to the silencing of some figures—in and out the biblical text—and the marginalization of minority voices in the enterprise of biblical interpretations. See, for example, E. Schüssler Fiorenza's watershed book, *In Memory of Her: A Feminist Reconstruction of Christian Origins* (New York: Crossroads, 1983). This study was published in order to challenge the androcentric presuppositions of much "malestream" scholarship, stimulating a wide range of feminist treatments of early Christian texts. See also Amy-Jill Levine, ed., *A Feminist Companion to Paul* (Cleveland: Pilgrim, 2004);FernandoF. Segovia and Rasiah S. Sugirtharajah, eds., *A Postcolonial Commentary on the New Testament Writings* (London: T & T Clark, 2007); Tat-siong Benny Liew, *What Is Asian American Biblical Hermeneutics? Reading the New Testament* (Honolulu: University of Hawaii Press, 2008).

5. On the origins of "the canon" and some of the issues surrounding the task of interpretation within cultural and canonical diversity, see James H. Charlesworth, "Reflections on the Canon, Its Origins, and New Testament Interpretation," in *Method and Meaning: Essays on New*

It is important that one consider Paul's identities, mission, and social relationships as a diaspora figure navigating different spaces in the first century. Locating Paul as a diasporic figure negotiating social realities and religious commitments allows one to observe how space is signified and how authority is asserted in the diaspora. If he is, as he understands it, a representative of Israel, who is called by God and not by humans (οὐκ ἀπ᾽ ἀνθρώπων οὐδὲ δι᾽ ἀνθρώπου, Gal. 1:1) to preach to the ἔθνη a gospel not of human origin (ὅτι οὐκ ἔστιν κατὰ ἄνθρωπον, 1:11), then it makes perfect sense for him to be very concerned for those sharing the same hope as he does and languishing in poverty in the recognized theological center—Jerusalem.[6] Demarcating the geographical significance of Jerusalem and downplaying the importance of recognized leaders coming from Jerusalem in Galatians, for example (Gal. 4:25; 2:6; 2:9), could not stop the real connotation of what his association with Jerusalem still signifies to him and to his converts. Accordingly, he plays with the place of origins to, in turn, help those in financial needs to be "blessed" by those who have been "blessed" by them. By presenting his arguments for a translocal obligation that the local Christ associations have vis-à-vis the poor in Christ physically located in Jerusalem, Paul is not so much building an international alternative and egalitarian society. Rather, he strives on the one hand to consolidate the prior understanding of labor division and autonomy by which he has jurisdiction over the whole gentile world, and, on the other hand, to show that the whole gentile world can be motivated to serve those in need at "home."

Testament Interpretation in Honor of Harold W. Attridge, ed. Andrew B. McGowan and Kent Harold Richards (Atlanta: Society of Biblical Literature, 2011), 505–29.

6. Paul is, in spite of his largely successful mission among the nations, not boasting but in anguish because, if we follow E. P. Sanders's reflections—themselves based on Johannes Munck's analysis of Romans 9–11—the mission to the Jews by Peter and others was largely unsuccessful. See Ed P. Sanders, *Paul, the Law, and the Jewish People* (Minneapolis: Fortress Press, 1983), 185.

Locating Paul's discursive negotiations as a diasporic figure who struggles to empower the communities of the poor scattered on the margins is important, if one deems it significant to situate him in larger and much more diverse as well as interesting conversations. He is one of the many marginalized voices of the early Jesus movement, although he might, at times, present himself as the sole authorized or authoritative prophetic voice (e.g., Gal. 1:15-16) of his socioreligious and ethnic group to the non-Jews. This way of revisiting Paul, as one trying to negotiate his diasporic spaces and make sense of it all, disrupts, complicates, reframes, redirects, redescribes, reimagines, and opens up the possibilities of looking at him "as embedded in a contested, complex, and shifting context that includes both ancient empire and modern neocolonialism, thus allowing an engagement with the present to revise our approach of the past."[7] We may imagine Paul much as we imagine ourselves at points: a little vague about what exactly we are "trying to do," all the more so sometimes when we think we really know what we are up to (the world being so mysterious, letting us fall so often into unexpected consequences, etc.). We are in flux, intuitive, and we are participating in the becoming of much more than we generally think about consciously. This way of approaching him, as one voice among many, has the advantage of helping us problematize his authoritarian and sexualized rhetorics—the nations are "the foreskin" (τῆς ἀκροβυστίας!) (Gal. 2:7), for example—that are manufactured as one totally in control of his gospel and totally in charge of the ways his assemblies functioned, with his missionary activities clearly defined. Worthy of mention is also Paul's extravagant language concerning his successful mission to the gentiles, leaving no more room for preaching in the regions

---

7. Melanie Johnson-Debaufre and Laura S. Nasrallah, "Beyond the Heroic Paul," in *The Colonized Apostle: Paul through Postcolonial Eyes*, ed. Christopher D. Stanley (Minneapolis: Fortress Press, 2011),167.

"from Jerusalem around all the way to Illyricum" (Rom.15:19, 23) and concerning the reality of the few struggling communities he has founded.[8] Decentring Paul requires that we reimagine him as a diasporic male Jew, traveling artisan, often sick, seen by many antagonizing Judeans in various communities as dangerous and an apostate; generally treated with great suspicion by those with certain political positions in the different synagogues in the Diaspora; subject of the Roman Empire, who imagines himself to be one called for a particular task in the series of events to be accomplished in the final days of this world.

Paul's social consciousness, as it manifested itself in the disjunction between his ideal claims and his diasporic social reality, seems to have placed him in a position to fantasize about another reality that is to come. Paul believed that the new was there already, but not in its final form; that the present time is one of transition, politically and sociologically. As an apocalyptic person knowing that he lives in an in-between time and that he is "not at home," he lives a mythic diaspora existence without complaining about the status quo, since he thought he and his communities were living in a hope that was already coming to realization, but not yet fully materialized.[9] The different imperial subjects to whom Paul, as a diaspora figure, is writing are not offered any clear "down to earth" alternative to deal meaningfully with their situation in the here and now. Paul, in other

8. See the article by Terence L. Donaldson, "The Field God Has Assigned: Geography and Mission in Paul," in *Religious Rivalries in the Early Roman Empire and the Rise of Christianity*, ed. Leif E. Vaage, Studies in Christianity and Judaism/Études sur le christianisme et le judaïsme ;(Waterloo, ON: Wilfrid Laurier University Press, 2006). See also Ryan Schellenberg, "'Danger in the Wilderness, Danger at Sea': Paul and Perils of Travel," in *Travel and Religion in Antiquity*, ed. Philip A. Harland, Studies in Christianity and Judaism 21(Waterloo, ON: Wilfrid Laurier University Press, 2011), 141–61.

9. This is what George E. Ladd has very aptly dubbed "fulfillment without consummation" in his now-classic *The Presence of the Future* (Grand Rapids: Eerdmans, 1974). See also J. Paul Sampley, *Walking Between the Times: Paul's Moral Reasoning* (Minneapolis: Fortress Press, 1991), 7–24.

words, is a good Roman subject who is at pains to negotiate religious ideals and social reality.

Having said that, one may not uncritically lump Paul into the category of a partisan of empire—the scars of Roman punishment were visible in his body (2 Cor. 11:25; Gal. 6:17)—but his clear message of conformity to the status quo is no less telling and genuine. Because of this eschatological standpoint—wherein the cosmic battle is of far greater importance than the sociopolitical reality of the present—Paul was, in a sense, minimizing and relativizing the powers ruling in society. The empire and the present political turmoil are thus seen as transient, while the power of God has dawned already in the community of the elect. From this understanding, one could argue that the millenary character deducible in Paul's message is highly political, in the sense that it uses social imagination to challenge the very social structure within which he was operating by giving marginal voices (slaves, women, and children) a platform to dream, exercise certain leadership abilities, and be viewed differently within the Christ-followers communities. And the millenarian view he presents offers the communities he is addressing great hope for the future in the sense of reversal of the present social order, providing an upsurge and release of emotional enthusiasm that helps the largely unprivileged and marginalized to cope with life in this world. But, again, that does not resolve the tension, in Paul, of negotiating life with the empire in the actuality of things (be it passing away by the alleged new creation or not). Paul is offering a temporal solution—wait for the Parousia (1 Thess. 4:13-5:11)! That is, be ready like soldiers for the arrival of Christ as the new emperor since, apparently for Paul, life cannot be conceived without empire.

Because of his belief in the imminence of the Parousia, and in his understanding in Phil. 3:20 that his home and constitutive government, alongside the Philippians, is in heaven, Paul anticipated that the Roman Empire would not persist for much longer. This is probably why he encouraged his followers to subject themselves to the existing governments and to be good citizens (Rom. 13:1-7). If what Paul offered his communities composed of both dispersed and nondiaspora peoples did give them hope in the times under the imperial power, his message still resonates well with the Roman regime. In these exhortations, the communities he is addressing are encouraged to stay in their normal roles as subalterns outside of the political spheres of influence. As long as Paul continued to encourage communities with which he was associated to keep a low profile and go unnoticed, he and these communities would be probably safe. But, of course, the picture is more complicated than that. What we have is that, on the one hand, Paul seems to embrace the Roman Empire, especially in how his discourse with the Galatians (see chapter 4 of this study for more on that) seems to mimic the very gendered discourse of the Roman Empire, but on the other hand he also seems to challenge the body politic of the imperial system as well. The community of Christ followers he is addressing in the Epistle to the Romans, for example, is called to be a body politic that is rooted in the offering of one's very body as living sacrifices to God (Rom. 12:1), instead of participating in the pagan sacrifices of the empire. Paul is appealing to this community to undermine the status system of honour in the empire by deliberately associating with the lowly and exercising hospitality to the outsider. Honor and shame should refer not to Jewish identity markers or one's rank within the Roman's social stratum, but to Christ.

On the other hand, if communities associated with Paul are deemed to challenge the norms and values of the ancient world, then one must give him credit as one Jewish male itinerant preacher and worker among others who has negotiated, accommodated, and empowered different communities of Christ followers to live life meaningfully and subversively as a diasporic subject. For these communities to adopt a kinship, unconventional gender roles for women, admit slaves as full members of different Christ communities, override ethnic identities within their alternative groups, and to portray a criminal executed by the state as a conqueror was clearly creating social tension that would, admittedly, constitute a source of local—and growing imperial—persecutions. For Paul, to contrast the grace and peace of Christ, even at a veiled polemical level, to the grace and peace (*pax Romana*) with which Emperor Augustus was associated, makes him an important and difficult socioreligious and diaspora figure to locate. It is necessary, then, to embrace him as a diasporic subject in his ambivalence, in his 'Third Space of enunciation' à la Bhabha, in rejecting, negotiating, mimicking, and embracing the Roman Empire at the same time, for different reasons, instead of trying to place him under a neat category.

Paul was a diaspora figure expressing his understanding of Judaism in light of his socioeconomic religious experiences, and he struggled to convince others of his own ethnic group that he was still operating within the parameters of a Judaism redeployed around Jesus. Paul was seeking to resolve what might have seemed to be quite ordinary problems for a Jew living in the Diaspora, speaking Greek, trying to make a living and trying to make sense of his world. The difference is that some of the letters he wrote to those with whom he believed he had discovered the solution have survived until today and, in fact, became canonical texts. Thus, besides an interest and curiosity about some figures in antiquity that may draw one to study Paul in his worlds, he is important particularly for theological reasons; he remains a source of endless fascination mainly because of his central authority for contemporary Christians, who seek to ground their own theological, political and historical-cultural projects in his authority.[10] Various social, ethnic, and religious communities around the globe today refer to Paul's epistles—irrespective of which ones scholars deem authentic or inauthentic—for guidance in different aspects of their lives. Many, if not most, in these communities and churches would not care less about what academics furiously debate concerning Paul and the movement of which he was a part of, or, as a matter of fact, regarding the present study. The nonheroic Paul of the first-century that was of interest to us in these pages is not the same as the sanctified and symbolic Christian Paul of today.

10. Stating that, I acknowledge that Paul continues to be a fascinating figure for other reasons as well. For example, the celebrated French philosopher Alain Badiou admires him. For Badiou, "Paul is not an apostle or a saint. I care nothing for the Good News he declares, or the cult dedicated to him. But he is a subjective figure of primary importance. . . . For me, Paul is a poet-thinker of the event, as well as one who practices and states the invariant traits of what can be called the militant figure. He brings forth the entirely human connection, whose destiny fascinates me, between the general idea of a rupture, an overturning, and that of a thought-practice that is this rupture's subjective materiality." See Alain Badiou, *Saint Paul: The Foundation of Universalism*, trans. Ray Brassier (Stanford, CA.: Stanford University Press, 2003), prologue, 1, 2.

Epilogue

The extent to which I come closer to understanding Paul as a diasporic subject, caught between his grand theological ideals, on one hand, and the nitty-gritty social realities of life as an itinerant worker, preacher and as a contested leader of Christ believers in his diasporic space(s) under the Roman Empire, on the other hand, is difficult for me to assess. But it has been an exercise worth pursuing and it certainly provided me with a lot of intellectual pleasures. The present project has led me to challenge my own Christian upbringing, ready answers, and theological preunderstandings on many Pauline issues and, hopefully, it will help others interested in Paul and in his social relationships as an itinerant diasporic figure to be similarly challenged in their paradigms and in their (mis)understandings. The hope is to continue to explore these and some other important issues in the Pauline corpus by not being (too) preoccupied with theology, and that this study will stimulate further research into Paul and the fragmented communities of which he was a part. That means continuing to study Paul as one social agent among others, who engages in mythmaking, social formations, and the rearranging and remapping of spaces and narratives in the messiness of social and cultural relationships within the complexities of first-century Diaspora Judaism.

It was also my goal to be as honest as I possibly could in following the arguments wherever they might lead, and not be (too) preoccupied by ready and easy theological answers in the texts (as well as in my head), while also not being swayed or discouraged by any real life pressures, such as whether some of the conclusions and analysis reached in the present study might not jeopardize my fragile and burgeoning academic career. I am thinking, for example, of some readers who might not quite understand or value the type of gender analysis undertaken in chapter 4. This concern is a serious one in an academic discipline still so much attached to theological Christian colleges, seminaries, and divinity schools—admittedly, there are countless such institutions and they vary in terms of theology, structures, and political and social concerns—alongside powerful religious and academic authorities in and out of the academic world. These powerful forces can place ideology and conformity to certain theological and religious or methodological traditions at the forefront, before creative, yet serious scholarship, by discouraging, by not hiring, by intimidating, by punishing, by weeding out, by firing any perceived as dissidents from manufactured norms, theologies, ideological investments, and petty, partisan politics. Systems of control and coercion can never facilitate serious and creative research that push boundaries and dare challenge some status quos, taboos, saintly figures, highly held theories and methods in the academic field one is engaged in. The various scholarly conversations we are engaged in, one would have hoped, should be the priority for institutions of higher learning.

I have tried to be as careful as I could in my research to not be defined by scholarly identities; or to not play the game of certain types of scholarship that pretend to be utterly impartial, neutral; or to not be defined by camps of Pauline scholarship that view Paul as either not interested in politics, or as an apostle of liberty undermining Caesar (of old, as well as his modern representatives), or as an emissary of God siding with the poor and the marginalized of his time, as well as those of today. Stating that, I also value W. Arnal's cautious words: "Our scholarly identities will best be served by hard work and honesty; not by facile repudiation of all the work of the past."[1] I choose to remain a stranger out of place without denying the value of what I can learn from those who inhabit different homes. Inevitably, such homelessness will annoy many readers invested in New Testament and Christian origins scholarship, who are "insistent on saving home, homeland, and *Heimat* at all costs."[2]

Does a reading of Paul from either side of the scholarly divide really matter in the concrete social, political, and economic realities of those excluded in the "lost" places of the global south, and in the messy, fragile, complex and complicated realities of those unwelcome refugees and immigrants, exploited nannies, subjugated poor, or abused migrant domestic laborers in the urban centers in the West? Frankly, where is "Paul"—both the constructed rhetorical persona and the stable Christian construct—in the struggles for survival of various children, women, and men in a place like Haiti today? Having lived under dictatorships, economic embargos, and having tried to express my faith in the God professed by Paul in the stricken-poor, complex Haiti, with the remarkable, resilient people of my tortured land, I have witnessed how Pauline texts can both affect and determine the space of real bodies in systems of male domination and political struggles.

Finally, does this study—apart from pursuing some intellectual interests, questions, curiosities about *our* scholarly understanding of

1. See Arnal, *The Symbolic Jesus: Historical Scholarship, Judaism and the Construction of Contemporary Identity* (London: Equinox, 2005), 46.
2. See Todd Penner and Davina C. Lopez, "Homelessness as a Way Home," in *Holy Land as Homeland? Models for Constructing the Historic Landscapes of Jesus*, ed. Keith W. Whitelam, The Social World of Biblical Antiquity, Second Series, 7 (Sheffield: Sheffield Phoenix, 2011), 176.

Paul's circumstances, and some of the issues that were crucially formed by the diasporic conditions he faced—matter, after all, in the grand scheme of things?

I really hope it does.

Bibliography

Aasgaard, Reidar. '*My Beloved Brothers and Sisters!*' *Christian Siblingship in Paul.* JSNTSup 265. London/New York: T&T Clark, 2004.

Agamben, Giorgio. *The Time that Remains: A Commentary on the Letter to the Romans.* Translated by Patricia Dailey. Palo Alto, CA: Stanford University Press, 2005.

Albl, Martin. ""For Whenever I Am Weak, Then I Am Strong": Disability in Paul's Epistles." In *This Abled Body: Rethinking Disabilities in Biblical Studies*, edited by Hector Avalos, Sarah J. Melcher, and Jeremy Schipper, 145–48. Atlanta: SBL, 2007.

Alles, Gregory D. *The Iliad, the R_M_YANA, And The Work Of Religion: Failed Persuasion and Religious Mystification.* University Park: The Pennsylvania State University Press, 1994.

Ando, Clifford. *Imperial Ideology and Provincial loyalty in the Roman Empire.* Berkeley, Los Angeles and London: University of California Press, 2000.

Antonaccio, C. "Hybridity and the Cultures within Greek Culture." In *The Cultures within Greek Culture*, edited by L. Kurke and C. Dougherty, 57–74. Cambridge: Cambridge University Press, 2003.

Arnal, William E. *The Symbolic Jesus: Historical Scholarship, Judaism and the Construction of Contemporary Identity.* London: Equinox, 2005.

———. "A Parting of the Ways? Scholarly Identities and a Peculiar Species of Ancient Mediterranean Religion." In *Identity and Interaction in the Ancient*

Mediterranean: Jews, Christians, and Others, edited by Zeba Crook and Philip Harland, 253–75. Sheffield: Sheffield Phoenix Press, 2007.

———. "Bringing Paul and the Corinthians Together? A Rejoinder and some proposals on Redescribing and Theory." In *Redescribing Paul and the Corinthians*, 75–104. Atlanta: SBL, 2011.

———. "The Collection and Synthesis of 'Tradition' and the Second-Century Invention of Christianity." *MTSR* 23 (2011): 193–215.

———, Willi Braun, and Russell T. McCutcheon. *Failure and Nerve in the Academic Study of Religion*. London: Equinox, 2012.

Ascough, Richard S. "The Completion of a Religious Duty: The Background of 2 Cor 8:1-15." *NTS* 42 (1996): 584–99.

———. "Translocal Relationship among Voluntary Associations and Early Christianity." *JECS* 5 (1997): 223–41.

———. "The Thessalonian Christian Community as a Professional Voluntary Association." *JBL* 119/2 (2000): 311–28.

———. *Paul's Macedonian Associations: The Social Context of Philippians and 1 Thessalonians*. WUNT 2:161. Tübingen: Mohr Siebeck, 2003.

———. "'Voluntary Associations and the Formation of Pauline Churches: Addressing the Objections." In Vereine, Synagogen und Gemeinden im kaiserzeitlichen Kleinasien, edited by Andreas Gutsfeld and Dietrich-Alex Koch, 149–83. STAC 25. Tübingen: Mohr Siebeck, 2006.

Ashcroft, Bill, Gareth Griffiths, and Helen Tiffin, eds. *The Post-Colonial Studies Reader*. New York: Routledge, 1995.

Atsuhiro, Asano. *Community-Identity Construction in Galatians: Exegetical, Social-Anthropological and Socio-Historical Studies*. London: T&T Clark, 2005.

Aus, Roger D. "Paul's Travel Plans to Spain and the 'Full Number of the Gentiles of Rom. XI 25." *NovT* 21 (1979): 232–62.

Badiou, Alain. *Saint Paul: The Foundation of Universalism*. Translated by Ray Brassier. Palo Alto, CA: Stanford University Press, 2003.

Bailey, Randall C. "They're Nothing But Incestuous Bastards: The Polemical Use of Sex and Sexuality in Hebrew Canon Narratives." In *Reading from This Place*. Vol 1, *Social Location and Biblical Interpretation in the United States*. Edited by Fernando F. Segovia and Mary Ann Tolbert, 121–38. Minneapolis: Fortress Press, 1995.

Barclay, John M. G. "Paul among Diaspora Jews: anomaly or apostate." *JSNT* 60 (1995): 89–120.

———. *Jews in the Mediterranean Diaspora: From Alexander to Trajan 323 B.C.E. – 117 C.E.* Berkeley: University of California Press, 1996.

———. "Paul and Philo on Circumcision: Romans 2.25–9 in Social and Cultural Context." *NTS* 44 (1998): 536–56.

———, ed. *Negotiating Diaspora: Jewish Strategies in the Roman Empire*. London: T&T Clark, 2004.

———. "The Empire Writes Back: Josephan Rhetoric in Flavian Rome." In *Flavius Josephus and Flavian Rome*, edited by J. Edmonson et al, 315–32. Oxford: Oxford University Press, 2005.

———. "Money and Meetings: Group Formation among Diaspora Jews and Early Christians." In *Vereine, Synagogen und Gemeinde im Kaiserzeitlichen Kleinasien*, edited by Andreas Gutsfeld and Dietrich-Alex Koch, 121–22. Studien und Texte zu antike und Christentum 25. Tübingen: Mohr Siebeck, 2006.

———. "Stoic Physics and the Christ-event: A Review of Troels Engberg-Pedersen." *JSNT* 33, no. 4 (2011): 406–14.

———. *Pauline Churches and Diaspora Jews*. Tübingen: Mohr Siebeck, 2011.

———, and S. J. Gathercole, eds. *Divine and Human Agency in Paul and His Cultural Environment*. London: T&T Clark, 2006.

Barnett, Paul. *The Second Epistle to the Corinthians*. NICNT. Grand Rapids: Eerdmans, 1997.

Barton, Lester J. *The City in The Ancient World*. Cambridge, MA: Harvard University Press, 1972.

Beaude, Pierre-Marie. *Saint Paul: L'oeuvre de Métamorphose*. Paris: Éditions du Cerf, 2011.

Beavis, Mary Ann L. "Anti-Egyptian Polemic in the Letter of Aristeas 130-165 The High Priest's Discourse."*JSJ* 18 (1987): 145–51.

Beker, J. Christiaan. *Paul the Apostle: The Triumph of God in Life and Thought*. Minneapolis: Fortress Press, 1980.

———. *Paul's Apocalyptic Gospel: The Coming Triumph of God*. Minneapolis: Fortress Press, 1982.

Benny Liew, Tat-siong. *What is Asian American Biblical Hermeneutics? Reading the New Testament*. Honolulu: University of Hawaii Press, 2008.

———. "Queering Closets and Perverting Desires: Cross-examining John's Engendering and Trans-gendering Word across Different Worlds." In *They Were all Together in One Place? Toward Minority Biblical Criticism*, edited by Randall C. Bailey et al, 251–88. Atlanta: SBL Press, 2009.

———. "Redressing Bodies at Corinth: Racial/Ethnic Politics and Religious Difference in the Context of Empire." In *The Colonized Apostle*, 127–45.

Berger, K. "Almosen für Israel." *NTS* 23 (1977): 180–204.

Berger, L. Peter. *The Sacred Canopy: Elements of a Sociological Theory of Religion*. New York: Anchor 1967, 1990.

Berns-McGown, Rima. "Redefining 'Diaspora': The Challenge of Connection and Inclusion." *International Journal* (Winter 2007–8): 3–20.

Betz, Hans Dieter. *Galatians: A Commentary on Paul's Letter to the Churches in Galatia*. Philadelphia: Fortress Press, 1979.

Bhabha, Homi K. "Cultural diversity and Cultural differences." In *The Post-Colonial Studies Reader*, edited by Bill Ashcroft, 206–9. London: Routledge, 1988.

———. "Cultural Identity and Diaspora." In *Identity: Community Culture and Difference*, edited by J. Rutherford. London: Lawrence and Wishart, 1990.

———. *Location of Culture*. London: Routledge, 1994.

———. "Culture's in Between." In *Artforum International* 32 (1993): 167–71.

Bird, Michael F., and Preston M. Sprinkle. *The Pistis Christou Debate: The Faith of Jesus Christ.* Peabody,MA: Hendrickson, 2009.

Birnbaum, Ellen. *The Place of Judaism in Philo's Thought: Israel, Jews, and Proselytes.* Brown Judaic Series 290. Studia Philonica Monographs 2. Atlanta: Scholars Press, 1996.

Bockmuehl, Markus N. A. *Jewish Law in Gentile Churches. Halakhah and the Beginning of Public Ethics.* Edinburgh: T&T Clark, 2000.

Bohak, Gideon. 'Review of J.M.G. Barclay, *Jews in the Mediterranean Diaspora*.' *The Classical Journal* 99, no. 2 (2003/4): 195–202.

Bondanella, Peter. *Umberto Eco and the Open Text, Semiotics, Fiction, Popular Culture.* Cambridge: Cambridge University Press, 1997.

Borgen, Peder. "Observations on the Theme 'Paul and Philo': Paul's Preaching of Circumcision in Galatia Gal 5:11 and Debates on Circumcision in Philo." In *Die Paulinische Literatur und Theologie*, edited by Sigfred Pedersen, 85–102. Arhus: Forlaget Aros, 1980.

———. *Philo, John and Paul: New Perspectives on Judaism and Early Christianity.* Brown Judaic Studies. Atlanta: Scholars Press, 1987.

———. "Some Hebrew and Pagan Features in Philo's and Paul's Interpretation of Hagar and Ishmael." In *The New Testament and Hellenistic Judaism*, edited by Peder Borgen and Sören Giversen, 151–64. Aarhus: Aarhus University Press, 1995.

Boyarin, Daniel. *Paul: A Radical Jew: Paul and the Politics of Identity.* Contraversions: Critical Studies in Jewish Literature, Culture, and Society. Berkeley/Los Angeles: University of California Press, 1994.

———. "Unheroic Conduct: The Rise of Heterosexuality and Jewish Masculinity." In *Men and Masculinities in Christianity and Judaism: A Critical Reader*, 79–95. London: SCM, 2009.

———, and Boyarin, Jonathan. "Diaspora: Generation and the Ground of Jewish Identity." In *Theorizing Diaspora: A Reader*, edited by Jana Evans Braziel and Anita Mannur. Oxford: Blackwell, 2003.

——, and Virginia Burrus. "Hybridity as Subversion of Orthodoxy? Jews and Christians in Late Antiquity." *Social Compass* 52 (2005): 431–41.

Brah, Avtar. *Cartographies of Diaspora: Contesting Identities.* London/New York: Routledge, 1996.

——. "Diaspora, Border and Transnational Identities." In *Feminist Postcolonial Theory: A Reader,* edited by R. Lewis and S. Mills, 613–34. New York: Routledge, 1995, 2003.

——. "Cartographies of diaspora: contesting identities." In *Theories of Memory: A Reader,* edited by Michael Rossington and Anne Whitehead, 286–89. Baltimore: John Hopkins University Press, 2007.

Braun, Willi, and Russell T. McCutcheon. *Introducing Religion: Essays in Honor of Jonathan Z. Smith.* London: Equinox, 2008.

Braund, David. *Rome and the Friendly King: The Character of the Client Kingship.* London: Croom Helm; New York: St Martin's Press, 1984.

Braziel, Jana Evans. *Diaspora: An Introduction.* Oxford: Blackwell, 2008.

——, and Anita Mannur. *Theorizing Diaspora: A Reader.* Oxford: Blackwell, 2003.

Breton, Raymond. *Ethnic Relations in Canada: Institutional Dynamics,* edited by Jeffrey G. Reitz. Montreal/Kingston: McGill-Queen's University Press, 2005.

Brubaker, Rogers, and Frederick Cooper. "Beyond 'Identity.'" *Theory and Society* 29 (2000): 1–47.

Bruce, F. F. "Paul and Jerusalem." *Tyndale Bulletin* 19 (1968): 3–25.

——. *Paul: Apostle of the Heart Set Free.* Grand Rapids: Eerdmans, 1977.

——. "'All Things to All Men': Diversity in Unity and Other Pauline Tensions." In *Unity and Diversity in New Testament Theology: Essays in Honor of George E. Ladd,* edited by Robert A. Guelich, 82–99. Grand Rapids: Eerdmans, 1978.

Bryce, James. *The Ancient Roman Empire and the British Empire in India.* London: Oxford University Press, 1914.

Buell, Denise K. *Why This New Race: Ethnic Reasoning in Early Christianity.* New York: Columbia University Press, 2005.

Buell, Denise K., and Hodge, Caroline J. "The Politics of Interpretation: The Rhetoric of Race and Ethnicity in Paul." *JBL* 123: 235–51.

Burrus, Virginia. "Macrina's Tattoo." In *The Cultural Turn in Late Ancient Studies: Gender, Asceticism, and Historiography,* edited by Dale B. Martin and Patricia C. Miller. Durham, NC: Duke University Press, 2005.

Burton, Ernest DeWitt. *A Critical and Exegetical Commentary on the Epistle to the Galatians.* New York: Schribner, 1920.

Butler, Judith. *Gender Trouble.* New York/London: Routledge, 1990, 2006.

Callaway, Helen. *Gender, Culture, and Empire.* Urbana: University of Illinois Press, 1987.

Cameron, Averil. *Christianity and the Rhetoric of Empire: The Development of Christian Discourse.* Berkeley/Los Angeles: University of California Press, 1991.

Cameron, Ron, and Merrill P. Miller. *Redescribing Christian Origins.* SBLSyms 28. Atlanta: SBL; Leiden: Brill, 2004.

———. "Redescribing Paul." In *Redescribing Paul and the Corinthians,* 245–302. Atlanta: SBL, 2011.

Campbell, W. S. *Paul and the Creation of Christian Identity.* New York, T&T Clark, 2006.

Carl R. Holladay. "Paul and His Predecessors in the Diaspora: Some Reflections on Ethnic Identity in the Fragmentary Hellenistic Jewish Authors." In *Early Christianity and Classical Culture: Comparative Studies in Honor of Abraham J. Malherbe,* edited by John T. Fitzgerald et al., 429–60. New York: Brill, 2003.

Carr, David. *Writing on the Tablet of the Heart: Origins of Scripture and Literature.* New York: Oxford University Press, 2005.

Carter, Warren. *The Roman Empire and the New Testament: An Essential Guide.* Nashville: Abingdon, 2006.

Casson, Lionel. *Travel in the Ancient World*. London: Allen & Unwin, 1974.

Castelli, Elizabeth A. "Interpretations of Power in 1 Corinthians." In *Michel Foucault and Theology: The Politics of Religious Experience*, edited by James Bernauer and Jeremy Carrette, 19–38. London: Ashgate, 2004.

Charles, Ronald. "A Postcolonial Reading of *Joseph and Aseneth*." *JSP* 18, no. 4 (2009): 265–83.

Charlesworth, James H. "Reflections on the Canon, its Origins, and New Testament Interpretation." In *Method and Meaning: Essays on New Testament Interpretation in Honor of Harold W. Attridge*, edited by Andrew B. McGowan and Kent Harold Richards, 505–29. Atlanta: SBL Press, 2011.

Chomsky, Noam. *Language and Problems of Knowledge: The Managua Lectures*. Cambridge, MA: MIT Press, 1988.

Christopher, Stanley D., ed. *The Colonized Apostle: Paul Through Postcolonial Eyes*. Minneapolis: Fortress Press, 2011.

Clifford, James. *Routes: Travel and Translation in the Late Twentieth Century*. Cambridge, MA: Harvard University Press, 1997.

Cohen, Robin. *Global Diasporas: An Introduction*. Seattle: University of Washington Press, 1997, 2008.

Cohen, Shayne J. D. *Josephus in Galilee and Rome: His Vita and Development As a Historian*. Leiden: Brill, 1979.

———. "Was Judaism in Antiquity a Missionary Religion?" In *Jewish Assimilation, Acculturation, and Accommodation: Past Traditions, Currents Issues, and Future Prospects*, edited by Menachem Mor, 14–23. Lanham, MD: University Press of America, 1992.

———. *The Beginnings of Jewishness: Boundaries, Varieties, Uncertainties*. Berkeley: University of California Press, 1999.

———. *From the Maccabees to the Mishnah*. 2nd ed. Louisville: Westminster John Knox, 2006.

———, and Frerichs, E. S., eds. *Diasporas in Antiquity: Brown Judaic Studies.* Vol. 288. Atlanta: Scholars Press, 1993.

Collins, John J. *Between Athens and Jerusalem: Jewish Identity in the Hellenistic Diaspora.* 2nd ed. Grand Rapids: Eerdmans, 2000.

———. *Jewish Cult and Hellenistic Culture: Essays on the Jewish Encounter with Hellenism and Roman Rule. JSJ*Sup 100. Leiden: Brill, 2005.

Crenshaw, Kimberlé. "Demarginalizing the Intersection of Race and Sex: A Black Feminist Critique of Antidiscrimination Doctrine, Feminist Theory and Antiracist Politics." *University of Chicago Legal Forum* (1989), 139–67. Reprinted in *The Politics of Law: A Progressive Critique.* 2nd ed. Edited by David Kairys. New York: Pantheon, 1990, 195–217.

———. "Mapping the Margins: Intersectionality, Identity Politics, and Violence Against Women of Color." *Stanford Law Review* 43 (1991): 1241–99.

Cromer, Baring, E. *Ancient and Modern Imperialism.* London: Oxford University Press, 1910.

Crossan, J. D., and Reed, J. L. *In Search of Paul: How Jesus's Apostle Opposed Rome's Empire with God's Kingdom.* New York: HarperCollins, 2004.

Cullmann, Oscar. "The Early Church and the Ecumenical Problem." *Anglican Theological Review* 40 (1958): 181–89, 294–301.

Cummins, Stephen. A. *Paul and the Crucified Christ in Antioch: Maccabean Martyrdom and Galatians 1 and 2.* Cambridge: Cambridge University Press, 2001.

Danticat, Edwidge, ed. *The Butterfly's Way: Voices from the Haitian Dyaspora [sic] in the United States.* New York: Soho Press, 2001.

Davies, Philip R. "Didactic Stories." In *The Complexities of Second Temple Judaism,* edited by D. A. Carson et al, 99–134. Vol. 1, *Justification and Variegated Nomism.* Tübingen: Mohr, Siebeck, 2001.

Dawson, David. *Allegorical Readers and Cultural Revision in Ancient Alexandria.* Berkeley: University of California Press, 1992.

De Boer, Martinus C. *Galatians: A Commentary*. Louisville: Westminster John Knox, 2011.

Deines, Roland, and Karl-Wilhlem Niebuhr, eds. *Philo und das Nue Testament*. WUNT 172. Tübingen: Mohr Siebeck, 2004.

Deissmann, Gustav A. *St. Paul: A Study in Social and Religious History*. First English ed. Translated by Lionel R. M. Strachan. New York/London: Hodder & Stoughton, 1912.

Deming, Will. *Paul on Marriage and Celibacy: The Hellenistic Background of 1 Corinthians 7*. Cambridge: Cambridge University Press, 1995.

Derrida, Jacques. "Structure, Sign and Play in the Discourse of the Human Sciences." In *Writing and Difference*, 278–94. London: Routledge, 1980.

Donaldson, Terence L. "The 'Curse of the Law' and the Inclusion of the Gentiles: Galatians 3.13-14." *NTS* 32 (1986): 94–112.

———. *Paul and the Gentiles: Remapping the Apostle's Convictional World*. Minneapolis: Fortress Press, 1997.

———. "The Field God Has Assigned: Geography and Mission in Paul." In *Religious Rivalries in the Early Roman Empire and the Rise of Christianity*, edited by Leif E. Vaage, 109–37. Studies in Christianity and Judaism/ Études sur le christianisme et le judaïsme. Waterloo, ON: Wilfrid Laurier University Press, 2006.

———. *Judaism and the Gentiles: Jewish Patterns of Universalism to 135 CE*. Waco, TX: Baylor University Press, 2007.

———. "Introduction to the Pauline Corpus." In *The Pauline Epistles*,edited by John Muddiman and John Barton, 27–56. The Oxford Bible Commentary. Oxford: Oxford University Press, 2010.

Downey, Glanville. *A History of Antioch in Syria: from Seleucus to the Arab Conquest*. Princeton, NJ: Princeton University Press, 1961.

Downing, Francis G. *Cynics, Paul and the Pauline Churches*. London/New York: Routledge, 1998.

Downs, David J. *The Offering of the Gentiles.* WUNT 248. Tübingen: Mohr Siebeck, 2008.

Dube, Musa W. *Postcolonial Feminist Interpretation of the Bible.* St. Louis: Chalice, 2000.

Dufoix, Stéphane. *Diasporas.* Translated by William Rodarmor. Berkeley: University of California Press, 2008.

———. "Notion, Concept ou Slogan: Qu'y a-t-il sous le terme de «Diaspora »? " In *Les diasporas: 2000 ans d'histoire,* edited by Lisa Anteby-Yemini, William Berthomière, and Gabriel Sheffers, 53–63. Rennes: Presses Universitaires de Rennes, 2005.

———. *La Dispersion: Une histoire des usages du mot diaspora.* Paris: Éditions Amsterdam, 2012.

Dunn, James D. G. *Jesus, Paul and the Law: Studies in Mark and Galatians.* Louisville: Westminster John Knox, 1990.

———. *The Theology of Paul's Letter to the Galatians.* Cambridge: Cambridge University Press, 1993.

Eco, Umberto. *The Role of the Reader: Explorations in the Semiotics of Texts.* Bloomington: University of Indiana Press, 1979.

Edwards, Douglas R., and Thomas C. McCollough, eds. *The Archaeology of Difference: Gender, Ethnicity, Class and the "Other" in Antiquity: Studies in Honor of Eric M. Meyers.* Annual of the American Schools of Oriental Research 60/61. Boston: American Schools of Oriental Research, 2007.

Ehrensperger, Kathy. 'Speaking Greek under Rome: Paul, the Power of language.' *Neotestamentica* 46, no. 1 (2012): 10–31.

———. *Paul at the Crossroads of Cultures: Theologizing in the space Between.* London: T&T Clark, 2013.

Ehrensperger, Kathy, and J. Brian Tucker. *Reading Paul in Context: Explorations in Identity Formation: Essays in Honour of William S. Campbell.* London: T&T Clark, 2010.

Eisenbaum, Pamela. *Paul Was Not a Christian: The Original Message of a Misunderstood Apostle*. New York: HarperCollins, 2009.

———. "Jewish Perspectives: A Jewish Apostle to the Gentiles." In *Studying Paul's Letters: Contemporary Perspectives and Methods*, 135–53. Minneapolis: Fortress Press, 2012.

Eliade, Mircea. *Myth and Reality*. New York: Harper & Row, 1963.

Elmer, Ian J. *Paul, Jerusalem and the Judaisers*. Tübingen: Mohr Siebeck, 2009.

Elsner, Jaś, and Ian Rutherford, eds. *Pilgrimage in Graeco-Roman & Early Christian Antiquity: Seeing the Gods*. Oxford: Oxford University Press, 2005.

Esler, Philip F. *Galatians*. New Testament Readings. London: Routledge, 1998.

Faltin, Lucia, and Melanie J. Wright, eds. *The Religious Roots of Contemporary European Identity*. London: Continuum, 2007.

Fanon, Fanon. *Black Skin, White Masks*. New York: Grove, 1967.

———. *Les Damnés de la Terre*. Paris: Librairie François Maspero, 1961, 1970.

Feldman, Louis H. "Palestinian and Diaspora Judaism in the First Century." In *Christianity and Rabbinic Judaism*, 1–39, 327–36. Washington, DC: Biblical Archaeology Society, 1992.

———. *Studies in Josephus' Rewritten Bible*. Leiden: Brill, 1998.

———. *Josephus's Interpretation of the Bible*. Berkeley: University of California Press, 1998.

Ferguson, James, and Akhil Gupta. "Spatializing States: Toward an Ethnography of Neoliberal Governmentality." *American Ethnologist* 29, no. 4 (2002): 981–1002.

———. "Beyond "Culture": Space, Identity, and the Politics of Difference." *Cultural Anthropology* 7, no. 1 (1992): 6–23.

Fiorenza, Elisabeth Schüssler. *In Memory of Her: A Feminist Reconstruction of Christian Origins*. New York: Crossroads, 1983.

———. *The Power of the Word: Scripture and the Rhetoric of Empire*. Minneapolis: Fortress Press, 2007.

Fitzgerald, John T. *Cracks in an Earthen Vessel: An Examination of the Catalogues of Hardships in the Corinthian Correspondence*. SBLDS 99. Atlanta: Scholars Press, 1988.

Focant, Camille. « L'expérience paulinienne d'une identité en tension. » *Revue d'Éthique et de Théologie morale*, no. 271 (2012): 143–64.

Foucault, Michel. *Discipline and Punish: The Birth of the Prison*. Translated by Alan Sheridan. New York: Vintage, 1977.

Fox, Kenneth A. *Paul's attitude toward the Body in Romans 6-8: Compared with Philo of Alexandria*. Unpublished Ph.D. diss. University of St. Michael's College, 2001.

Frey, Jörg. "Paul's Jewish Identity." In *Jewish Identity in the Greco-Roman World*, edited by J. Frey, D. R. Schwartz, and S. Gripentrog, 285–322. Ancient Judaism and Early Christianity 72. Leiden: Brill, 285–322.

Friesen, Steven. "Poverty in Pauline Studies: Beyond the So-called New Consensus." *JSNT* 26, no. 3 (2004): 323–61.

Gadamer, Hans-Georg. *Truth and Method*. 2nd rev. Edited by Trans. J. Weinsheimer and D. G. Marshall. New York: Crossroad, 1989.

Gafni, Isaiah M. *Land, Center and Diaspora: Jewish Constructs in Late Antiquity*. JSPSup, 21. Sheffield: Sheffield Academic Press, 1997.

Gager, John G. *Kingdom and Community: The Social World of Early Christianity*. Englewood Cliffs: Prentice-Hall, 1975.

———. *Reinventing Paul: Israel and Gentiles in Paul's Gospel*. New York: Oxford University Press, 2000.

Gager, John G., and E. Leigh Gibson. "Violent Acts and Violent Language." In *Violence in the New Testament*, edited by Shelly Matthews and E. Leigh Gibson, 13–21. New York: T&T Clark, 2005.

Garlington, Don. *An Exposition of Galatians: A Reading from the New Perspective*. 3rd ed. Eugene, OR: Wipf & Stock, 2007.

Garnsey, Peter D. A., and C. R. Whitaker. *Imperialism in the Ancient World.* Cambridge: Cambridge University Press, 1978.

Garnsey, Peter D. A., and Richard Saller. *The Roman Empire: Economy, Society and Culture.* London: Duckworth; Berkeley: University of California Press, 1987.

Georgi, Dieter. *Remembering the Poor: The History of Paul's Collection for Jerusalem.* Nashville: Abingdon, 1965.

Gilroy, Paul. *The Black Atlantic: Modernity and the Double Consciousness.* Cambridge, MA: Harvard University Press, 1992.

———. *Between Camps: Nations, Culture and the Allure of Race.* London: Allen Lane, Penguin Press, 2000.

Glick Schiller, Nina, and Georges Fouron. *Woke up Laughing: Long-Distance Nationalism and the Search for Home.* Durham, NC: Duke University Press, 2001.

Goldstein, Jonathan A. "The Message of Aristeas to Philokrates in the Second Century BCE: Obey the Torah, Venerate the Temple of Jerusalem, but Speak Greek, and Put Your Hopes in the Ptolemaic Dynasty." In *Eretz Israel, Israel, and the Jewish Diaspora: Mutual Relations: Proceedings of the First Annual Symposium of the Philip M. and Ethel Klutznick Chair in Jewish Civilization, held on Sunday-Monday, October 9-10, 1988,* edited by Menachem Mor, 1–23. Lanham, MD: University Press of America, 1991.

Goodenough, Erwin R. *An Introduction to Philo Judaeus.* 2nd ed. New York: Oxford University Press, 1962.

Goodman, Martin. *Mission and Conversion: Proselytizing in the Religious History of the Roman Empire.* Oxford: Clarendon, 1994.

Gourgues, M., and M. Talbot, ed. *Partout où tu iras . . . Conceptions et expériences bibliques de l'espace.* Sciences bibliques 12. Montréal: Médiaspaul, 2003.

Grewal, Inderpal. *Home and Harem: Nation, Gender, Empire, and the Cultures of Travel.* Post-Contemporary Interventions. Durham, NC: Duke University Press, 1996.

Gruen, Erich S. *Diaspora: Jews Amidst Greeks and Romans.* Cambridge, MA: Harvard University Press, 2002.

———. "Diaspora and Homeland." In *Diaspora and Exiles: Varieties of Jewish Identity*, edited by Howard Wettstein, 18–46. Berkeley: University of California Press, 2002.

Haacker, Klaus. "Die Geschichtstheologie von Röm 9–11 im Lichte philonischer Schriftauslegung." *NTS* 43 (1997): 209–22.

Hadas-Lebel, Mireille. "Flavius Josephus, Historian of Rome." In *Josephus and the History of the Greco-Roman Period: Essays in Memory of Morton Smith*, edited by Fausto Parente and Joseph Sievers, 99–106. Leiden: Brill, 1994.

Hahne, Harry A. *The Corruption and Redemption of Creation. Nature in Romans 8:19-22 and Jewish Apocalyptic Literature.* London: T&T Clark, 2006.

Hall, Stuart. "The Question of Cultural Identity." In *Modernity and Its Futures*, edited by S. Hall, D. Held, and A. McGrew, 273–316. Cambridge: Polity, 1992.

Hammond, Mason. *The City in the Ancient World.* Cambridge, MA: Harvard University Press, 1972.

Hanges, James C. *Paul, Founder of Churches: A Study in Light of the Evidence for the Role of "Founder-Figures" in the Hellenistic-Roman Period.* Tübingen: Mohr Siebeck, 2012.

Hardin, Justin K. *Galatians and the Imperial Cult: A Critical Analysis of the First-Century Social Context of Paul's Letter.* WUNT 2.237. Tübingen: Mohr Siebeck, 2008.

Harland, Philip A. *Associations, Synagogues and Congregations: Claiming a Place in Ancient Mediterranean Society.* Minneapolis: Fortress Press, 2003.

———. "Acculturation and Identity in the Diaspora: A Jewish Family and 'Pagan' Guilds at Hierapolis." *JJS* 57, no. 2 (2006): 222–44.

——. "Familial Dimensions of Group Identity: 'Brothers' ΑΔΕΛΦΟΙ in Associations of the Greek East." *Journal of Biblical Literature* 124 (2005): 491–513.

——. "Familial Dimensions of Group Identity II: 'Mothers' and 'Fathers' in Associations and Synagogues of the Greek World." *Journal for the Study of Judaism in the Persian, Hellenistic, and Roman Period* 38 (2007): 57–79.

——. *Dynamics of Identity in the World of the Early Christians: Associations, Judeans, and Cultural Minorities*. London: T&T Clark, 2009.

Harrison, Thomas. "Ancient and Modern Imperialism." *Greece and Rome* 55 (2008): 1–22.

Harvey, David. *Cosmopolitanism and the Geographies of Freedom. Wellek Library Lectures in Critical Theory*. New York: Columbia University Press, 2009.

——. "Space as a Key Word." In *The David Harvey Reader*, edited by Noel Castree and Derek Gregory, 272–74. Oxford: Blackwell, 2006.

Hengel, Martin. *Die Zeloten: Untersuchungen zur Jüdischen Freiheits-Bewegung in der Zeit von Herodes 1. Bis 70 n. Chr.* Leiden: Brill, 1961.

Hill, Craig C. *Hellenists and Hebrews: Reapprasing Division within the Earliest Church*. Minneapolis: Fortress Press, 1992.

Himmelfarb, Martha. "Review of J.M.G. Barclay, *Jews in the Mediterranean Diaspora*." *AJS* 23, no. 2 (1998): 247–50.

Hock, Ronald F. *The Social Context of Paul's Ministry: Tentmaking and Apostleship*. Philadelphia: Fortress Press, 1980.

——. "A Support for His Old Age: Paul's Plea on Behalf of Onesimus." In *The Social World of the First Christians: Essays in Honor of Wayne A. Meeks*, edtied by L. Michael White and O. Larry Yarbrough, 67–81. Minneapolis: Fortress Press, 1995.

——. "Paul and Greco-Roman Education." In *Paul in the Greco-Roman World: A Handbook*, edited by J. Paul Sampley, 198–227. Harrisburg, PA: Trinity Press International, 2003.

———. "The Problem of Paul's Social Class: Further Reflections." In *Paul's World*, edited by Stanley E. Porter, 7–18. Pauline Studies 4. Leiden: Brill, 2008.

———. *The Chreia and Ancient Rhetoric: Classroom Exercises.* Atlanta: SBL, 2002.

———, and O'Neil, Edward N. *The Chreia in Ancient Rhetoric.Vol I. The Progymnasmata*, SBLTT 27. Atlanta: Scholars Press, 1986.

Hodge, Caroline J. *If Sons, then Heirs: A Study of Kinship and Ethnicity on the Letters of Paul.* Oxford: Oxford University Press, 2007.

Holl, Karl. "Der Kirchenbegriff des Paulus in seinem Verhältnis zu dem der Urgemeinde." In *Gesammelte Aufsätze zur Kirchengeschichte*, 44–67. Tübingen: Mohr Siebeck, 1928.

Holladay, Carl R. "Paul and His Predecessors in the Diaspora: Some Reflections on Ethnic Identity in the Fragmentary Hellenistic Jewish Authors." In *Early Christianity and Classical Culture: Comparative Studies in Honor of Abraham J. Malherbe*, edited by John T. Fitzgerald et al., 77–89. SNT. New York: Brill Academic, 2003.

Holmberg, Bengt. *Paul and Power.* Lund: CWK Gleerup, 1978.

Honigman, Sylvie. *The Septuagint and Homeric Scholarship in Alexandria: A Study in the Narrative of the Letter of Aristeas.* New York: Routledge, 2003.

———. "The Narrative Function of the King and the Library in the *Letter of Aristeas.*" In *Jewish Perspectives on Hellenistic Rulers*, edited by Rajak T. et al., 128–46.

Hopkins, Keith. *A World full of Gods: Pagans, Jews and Christians in the Roman Empire.* Weidenfeld & Nicolson: London, 1999.

Horrell, David. "Paul's Collection: Resources for a Materialist Theology." *Epworth Review* 22 (1995): 74–83.

———. "'The Lord Commanded . . . But I Have Not Used': Exegetical and Hermeneutical Reflections on 1 Cor 9:14-15." *NTS* 43 (1997): 587–603.

Horsley, Richard A. *Paul and Empire: Religion and Power in Roman Imperial Society*. Harrisburg, PA: Trinity Press International, 1997.

———. *Paul and Politics: Ekklesia, Israel, Imperium, Interpretation: Essays in Honor of Krister Stendhal*. Harrisburg, PA: Trinity Press International, 2000.

———. *Paul and the Roman Imperial Order*. Harrisburg, PA: Trinity Press International, 2004.

———. "Commentary on 1 Corinthians." In *Postcolonial Commentary on the New Testament Writings*, edited by Fernando F. Segovia and R. S. Sugirtharajah. London: T&T Clark, 2007.

Howard, George E. "The Letter of Aristeas and Diaspora Judaism." *JTS* 22 (1971): 337–48.

Hurtado, Larry W. "The Book of Galatians and the Jerusalem Collection." *JSNT* (1979): 46–62.

———. "Does Philo help explain Early Christianity." In *Philo und das Neue Testament: Wechselseitige Wahrnehmungen*, Internationales Symposium zum Corpus Judaeo-Hellenisticum, 1.-4. Mai 2003, Eisenach, edited by Jena. R. Deines and K. W. Niebuhr, 73–92. WUNT 172, Tübingen: Mohr Siebeck, 2004.

Ivarsson, Fredrik. "Christian Identity as True Masculinity." In *Exploring Early Christian Identity*, edited by Bengt Holmberg. WUNT 172. Tübingen: Mohr Siebeck, 2008.

Jackson, Ryan T. *New Creation in Paul*. WUNT 272. Tübingen: Mohr Siebeck, 2010.

James, Carl E. "'I feel like a Trini': Narrative of a Generation-and-a-Half Canadian." In *Diaspora, Memory, and Identity: A Search for Home*, edited by Vijay Agnew, 247–48. Toronto: Toronto Press Inc., 2005.

Jeffers, James S. *The Greco-Roman World of the New Testament Era: Exploring the Background of Early Christianity*. Downers Grove, IL: InterVarsity, 1999.

Jeffreys, Elizabeth, Michel Jeffreys, and Roger Scott, ed. *The Chronicle of John Malalas: A Translation.* Sydney: Australian Association for Byzantine Studies, 1986.

Jervis, Ann L. "Reading Romans 7 in Conversation with Post-Colonial Theory: Paul's Struggle toward a Christian Identity of Hybridity." *Theoforum* 35 (2004): 173–94.

Jewett, Robert. "The Agitators and the Galatian Congregation." *NTS* 17 (1970–71): 198–212.

———. *Romans: A Commentary.* Roy D. Kotansky and Eldon J. Epp, eds. Minneapolis: Fortress Press, 2007.

Johnson-Debaufre, Melanie, and Laura S. Nasrallah, "Beyond the Heroic Paul." In *The Colonized Apostle: Paul Through Postcolonial Eyes,* edited by Christopher D. Stanley, 161–74. Minneapolis: Fortress Press, 2011.

Jones, Siân, and Pearce, Sarah, eds. *Jewish Local Patriotism and Self-Identification in the Graeco-Roman Period.* JSPSup, vol. 31. Sheffield: Sheffield Academic, 1998.

Josephus, Flavius. *The Antiquities of the Jews,* trans. Ralph Marcus. Loeb Classical Library. Cambridge, MA: Harvard University Press, 1943.

———. *The Jewish War.* Translated by H. St. J. Thackery. 2 vols. Loeb Classical Library. Cambridge: Harvard University Press, 1927–28.

Joubert, Stephan. *Paul as Benefactor: Reciprocity, Strategy and Theological Reflection in Paul's Collection.* WUNT 124, Tübingen: Mohr Siebeck, 2000.

Kaden, David A. "Flavius Josephus and the *Gentes Devictae* in Roman Imperial Discourse: Hybridity, Mimicry, and Irony in the Agrippa II Speech *Judean War* 2.345-402." *JSJ* 42 (2011): 481–507.

Kahl, Brigitte. *Galatians Re-Imagined: Reading With The Eyes Of The Vanquished.* Minneapolis: Fortress Press, 2010.

———. "Galatians and the 'Orientalism' of Justification by Faith: Paul among Jews and Muslims." In *The Colonized Apostle,* 209–17.

Kelly, Christopher. *The Roman Empire: A Very Short Introduction*. London: Oxford University Press, 2006.

Knott, Kim, and Seán McLoughlin, eds. *Diasporas: Concepts, Intersections, Identities*. London: Zed, 2010.

Kloppenborg, John S. "Greco-Roman *Thiasoi, the Ekklēsia* at Corinth, and Conflict Management." In *Redescribing Paul and the Corinthians*, edited by Ron Cameron and Merrill P. Miller, 187–218. Atlanta: Society of Biblical Literature, 2011.

———. "Judaeans or Judaean Christians in James?" In *Identity & Interaction in the Ancient Mediterranean: Jews, Christians and Others, Essays in Honor of Stephen G. Wilson*, edited by Zeba Crook and Philip Harland, 113–35. Sheffield: Sheffield Phoenix, 2007.

———, and Richard S. Ascough. *Greco-Roman Associations: Texts, Translations, and Commentary I. Attica, Central Greece, Macedonia, Thrace*. Berlin: Walter de Gruyter, 2011.

Knust, Jennifer W. "Paul and the Politics of Virtue and Vice." In *Paul and the Imperial Order*, edited by Richard Horsley, 155–73. Harrisburg, PA: Trinity Press International, 2004.

———. *Unprotected Sex: The Bible's Surprising Contradictions About Sex and Desire*. New York: HarperOne, 2011.

Koch, Dietrich-Alexander. *Die Schrift als Zeuge des Evangeliums, Untersuchung zur Verwendung und zum Verständnis der Schrift bei Paulus*. Tübingen: Mohr Siebeck, 1986.

Kondo, Dorinne. "The Narrative Production of "Home" Community, and Political Identity in Asian American Theater." In *Displacement, Diaspora, and Geographies of Identity*, edited by Smadar Lavie and Ted Swedenburg. Durham, NC: Duke University Press, 1996.

Kovelman, Andrew. *Between Alexandria and Jerusalem: The Dynamic of Jewish and Hellenistic Culture*. The Brill Reference Library of Judaism21. Leiden: Brill, 2005.

Kovelman, Arkady. *Between Alexandria and Jerusalem: The Dynamic of Jewish and Hellenistic Culture.* Leiden: Brill, 2005.

Kraabel, Thomas A. "The Roman Diaspora: Six Questionable Assumptions." In *Diaspora Jews and Judaism: Essays in Honor of, and in Dialogue with, A. Thomas Kraabel,* edited by Andrew J. Overman, 1–20. South Florida Studies in the History of Judaism, 41. Atlanta: Scholars Press, 1992.

Kraeling, Carl H. "The Jewish Community at Antioch." *JBL* 51 (1932): 130–60.

Ladd, George E. *The Presence of the Future.* Grand Rapids: Eerdmans, 1974.

Laguerre, Michel S. *Diaspora, Politics, and Globalization.* New York: Palgrave Macmillan, 2006.

Lamour, Denis. *Flavius Josèphe.* Paris: Les Belles Lettres, 2000.

Lassus, Jean. "*La ville d'Antioche à l'époque romaine d'après l'archéologie.*" In *Aufstieg und Niedergang der römischen Welt,* II, *Principat,* b. 8, edited by H. Temporini and W. Haase, 55–102. Berlin, New York: Walter de Gruyer, 1977.

Leal, Roxana B. "What are the different ways in which we can understand gendered diasporic identities?" *Zona Próxima,* no. 1 (2009): 170–83.

Lee, Jae Won. "Justification of Difference in Galatians." In *Character Ethics and the New Testament,* edited by Robert Brawley, 191–209. Louisville: Westminster John Knox, 2007.

———. "Paul, Nation, and Nationalism: A Korean Postcolonial Perspective." In *The Colonized Apostle: Paul Through Postcolonial Eyes.* Minneapolis: Fortress Press, 2011.

Levine, Amy-Jill, ed. *A Feminist Companion to Paul.* Cleveland: Pilgrim, 2004.

Levinskaya, Irina. *The Book of Acts in Its First Century Setting.* Grand Rapids: Eerdmans, 1996.

Levy, André, and Alex Weingrod, eds. *Homelands and Diasporas: Holy Lands and Other Places.* Palo Alto, CA: Stanford University Press, 2005.

Lieber, Andrea. "Between Motherland and Fatherland: Diaspora, Pilgrimage and the Spiritualization of Sacrifice in Philo of Alexandria." In *Heavenly Tablets: Interpretation, Identity and Tradition in Ancient Judaism*, edited by Lynn LiDonnici and Andrea Lieber, 193–210. Leiden: Brill, 2007.

Lieu, Judith. *Christian Identity in the Jewish and Graeco-Roman World*. Oxford: Oxford University Press, 2004.

Lintott, Andrew W. *Imperium Romanum: Politics and Administration*. London: Routledge, 1993.

Longenecker, Bruce W. *Remember the Poor: Paul, Poverty, and the Greco-Roman World*. Grand Rapids: Eerdmans, 2010.

Longenecker, Richard N. *Galatians*. WBC 41. Dallas: Word Books, 1990.

Loomba, Ania, et al., eds., *Postcolonial Studies and Beyond*. Durham, NC: Duke University Press, 2005.

Lopez, Davina C. *Apostle to the Conquered: Reimagining Paul's Mission*. Minneapolis: Fortress Press, 2008.

———. "Visual Perspectives." In *Studying Paul's Letters: Contemporary Perspectives and Methods*, 93–116. Minneapolis: Fortress Press, 2012.

———. "Visualizing Significant Otherness: Reimagining Pauline Studies through Hybrid Lenses." In *The Colonized Apostle*, 74–94.

Maccoby, Hyam. *The Mythmaker: Paul and the Invention of Christianity*. New York: Harper & Row, 1986.

———. *Paul and Hellenism*. London: SCM, 1991.

MacDonald, Margaret Y. *The Pauline Churches: A Socio-Historical Study of Institutionalization in the Pauline and Deutero-Pauline Writings*. Cambridge: Cambridge University Press, 1988.

Mack, Burton. *Myth and the Christian Nation: A Social Theory of Religion*. London: Equinox, 2008.

———. *Who Wrote the New Testament? The Making of the Christian Myth*. San Francisco: HarperSanFrancisco, 1995.

Malina, Bruce J. *The New Testament World: Insights from Cultural Anthropology*. Nashville: Westminster John Knox, 2001.

———, and Jerome H. Neyrey. *Portraits of Paul: An Archeology of Ancient Personality*. Louisville: Westminster John Knox, 1996.

Malkki, Lisa. "National Geographic: The Rooting of Peoples and the Territorialization of National Identity Among Scholars and Refugees." *Cultural Anthropology* 7, no. 1 (1992): 24–38.

Marchal, Joseph A. *Hierarchy, Unity, and Imitation: A Feminist Rhetorical Analysis of Power Dynamics in Paul's Letter to the Philippians*. Atlanta: SBL Press, 2006.

———. *The Politics of Heaven: Women, Gender, and Empire in the Study of Paul*. Minneapolis: Fortress Press, 2008.

———, ed. *Studying Paul's Letters: Contemporary Perspectives and Methods*. Minneapolis: Fortress Press, 2012.

Marquis, Timothy Luckritz. *Transient Apostle: Paul, Travel, and the Rhetoric of Empire*. Synkrisis. New Haven: Yale University Press, 2013.

Marshall, John W. *Parables of War: Reading John's Jewish Apocalypse*. ESCJ, Studies in Christianity and Judaism/Études sur le christianisme et le judaïsme. Waterloo, ON: Wilfrid Laurier University Press, 2001.

———. "Hybridity and Reading of Romans 13." *JSNT* 31 (2008): 157–78.

Martin, Dale B. *Slavery as Salvation*. New Haven: Yale University Press, 1990.

Martin, Luther H. "Redescribing Christian Origins: Historiography or Exegesis?" In *Redescribing Christian Origins*, edited by R. Cameron and M. Miller, 475–81. Leiden: Brill, 2004.

Mason, Steve. "Figured Speech and Irony in T. Flavius Josephus." In *Flavius Josephus and Flavian Rome*, edited by Jonathan Edmondson, Steve Mason, and James Rives, 243–88. Oxford: Oxford University Press, 2005.

————. "Should any wish to enquire further' *Ant.* 1. 25: The aim and audience of Josephus' *Judean Antiquities/Life.*" In *Understanding Josephus: Seven Perspectives,* 64–103. Sheffield: Sheffield Academic, 1998.

————. "The aim and audience of Josephus': Judean *Antiquities/Life.*" Sheffield: Sheffield Academic Press, 1998.

————, and James Rives. *Flavius Josephus and Flavian Rome.* Oxford: Oxford University Press, 2005, 244–88.

Matthews, Basil. *Paul the Dauntless: The Course of a Great Adventure.* New York: Revell, 1916.

Mattingly, David J., ed. *Dialogues in Roman Imperialism: Power, Discourse, and Discrepant Experience in the Roman Empire.* Journal of Roman Archaeology Supplementary Series 23. Portsmouth, RI: *Journal of Roman Archaeology,* 1997.

————. *Imperialism, Power, and Identity: Experiencing the Roman Empire.* Princeton, NJ: Princeton University Press, 2011.

McCutcheon, Russell T. *Critics Not Caretakers: Redescribing the Public Study of Religion.* Albany: State University of New York Press, 2001.

————. "A Direct Question Deserves a Direct Answer: A Response to Atalia Omer's 'Can a Critic Be a Caretaker Too?'" *JAAR* 80, no. 4: 1077–81.

McLay, Timothy R. *The Use of the Septuagint in New Testament Research.* Grand Rapids, Eerdmans, 2003.

McLoughlin, S. "Muslim Travellers: Homing Desire, the *Umma* and British-Pakistanis." In *Diasporas: Concepts, Intersections, Identities,* edited by Kim Knott and Seán McLoughlin, 223–29. London: Zed, 2010.

Meeks, Wayne A. *The First Urban Christians: The Social World of the Apostle Paul.* New Haven: Yale University Press, 1983.

Meggitt, Justin. *Paul, Poverty and Survival.* Edinburgh: T&T Clark, 1998.

Michel, Margaret M. "Peter's 'Hypocrisy' and Paul's: Two 'Hypocrites' at the Foundation of Earliest Christianity?" *NTS* 58 (2012): 213–34.

Miller, Christopher L. *Blank Darkness: Africanist Discourse in French*. Chicago: The University of Chicago Press, 1985.

Miller, Merrill P. "Antioch, Paul, and Jerusalem: Diaspora Myths of Origins in the Homeland." In *Redescribing Christian Origins*, edited by Ron Cameron and Merril P. Miller, 177–236. SBLSymS 28. Atlanta: Society of Biblical Literature, 2004.

———. "Re: Paul." In *Introducing Religion: Essays in Honor of Jonathan Z. Smith*, edited by Willi Braun and Russell T. McCutcheon, 340–57. London: Equinox, 2008.

Modrejewski, Mélèze J. "How to be a Jew in Hellenstic Egypt?" In *Diaspora in Antiquity*, edited by Shaye J. D. Cohen and Ernest S. Frerichs, 65–91. Atlanta: Scholars Press, 1993.

———. *The Jews of Egypt: From Rameses II to Emperor Hadrian*. Princeton, NJ: Princeton University Press. Edition Paperback, 1997.

Moore, Stephen D. *God's Beauty Parlor: And Other Queer Spaces in and around the Bible*. Contraversions. Palo Alto, CA: Stanford University Press, 2001.

———. *Empire and Apocalypse: Postcolonialism and the New Testament*. The Bible in the Modern World 12. Sheffield: Sheffield Phoenix, 2006.

———. *The Bible in Theory: Critical and Postcritical Essays*. Atlanta: SBL, 2010.

———. "Paul after Empire." In *The Colonized Apostle*, 9–23. Minneapolis: Fortress Press, 2011.

Moxnes, Halvor. *Theology in Conflict: Studies in Paul's Understanding of God in Romans*. Supplements to Novum Testamentum. Leiden: Brill, 1980.

———, ed. *Constructing Early Christian Families: Family as Social Reality and Metaphor*. London: Routledge, 1997.

Mudimbe, Valentin Y. *The Idea of Africa*. Bloomington: Indiana University Press, 1994.

Munck, Johannes. *Paul and the Salvation of Mankind*. Richmond: John Knox, 1959.

Murphy-O'Connor, Jerome. *Paul: A Critical Life*. Oxford: Clarendon, 1996.

Nanos, Mark D. *The Irony of Galatians: Paul's Letter in First-Century Context* Minneapolis: Fortress Press, 2002.

———. "What Was at Stake in Peter's 'Eating with Gentiles' at Antioch?" In *The Galatians Debate: Contemporary Issues in Rhetorical and Historical Interpretation*, edited by Mark D. Nanos, 282–318. Peabody, MA: Hendrickson, 2002b.

Nasrallah, Laura S. "Spatial Perspectives: Space and Archeology in Roman Philippi." In *Studying Paul's Letters*, 53–74.

———. *Christian Responses to Roman Art and Architecture: The Second Century Church amid the Spaces of Empire*. Cambridge: Cambridge University Press, 2010.

Neusner Jacob, and Frerichs, Ernest S., eds. *"To See Ourselves as Others see Us": Christians, Jews, "Others" in Late Antiquity*. Chico, CA: Scholars Press, 1985.

Newton, Michael. *The Concept of Purity at Qumran and in the Letters of Paul*. London: Cambridge University Press, 1985.

Niang, Aliou C. *Faith and Freedom in Galatia and Senegal: The Apostle Paul, Colonists and Sending Gods*. Leiden: Brill, 2009.

Nickelsburg, George W. E. *Jewish Literature between the Bible and the Mishnah*. 2nd ed. Minneapolis: Fortress Press, 2005.

Nickle, Keith F. *The Collection: A Study in Paul's Strategy*. London: SCM, 1966.

Noack, Christian. "'Haben oder Empfangen' Antithetische Charakterisierungen von Torheit und Weisheit bei Philo und bie Paulus." In *Philo und das Nue Testament*, edited by Roland Deines and Karl-Wilhelm Niebuhr, 283–307. WUNT 172. Tübingen: Mohr Siebeck, 2004.

Nordgaard, Stefan. "Paul's Appropriation of Philo's Theory of 'Two Men' in 1 Corinthians 15.45-49." *NTS* (2011): 348–65.

Ogereau, Julien M. "The Jerusalem Collection as Κοινωνία: Paul's Global Politics of Socio-Economic Equality and Solidarity." *NTS* 58, no. 3: 360–78.

Osiek, Carolyn, and David L. Balch, eds, *Early Christian Families in Context: An Interdisciplinary Dialogue.* Grand Rapids: Eerdmans, 2003.

Overman, Andrew J., and Robert S. MacLennan, eds. *Diaspora Jews and Judaism: Essays in Honor of, and in Dialogue with, A. Thomas Kraabel.* South Florida Studies in the History of Judaism, 41. Atlanta: Scholars Press, 1992.

Pascal, Blaise. *Pensées.* Texte établi par Léon Brunschvicg. Paris: Éditions Hachette, 1897. Paris: Garnier-Flammarion, 1976.

Penner, Todd, and Davina Lopez. "Homelessness as a Way Home." In *Holy Land as Homeland? Models for Constructing the Historic Landscapes of Jesus,* edited by Keith W. Whitelam, 151–76. The Social World of Biblical Antiquity, Second Series, 7. Sheffield: Sheffield Phoenix, 2011.

Pearce, Sarah. "Translating for Ptolemy: Patriotism and Politics in the Greek Pentateuch?" In *Jewish Perspectives on Hellenistic Rulers,* edited by Tessa Rajak et al., 165–89. London: University of California Press, 2007.

———. "Jerusalem as Mother City in the Writings of Philo of Alexandria." In *Negotiating Diaspora: Jewish Strategies in the Roman Empire,* edited by J. M. Barclay, 19–37. Library of Second Temple Studies 45. London: T&T Clark, 2004.

Pelletier, André. *Flavius Josèphe adapteur de la Lettre d'Aristée. Une réaction Atticisante contre la Koinè.* Paris: Librairie C. Klincksieck, 1962.

———. *Lettre D'Aristée à Philocrate.* Paris: Éditions du Cerf, 1962.

Philo. *De Specialibus legibus.* Books 1-3. Translated by F. H. Colson. Loeb Classical Library. Cambridge, MA: Harvard University Press, 1937.

———. *Legatio ad Gaium.* Book X. Translated by F. H. Colson. Loeb Classical Library; Cambridge, MA: Harvard University Press, 1962.

Pope, Robert M. *On Roman Roads with St. Paul.* London: Epworth, 1939.

Porter, Stanley. "Review of J.M.G. Barclay, *Jews in the Mediterranean Diaspora.*" *JSNT* 72 (1998): 126–28.

Pratt, Louise M. *Imperial Eyes: Travel Writing and Transculturation.* London: Routledge, 1992.

Punt, Jeremy. "Identity, Memory, and Scriptural Warrant: Arguing Paul's Case." In *Paul and Scripture: Extending the Conversation*, edited by Christopher D. Stanley, 25–53. Atlanta: SBL, 2012.

———. "Paul, Body, and Resurrection in an Imperial Setting: Considering Hermeneutics and Power." *Neotestamentica* 45, no. 2 (2011): 311–30.

Quayson, Ato. "Colonial space-making and hybridizing history, or 'Are the Indians of East Africa Africans or Indians?'" In *Diasporas: Concepts, Intersections, Identities*, edited by Kim Knott and Seán McLoughlin, 243–48. London: Zed, 2010.

Radhakrishnan, R. "Ethnicity in an Age of Diaspora." In *Theorizing Diaspora: A Reader Key Works in Cultural Studies*, edited by Jana Evans Braziel and Anita Mannur, 119–31. Oxford: Blackwell, 2003.

Räisänen, Heikki. "A Controversial Jew and his Conflicting Convictions." In *Redefining First-Century Jewish and Christian* Identities, edited by Duo Herschel and Chancey Tatum, 319–35. Notre Dame, IN: University of Notre Dame Press, 2008.

Rajak, Tessa. "Josephus in the Diaspora." In *Flavius Josephus and Flavian Rome*, edited by Jonathan Edmondson, Steve Mason, and James Rives, 79–97. Oxford: Oxford University Press, 2005.

———. *The Jewish Dialogue with Greece and Rome: Studies in Cultural and Social Interaction.* Leiden: Brill, 2001.

———. *Translation and Survival: The Greek Bible of the Ancient Jewish Diaspora.* Oxford: Oxford University Press, 2009.

———. "Surviving by the Book: The Language of the Greek Bible and Jewish Identity." In *Cultural Identity in the Ancient Mediterranean*, edited by Erich S. Gruen, 273–87. Los Angeles: Getty Research Institute, 2011.

Ramsay, William. *St. Paul the Traveler and Roman Citizen.* London: Hodder & Stoughton, 1896.

Reynier, Chantal. *Saint Paul sur les routes du monde romain: Infrastructures, Logistique, Itinéraire.* Paris: Éditions du Cerf, 2009.

Richardson, Peter. "Pauline Inconsistency: 1 Cor. 9:19-23 and Gal. 2:11-14." *NTS* 26 (1979–80): 347–62.

Riesner, Rainer. *Paul's Early Period: Chronology, Mission Strategy, Theology.* Translated by Doug Stott. Grand Rapids: Eerdmans, 1998.

Roetzel, Calvin. "Response: How anti-imperial was the collection and how emancipatory was Paul's project?" In *Paul and Politics*, 227–30. Harrisburg, PA: Trinity Press International, 2000.

———. "*Oikoumene* and the Limits of Pluralism in Alexandria Judaism and Paul." In *Diaspora Jews and Judaism: Essays in Honor of, and in Dialogue with, A. Thomas Kraabel*, edited byAndrew J. Overman and Robert S. MacLenan, 163–82. SFSHJ 41. Atlanta: Scholars Press, 1992.

———. "The Language of War 2 Cor. 10:1-6 and the Language of Weakness 2 Cor. 11:21b-13:10." In *Violence, Scripture and Textual Practice in Early Judaism and Christianity*, edtied by Ra'anan S. Boustan, Alex P. Jassen, and Calvin J. Roetzel, 77–98. Leiden: Brill, 2010.

———."Paul and Nomos in the Messianic Age." In *Reading Paul in Context: Explorations in Identity Formation: Essays in Honour of William S. Campbell*, edited by Kathy Ehrensperger and Brian J. Tucker, 120–27. London. New York: T&T Clark, 2010.

———. *The Letters of Paul: Conversations in Context.* 5th ed. Louisville: Westminster John Knox, 2009.

Runesson, Anders. *The Origins of the Synagogue: A Socio-Historical Study.* Stockholm: Almqvist & Wiksell International, 2001.

———. "Inventing Christian Identity: Paul, Ignatius, and Theodosius I." In *Exploring Early Christian Identity*, edited by Bengt Holmberg, 59–92. WUNT 172, Tübingen: Mohr Siebeck, 2008.

———, Donald D. Binder, and Birger Olsson, eds. *The Ancient Synagogue from its Origins to 200 C.E.: A Source Book.* Leiden. Boston: Brill, 2008.

Rutgers, Leonard V. *The Hidden Heritage of Diaspora Judaism, Contributions to Biblical Exegesis and Theology.* Vol. 20. Leuven: Peeters, 1998.

Said, Edward W. "Orientalism Reconsidered." *Cultural Critique* 11 (1985): 89–107.

———. *Out of Place.* New York: Vintage, 1999.

———. *Orientalism.* 25th anniversary ed. New York: Vintage, 2003.

Salih, R. *Gender in Transnationalism: Home, Longing and Belonging among Moroccan Migrant Women.* London and New York: Routledge, 2003.

Samosata, Lucian of. *The Carousal (Symposium) or The Lapiths* 46. Loeb Classical Library No. 14. Translated by A. M. Harmon. Cambridge, MA: Harvard University Press, 1913.

Sampley, J. Paul. *Walking Between The Times: Paul's Moral Reasoning.* Minneapolis: Fortress Press, 1991.

Sandelin, Karl-Gustav. "Philo and Paul on Alien Religion: A Comparison." In *Lux Humana, Lux Aeterna. Essays on Biblical and Related Themes in Honour of Lars Aejmelaeus,* edited by Antti Mustakallio, 213–46. Publications of the Finnish Exegetical Society 89. Helsinki: Finnish Exegetical Society; Göttingen: Vandenhoeck & Ruprecht, 2005.

Sanders, E. P. *Paul and Palestinian Judaism: A Comparison of Patterns of Religion.* London: SCM, 1977.

———. *Paul, the Law, and the Jewish People.* Minneapolis: Fortress Press, 1983.

Schreiner, Thomas R. *Romans.* BECNT. Grand Rapids: Baker, 1998.

Sandwell, Isabella. *Religious Identity in Late Antiquity: Greeks, Jews and Christians in Antioch.* New York: Cambridge University Press, 2007.

Schäfer, Peter. *Judeophobia: Attitudes Toward the Jews in the Ancient World.* Cambridge, MA: Harvard University Press, 1997.

Schellenberg, Ryan. "'Danger in the Wilderness, Danger at Sea": Paul and Perils of Travel.' In *Travel and Religion in Antiquity,* edited by Philip A.

Harland, 141–61. Studies in Christianity and Judaism. Vol. 21. Waterloo, ON: Wilfrid Laurier University Press, 2011.

Schneiders, Sandra M. *The Revelatory Text: Interpreting the New Testament as Sacred Scripture*. San Francisco: Harper, 1991.

Schreckenberg, Heinz. *Rezeptionsgeschichtliche und Textkritische Untersuchungen zu Flavius Josephus*. Leiden: Brill, 1977.

Schwartz, Daniel R. "Josephus on the Jewish Constitutions and Community." *SCI* 7 (1983–84): 30–52.

———. "Temple or City: What did Hellenistic Jews See in Jerusalem?" In *The Centrality of Jerusalem: Historical Perspectives*, edited by M. Poorthuis and C. Safrai, 114–27. Kampen: Peeters, 1996.

———. "How at Home Were Jews of the Hellenistic Diaspora?" *CP* 95 (2000): 349–57.

———. "Review of J.M.G. Barclay, *Jews in the Mediterranean Diaspora*." *Classical Philology* 95, no. 3 (2000): 349–57.

———. "From Punishment to Program, From Program to Punishment: Josephus and the Rabbis on Exile." In *For Uriel. Studies in the History of Israel in Antiquity Presented to Professor Uriel Rappaport*, edited by M. Mor and J. Pastor, 205–26. Jerusalem: Zalman Shazar Center for Jewish History, 2005.

Scott, James M. *Paul and the Nations: The Old Testament and Jewish Background of Paul's Mission to the Nations with Special Reference to the Destination of Galatians*. Tübingen: Mohr Siebeck, 1995.

Seesengood, Robert. "Hybridity and the Rhetoric of Endurance: Reading Paul's Athletic Metaphors in a Context of Postcolonial Self-Construction." *Bible and Critical Theory* 1, no. 3 2005.

———. "Wrestling with the "Macedonian Call": Paul, Pauline Scholarship, and Nineteenth-Century Colonial Missions." In *The Colonized Apostle: Paul Through Postcolonial Eyes*, edited by Christopher D. Stanley, 189–205. Minneapolis: Fortress Press, 2011.

Segal, Alan F. "The History Boy: The Importance of Perspective in the Study of Early Judaism and Christianity." In *Identity and Interaction in the Ancient Mediterranean: Jews, Christians and Others, Essays in Honor of Stephen G. Wilson*, edited by Zeba Crook and Philip Harland. Sheffield: Sheffield Phoenix, 2007.

Segovia, Fernando F. *Decolonizing Biblical Studies: A View from the Margins.* Maryknoll, NY: Orbis, 2004.

———. "Interpreting beyond Borders: Postcolonial Studies and Diasporic Studies in Biblical Criticism." In *Interpreting Beyond Borders*, edited by Fernando F. Segovia, 11–34. Sheffield: Sheffield Academic, 2000.

———, and Rasiah S. Sugirtharajah, eds. *A Postcolonial Commentary on the New Testament Writings.* London: T&T Clark, 2007.

Shahid, Amin, and Dipesh Chakrabarty, eds. *Subaltern Studies: Writings on South Asian History and Society.* Vol. 9. Delhi: Oxford University Press, 1996.

Shutt, R. J. H. "Letter of Aristeas." In *The Old Testament Pseudepigrapha*, 1:12–34. 2 vols. James H Charlesworth, ed. Garden City, NY: Doubleday, 1983–1985.

Siegert, Folker. "Philo and the New Testament." In *The Cambridge Companion to Philo*, edited by Adam Kamesar, 175–209. Cambridge: Cambridge University Press, 2009.

Smith, Dennis E. "What Do We Really Know about the Jerusalem Church? Christian Origins in Jerusalem according to Acts and Paul." In *Redescribing Christian Origins*, edited by Ron Cameron and Merrill P. Miller, 237–52. Atlanta: SBL, Symposium Series, no. 28.

Smith, Jonathan Z. *Drudgery Divine: On the Comparison of Early Christianities and the Religions of Late Antiquity.* Chicago: The University of Chicago Press, 1990.

———. *Map Is Not Territory: Studies in the History of Religion.* Chicago: University of Chicago Press, 1993 [1978].

———. "What a Difference a Difference Makes." In *Relating Religion: Essays in the Study of Religion*, 251–302. Chicago: University of Chicago Press, 2004.

Stegemann, Ekkehard W., and Wolfgang Stegemann. *The Jesus Movement: A Social History of Its First Century*. Minneapolis: Fortress Press, 1999.

Stern, Menahem. "The Jewish Diaspora." In *The Jewish people on the First Century*, edited by S. Safrai and M. Stern, 117–83. 2 vols. Philadelphia: Fortress Press, 1974.

Stowers, Stanley K. "Paul and Slavery: A Response." *Semeia* 83–84 (1998): 295–311.

———. *A Rereading of Romans: Justice, Jews, and Gentiles*. New Haven: Yale University Press, 1994.

———. "Does Pauline Christianity Resemble a Hellenistic Philosophy?" In *Paul Beyond the Judaism/Hellenism Divide*, edited by T. Engberg-Pedersen. Louisville: Westminster John Knox, 2001.

Syed, Yasmin. *Vergil's Aeneid and the Roman self: Subject and Nation in LiteraryDiscourse*. Ann Arbor: University of Michigan Press, 2005.

Taussig, Hal. *In The Beginning Was the Meal: Social Experimentation and Early Christian Identity*. Minneapolis: Fortress Press, 2009.

Taylor, J. "Why Were the Disciples First Called "Christians" at Antioch? (Acts 11:26)." *RB* 101, no. 1 (1994): 75–94.

Taylor, Nicholas. *Paul, Antioch and Jerusalem: A Study in Relationships and Authority in Earliest Christianity*. Sheffield: JSOT Press, 1992.

Tcherikover, Victor. "The Ideology of the Letter of Aristeas." *HTR* 51 (1958): 59–85.

ter Haar, Gerrie, ed. *Strangers and Sojourners: Religious Communities in the Diaspora*. Study of Religion and Mythology. Leuven: Peeters, 1998.

Theissen, Gerd. *The Social Setting of Pauline Christianity: Essays on Corinth*. Philadelphia: Fortress Press, 1982.

Thiessen, Matthew. *Contesting Conversion: Genealogy, Circumcision, and Identity in Ancient Judaism and Christianity.* Oxford: Oxford University Press, 2011.

Thomas, Harrison. "Ancient and Modern Imperialism." *Greece and Rome* 55, no. 1, *The Classical Association,* 2008.

Trebilco, Paul R. *Jewish Communities in Asia Minor.* Society for New Testament Studies Monograph Series 69. Cambridge: Cambridge University Press, 1991.

Trocmé, Etienne. "Le Christianisme primitif, un mythe historique ?" *ETR* 49, no. 1 (1974): 15–29.

Troels, Engberg-Pedersen. *Paul and the Stoics.* Nashville: Westminster John Knox, 2000.

———. *Cosmology and Self in the Apostle Paul.* Oxford: Oxford University Press, 2010.

Vaage, Leif E. "Why Christianity Succeeded in the Roman Empire." In *Religious Rivalries in the Early Roman Empire and the Rise of Christianity,* edited by Leif E. Vaage. Studies in Christianity and Judaism/Études sur le christianisme et le judaïsme. Waterloo, ON: Wilfrid Laurier University Press, 2006.

van Unnik, W. C. *Das Selbstverständnis der jüdischen Diaspora in der hellenistisch-römischen Zeit.* Leiden: Brill, 1993.

Vassiliadis, P. "The Collection Revisited." *Deltion Biblikon Meleton* 11 (1992): 42–48.

———. "Equality and Justice in Classical Antiquity and in Paul: The Social Implications of the Pauline Collection." *St Vladimir's Theological Quarterly* 36 (1992): 42–48.

Vertovec, Steven. "Religion and Diaspora." In *New Approaches to the Study of Religion,* 275–303. Vol. 2 of *Textual, Comparative, Sociological, and Cognitive Approaches.* Berlin: Walter de Gruyter, 2004.

Vouga, François. *An die Galater.* HZNT 10. Tübingen: Mohr Siebeck, 1998.

Wallace, Richard. *The Three Worlds of Paul of Tarsus*. New York: Routledge, 1998.

Wan, Sze-kar. "Collection for the Saints as Anticolonial Act: Implications of Paul's Ethnic Reconstruction." In *Paul and Politics: Ekklesia, Israel, Imperium, Interpretation: Essays in Honor of Krister Stendahl*, edited by Richard H. Horsley, 191–215. Harrisburg, PA: Trinity Press International, 2000.

———. "'To the Jew First and to the Greek': Reading Romans as Ethnic Construction." In *Prejudice and Christian Beginnings: Investigating Race, Gender, and Ethnicity in Early Christian Studies*, edited by Laura Nasrallah and Elisabeth Schüssler Fiorenza, 129–55. Minneapolis: Fortress Press, 2009.

———. "Asian American Perspectives: Ambivalence of the Model Minority and Perpetual Foreigner." In *Studying Paul's Letters: Contemporary Perspectives and Methods*, 175–90. Minneapolis: Fortress Press, 2012.

———. "Does Diaspora Identity Imply Some Sort of Universality? An Asian-American Reading of Galatians." In *Interpreting Beyond Borders*, edited by Fernando F. Segovia, 107–31. Sheffield: Sheffield Academic, 2000.

———. "Galatians Commentary." In *Postcolonial Commentary on the New Testament Writings*, edited by Fernando F. Segovia and R. S. Sugirtharajah, 246–64. London: T&T Clark, 2007.

Wasserman, Emma. "Paul among the Philosophers: The Case of Sin in Romans 6-8." *JSNT* 30 (2008): 387–415.

———. "The Death of the Soul in Romans 7: Revisiting Paul's Anthropology in Light of Hellenistic Moral Psychology." *JBL* 126, no. 4 (2007): 793–816.

Wenham, David. *Paul: Follower of Jesus or Founder of Christianity?* Grand Rapids: Eerdmans, 1995.

Wiebe, Donald. "The Failure of Nerve in the Academic Study of Religion." *Studies in Religion* 13, no. 4 (1984): 401–22.

Winter, Bruce W. *Philo and Paul Among the Sophists.* Society of the New Testament Studies Monograph Series 96. Cambridge: Cambridge University Press, 1997.

Wire, Antoinette C. *The Corinthian Women Prophets: A Reconstruction through Paul's Rhetoric.* Minneapolis: Fortress Press, 1990.

Witherington, Ben. *The Paul Quest, The Renewed Search for the Jew of Tarsus.* DownersGrove, IL: InterVarsity Press, 1998.

Worthington, Jonathan D. *Creation in Paul and Philo: The Beginning and Before.* WUNT II 317. Tübingen: Mohr Siebeck, 2011.

Wrede, William. *Paul.* London: Philip Green, 1907.

Wright, N. T. *The Climax of the Covenant: Christ and the Law in Pauline Theology.* Minneapolis: Fortress Press, 1991.

———. *What Saint Paul Really Said.* Grand Rapids: Eerdmans 1997.

———. *Paul in Fresh Perspectives.* Minneapolis: Fortress Press, 2005.

Yinger, Milton J. *Ethnicity: Source of Strength? Source of Conflict?* Albany: State University of New York, 1994.

Yonge, C. D., trans. *Athenaeus: The Deipnosophists: Book 13.* n.p. 1854.

Young, Robert J. C. *Postcolonialism: An Historical Introduction.* Oxford: Blackwell, 2001.

Zacaïr, Philippe. *Haiti and the Haitian Diaspora in the Wider Caribbean.* Gainesville: University Press of Florida, 2010.

Zerbe, Gordon M. "Constructions of Paul in Filipino Theology of Struggle." In *The Colonized Apostle,* 236–55.

Zetterholm, Magnus. *The Formation of Christianity in Antioch: A Social-Scientific Approach to the Separation between Judaism and Christianity.* Routledge Early Church Monographs. London: Routledge, 2003 [paperback edition 2005].

Zuntz, Günther. "Aristeas Studies I: 'The Seven Banquets.'" *JSS* 4 (1959): 21–36.

Index